KNOWLEDGE-BASED SYSTEMS
for Engineers and Scientists

ADRIAN A. HOPGOOD
The Open University

CRC Press
Boca Raton   Ann Arbor   London   Tokyo

Library of Congress Cataloging-in-Publication Data

Hopgood, Adrian A.
  Knowledged-based systems for engineers and scientists / Adrian A. Hopgood
    p.   cm.
  Includes bibliographical references and index.
  ISBN 0-8493-8616-0
  1. Expert systems (Computer science). 2. Computer-aided engineering. I. Title.
  Qa76.76.E95H68   1993
  006.3'3'02462—dc20   92-42809
                                                                                        CIP

International Standard Book Number 0-8493-8616-0

Printed in the United States   4 5 6 7 8 9 0
Printed on acid-free paper

This book is dedicated to my mother, who sadly did not live to see it completed.

Preface

Plenty of books have been written on knowledge-based systems, but I hope that this one is substantially different from previous ones. An emphasis has been placed on showing how knowledge-based systems and related techniques can solve practical engineering and scientific problems. I have therefore tried to describe a range of techniques with the help of realistic examples. Although various applications are explored, I have avoided merely surveying past engineering examples of knowledge-based systems. Instead, examples have been selected on the basis of the lessons that can be drawn from them.

In an attempt to make the book more readable than most of the computing literature, my initial intention was to introduce all of the techniques as separate aspects of case studies in interpretation, diagnosis, design, planning and control. After deciding that diagnosis is simply a special case of interpretation, I had four distinct application areas to discuss, with the intention of introducing appropriate techniques along the way. Nonetheless, there was still some fundamental knowledge of tools and techniques that I needed to assume. Therefore I finally settled on dividing the book into two parts. Chapters 1 to 6 describe the tools and techniques with appropriate examples, while chapters 7 to 10 look at some applications in detail.

The four chapters on applications cover "interpretation and diagnosis", "design and selection", "planning" and "control". In the course of writing, it became apparent to me that these applications had more in common than I had initially suspected. All of them are about making decisions automatically, using the information available. In some applications, particularly control, the decision must be taken within the time available. In these circumstances, a suboptimal decision made quickly may be preferable to a well-informed decision made too late. Interpretation involves deciding the meaning of a set of data. In the specific case of diagnosis, symptoms are interpreted in terms of their causes. Control is similar, but involves the additional decision of what action to take on the basis of the interpretation. Control therefore involves interpreting the data and deciding upon an action (i.e., planning), performing the action, and responding to whatever happens next. Thus the planning and execution of actions are interleaved. The chapter on planning, on the other hand, describes techniques for drawing up a plan to be executed at some later time. Planning and design are also closely related, as both involve devising a means of achieving a goal while meeting the constraints that are imposed. In planning, those constraints are time and resources, while in design the constraints might include function, cost, weight, shape and size of the product being designed. The general problem of selection between alternatives is discussed as one aspect of design.

Since the applications are similar in many ways, the techniques introduced under one application heading are often relevant to others too. Blackboard systems are an important example. These are introduced in a case study on interpretation, but they are often used in other application areas as well.

I hope that the book will appeal to a wide readership. As knowledge-based systems and related techniques increase in importance, postgraduates and final year undergraduates in science or engineering may have an opportunity to study this fascinating area of computing. Outside of academia, the book will appeal to practicing engineers and scientists who are building knowledge-based systems or who simply want to know more about such systems.

I joined the Open University as a lecturer in 1986, and I started to think about the contents of this book during 1989. Events soon overtook me when I was offered work at the Research Laboratories of Telecom Australia in Melbourne. There I stayed for a little over two years between 1990 and 1992. Virtually all of the book was written during my spare time while I lived in Melbourne. The finishing touches were made after my return to the Open University in April 1992.

Many people have helped me, and I am grateful to them all. Philip Sargent has kindly reviewed all of my draft chapters and made many incisive comments and suggestions. I have also received helpful comments on specific parts of the book from (in alphabetical order) Mike Brayshaw, David Hopgood, Adam Kowalzyk, Sean Ogden, Phil Picton, Chris Price, Peter Richardson, Neil Woodcock and John Zucker. I am also indebted to Phil Picton for his time spent discussing some of the finer points of neural networks, fuzzy logic and control systems. The case study on ultrasonic image interpretation that appears in chapter 7 is based upon research carried out by Nicholas Hallam, Neil Woodcock and myself. Alan Hopson and others contributed towards the Common Traffic Model described in chapter 8. The case study on the design of load-bearing beams, also in chapter 8, was inspired by an Open University summer school activity. Thanks are due to Navin Sullivan of the CRC Press for organizing the publication of the book, and to David Carpenter for proof reading the final draft. Various people at Telecom Australia and at the Open University have also given their support and encouragement.

Finally, I am indebted to Sue for taking on my share of the domestic chores while I sat hunched in front of my computer screen for hours at a time. Not content with that additional workload, she has also read my drafts, helped with the final preparations, and made many useful suggestions.

The book was typeset by myself using Microsoft Word™ on an Apple Macintosh™ computer. The figures were prepared using MacDrawII™, Canvas™, and Mathematica™.

Adrian Hopgood
August 1992

Contents

chapter one

Introduction

1.1 Artificial intelligence

Over many centuries, tools of increasing sophistication have been developed to serve the human race. Physical tools such as chisels, hammers, spears, arrows, guns, carts, cars and aircraft all have their place in the history of civilization. The human race has also developed tools of communication - spoken language, written language and the language of mathematics. These tools have not only enabled the exchange and storage of information, but have also allowed the expression of concepts that simply could not exist outside of the language.

The last few decades have seen the arrival of a new tool - the digital computer. Computers are able to perform the same sort of numerical and symbolic manipulations that an ordinary person can, but faster and more reliably. They have therefore been able to remove the tedium from many tasks that were previously performed manually, and have allowed the achievement of new feats. Such feats range from huge scientific "number-crunching" experiments to the more familiar electronic banking facilities.

Although these uses of the computer are impressive, the computer is actually only performing quite simple operations, albeit rapidly. It is still therefore only a complex calculating machine. The intriguing idea now is whether we can build a computer (or a computer program) that can *think*. As Penrose [1] has pointed out, most of us are quite happy with machines that enable us to do physical things more easily or more quickly, such as digging a hole or traveling along a freeway. We are also happy to use machines that enable us to do physical things that would otherwise be impossible, such as flying. However, the idea of a machine that can think for us is a huge leap forward in our ambitions, and one which raises many ethical and philosophical questions.

Research in artificial intelligence (or simply AI) is directed towards building such a machine and improving our understanding of intelligence. The ultimate achievement in this field would be to construct a machine that can mimic or exceed human mental capabilities including reasoning, understanding, imagination, recognition, creativity and emotions. We are a long way from achieving this, but some successes have been achieved in mimicking specific areas of human mental activity. For instance, machines are now able to play chess at the highest level, to interpret spoken sentences and to diagnose medical complaints. An objection to these claimed successes might be that the machine does not tackle these problems in the same way that a human would. This objection will not concern us in this book, which is intended as a guide to practical systems and not a philosophical thesis.

In achieving these modest successes, research into artificial intelligence (together with other branches of computer science) has resulted in the development of several useful computing tools, which form the basis of this book. These tools have a range of potential applications, and we will emphasize their use in engineering and science. The tools of particular interest are knowledge-based systems (including expert, rule-based and blackboard systems), object-oriented and frame-based systems, neural networks, and novel algorithms (e.g., simulated annealing and genetic algorithms). While these may not have solved the problem of building an artificial mind, they have enabled a range of problems to be tackled that were previously considered too difficult, and have enabled a large number of other problems to be tackled more effectively.

1.2 Knowledge-based systems

The principal difference between a knowledge-based system and a conventional program lies in its structure. In a conventional program, domain knowledge is intimately intertwined with software for controlling the application of that knowledge. In a knowledge-based system, the two roles are explicitly separated. In the simplest case there are two modules - the knowledge module is called the *knowledge base*, and the control module is called the *inference engine* (Figure 1.1). In more complex systems the inference engine itself may be a knowledge-based system containing meta-knowledge, i.e., knowledge of how to apply the domain knowledge.

The explicit separation of knowledge from control makes it easier to add new knowledge either during program development or in the light of experience during the program's lifetime. There is an analogy with the brain, whose control processes (the inference engine) are approximately unchanging in their nature, even though individual behavior is continually modified by new knowledge and experience (updating the knowledge base).

Suppose that a professional engineer uses a conventional program to support his or her everyday work. Altering the behavior of the program would

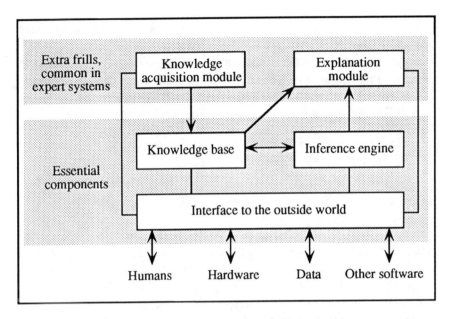

Figure 1.1 The main components of a knowledge-based system.

require him or her to become immersed in the details of the program's implementation. Typically this would involve altering control structures of the form:

```
IF..THEN...ELSE
```
or
```
FOR X FROM A TO B.
```

To achieve these changes requires the engineer to be a proficient programmer. Even if he or she does have this skill, modifications of the kind described are unwieldy and are difficult to make without unwittingly altering some other aspect of the program's behavior.

The knowledge-based system approach is more straightforward. The knowledge is represented *explicitly* in the knowledge base, not *implicitly* within the structure of a program. Thus the knowledge can be altered with relative ease. The inference engine uses the knowledge base to tackle a particular task in an analogous fashion to a conventional program using a data file.

1.3 The knowledge base

The knowledge base may be rich with diverse forms of knowledge. For the time being, we will simply state that the knowledge base contains rules and facts.   However, the rules may be complex, and the facts may include sequences, structured entities, attributes of such entities and the relationships between them. The details of the representation used vary from system to system, so the syntax shown in the following examples is chosen arbitrarily. Let us consider a knowledge-based system for dealing with the payroll of ACME inc. A fact and a rule in the knowledge base may be:

```
/* Fact 1.1 */
Joe Bloggs works for ACME

/* Rule 1.1 */
IF ?X works for ACME THEN ?X earns a large salary.
```

The question marks are used to indicate that X is a variable which can be replaced by a constant value, such as Joe Bloggs or Mary Smith.

Let us now consider how we might represent the fact and the rule in a conventional program. We might start by creating a "record" (a data structure for grouping together different data types) for each employee. The rule could be expressed easily enough as a conditional statement (IF...THEN), but it would need to be carefully positioned within the program so that:

- the statement is applied whenever it is needed;

- all relevant variables are in scope (the scope of a variable is that part of the program to which the declaration of the variable applies);

- any values that are assigned to variables remain active for as long as they are needed; and

- the rest of the program is not disrupted.

In effect, the fact and the rule are "hard-wired", so that they become an intrinsic part of the program. As many systems need hundreds or thousands of facts and rules, slotting them into a conventional program is a difficult task. This can be contrasted with a knowledge-based system in which the rule and the fact are represented explicitly and can be changed at will.

Rules like rule 1.1 are a useful way of expressing many types of knowledge, and are discussed in more detail in chapter 3. It has been assumed so far that we are dealing with certain knowledge. This is not always the case, and chapter 4 discusses the use of uncertainty in rules. In the case of rule 1.1, uncertainty may arise from three distinct sources:

- *uncertain evidence*
  (Perhaps we are not certain that Joe Bloggs works for ACME)

- *uncertain link between evidence and conclusion*
  (We cannot be certain that an ACME employee earns a large salary, we
  just know that it is likely)

- *vague rule*
  (what is a "large" salary anyway?)

The first two sources of uncertainty can be handled by Bayesian updating, or
variants of this idea. The last source of uncertainty can be handled by fuzzy
sets and fuzzy logic.

Let us now consider facts in more detail. Facts may be static, in which
case they can be written into the knowledge base. Fact 1.1 falls into this
category. Note that static facts need not be permanent, but they change
sufficiently infrequently that changes can be accommodated by updating the
knowledge base when necessary. In contrast, some facts may be transient.
Transient facts (e.g., "Oil pressure is 3000 Pa", "the user of this program is
Adrian") apply at a specific instance only, or for a single run of the system.
The knowledge base may contain defaults, which can be used as facts in the
absence of transient facts to the contrary. Here is a collection of facts about
my car:

```
My car is a car              (static relationship)
A car is a vehicle           (static relationship)
A car has four wheels        (static attribute)
A car's speed is 0mph        (default attribute)
My car is green              (static attribute)
My car is in my garage       (default relationship)
My garage is a garage        (static relationship)
A garage is a building       (static relationship)
My garage is made from brick (static attribute)
My car is in the High Street (transient relationship)
The High Street is a street  (static relationship)
A street is a road           (static relationship)
```

Notice that in this list we have distinguished between attributes and
relationships. Attributes are properties of objects (such as my car) or classes of
object (such as cars in general). Relationships exist between objects and
classes of object. In this way we can begin to build a model of the subject area
of interest, and this reliance on a model will be a recurring topic throughout
this book. Attributes and relationships can be represented as a network, known
as an *associative or semantic network*, as shown in Figure 1.2. In this
representation, attributes are treated in the same way as relationships. In
chapter 4 we will explore object-oriented systems, in which relationships and

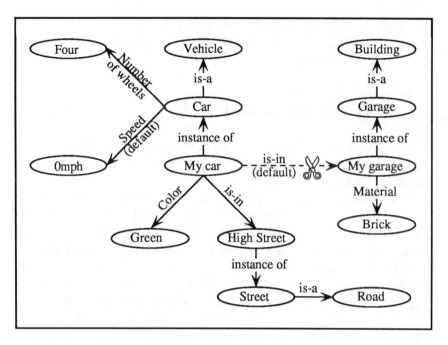

Figure 1.2   A semantic network with an overridden default.

attributes are represented explicitly in a formalized manner. Object-oriented
systems offer many other benefits besides, which will also be discussed.

The facts that have been described so far are all made available to the
knowledge-based system either at the outset (static facts), or while the system
is running (transient facts). Both may therefore be described as "given" facts.
One or more given facts may satisfy the condition of a rule, resulting in the
generation of a new fact, known as a derived fact. For example, by applying
rule 1.1 to fact 1.1, we can derive:

```
/* Fact 1.2 */
Joe Bloggs earns a large salary
```

The derived fact may satisfy, or partially satisfy, another rule, such as

```
/* Rule 1.2 */
IF ?X earns a large salary OR ?X has job satisfaction
THEN ?X is professionally content
```

This in turn may lead to the generation of a new derived fact. Rules 1.1 and
1.2 are interdependent, since the conclusion of one can satisfy the condition of
another. The interdependencies amongst the rules define a network, as shown
in Figure 1.3, known as an *inference network*.

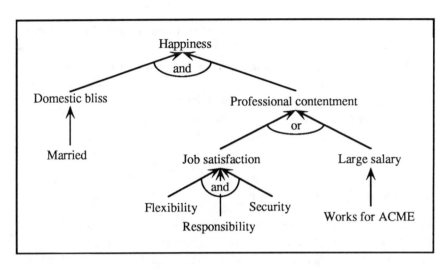

Figure 1.3 An inference network.

1.4 Deduction, abduction and induction

The rules that make up the inference network in Figure 1.3, and the network taken as a whole, are used to link cause and effect:

```
IF <cause> THEN <effect>.
```

Using the inference network, we can infer that if Joe Bloggs works for ACME and is married (the causes) then he is happy (the effect). This is the process of *deduction*. Many problems, such as diagnosis, involve the reasoning in the reverse direction, i.e., we wish to ascertain a cause, given an effect. This is *abduction*. Given the observation that Joe Bloggs is happy, we can infer by abduction that Joe Bloggs enjoys domestic bliss and professional contentment. However, this is only a valid conclusion if the inference network shows *all* of the ways in which a person can find happiness. This is the *closed world assumption*, the implications of which are discussed in chapters 3 and 7.

If we have many examples of cause and effect, we can infer the rule (or inference network) that links them. For instance, if every employee of ACME that we have met earns a large salary, then we might infer rule 1.1:

```
/* Rule 1.1 */
IF ?X works for ACME THEN ?X earns a large salary
```

Inferring a rule from a set of example cases of cause and effect is termed *induction*.

We can summarize deduction, abduction and induction as follows:

deduction: cause + rule   ⇒ effect;
abduction: effect + rule   ⇒ cause;
induction: cause + effect ⇒ rule.

1.5 The inference engine

Inference engines vary greatly according to the type and complexity of knowledge with which they deal. Two important types of inference engine can be distinguished, namely forward-chaining and backward chaining. These may also be known as data-driven and goal-driven respectively. A knowledge-based system working in data-driven mode takes the available information (the "given" facts) and generates as many derived facts as it can. The output is therefore unpredictable. This may either have the advantage of leading to novel or innovative solutions to a problem, or the disadvantage of wasting time generating irrelevant information. The data-driven approach might typically be used for problems of interpretation, where we wish to know whatever the system can tell us about some data. A goal-driven strategy is appropriate when a more tightly-focused solution is required. For instance, a planning system may be required to generate a plan for manufacturing a widget. Any other plans are irrelevant. A backward chaining system might be presented with the proposition "a plan exists for manufacturing a widget". It will then attempt to ascertain the truth of this proposition by generating the plan (or it may conclude that the proposition is false and no plan is possible). Forward and backward chaining are discussed in more detail in chapter 3. Planning is discussed in chapter 9.

1.6 Expert systems

Expert systems are a type of knowledge-based system designed to embody expertise in a particular specialized domain. Example domains might be configuring computer networks, diagnosing faults in telephones, or mineral prospecting. An expert system is intended to act like a human expert who can be consulted on a range of problems that fall within his or her domain of expertise. Typically the user of an expert system will enter into a dialogue in which he or she describes the problem (such as the symptoms of a fault) and the expert system offers advice, suggestions or recommendations. The dialogue may be led by the expert system, so that the user responds to a series of questions or enters information into a spreadsheet. Alternatively, the expert system may allow the user to take the initiative in the consultation by allowing him or her to supply information without necessarily being asked for it.

Since an expert system is a knowledge-based system that acts as a specialist consultant, it is often proposed that an expert system must offer certain capabilities that mirror those of a human consultant. In particular, it is often claimed that an expert system must be capable of justifying its current line of inquiry and explaining its reasoning in arriving at a conclusion (Figure 1.1). However, the best that most expert systems can achieve is to produce a trace of the facts and rules that have been used. This is equivalent to a trace of the execution path for a conventional program, a facility which is normally regarded as standard and not particularly noteworthy.

An expert system shell is an expert system with an empty knowledge base. These are sold as software packages of varying complexity. In principle, it should be possible to buy an expert system shell, build up a knowledge base, and thereby produce an expert system. However, all domains are different and it is difficult for a software supplier to build a shell that adequately handles them all. The best shells are flexible in their ability to represent and apply knowledge. Without this flexibility, it may be necessary to generate rules and facts in a convoluted style in order to fit the syntax or to force a certain kind of behavior from the system. This situation is scarcely better than building a conventional program.

1.7 Knowledge acquisition

The representation of knowledge in a knowledge base can only be addressed once the knowledge is known. There are three distinct approaches to acquiring the relevant knowledge for a particular domain:

- the knowledge is teased out of a domain expert;
- the builder of the knowledge-based system *is* a domain expert; or
- the system learns automatically from examples.

The first approach is commonly used, but is fraught with difficulties. The person who extracts the knowledge from the expert and encodes it in the knowledge base is termed the "knowledge engineer". Typically the knowledge engineer interviews one or more domain experts and tries to make them articulate their in-depth knowledge in a manner that the knowledge engineer

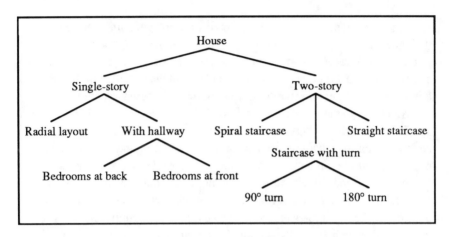

Figure 1.4 A search tree for house designs.

can understand. The inevitable communication difficulties can be avoided by
the second approach, in which the domain expert becomes a knowledge
engineer or the knowledge engineer becomes a domain expert.

Finally, there are many circumstances in which the knowledge is either
unknown or cannot be expressed explicitly. In these circumstances it may be
preferable to have the system generate its own knowledge base from a set of
examples. Techniques for automatic learning are discussed in chapter 6.

1.8 Search

Search is the key to practically all problem-solving tasks, and has been a major
focus of research in artificial intelligence and knowledge-based systems.
Problem-solving concerns the search for a solution. The detailed engineering
applications discussed in this book include the search for a design, plan,
control action, or diagnosis of a fault. All of these applications involve
searching through the possible solutions (the *search space*) to find one or more
that are optimal or satisfactory. Search is also a key issue for the internal
workings of a knowledge-based system. The knowledge base may contain
hundreds or thousands of rules and facts. The principal role of the inference
engine is to search for the most appropriate item of knowledge to apply at any
given moment (see chapter 3).

In the case of searching the knowledge base, it is feasible (though not very
efficient) to test all of the alternatives before selecting one. This may not be a
practical option in the search space of the application. For many applications,
such as design, the search space may be infinitely large. For other problems,
such as diagnosis, there may be a finite but very large search space

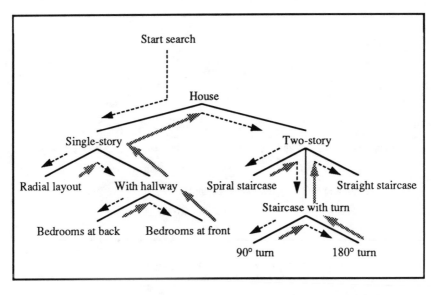

Figure 1.5 Depth-first search (the gray arrows indicate backtracking).

representing all possible causes of faults. In these cases the search has to be selective. The alternatives that are examined in the search process make up the *search tree*. Unless the search is exhaustive, the search tree is a sub-set of the search space.

The expression "search tree" indicates that solutions can be categorized in some fashion, so that similar solutions are clustered together on the same branch of the tree. Figure 1.4 shows a possible search tree for designing a house. Unlike a real tree, the tree shown here has its root at the top and its leaves at the bottom. As we progress towards the leaves, the differences between the designs become less significant. Each alternative design is either generated automatically or found in a database, and tested for suitability. In either case, this is described as a "generate and test" strategy. If a solution passes the test, the search may continue in order to find further acceptable solutions, or it may stop.

Two alternative strategies for systematically searching the tree are depth-first and breadth-first searches. An example of *depth-first* search is shown in Figure 1.5. In the example shown, a progressively more detailed description of a single story house is built up and tested before other classifications, such as a two-story house, are considered. When a node fails the test, the search resumes at the previous node at which a branch was selected. This process of *backtracking* (see sections 2.6.3 and 3.9) is indicated in figure 1.5 by the gray arrows, which are directed towards the root rather than the leaves of the tree.

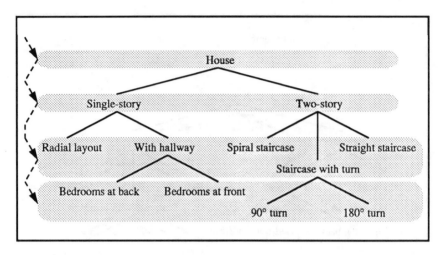

Figure 1.6 Breadth-first search.

In contrast, the *breadth-first* approach (Figure 1.6) involves examining all nodes at a given level in the tree before progressing to the next level. Each node is a generalization of the nodes on its subbranches. Therefore, if a node fails the test, all subcategories are assumed to fail the test and are eliminated from the search.

The systematic search strategies described above are examples of *blind search*. The search can be made more efficient either by eliminating unfeasible categories ("pruning the search tree") or by ensuring that the most likely alternatives are tested before less likely ones. To achieve either of these, we need to apply heuristics to the search process. Blind search is thereby modified to *heuristic search*. Barr and Feigenbaum [2] have surveyed the use of the word "heuristic", and produced this general description:

> *A heuristic is a rule of thumb, strategy, trick, simplification, or any other kind of device which drastically limits search for solutions in large search spaces. Heuristics do not guarantee optimal solutions; in fact they do not guarantee any solution at all; all that can be said for a useful heuristic is that it offers solutions which are good enough most of the time.*

In a diagnostic system for plumbing, a useful heuristic may be that pipes are more likely to leak at joints than along lengths. This heuristic defines a search strategy, namely to look for leaking joints first. In a design system for a house, we might use a heuristic to eliminate all designs that would require us to walk through a bedroom to reach the bathroom. In a short-term planning system, a heuristic might be used to ensure that no plans looked ahead more

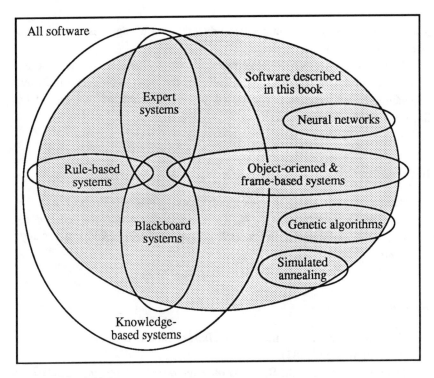

Figure 1.7 Categories of software covered in this book.

than a week. In a control system for a nuclear reactor, a heuristic may ensure that the control rods are never raised while the coolant supply is turned off.

1.9 Integration with other software

This book will take a very broad view of knowledge-based systems, and will stress the importance of related techniques such as object-oriented systems, neural networks, simulated annealing, genetic algorithms, and conventional programming (Figure 1.7). These techniques do not necessarily represent exclusive alternatives, but can often be used cooperatively. For example, a designer may already have an excellent conventional program for simulating the aerodynamic properties of a car. In this case, a knowledge-based system might be used as an interface to the program, allowing the program to be used to its full potential.

If a problem can be broken down into subtasks, a blackboard system (described in chapter 7) might provide an ideal way of tackling it. Blackboard systems allow each subtask to be handled using an appropriate technique, thereby contributing most effectively to the overall solution. A typical blackboard system may contain several different knowledge bases, each with its own inference engine.

As with any other technique, knowledge-based systems are not suitable for all types of problem. Each problem calls for the most appropriate tool, but knowledge-based systems can be used for many problems that would be impracticable by other means.

References

1. Penrose, R., *The emperor's new mind*, Oxford University Press (1989).
2. Barr, A. and Feigenbaum, E. A., *The handbook of artificial intelligence - volume 1*, William Kaufmann (1981) (republished by Addison-Wesley, 1986).

Further reading

*   Charniak, E. and McDermott, D. V., *Introduction to artificial intelligence*, Addison-Wesley (1985).
*   Dym, C. L. and Levitt, R. E., *Knowledge-based systems in engineering*, McGraw-Hill (1991).
*   Famili, A. F., Kim, S. H. and Nau, D. S. (ed.), *Applications of AI in manufacturing*, AAAI Press (1991).
*   Frost, R. A., *Introduction to knowledge base systems*, Collins (1986).
*   Kusiak, A. (ed.), *Knowledge-based systems in manufacturing*, Taylor & Francis (1989).
*   Pham, D. T. (ed.), *Expert systems in engineering*, IFS/Springer-Verlag (1988).

chapter two

Tools and languages

2.1 Declarative versus procedural programming

We have already seen that a distinctive characteristic of a knowledge-based system is that knowledge is separated from reasoning. Within the knowledge base, the programmer expresses information about the problem to be solved. Often this information is declarative, i.e., the programmer states some facts, rules or relationships without having to be concerned with the detail of *how* and *when* that information is applied. The following are all examples of declarative programming:

```
/* Rule 2.1 */
IF pressure is above threshold THEN close valve

/* Fact 2.1 */
valve A is shut                          /* a simple fact */

/* Fact 2.2 */
valve B is connected to tank 3           /* a relation */
```

Each example represents a piece of knowledge that could form part of a knowledge base. The declarative programmer does not necessarily need to state explicitly how, when and if the knowledge should be used. These details are implicit in the inference engine. An inference engine is normally programmed procedurally - a set of sequential commands are obeyed, which involve extracting and using information from the knowledge base. This task can be made explicit by using *meta-knowledge* (knowledge about knowledge), e.g.,

```
/* Meta-rule 2.1 */
Examine rules about valves before rules about pipes.
```

Most conventional programming is procedural. Consider, for example, the following C program:

```
/* A program in C to read 10 integers from a file and */
/* print them out */
#include <stdio.h>
FILE *openfile;
main()
{ int j, mynumber;
  openfile = fopen("myfile.dat", "r");
  if (openfile == NULL)
    printf("error opening file");
  else
  {
    for (j=1; j<=10; j=j+1)
    {
      fscanf(openfile,"%d",&mynumber);
      printf("Number %d is %d\n", j, mynumber);
    }
    fclose(openfile);
  }
}
```

This program contains explicit step-by-step instructions telling the computer to perform the following actions:

i   open a data file;
ii   print a message if it cannot open the file, otherwise perform the remaining steps;
iii   set the value of j to 1;
iv   read an integer from the file and store it in the variable mynumber;
v   print out the value of mynumber;
vi   add 1 to j;
vii   if $j \leq 10$ to repeat steps iv-vi, otherwise move on to step viii;
viii close the data file.

The data file, on the other hand, contains no instructions for the computer at all, just information in the form of a set of integers. The procedural instructions for determining what the computer should do with the integers resides in the program. The data file is therefore declarative, while the program is procedural. The data file is analogous to a trivial knowledge base, and the program is analogous to the corresponding inference engine. Of course, a proper knowledge base would be richer in content, perhaps containing a combination of rules, facts, relations and data. The corresponding inference engine would be expected to interpret the knowledge, to combine it to form an overall view, to apply the knowledge to data, and to make decisions.

It would be an oversimplification to think that all knowledge bases are written declaratively and all inference engines are written procedurally. In real systems, a collection of declarative information, such as a rule set, often needs to be embellished by some procedural information. Similarly, there may be some inference engines that have been programmed declaratively, notably those implemented in Prolog (described in section 2.6). Nonetheless, the declarative instructions must eventually be translated into procedural ones, as the computer can only understand procedural instructions at the machine code level.

The facilities available to assist in constructing knowledge-based systems can be roughly divided into four categories:

- expert system shells;
- toolkits: e.g., ART™, KEE™ and Goldworks™;
- programming languages for artificial intelligence: e.g., Lisp, Prolog and Pop-11;
- conventional programming languages: e.g., C, Pascal and Fortran.

Most expert system shells (see section 2.2) provide facilities for declarative programming in the form of rules, but little else. The programming languages offer the flexibility of programming procedurally, and can be used to build tools which allow declarative programming. The Prolog language permits both procedural and declarative programming. The toolkits typically offer a mixture of facilities so that the programmer has free access to the underlying language and also to tools such as rule-based programming (see chapter 3) and object-oriented programming (see chapter 5). The provision of these tools can save considerable programming effort, while the ability to access the underlying language gives the freedom to build extra facilities.

2.2 Expert system shells

An expert system shell is an expert system that is complete except for the knowledge base. Thus a shell includes an inference engine, a user interface for programming, and a user interface for running the system. Typically the programming interface will comprise a specialized editor for creating rules in a predetermined format, and some debugging tools. The user of the shell enters rules in a declarative fashion, and ideally should not need to be concerned with the workings of the inference engine. In practice this ideal is rarely met, and a typical difficulty in using a shell lies in ensuring that a rule is applied when it is expected to be. As the user has no direct control over the inference engine, it is normally necessary to gain some insight into its workings and to tailor the rules in order to achieve the desired effect. This is not necessarily easy, and detracts from the advantages of having a separate knowledge base. Nonetheless, shells are easy to use in other respects and allow a simple knowledge-based system to be constructed quickly. However, their inflexible facilities for knowledge representation and inference are often a major drawback.

2.3   Artificial intelligence toolkits

Artificial intelligence toolkits offer the facilities of expert system shells, object-oriented programming (see chapter 5) and artificial intelligence languages (sections 2.4-2.7). While this may sound like the best of all worlds, there are penalties to be paid for the rich programming power of the AI toolkits. The most important penalties are that they require a powerful processor, large amounts of disk space and memory (RAM), and that the licence fee must be paid. Three of the best known AI toolkits are KEE™, ART™ and Goldworks™. Some toolkits are now available (e.g., Nexpert™ and ProKappa™) which have been built using C or C++ rather than an AI language. These products are likely to grow in importance since they benefit from the widespread popularity of C and C++.

2.4   Artificial intelligence languages

The two most widely used artificial intelligence (AI) languages are Lisp and Prolog. Our discussion will also include Pop-11, a language with many common features to Lisp. Two important features of the AI languages are:

- the ability to manipulate symbolic data (characters and words) as well as numerical data; and
- an interactive programming environment is provided.

2.4.1   Lists
A knowledge base may contain a mixture of numbers, letters, words, punctuation and complete sentences. Most computer languages can handle such a mixture of characters, provided that the general layout or format can be anticipated in advance. So it is possible in C to declare a structure which, for instance, could contain five elements: a string, an integer, another string, a real number and a third string. This structure would be fine for declaring a simple fact such as:

```
pressure in valve 2 is 12.8 MPa.
```

One possible C implementation of this fact is shown below. A data structure called `state_of_device` is defined, and then a structure of this type, called `device1` is created. Each of the five parts, or *fields*, of `device1` is then set to an appropriate value.

```
type def struct
{
    char* device_type[10];
    int device_number;
    char* property[10];
    double value;
    char* units[10]
} state_of_device;

state_of_device device1;
device1.device_type = valve;
device1.device_number = 2;
device1.property = pressure;
device1.value = 12.8;
device1.units = MPa;
```

Although `state_of_device` has been defined in a generic way, so that it can be applied to components other than valves, a completely new structure would need to be defined for a fact or rule having a different format, such as:

```
if pressure is above 10 MPa then close valve.
```

A data structure is needed that can represent unpredictable combinations of words, numbers and symbols. The *list* is such a structure, and is a feature of Lisp, Prolog or Pop-11. Lists allow different types of data to be freely mixed, and are therefore a useful tool for symbol manipulation. The two examples above could each be represented as lists:

```
[pressure in valve 2 is 12.8 MPa]
[if pressure is above 10 MPa then close valve]
```

Prolog and Pop-11 both use square brackets (as shown) to denote lists, whereas Lisp uses round brackets. Both Lisp and Pop-11 use the key word *nil* to denote an empty list. Thus in Lisp, () and *nil* are equivalent, and in Pop-11 [] and *nil* are equivalent. The word *nil* does not have any special meaning attached to it in Prolog.

It should be noted that C is a versatile language, and that lists can be implemented in C by creating pairs of values and pointers, forming a so-called linked list. However, a strength of the AI languages is the integration of lists into the language, together with the necessary facilities for manipulating those lists.

2.4.2 Other data types

As well as lists, there are a number of other data types available in the AI languages. Unlike conventional languages, variables in the AI languages can be used to store any type of data. This is illustrated by the following Pop-11 code:

```
vars myvariable;                       /* declare myvariable */
[a list] -> myvariable;        /* assign a list to myvariable */
pr(myvariable);      /* print the value assigned to myvariable */
3.141593 -> myvariable; /* assign a real number to myvariable */
pr(myvariable);      /* print the value assigned to myvariable */
```

The comments at the end of each line of code explain the operation being performed. The declaration in the first line creates a new variable, but does not state what type of data will be stored under that variable name. In the example shown, a list is firstly assigned to the variable and printed, followed by a real (or floating point) number. The declaration of variables is not always necessary in the AI languages, but in the case of Lisp and Pop-11 declarations are normally made in order to specify explicitly the scope of a variable. Undeclared variables are assumed to be global in Pop-11 and Lisp (i.e., memory is allocated for the whole duration of a program or interactive session). In Pop-11 an appropriate warning is generated whenever this assumption is made.

Type	Examples
integers	0, 23, -15
real (floating point) numbers	3.1415927, -1.24
strings	"a string in Lisp" "a string in Prolog" 'a string in Pop-11'
words	myword, x, z34
lists	(a list of words in Lisp) [a, list, in, Prolog] [a list in Pop-11]

Table 2.1 Some data types.

Although the assignment of different types of data to variables is transparent to the programmer, the computer nevertheless needs to know the type of the data in order to handle it correctly. There are various techniques for achieving this. Typically the value associated with a variable includes a tag, hidden from the programmer, which labels its type. Some commonly used data types in the AI languages are shown in table 2.1.

Pop-11 and Lisp also allow the creation of arrays and structures, similar to those used in C. Strings can be made up of any printable characters, including numbers and spaces, enclosed in quotation marks. Words are less well defined, but in general can be regarded as a sequence of one or more characters without any spaces, since spaces and certain other characters (depending on the language) act as separators for words. Examples of words include variable names and the elements of the lists shown in table 2.1. List elements are not always words, as lists can contain embedded lists or numbers. The term *atom* is used in all three languages to denote a fundamental data type, which cannot be made up from other data types. For example, numbers and words are atoms, but lists are not.

During the execution of a program, various data structures may be created. There is therefore a need for management of the computer memory, i.e., memory must be allocated when needed and subsequently reclaimed. In languages such as C, the responsibility for memory management rests with the programmer, who must allocate and reclaim memory at appropriate places in the program using the `malloc` and `free` commands (or their equivalent). In the AI languages (and some others such as Smalltalk - see chapter 5) the memory is managed *automatically*. The programming environment must therefore be capable of both dynamically allocating memory and freeing memory that is no longer required. The latter process is called *garbage collection*, and may result in a momentary pause in the computer's response.

2.4.3 AI language environments

A conventional program is firstly designed and then typed into the computer using a text editor. The programmer then runs two standard programs, a compiler and linker, which convert his or her program code into an "executable image". Often the editor, compiler, and linker are provided as a single software package. If the code contains no mistakes, the program is then ready to run. If the compilation or linking fail, or the program does not act as intended, the programmer has to modify the program repeatedly until it compiles, links and works properly.

In general, the three AI languages (and some other languages) can be used interactively. The user starts by "calling up" Lisp, Prolog, or Pop-11. After a short pause, the user is presented with a symbol (the *prompt*), which signifies that the computer is ready to accept code on-line. Instructions are interpreted and obeyed as soon as they have been typed, and the output, if any, is printed on the screen. As we shall see in section 2.5, there is always a result to print in the case of Lisp.

Typing commands after the prompt is a useful way of inspecting the values of variables and testing ideas, but is not a practical way of writing a program. Most AI environments include a text editor which allows the user to type code which can subsequently be modified, saved and run. However, unlike editing and compiling conventional languages, at no stage does the programmer have to leave the AI language environment. Indeed, program code can often be evaluated or compiled from within the editor. Debugging programs is also easier. Like some implementations of conventional languages, the computer can be made to halt at a nominated point, or when an error occurs, so that the assignments up to that point to be examined. However, in an AI language, the programmer has more options at this stage. For instance, he or she may even be able to repair the code there and then so that the program can carry on running.

Code which has been written in an AI language will, in general, run more slowly than a compiled C program. However, the appeal of the AI languages is their power in terms of flexibility for the programmer, rather than computational or memory efficiency.

2.5 Lisp

2.5.1 Background

It has already been noted that a feature of the AI languages is the integration of lists and list manipulation into the language. This is particularly so in the case of Lisp, since a Lisp program is itself a list made up of many lists. Indeed the name Lisp is derived from the phrase "list processing".

Historically, Lisp has developed in an unregulated fashion. Different syntax and features were introduced into different implementations, partly as a consequence of the surrounding hardware and software environment. As a result, many different Lisp dialects such as Interlisp, Franzlisp, Maclisp, Zetalisp and Scheme were developed. A dialect called Common Lisp has now been produced, which aims to combine the most useful and the most portable features of the previous dialects into one machine-independent language [1]. All the examples introduced here are based upon the definition of Common Lisp, and should work on any Common Lisp system.

A list is a collection of words, numbers, strings, functions and further lists, enclosed in parentheses. The following are all examples of lists:

```
(a b c d)
(My car is 10 years old)
(a list (a b c) followed by an empty list ())
```

Lisp extends the idea of a language based upon list manipulation to the point where everything is either a list or an element of a list. There are only a few basic rules to remember in order to understand how Lisp works. However, because its structure is so different from other languages, Lisp may seem rather strange to the novice.

2.5.2 Lisp functions

While it is valid to describe Lisp as a procedural language (i.e., the computer is told exactly what to do), a more precise description would be that it is a *functional* language. This is because a Lisp program is made up of lists that are interpreted as functions and which, by definition, return a single value.

The three key rules to understanding Lisp are:

- each item of a list is evaluated;
- the first item is interpreted as a function name; and
- the remaining items are the parameters (or arguments) of the function.

Some of the functions with which we will be dealing are strictly speaking *macros*, which are predefined combinations of functions. However, the distinction need not concern us here. With a few exceptions, the parameters to a function are always evaluated before the function itself. The parameters themselves may also be functions, and can even be the same function (thereby permitting recursion). The following example would be a valid Lisp call to the function *print*. The computer's prompt which precedes user input will be shown as "lisp>":

```
lisp> (print "hello world")
hello world
hello world
```

The first element in the list was interpreted as a function name, and the second item as its argument. The argument evaluates to the string "hello world". It might seem surprising that "hello world" is printed twice. It is firstly printed because we instructed Lisp to do so. It is then printed again because Lisp always prints out the value of the function that it is given. In this example the function *print* returned as its value the item that it had printed. Consider what will happen if we type the following:

```
lisp> (print hello)
Error: Unbound variable: HELLO.
```

This error message has come about because Lisp evaluates every item in the list. In this example, the interpreter tried to evaluate `hello`, but found it to be undefined. A defined variable is one which has a value (perhaps another function) assigned to it. However, in this case we didn't really want `hello` to be evaluated. There are many instances when writing Lisp code when we would like to suppress Lisp's habit of evaluating every argument. A special function, *quote*, is provided for this specific purpose.

The *quote* function takes only one argument, which it does not evaluate but simply returns in the same form that it is typed:

```
lisp> (quote hello)
hello

lisp> (print (quote hello))
hello
hello
```

The *quote* function is used so often that a shorthand form has been made available, so that:

```
lisp> (quote hello)
```

and

```
lisp> 'hello
```

are equivalent.

Another occasion when we would wish to suppress the habit of functions evaluating their arguments is when making assignments. Here is an assignment in C:

```
my_variable=2.5; /* C code to assign value 2.5 to my_variable */
```

A value of 2.5 is assigned to `my_variable`. Lisp provides various functions for achieving this, one of which is *setf*:

```
lisp> (setf my_variable 2.5)
2.5
```

Since the first argument is a variable name, only the second argument to *setf* is evaluated. This is because we want to make an assignment to the variable

name and not to whatever was previously assigned to it. The second parameter
of *setf*, namely 2.5, evaluates to itself, and this value is then assigned to
my_variable. Like all Lisp functions, *setf* returns a value, in this case 2.5,
and this value is printed on the screen by the Lisp interpreter.

As we noted earlier, Lisp usually tries to evaluate the parameters of a
function before attempting to evaluate the function itself. The parameters may
be further functions with their own parameters. There is no practical limit to
the embedding of functions within functions in this manner, so complex
composite functions can easily be built up, and perhaps given names so that
they can be reused. The important rule for reading or writing Lisp code is that
list elements are interpreted as a function name and its parameters (unless the
list is the argument to *quote*, *setf* or a similar function), and that a function
always returns a value.

Lisp code is entirely constructed from lists, and lists also represent an
important form of data in Lisp. Therefore it is hardly surprising that built-in
functions for manipulating lists form an important part of the Lisp language.
Two basic functions for list manipulation are *first* and *rest*. For historical
reasons, the functions *car* and *cdr* are also available to perform the same tasks.
The *first* function returns the first item of that list, while *rest* returns the
list but with the first item removed. Here are some examples:

```
Lisp>(first '(a b c d))
a

Lisp>(rest '(a b c d))
(b c d)

Lisp>(first (rest '(a b c d)))
b

Lisp>(first '((a b)(c d)))
(a b)
```

Used together, *first* and *rest* can find any element in a list. However, two
convenient functions for finding parts of a list are *nth* and *nthcdr*.

```
(nth 0 x)    finds the 1st element of list x.
(nth 1 x)    finds the 2nd element of list x.
(nth 2 x)    finds the 3rd element of list x.
(nthcdr 2 x) is the same as (rest (rest x)).
(nthcdr 3 x) is the same as (rest (rest (rest x))).
```

In chapter 8, the problem of selecting materials is discussed. One approach involves (among other things) finding those materials which meet a specification or list of specifications. This task is used here as an illustration of the features of the three main AI languages. The problem is to define a Lisp function, Prolog relation or Pop-11 procedure called accept. When a materials specification or set of specifications are passed as parameters to accept, it should return a list of materials in the database which meet the specification(s). The list returned should contain pairs of material names and types. Thus, in Pop-11 syntax, the following would be a valid result from accept:

```
[[polypropylene thermoplastic]
 [polyurethane_foam thermoset]]
```

In this case, the list returned contains two elements, corresponding to the two materials that meet the specification. Each of the two elements is itself a list of two elements: a material name and its type.
The specification that is passed to accept as a parameter will have a predefined format. If just one specification is to be applied, this will be in the form of a list of the form:

```
[property_name  minimum_value  tolerance]
```

The representation of lists varies slightly between the AI languages. An example specification would be:

```
[flexural_modulus 1.0 0.1]
```

For a material to meet this specification, its flexural modulus must be at least (1.0 - 0.1). The units of flexural modulus are assumed to be GPa. If more than one specification is to be applied, the specifications will be grouped together into a list of the form:

```
[[property1  minimum_value1  tolerance1]
 [property2  minimum_value2  tolerance2]
 [property3  minimum_value3  tolerance3]]
```

When presented with a list of this type, accept should find those materials in the database which meet all of the specifications.

Box 2.1 Problem definition: finding materials which meet some specifications.

Note that `rest` and `nthcdr` both return a list, while `first` and `nth` may return a list or an atom. When `rest` is applied to a list which contains only one element, an empty list is returned, which is written as () or `nil`. When either `first` or `rest` is applied to an empty list, they both return `nil`.

There are many other functions provided in Lisp for list manipulation and program control. It is not intended that this overview of Lisp should introduce them all. The purpose of this section is not to replace the many texts on Lisp, but to give the reader a feel for the unusual syntax and structure of Lisp programs. However, we will show by means of a worked example how Lisp programs can be constructed, and in so doing will introduce some of the important functions in Lisp.

2.5.3 A worked example

We will discuss in chapter 8 the application of knowledge-based systems to problems of selection. One of the selection tasks that will be discussed in some detail is the selection of an appropriate material from which to manufacture a product or component. For the purposes of this worked example, let us assume that we wish to build a shortlist of polymers that meet some numerical specifications. We will endeavor to solve this problem using Lisp, and later in this chapter will encode the same example in Prolog and in Pop-11. The problem is specified in detail in box 2.1.

The first part of our program will be the setting up of some appropriate materials data. There are a number of ways of doing this, including the creation of a list called `materials_database`:

```
(defvar materials_database nil)
(setf materials_database '(
                    (abs thermoplastic
                            (impact_resistance 0.2)
                            (flexural_modulus 2.7)
                            (maximum_temperature 70))
                    (polypropylene thermoplastic
                            (impact_resistance 0.07)
                            (flexural_modulus 1.5)
                            (maximum_temperature 100))
                    (polystyrene thermoplastic
                            (impact_resistance 0.02)
                            (flexural_modulus 3.0)
                            (maximum_temperature 50))
                    (polyurethane_foam thermoset
                            (impact_resistance 1.06)
                            (flexural_modulus 0.9)
                            (maximum_temperature 80))
                    (pvc thermoplastic
```

```
                          (impact_resistance 1.06)
                          (flexural_modulus 0.007)
                          (maximum_temperature 50))
              (silicone thermoset
                          (impact_resistance 0.02)
                          (flexural_modulus 3.5)
                          (maximum_temperature 240))))
```

The function *defvar* is used to declare the variable materials_database and to assign to it an initial value, in this case *nil*. The function *setf* is used to assign the list of materials properties to materials_database. In a real application we would be more likely to read this information from a file than to have it "hard-coded" into our program, but this representation will suffice for the moment. The variable materials_database is used to store a list, each element of which is also a list. Each of these sublists contains information about one polymer. The information is in the form of a name and category, followed by further lists in which property names and values are stored. Since materials_database does not have a predeclared size, materials and materials properties can be added or removed with ease.

Our task is to define a Lisp function, to be called accept, which takes a set of specifications as its parameters and returns a list of polymers (both their names and types) which meet the specifications. To define accept, we will use the function *defun*, whose purpose is to define a function. Like *quote*, *defun* does not evaluate its arguments. We will define accept as taking a single parameter, spec_list, which is a list of specifications to be met. Comments are indicated by a semi-colon.

```
(defun accept (spec_list)
   (let ((shortlist (setup)))
     (if (atom (first spec_list))
;if the first element of spec_list is an atom then consider the
;specification
       (setf shortlist (meets_one spec_list shortlist))
;else consider each specification in turn
       (dolist (each_spec spec_list)
         (setf shortlist (meets_one each_spec shortlist))))
     shortlist))                                        ;return shortlist
```

In defining accept, we have assumed the form that the specification, spec_list, will take. It will either be a list of the form:

```
(property minimum_value tolerance)
```

or a list made up of several such specifications:

```
((property1 minimum_value1 tolerance1) (property2
minimum_value2 tolerance2) (property3 minimum_value3
tolerance3)).
```

Where more than one specification is given within spec_list, they must all be met.

The first function of accept is *let*, a function which allows us to declare and initialize local variables. In our example the variable shortlist is declared and assigned the value returned by the function setup, which we have still to define. The variable shortlist is local in the sense that it only exists between "(let" and the matching closing bracket.

There then follows a Lisp conditional statement. The *if* function is used to test whether spec_list comprises one or many specifications. It does this by ascertaining whether the *first* element of spec_list is an atom. If it is, then spec_list contains only one specification, and the *first* element of spec_list is expected to be the name of the property to be considered. If on the other hand spec_list contains more than one specification, then its *first* element will be a list representing the first specification, so the test for whether the *first* element of spec_list is an atom will return *nil* (meaning "false").

The general form of the *if* function is:

```
(if condition function1 function2)
```

which is interpreted as:

```
IF condition is true THEN do function1 ELSE do function2.
```

In our example, function1 involves setting the value of shortlist to the value returned by the function meets_one (yet to be defined), which is passed the single specification and the current shortlist of materials as its parameters. The "else" part of the conditional function (function2) is more complicated, and comprises the *dolist* control function. In our example, *dolist* initially assigns the first element of spec_list to the local variable each_spec. It then evaluates all functions up to the ")" which is paired with "(dolist". In our example this is just one function, which sets shortlist to the value returned from the function meets_one. Since *dolist* is an iterative control function, it will then repeat the process with the second element of spec_list, and so on until there are no elements left.

It is our intention that the function accept should return a list of polymers which meet the specification or specifications. When a function is made up of many functions, the value returned is the last value to be evaluated. In order to ensure that the value returned by accept is the final shortlist of polymers, shortlist is evaluated as the last line of the definition of accept. Note that the bracketing is such that this evaluation takes place within the scope of the `let` function, within which `shortlist` is a local variable.

We have seen that the first task performed within the function `accept` was to set up the initial shortlist of polymers by evaluating the function `setup`. This function produces a list of all polymers (and their types) which are known to the system through the definition of `materials_database`. The `setup` function is defined as follows:

```
(defun setup ()
  (let ((shortlist nil))
    (dolist (material materials_database)
      (setf shortlist (cons (cons (first material) (nth 1
                    material)) shortlist)))
    shortlist))
```

The empty brackets at the end of the first line of the function definition signify that `setup` takes no parameters. As in the definition of `accept`, *let* is used to declare a local variable and to give it an initial value of *nil*, i.e., the empty list. Then *dolist* is used to consider each element of `materials_database` in turn and to assign it to the local variable `material`. Each successive value of `material` is a list comprising the polymer name, its type, and lists of properties and values. The intention is to extract from this a list comprising a name and type only, and to collect all such two-element lists together into the list `shortlist`. The Lisp function *cons* adds an element to a list, and can therefore be used to build up `shortlist`.

Assuming that its second parameter is a list, *cons* will return the result of adding its first parameter to the front of that list. This can be illustrated by example:

```
lisp>(cons 'a '(b c d))
(a b c d)
```

However, the use of *cons* is still valid even if the second parameter is not a list. In such circumstances, a special type of two-element list, called a dotted pair, is produced:

```
lisp>(cons 'a 'b)
(a.b)
```

In our definition of `setup` we have used two embedded calls to *cons*, one of which produces a dotted pair while the other produces an ordinary list. The most deeply embedded (or *nested*) call to *cons* is called first, as Lisp always evaluates parameters to a function before evaluating the function itself. So the first *cons* to be evaluated returns a dotted pair comprising the *first* element of material (which is a polymer name) and the second element of material (which is the polymer type). The second *cons* to be evaluated returns the result of adding the dotted pair to the front of shortlist. Then shortlist is updated to this value by the call of *setf*. As in the definition of accept, shortlist is evaluated after the *dolist* loop has terminated, to ensure that setup returns the last value of shortlist.

As we have already seen, accept passes a single specification, together with the current shortlist, as parameters to the function meets_one. It is this function which performs the most important task in our program, namely deciding which materials in the shortlist meet the specification:

```
(defun meets_one (spec shortlist)
   (dolist (material shortlist)
     (let ((actual (get_database_value (first spec) (first
                     material))))
       (if (< actual (- (nth 1 spec) (nth 2 spec)))
         (setf shortlist (remove material shortlist)))))
           ;;pseudo-C equivalent:
           ;;if actual < (value - tolerance)
           ;;shortlist=shortlist without material
shortlist)
```

We have already met most of the Lisp functions that make up meets_one. In order to consider each material-type pair in the shortlist, *dolist* is used. The actual value of a property (such as maximum operating temperature) for a given material is found by passing the property name and the material name as arguments to the function get_database_value, which has yet to be defined. The value returned from get_database_value is stored in the local variable actual. The value of actual is then compared with the result of subtracting the specified tolerance from the specified target value. In our example, the tolerance is simply used to make the specification less severe. It may be surprising at first to see that subtraction and arithmetic comparison are both dealt with in Lisp as functions. Nonetheless this treatment is consistent with other Lisp operations. The code includes a comment showing the conventional positioning of the operators in other languages such as C. Note that *nth* is used in order to extract the second and third elements of spec, which represent the specification value and tolerance respectively.

If the database value, actual, of the property in question is less than the specification value minus the tolerance, then the material is removed from the shortlist. The Lisp function *remove* is provided for this purpose. Since the arguments to the function are evaluated before the function itself, it follows that *remove* is not able to alter shortlist itself. Rather it returns the list that would be produced if material were removed from a copy of shortlist. Therefore *setf* has to be used to set shortlist to this new value.

As in our other functions, shortlist is evaluated so that its value will be returned as the value of the function meets_one. At a glance, it may appear that this is unnecessary, as *setf* would return the value of shortlist. However, it is important to remember that this function is embedded within other functions. The last function to be evaluated is in fact *dolist*. When *dolist* terminates by reaching the end of shortlist, it returns the empty list, (), which is clearly not the desired result.

There now only remains one more function to define in order to make our Lisp program work, and that function is get_database_value. As mentioned previously, get_database_value should return the actual value of a property for a material, when the property and material names are passed as arguments. Common Lisp provides us with the function *find*, which is ideally suited to this task. The syntax of *find* is best illustrated by example. The following function call will search the list materials_database until it finds a list whose *first* element is identically equal (*eq*) to the value of material:

```
(find material materials_database :test #'eq :key #'first)
```

Other tests and keys can be used in conjunction with *find*, as defined in [1]. Having found the data corresponding to the material of interest, the name and type can be removed using *nthcdr*, and *find* can be called again in order to find the list corresponding to the property of interest. The function get_database_value can therefore be written as follows:

```
(defun get_database_value (prop_name material)
  (nth 1 (find prop_name
            (nthcdr 2
              (find material materials_database :test #'eq :key
                #'first))
            :test #'eq :key #'first)))
```

We are now in a position to put our program together, as shown in box 2.2 and to ask Lisp some questions about polymers:

```
lisp> (accept'(maximum_temperature 100 5))
((SILICONE . THERMOSET) (POLYPROPYLENE . THERMOPLASTIC))

lisp> (accept '((maximum_temperature 100 5) (impact_resistance
      0.05 0)))
((POLYPROPYLENE . THERMOPLASTIC))
```

```lisp
(defvar materials_database nil)
(setf materials_database '(
                            (abs thermoplastic
                                       (impact_resistance 0.2)
                                       (flexural_modulus 2.7)
                                       (maximum_temperature 70))
                            (polypropylene thermoplastic
                                       (impact_resistance 0.07)
                                       (flexural_modulus 1.5)
                                       (maximum_temperature 100))
                            (polystyrene thermoplastic
                                       (impact_resistance 0.02)
                                       (flexural_modulus 3.0)
                                       (maximum_temperature 50))
                            (polyurethane_foam thermoset
                                       (impact_resistance 1.06)
                                       (flexural_modulus 0.9)
                                       (maximum_temperature 80))
                            (pvc thermoplastic
                                       (impact_resistance 1.06)
                                       (flexural_modulus 0.007)
                                       (maximum_temperature 50))
                            (silicone thermoset
                                       (impact_resistance 0.02)
                                       (flexural_modulus 3.5)
                                       (maximum_temperature 240))))

(defun accept (spec_list)
  (let ((shortlist (setup)))
    (if (atom (first spec_list))
;;if the first element of spec_list is an atom then consider the
;;specification
      (setf shortlist (meets_one spec_list shortlist))
;;else consider each specification in turn
      (dolist (each_spec spec_list)
        (setf shortlist (meets_one each_spec shortlist))))
      shortlist))                                       ;return shortlist

(defun setup ()
  (let ((shortlist nil))
    (dolist (material materials_database)
      (setf shortlist (cons (cons (first material) (nth 1 material))
shortlist)))
    shortlist))

(defun meets_one (spec shortlist)
  (dolist (material shortlist)
    (let ((actual (get_database_value (first spec) (first material))))
      (if (< actual (- (nth 1 spec) (nth 2 spec)))
        (setf shortlist (remove material shortlist)))))
          ;;pseudo-C equivalent:
          ;;if actual< (value - tolerance)
          ;;shortlist=shortlist without material
shortlist)

(defun get_database_value (prop_name material)
  (nth 1 (find prop_name
           (nthcdr 2
              (find material materials_database :test #'eq :key
                  #'first))
           :test #'eq :key #'first)))
```

Box 2.2 A worked example in Lisp.

Once the function definitions have been evaluated, each function (such as `accept`) becomes known to Lisp in the same way as all of the predefined functions such as `setf` and `dolist` .   Therefore we have extended the Lisp language so that it has become specialized for our own specific purposes.   It is this ability that makes Lisp such a powerful and flexible language.   If a programmer doesn't like the facilities that Lisp offers, he or she can alter the syntax by defining his or her own functions, thereby producing an alternative language.   This is the basis upon which the sophisticated and expensive AI environments such as Goldworks™, KEE™ and ART™ are built.   These environments not only offer the programmer a Lisp interpreter, but also a vast number of Lisp functions which together provide a language for object-oriented programming (chapter 5) and rule-based programming (chapter 3).   In addition, an attractive user interface is normally provided, and this too has been built up as an extension of the Lisp language.

2.6   Prolog

2.6.1   Background

Prolog is an AI language which can be programmed declaratively.   It is therefore very different from Lisp, which is a procedural language that can be used to build declarative applications such as expert system shells.   As we will see, although Prolog can be used declaratively, an appreciation of the procedural behavior of the language is needed.   In other words, programmers need to understand how Prolog uses the declarative information that they supply.

Prolog is suited to symbolic (rather than numerical) problems, particularly logical problems involving relations between things.   It is also suitable for tasks that involve data look-up and retrieval, since pattern-matching is fundamental to the functionality of the language.   Because Prolog is so different from other languages in its underlying concepts, many newcomers find it a difficult language.   Whereas most languages can rapidly be learned by someone with computing experience, Prolog is perhaps more easily learnt by someone who has never programmed before.

2.6.2   A worked example

The main building blocks of Prolog are lists (as in Lisp) and *relations*, which can be used to construct *clauses*.   We will demonstrate the declarative nature of Prolog programs by constructing a small program for selecting polymers from a database of polymer properties.   The task will be identical to that used to illustrate Lisp, namely selecting from a database those polymers which meet a numerical specification or set of specifications. The problem is described in more detail in box 2.1. We have already said that Prolog is good for data lookup, so let's begin by creating a small database containing some properties of materials. Our database will comprise a number of clauses like this one involving the relation `materials_database`:

```
materials_database(polypropylene, thermoplastic,
[maximum_temperature, 100]).
```

The above clause means that the three items in parentheses are related through the relation called `materials_database`. The third argument of the clause is a list (denoted by square brackets), while the first two arguments are atoms. The clause is our first piece of Prolog code, and it is purely declarative. We have given the computer some information about polypropylene, and this is sufficient to produce a working (though rather trivial) program. Even though we have not given Prolog any procedural information (i.e., we haven't told it how to use the information about polypropylene), we can still ask it some questions. Having typed the above line of Prolog code, not forgetting the full-stop, we can ask Prolog the question:

"What type of material is polypropylene?"

Depending on the Prolog implementation, queries are normally preceded with a question mark. Our query to Prolog could be expressed as:

```
prolog> ? materials_database(polypropylene, Family, _).
```

Prolog would respond:

```
Nº1    Family = thermoplastic
No more solutions
```

The computer's prompt is displayed as `prolog>`, although this will vary between Prolog installations. This simple example illustrates several features of Prolog. Firstly, our program comprised a single line of code, which stated that polypropylene is a material of type thermoplastic, and which has a maximum operating temperature of 100 (°C assumed). Thus the program is purely declarative. We have told Prolog what we know about polypropylene, but have given Prolog no procedural instructions about what to do with that information. Nevertheless we were able to ask a sensible question and receive a sensible reply. Our query includes some distinct data types. As `polypropylene` began with a lower case letter, it was recognized as a constant, whereas `Family` was recognized as a variable by virtue of beginning with an upper case letter. These distinctions stem from the following rules, which are always observed:

- variables in Prolog can begin either with an uppercase letter or with an underscore character (e.g., `X`, `My_variable`, `_another` are all valid variable names); and

- constants begin with a lower case letter (e.g., `adrian`, `polypropylene`, `pi` are all valid names for constants).

When presented with our query, Prolog has attempted to *match* the query to the relations (only one relation in our example) that it has stored. In order for any two terms to match, either:

i   the two terms must be identical; or

ii   it must be possible to set (or *instantiate*) any variables in such a way that the two terms become identical.

If Prolog is trying to match two or more clauses and comes across multiple occurrences of the same variable name, it will always instantiate them identically. The only exception to this rule is the underscore character, which has a special meaning when used on its own. Each occurrence of the underscore character appearing alone means:

"I don't care what '_' matches so long as it matches something".

Multiple occurrences of the character can be matched to different values. The '_' character is used when the value of a variable is not needed in the evaluation of a clause. Thus:

```
materials_database(polypropylene, thermoplastic,
[maximum_temperature, 100]).
```

matches

```
materials_database(polypropylene, Family, _).
```

The relation name, `materials_database`, and its number of arguments (or its *arity*) are the same in each case. The first argument to `materials_database` is identical in each case, and the remaining two can be made identical by instantiating the variable Family to t hermoplastic and the underscore variable to the list [maximum_temperature, 100]. We don't care what the solo underscore character matches, so long as it matches something.

Now let's see if we can extend our example into a useful program. Firstly we will make our database more useful by adding some more data:

```
materials_database(abs, thermoplastic,
  [[impact_resistance, 0.2],
  [flexural_modulus, 2.7],
  [maximum_temperature, 70]]).
materials_database(polypropylene, thermoplastic,
  [[impact_resistance, 0.07],
  [flexural_modulus, 1.5],
  [maximum_temperature, 100]]).
materials_database(polystyrene, thermoplastic,
  [[impact_resistance, 0.02],
  [flexural_modulus, 3.0],
  [maximum_temperature, 50]]).
materials_database(polyurethane_foam, thermoset,
  [[impact_resistance, 1.06],
  [flexural_modulus, 0.9],
  [maximum_temperature, 80]]).
materials_database(pvc, thermoplastic,
  [[impact_resistance, 1.06],
  [flexural_modulus, 0.007],
  [maximum_temperature, 50]]).
materials_database(silicone, thermoset,
  [[impact_resistance, 0.02],
  [flexural_modulus, 3.5],
  [maximum_temperature, 240]]).
```

Our aim is to build a program which can select from the database those materials which meet a set of specifications. This requirement can be translated directly into a Prolog rule:

```
accept(Material,Type,Spec_list):-
  materials_database(Material,Type,Stored_data),
  meets_all_specs(Spec_list,Stored_data).
```

The ':-' symbol stands for the word 'if' in the rule. Thus the above rule means:

accept a material, given a list of specifications, if that material is in the database and if the stored data about the material meet the specifications.

We now have to let Prolog know what we mean by a material meeting all of the specifications in the user's specification list. The simplest case is when there are no specifications at all, in other words the specification list is empty. In this case the (nonexistent) specifications will be met regardless of the stored data. This fact can be simply coded in Prolog as:

```
meets_all_specs([],_).
```

The next most straightforward case to deal with is when there is only one specification, which we can code as follows:

```
meets_all_specs(Spec_list, Data):-
  Spec_list= [Spec1|Rest],
  atom(Spec1),
  meets_one_spec([Spec1|Rest],Data).
```

This rule introduces the list separator |, which is used to separate the first element of a list from the rest of the list. As an example, consider the following Prolog query:

```
prolog> ? [Spec1|Rest] = [flexural_modulus, 1.0, 0.1]
   Nº1    Spec1 = flexural_modulus,   Rest = [1.0, 0.1]
   No more solutions
```

The assignments to the variables immediately before and after the list separator are analogous to taking the *first* and *rest* of a list in Lisp. Consistent with this analogy, the item immediately following a 'I' symbol will always be instantiated to a list. Returning now to our rule, the first condition requires Prolog to try to match Spec_list to the template [Spec1|Rest]. If the match were successful, Spec1 would become instantiated to the first element of Spec_list and Rest instantiated to Spec_list with its first element removed.

We could make our rule more compact by combining the first condition of the rule with the arguments to the goal:

```
meets_all_specs([Spec1|Rest], Data):-
  atom(Spec1),
  meets_one_spec([Spec1|Rest],Data).
```

If the match is successful, we wish to establish whether Spec_list contains one or many specifications. This can be achieved by testing the type of its first element. If the first element is an atom, the user has supplied a single specification, whereas if it is a list then more than one specification must have been supplied. All this assumes of course that the intended format was used for the query. The built-in Prolog relation *atom* succeeds if its argument is an atom, and otherwise it fails.

We have not yet told Prolog what is meant by the relation called meets_one_spec, but we will do so shortly. Next we will consider the general case of the user specifying several specifications:

```
meets_all_specs([Spec1|Rest],Data):-
  not atom(Spec1),
  meets_one_spec(Spec1,Data),
  meets_all_specs(Rest,Data).
```

An important feature demonstrated by this rule is the use of recursion, that is, the reuse of meets_all_specs within its own definition. Our rule says that the stored data meets the user's specification if each of the following are satisfied:

- we can separate the first specification from the remainder;
- the first specification is not an atom;
- the stored data meet the first specification; and
- the stored data meet all of the remaining specifications.

When presented with a list of specifications, individual specifications will be stripped off the list one at a time, and the rule will be deemed to have been satisfied if the stored data satisfy each of them.

Having dealt with multiple specifications by breaking down the list into a set of single specifications, it now remains for us to define what we mean by a specification being met. This is coded as follows:

```
meets_one_spec([Property, Spec_value, Tolerance], List):-
  member([Property, Actual_value], List),
  Actual_value>Spec_value-Tolerance.
```

As in the Lisp example, we explicitly state that a user's specification must be in a fixed format, i.e., the material property name, its target value and the tolerance of that value must appear in sequence in a list. A new relation called member is introduced in order to check that the stored data for a given material includes the property being specified, and to assign the stored value for that property to Actual_value. Member is not a built-in Prolog relation, so we will have to define it ourselves. Finally, the stored value is deemed to meet the specification if it is greater than the specification minus the tolerance.

The definition of member (taken from [2]) is similar in concept to our definition of meets_all_specs. The definition is that an item is a member of a list if that item is the first member of the list or if the list may be split so that the item is the first member of the second part of the list. This can be expressed more concisely and elegantly in Prolog than it can in English:

```
member(A,[A|L]).
member(A,[_|L]):-member(A,L).
```

Our program is now complete and ready to be interrogated. The program is shown in full in box 2.3. In order to run a Prolog program, Prolog must be set a goal which it can try to prove. If successful it will return all of the sets of instantiations necessary to satisfy that goal. In our case the goal is to find the materials that meet some specifications.

Let's now test our program with some example queries (or goals). Firstly

```
materials_database(abs, thermoplastic,
   [[impact_resistance, 0.2],
    [flexural_modulus, 2.7],
    [maximum_temperature, 70]]).
materials_database(polypropylene, thermoplastic,
   [[impact_resistance, 0.07],
    [flexural_modulus, 1.5],
    [maximum_temperature, 100]]).
materials_database(polystyrene, thermoplastic,
   [[impact_resistance, 0.02],
    [flexural_modulus, 3.0],
    [maximum_temperature, 50]]).
materials_database(polyurethane_foam, thermoset,
   [[impact_resistance, 1.06],
    [flexural_modulus, 0.9],
    [maximum_temperature, 80]]).
materials_database(pvc, thermoplastic,
   [[impact_resistance, 1.06],
    [flexural_modulus, 0.007],
    [maximum_temperature, 50]]).
materials_database(silicone, thermoset,
   [[impact_resistance, 0.02],
    [flexural_modulus, 3.5],
    [maximum_temperature, 240]]).

accept(Material,Type,Spec_list):-
   materials_database(Material,Type,Stored_data),
   meets_all_specs(Spec_list,Stored_data).

meets_all_specs([],_).
meets_all_specs([Spec1|Rest],Data):-
   atom(Spec1),
   meets_one_spec([Spec1|Rest],Data).
meets_all_specs([Spec1|Rest],Data):-
   not atom(Spec1),
   meets_one_spec(Spec1,Data),
   meets_all_specs(Rest,Data).

meets_one_spec([Property, Spec_value, Tolerance], List):-
   member([Property, Actual_value], List),
   Actual_value>Spec_value-Tolerance.

member(A,[A|L]).
member(A,[_|L]):-member(A,L).
```

Box 2.3 A worked example in Prolog.

we will determine which materials have a maximum operating temperature of at least 100°C, with a 5°C tolerance:

```
prolog> ?accept(M, T, [maximum_temperature, 100, 5]).
   Nº1     M = polypropylene,  T = thermoplastic
   Nº2     M = silicone,  T = thermoset
   No more solutions
```

We can now extend our query to find all materials which, as well as meeting the temperature requirement, have an impact resistance of at least 0.05 kJ/m:

```
prolog> ?accept(M, T, [[maximum_temperature, 100, 5],
[impact_resistance, 0.05, 0]]).
   Nº1     M = polypropylene,  T = thermoplastic
   No more solutions
```

2.6.3 Backtracking in Prolog

So far we have seen how to program declaratively in Prolog, without giving any thought to how Prolog uses the declarative program to decide upon a sequential series of actions. In the example shown in section 2.6.2 it was not necessary to know how Prolog used the information supplied to arrive at the correct answer. This represents the ideal of declarative programming in Prolog. However, the Prolog programmer invariably needs to have an idea of the procedural behavior of Prolog in order to ensure that a program performs correctly and efficiently. In many circumstances it is possible to type a valid declarative program, but for the program to fail to work as anticipated because the programmer has failed to take account of how Prolog works.

Let us start by considering our last example query to Prolog:

```
prolog> ?accept(M, T, [[maximum_temperature, 100, 5],
[impact_resistance, 0.05, 0]]).
```

Prolog treats this query as a goal, whose truth it attempts to establish. As the goal contains some variables (M and T), these will need to be instantiated in order to achieve the goal. Prolog's first attempt at achieving the goal is to see whether the program contains any clauses which directly match the query. In our example it does not, but it does find a rule with the accept relation as its conclusion:

```
accept(Material, Type, Spec_list):-
  materials_database(Material, Type, Stored_data),
  meets_all_specs(Spec_list, Stored_data).
```

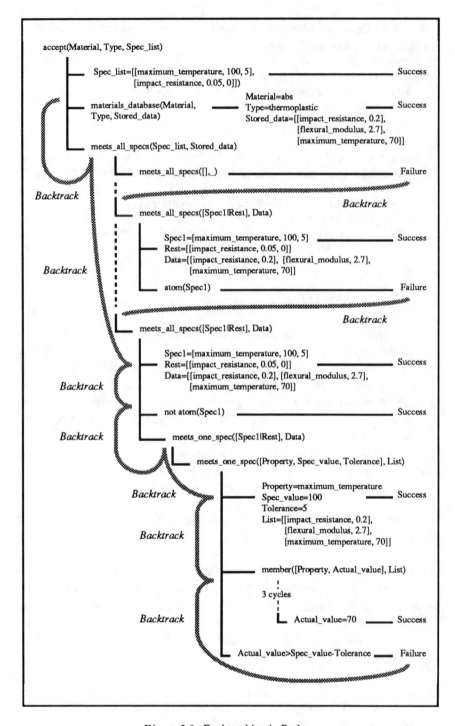

Figure 2.1 Backtracking in Prolog.

Prolog now knows that if it can establish the two conditions with M matched to Material, T matched to Type, and Spec_list instantiated to [[maximum_temperature, 100, 5], [impact_resistance, 0.05, 0]], then the goal is achieved. The two conditions then become goals in their own right. The first one, involving the relation materials_database is easily achieved, and the second condition:

```
meets_all_specs(Spec_list,Stored_data).
```

becomes the new goal. Prolog's first attempt at satisfying this goal is to look at the relation:

```
meets_all_specs([],_).
```

However, this doesn't help as Spec_list is not instantiated to an empty list. Prolog must at this point *backtrack* to try another way of achieving the current sub-goal. In other words, Prolog remembers the stage it was at before the failed attempt, and resumes its reasoning along another path from there. Figure 2.1 shows the reasoning followed by Prolog when presented with the goal:

```
prolog> ?accept(M,T,[[maximum_temperature, 100,
5],[impact_resistance, 0.05, 0]]).
```

The illustration shows Prolog's first attempt at a solution, namely M=abs and T=thermoplastic, and the steps that are followed before rejecting these particular instantiations as a solution. The use of backtracking is sensible up until the point where it is discovered that the maximum operating temperature of ABS (acrylonitrile-butadiene-styrene) is too low. When this has been determined, we would ideally like the program to reject ABS as a candidate material, and to move on to the next contender. However, Prolog does not give up so easily. Instead it backtracks through every step that it has taken, checking to see whether there may be an alternative solution (or set of instantiations) that could be used. Ultimately it arrives back at the materials_database relation, and Material and Type become reinstantiated.

Prolog provides two facilities for controlling backtracking, which can be used to increase efficiency and to alter the meaning of a program. These facilities are:

i   the *order* of Prolog code; and
ii   the use of the *cut* operator.

Prolog tries out possible solutions to a problem in the order in which they are coded. Thus in our example, Prolog always starts by assuming that the user has supplied a single materials specification. Only when it discovers that this is not the case does Prolog consider that the user may have submitted a list of several specifications. This is an appropriate ordering, as it is sensible to try the simplest solution first. In general, the ordering of code will affect the procedural meaning of a Prolog program (i.e., how the problem will be solved), but not its declarative meaning. However, as soon as the Prolog programmer starts to use the second facility, namely the cut operator, the order of Prolog clauses can affect both the procedural and the declarative meaning of programs.

In order to prevent Prolog from carrying out unwanted backtracking, the cut symbol ('!') can be used. Cuts can be inserted as though they were goals in their own right. When Prolog comes across a cut, backtracking is prevented. Cuts can be used to make our example program more efficient by forcing Prolog immediately to try a new material once it has established whether or not a given material meets the specification. The revised program, with cuts included, is shown in box 2.4 (the setting up of the materials_database relations is unchanged and has been omitted).

Although the discussion so far has regarded the cut as a means of improving efficiency by eliminating unwanted backtracking, cuts can also alter the declarative meaning of programs. This can be illustrated by referring once again to our materials selection program. The program contains three alternative means of achieving the meets_all_specs goal. The first deals with the case where the first argument is the empty list. The two others take identical arguments, and a distinction is made based upon whether or not the first element of the first argument (a list) is an atom. If the element is an atom, then the alternative case need not be considered, and this can be achieved using a cut ('%' symbols indicate comments):

```
meets_all_specs([Spec1|Rest],Data):-
   atom(Spec1),!,                   % cut placed here
   meets_one_spec([Spec1|Rest],Data).

meets_all_specs([Spec1|Rest],Data):-
   not atom(Spec1),                 % this test is now redundant
   meets_one_spec(Spec1,Data),
   meets_all_specs(Rest,Data).
```

Because of the positioning of the cut, if:

```
atom(spec1)
```

is successful, then the alternative rule will not be considered. Therefore the test:

```
accept (Material,Type,Spec_list):-
   materials_database(Material,Type,Stored_data),
   meets_all_specs(Spec_list,Stored_data).

meets_all_specs([],_):-!.

meets_all_specs([Spec1|Rest],Data):-
   atom(Spec1),!,
   meets_one_spec([Spec1|Rest],Data).

meets_all_specs([Spec1|Rest],Data):-
   meets_one_spec(Spec1,Data),
   meets_all_specs(Rest,Data).

meets_one_spec([Property, Spec_value, Tolerance], List):-
   member([Property, Actual_value], List),!,
   Actual_value>Spec_value-Tolerance.

member(A,[A|L]).
member(A,[_|L]):-member(A,L).
```

Box 2.4 A Prolog program with cuts.

```
not atom(spec1)
```

is now redundant and can be removed. However, this test can only be removed
provided that the cut is included in the previous rule. This example shows that
a *cut* can be used to create rules of the form:

```
IF .... THEN .... ELSE.
```

While much of the above discussion has concentrated on overcoming the
inefficiencies that backtracking can introduce, it is important to remember that
backtracking is essential for searching out a solution, and the elegance of
Prolog in many applications lies in its ability to backtrack without the
programmer needing to program this behavior explicitly.

2.7 Pop-11

2.7.1 Background
Lisp is probably the most widely used language for list processing, but Pop-11
is an alternative AI language which has gained some popularity. It has a
Pascal-like syntax and can perform most tasks of a structured language like
Pascal, but in addition it contains many functions for manipulating symbols
and lists. The Pop-11 language is rich in the sense that it has a large number of
built-in procedures which can greatly accelerate program development.

Although Pop-11 is available as an isolated language, it is mostly used as a part of Poplog™, which is a programming environment that includes Pop-11, Common Lisp, Prolog, a built in editor, and facilities for linking-in code written in other languages such as C. A built-in "help" facility is provided in order to help the Pop-11 programmer find his or her way around the large number of procedures provided. The language is very expressive, so that the meaning of Pop-11 code is generally quite clear and explicit. This can be contrasted to Lisp, which is elegant in its compact representation, but can be difficult to follow. The price that is paid for the clarity of Pop-11 code is that there are generally more words to type than in Lisp. A example of the relative verbosity of Pop-11 is that every expression which can act on a block of code (e.g., *define*, *if*, *for*) must be terminated by a corresponding terminating word (*enddefine*, *endif*, *endfor*, etc).

2.7.2 A worked example

The syntax and semantics of Pop-11 can be illustrated by programming the same example that we used with Lisp and Prolog - namely selecting from a database those polymers that meet a set of specifications. The problem is defined in box 2.1. As before, the first task will be to create the materials database. Let's start by declaring the maximum operating temperature of polypropylene. To do this we will use the Pop-11 assignment arrow (->) as shown:

```
pop-11>[polypropylene thermoplastic [maximum_temperature 100]]
    -> materials_database;
;;; DECLARING VARIABLE materials_database
```

The computer's prompt is displayed as pop-11>, although the more normal prompt is simply a colon (:). In the above expression, the variable name materials_database appears to the right of the assignment arrow. This is in contrast to languages like C, Pascal and Fortran, where the variable name is placed on the left-hand side of the assignment operator and an expression to the right. Note also that because we had not explicitly told Pop-11 of our intention to use the variable materials_database, the interpreter has declared the variable on our behalf and has provided a warning. This is useful because variable names would normally be declared, and so the warning message is often associated with a misspelt variable name. When Pop-11 automatically declares variables, it always assumes them to be global.

As with Prolog, the one line of code that we have typed so far is sufficient for us to ask Pop-11 some questions and in so doing to illustrate some of the features of the language. Firstly we can ask pop-11 to print on the computer screen the value of materials_database using the "pretty print" arrow (==>).

```
pop-11>materials_database==>
** [polypropylene thermoplastic [maximum_temperature 100]]
```

Pop-11 also provides some other ways of printing onto the screen, but ==> will suffice for our purposes.

One of Pop-11's greatest strengths is the provision of a powerful pattern-matcher for manipulating lists. We can use this facility to find out the maximum operating temperature of polypropylene:

```
pop-11>vars my_value;
pop-11>materials_database -->
        [polypropylene = [maximum_temperature ?my_value]];
pop-11>my_value==>

** 100
```

This time we have declared the variable that we intend to use (my_value) by means of the key word *vars*. Unlike conventional languages, it is sufficient to state that the variable will be used, without committing it to storing a particular type of data. We then match materials_database onto a template using the *match arrow* (-->). The template contains three items. The first is the polymer name, the next is the '=' sign, and the last is an embedded list. The matching process is similar to that in Prolog. The variable and the template match if:

- the two terms are identical; or

- it is possible to set (or *instantiate*) any variables preceded by a question mark ('?') in such a way that the two terms become identical.

Although Pop-11 is case-sensitive (my_variable is different from My_variable), it does not use case for any special purpose, unlike Prolog. However, for pattern matching, Pop-11 needs to be able to distinguish variables from constants. For this reason variables which can be instantiated are preceded with a question mark. As we shall see shortly, Pop-11 also provides the '^' symbol for forcing the current value of a variable to be used as though it were a constant. The '=' sign can be instantiated to any value, and multiple occurrences of '=' can stand for different values. It can therefore be interpreted as:

"I don't care what the symbol '=' matches, so long as it matches something".

The '=' sign serves an identical function to the solo underscore ('_') in Prolog.

As with the Prolog and Lisp examples, our first stage towards building a useful program will be to expand the database. We will create a list called materials_database which is identical in its structure to that used in the Lisp example:

```
[
 [abs thermoplastic
                [impact_resistance 0.2]
                [flexural_modulus 2.7]
                [maximum_temperature 70]]
 [polypropylene thermoplastic
                [impact_resistance 0.07]
                [flexural_modulus 1.5]
                [maximum_temperature 100]]
 [polystyrene thermoplastic
                [impact_resistance 0.02]
                [flexural_modulus 3.0]
                [maximum_temperature 50]]
 [polyurethane_foam thermoset
                [impact_resistance 1.06]
                [flexural_modulus 0.9]
                [maximum_temperature 80]]
 [pvc thermoplastic
                [impact_resistance 1.06]
                [flexural_modulus 0.007]
                [maximum_temperature 50]]
 [silicone thermoset
                [impact_resistance 0.02]
                [flexural_modulus 3.5]
                [maximum_temperature 240]]
]->materials_database;
```

Because Pop-11 is so close to Lisp in its functionality, we can build our Pop-11 program by defining procedures that perform identical tasks to the Lisp functions described in section 2.5.3. Whereas all Lisp functions must return a value, Pop-11 procedures may return a value (in which case they are functions) or they may not. We will define a procedure called accept, which, like its Lisp equivalent, takes as its parameter a list (spec_list) containing one or more specifications, and returns a list of polymers that meet the specifications:

```
define accept(spec_list) -> polymer_list;
  vars shortlist, each_spec;
  setup()->shortlist;
  if isword(spec_list(1)) then
    meets_one(spec_list, shortlist)->shortlist;
  else
    for each_spec in spec_list do
```

```
        meets_one(each_spec, shortlist)->shortlist;
     endfor;
  endif;
  shortlist -> polymer_list;
enddefine;
```

The fact that `accept` returns a value is made explicit by the assignment of the procedure name and of the final value of `shortlist` to `polymer_list`. Pop-11 also allows the less explicit technique of omitting the first assignment, and replacing the second with:

```
return (shortlist);
```

The latter technique has the disadvantage of burying within the procedure's definition the fact that the procedure returns a value.

The variables `shortlist` and `each_spec` are declared within the body of the definition of the procedure, which means that they are local to the procedure. Any values which are assigned to local variables within a procedure will be lost when the procedure finishes its execution.

The variable `shortlist` is initially assigned the value returned by the procedure `setup`. The call to `setup` is made explicit by the empty brackets after the procedure name, indicating that the procedure should be called with no arguments. In the absence of the empty brackets, the *definition* of the procedure called `setup` would merely be assigned to shortlist, and the procedure would not be made to run.

As in the Lisp program, we need to distinguish between the cases where `spec_list` is a single specification and when it is a list of several specifications each of which must be met. This is achieved by testing to see whether the first element of the list `spec_list` is a word. The test is implemented by means of the procedure *isword* which returns the value *true* if the argument is a word and otherwise returns *false*. Note that any element of a list can be accessed simply by specifying its position in the list as an integer in brackets after the list name. This notation can be confusing, as it can make a list appear to be behaving like a procedure. Accessing the first element of `spec_list` is equivalent to using *first* in Lisp. Pop-11 provides two functions *hd* and *tl* (meaning "head" and "tail") which are equivalent to *first* and *rest* in Lisp. Thus:

`hd(spec_list)` and `spec_list(1)` are equivalent, but:

`tl(spec_list)` is different from `spec_list(2)`

as the latter refers to the second element of `spec_list`.

If spec_list contains only one specification, then a final list of polymers that meet the specification is returned by a single call of meets_one, which has yet to be defined. Otherwise meets_one must be called once for every specification in spec_list, and this is achieved by use of a loop of the form:

```
for element in list do
    ;;;pop-11 code here
endfor;
```

The code which constitutes the body of the loop is executed with element set to each element of list in turn. If some of the elements of list are themselves lists, then these embedded lists will, in their turn, be assigned to element. The elements of the embedded lists will not be extracted by the *for* loop. This point may be illustrated by loading the following procedure:

```
define example;
  vars mylist, myelement;
  [a [embedded list] b c] -> mylist;
  for myelement in mylist do
    myelement==>
  endfor;
enddefine;
```

If this procedure is called, the four elements of mylist will be printed, as shown:

```
pop-11>example();
** a
** [embedded list]
** b
** c
```

The final value of shortlist, after all polymers which fail to meet the specification have been removed, is the value returned by accept.

We will now define the procedure setup, which creates a list of all polymers in the materials database, this list serving as the initial shortlist:

```
define setup()->shortlist;
  vars shortlist, material;
  [] -> shortlist;
  for material in materials_database do
    [[^(material(1)) ^(material(2))] ^^shortlist] ->shortlist;
  endfor;
enddefine;
```

We start off by assigning the empty list to the local variable shortlist. We then step through the elements of materials_database by means of a *for* loop, and add the polymer names and types to shortlist. There are a number of alternative ways of adding the polymer names and types to shortlist. The method shown exploits the ^ and ^^ symbols. When the ^ symbol is followed by an expression (which may be simply a variable name), Pop-11 evaluates the expression and inserts the value in place of the expression or name. The ^^ symbol is similar, but the expression which follows must evaluate to a list. The list is then inserted in place of the expression or name, but firstly has its outer brackets removed, with the result that several items may be inserted. In our example, a two-element list containing a polymer name and its type is created. Let us call this list1. The surrounding brackets of shortlist are now removed, and a new list created which has list1 at its head, followed by all the elements of shortlist. The list produced is then assigned to shortlist.

An alternative means of achieving the same result would be through the use of the <> symbol, which is used to join (or *concatenate*) two lists:

```
[[^(material(1)) ^(material(2))]] <> shortlist] -> shortlist;
```

With the definition of setup complete, the next task is to define the procedure meets_one, which takes as its parameters a single property specification and the current shortlist, and returns a new shortlist of all polymers that meet the property specification:

```
define meets_one(spec, shortlist) -> shortlist;
  vars material, actual;
  for material in shortlist do
    get_database_value(spec(1), material(1)) -> actual;
    if actual < (spec(2) - spec(3)) then
      delete(material, shortlist) -> shortlist;
    endif;
  endfor;
enddefine;
```

Two local variables are defined: material and actual. A *for* loop is used again, this time in order to extract each polymer in turn from the current shortlist, and to assign it to the local variable material. The value assigned to material is in fact a list, the first element of which is the polymer name. This name is passed together with the property name to a procedure called get_database_value, which will have to be defined so that it returns the property value for the polymer.

```
[ [abs thermoplastic
                    [impact_resistance 0.2]
                    [flexural_modulus 2.7]
                    [maximum_temperature 70]]
   [polypropylene thermoplastic
                    [impact_resistance 0.07]
                    [flexural_modulus 1.5]
                    [maximum_temperature 100]]
   [polystyrene thermoplastic
                    [impact_resistance 0.02]
                    [flexural_modulus 3.0]
                    [maximum_temperature 50]]
   [polyurethane_foam thermoset
                    [impact_resistance 1.06]
                    [flexural_modulus 0.9]
                    [maximum_temperature 80]]
   [pvc thermoplastic
                    [impact_resistance 1.06]
                    [flexural_modulus 0.007]
                    [maximum_temperature 50]]
   [silicone thermoset
                    [impact_resistance 0.02]
                    [flexural_modulus 3.5]
                    [maximum_temperature 240]]
 ]->materials_database;

define accept(spec_list) -> polymer_list;
  vars shortlist, each_spec;
  setup()->shortlist;
  if isword(spec_list(1)) then
    meets_one(spec_list, shortlist) -> shortlist;
  else
    for each_spec in spec_list do
      meets_one(each_spec, shortlist) -> shortlist;
    endfor;
  endif;
  shortlist -> polymer_list;
enddefine;

define meets_one(spec, shortlist) -> shortlist
  vars material, actual;
  for material in shortlist do
    get_database_value(spec(1), material(1)) -> actual;
    if actual < (spec(2) - spec(3)) then
      delete(material, shortlist) -> shortlist;
    endif;
  endfor;
enddefine;

define setup() -> shortlist;
  vars shortlist, material;  [] -> shortlist;
  for material in materials_database do
    [[^(material(1)) ^(material(2))] ^^shortlist] ->shortlist;
  endfor;
enddefine;

define get_database_value(prop_name, material) -> actual;
  vars value;
  if matches(materials_database,[==[^material == [^prop_name ?value]==]==])
    then value -> actual;
    else [] -> actual;
  endif;
enddefine;
```

Box 2.5 A worked example in Pop-11.

The database value returned is then compared with the specified value less the tolerance. If the database value is found to be the smaller, then the polymer in question is removed from the local copy of the shortlist by means of the `delete` procedure, which is built into Pop-11. The fact that it is only a local copy of `shortlist` that changes is an important point. The `shortlist` referred to in `accept`, and the `shortlist` referred to in `meets_one` are distinct, and local to the respective procedures. Thus the `shortlist` in the procedure `accept` only becomes updated when `meets_one` has finished its task, and the value returned is assigned to the copy in `accept`.

The only procedure now remaining to be defined is `get_database_value`, which, as the name implies, looks up the value of a given property for a given polymer. This job is rendered quite straightforward using the Pop-11 pattern matcher. All we need to do is to define a template describing the value we wish to extract, and match the template to the `materials_database`. We might choose to use the match arrow (-->) for this purpose:

```
materials_database -->
   [==[^material == [^prop_name ?value] ==]==]);
```

Here we have introduced a new "wildcard" symbol, '=='. This symbol performs a similar job to the = symbol, but whereas = can stand for any one item, the == symbol can stand for any number of items, including no items at all. The use of the match arrow in this context has a drawback - an error will be reported if the match fails, or in other words if the data being sought is not in the database. Fortunately Pop-11 provides the procedure *matches* for cases where we cannot be certain that a match will succeed. This procedure takes the template and list name (in our case `materials_database`) as parameters, and returns the value *true* if the match is successful, and otherwise returns the value *false*. If the match is successful, all "match variables", i.e., variables preceded with a '?' become defined appropriately. In our definition of `get_database_value`, we return the appropriate value from the database if a match is found, or otherwise we will return an empty list. The definition of `get_database_value` is reproduced below:

```
define get_database_value(prop_name, material) -> actual;
   vars value;
   if matches(materials_database, [==[^material == [^prop_name
      ?value] ==]==]) then
     value -> actual;
   else [] -> actual;
   endif;
enddefine;
```

The complete Pop-11 program is shown in box 2.5, and it can be tested with the same examples that we set for our Lisp and Prolog programs:

```
pop-11> accept([maximum_temperature 100 5])==>
** [[silicone thermoset]
   [polypropylene thermoplastic]]


pop-11> accept([[maximum_temperature 100 5][impact_resistance
0.05 0]])==>
** [[polypropylene thermoplastic]]
```

2.8 Comparison of AI languages

For each of the three AI languages, the worked example gives some feel for the the language structure and syntax. However, it does not form the basis for a fair comparison of their merit. The Prolog code is the most compact and elegant solution to the problem of choosing materials which meet a specification. This is because Prolog is particularly good at tasks which involve pattern matching and retrieval of data. However the language places a number of constraints on the programmer, particularly in committing him or her to one particular search strategy. As we have seen, the programmer can control this strategy to some extent by judicious ordering of clauses and use of the cut mechanism. Another significant limitation is the absence of a structure for iteration, like "FOR x FROM 1 TO 10". Instead, the programmer has to rely upon recursion in order to achieve the same effect.

Our Lisp and Pop-11 programs have a completely different structure from the Prolog example, as they have been programmed procedurally. Although the Lisp and Pop-11 examples look very different from each other syntactically, they are practically identical in their structure. The two languages provide similar facilities for manipulating symbols and lists of symbols. Pop-11 code is generally easier to understand, at least for the novice, but the price to be paid for this clarity is that the language is more verbose.

Both Lisp and Pop-11 are powerful languages which allow practically any reasoning strategy to be implemented. In fact they are so flexible that they can be reconfigured by the programmer, but the worked example does not do justice to this flexibility. In particular, the materials database took the form of a long flat list, whereas there are more structured ways of representing the data. As we will see in chapters 5 and 8, object-oriented programming allows a hierarchical representation of the materials properties.

2.9 Summary

Ease of use
The following tools and languages are arranged in order of increasing ease of use for building a *simple* knowledge-based system:

- conventional languages;
- AI languages;
- AI toolkits;
- expert system shells.

Sophistication
While expert system shells are suitable for some simple problems, most are inflexible and have only limited facilities for knowledge representation. They are difficult to adapt to complex "real world" problems, where AI languages or AI toolkits are usually more appropriate.

Characteristics of AI languages
The three AI languages discussed here (Lisp, Prolog and Pop-11) are all well suited to problems involving the manipulation of symbols. They are, however, less suited to numerical problems than conventional languages. In contrast with conventional languages, the same variable can be used to hold a variety of data types. The AI languages allow various types of data to be combined into lists, and they provide facilities for list manipulation.

Prolog can be used declaratively, and includes a backtracking mechanism which allows it to explore all possible ways in which a goal might be achieved. The programmer can exercise control over Prolog's backtracking by careful ordering of clauses and through the use of "cuts".

In Lisp, lists are not only used for data, but also constitute the programs themselves. Lisp functions are represented as lists containing a function name and its arguments. As every Lisp function returns a value, the arguments themselves can be functions. Lisp is a flexible, elegant and concise language.

Pop-11 is equivalent to Lisp in its functionality. However its syntax is closer to Pascal than Lisp. Pop-11 is well suited to list manipulation, and has facilities for pattern-matching built into the language.

References

1. Steele, G. L., *Common Lisp: the language - 2nd edition*, Digital Press (1990).
2. Bratko, I., *Prolog programming for artificial intelligence - 2nd edition*, Addison-Wesley (1990).

Further reading

- Barrett, R., Ramsay, A. and Sloman, A., *Pop-11: a practical language for artificial intelligence*, Ellis Horwood (1985).
- Bratko, I., *Prolog programming for artificial intelligence - 2nd edition*, Addison-Wesley (1990).
- Burton, M. and Shadbolt, N., *Pop-11 programming for artificial intelligence*, Addison-Wesley (1987).
- Clocksin, W. F. and Mellish, C. S., *Programming in Prolog*, Springer-Verlag (1981).
- Hasemer, T. and Domingue, J., *Common Lisp programming for artificial intelligence*, Addison-Wesley (1989).
- O'Keefe, R. A. (ed.), *The craft of Prolog*, MIT Press (1990).
- Steele, G. L., *Common Lisp: the language - 2nd edition*, Digital Press (1990).
- Sterling, L. and Shapiro, E., *The art of Prolog : advanced programming techniques*, MIT Press (1986).
- Sterling, L. (ed.), *The practice of Prolog*, MIT Press (1990).
- Winston, P. H. and Horn, B. K. P., *Lisp - 3rd edition*, Addison-Wesley (1988).

chapter three

Rule-based systems

3.1 Rules and facts

A rule-based system is a knowledge-based system where the knowledge base is represented in the form of a set (or sets) of *rules*. Rules are an elegant, expressive, straightforward and flexible means of expressing knowledge. The simplest type of rule is called a *production rule* and takes the form:

```
IF <condition> THEN <conclusion>.
```

An example of a production rule might be:

```
IF the tap is open THEN water flows.
```

Part of the attraction of using production rules is that they can often be written in a form which is close to natural language, as opposed to a computer language. A simple rule like the one above is intelligible to anyone who understands English. Although rules can be considerably more complex than this, their explicit nature still makes them more intelligible than conventional computer code.

In order for rules to be applied, and hence for a rule-based system to be of any use, the system will need to have access to *facts*. Facts are unconditional statements which are assumed to be correct at the time that they are used. For example, "the tap is open" is a fact. Facts can be:

- looked up from a database;
- already stored in computer memory;
- determined from sensors connected to the computer;
- obtained by prompting the user for information; or
- derived by applying rules to other facts.

Facts can be thought of as special rules whose condition part is always true. Therefore the fact "the tap is open" could also be thought of as a rule:

```
IF TRUE THEN the tap is open.
```

Given the rule "IF the tap is open THEN water flows" and the fact "the tap is open", the derived fact "water flows" can be generated. The new fact is stored in computer memory and can be used to satisfy the conditions of other rules, thereby leading to further derived facts. The collection of facts which are known to the system at any given time is called the fact base.

Rule-writing is a type of declarative programming (see section 2.1) because rules represent knowledge that can be used by the computer, without specifying how and when to apply that knowledge. Therefore the ordering of rules in a program should ideally be unimportant, and it should be possible to add new rules or modify existing ones without fear of side-effects. We will see by reference to some simple examples that these ideals cannot always be taken for granted. The rules that will be discussed in this chapter are no different from Prolog rules (see section 2.6) except that:

- we will use a different rule syntax; and
- we will not be constrained to using Prolog's backtracking inference engine.

3.2 A rule-based system for boiler control

Whereas the above discussion described rule-based systems in an abstract fashion, a physical example is introduced in this section. We will consider a rule-based system to monitor the state of a power station boiler and to advise appropriate actions. The boiler in our example (figure 3.1) is used to produce steam to drive a turbine and generator. Water is heated in the boiler tubes to produce a steam and water mixture that rises to the steam drum, which is a cylindrical vessel mounted horizontally near the top of the boiler. The purpose of the drum is to separate the steam from the water. Steam is taken from the drum, passed through the superheater and applied to the turbine that turns the generator. Sensors are fitted to the drum to monitor:

- the temperature of the steam in the drum;
- the voltage output from a transducer, which in turn monitors the level of water in the drum;
- the status of pressure release valve (i.e., open or closed); and
- the rate of flow of water through the control valve.

The following rules have been written for controlling the boiler:

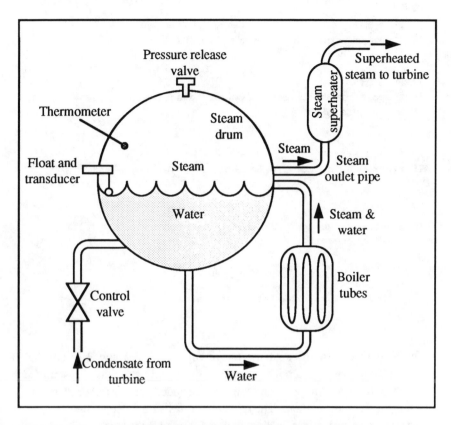

Figure 3.1   A power station boiler.

```
/* Rule 3.1 */
IF water level low THEN open control valve

/* Rule 3.2 */
IF temperature high and water level low
THEN open control valve AND shut down boiler tubes

/* Rule 3.3 */
IF steam outlet blocked THEN replace outlet pipe

/* Rule 3.4 */
IF release valve stuck THEN steam outlet blocked

/* Rule 3.5 */
IF pressure high AND release valve closed
THEN release valve stuck
```

```
/* Rule 3.6 */
IF steam escaping THEN steam outlet blocked


/* Rule 3.7 */
IF temperature high AND NOT(water level low)
THEN pressure high


/* Rule 3.8 */
IF transducer output low THEN water level low


/* Rule 3.9 */
IF release valve open AND flow rate high
THEN steam escaping


/* Rule 3.10 */
IF flow rate low THEN control valve closed
```

The conclusions of three of the above rules (3.1, 3.2 and 3.3) consist of recommendations to the boiler operators. In a fully automated system, such rules would be able to perform their recommended actions rather than simply making a recommendation. The remaining rules all involve taking a low level fact, such as a transducer reading, and deriving a higher level fact, such as the quantity of water in the drum. The input data to the system (sensor readings in our example) are low level facts; higher level facts are derived facts from them.

Most of the rules in our rule base are specific to one particular boiler arrangement, and would not apply to other situations. These rules could be described as *shallow*, as they represent shallow knowledge. On the other hand, rule 3.7 expresses a fundamental rule of physics, namely that the boiling temperature of a liquid increases with increasing applied pressure. This is valid under any circumstances, and is not specific to the boiler shown in figure 3.1. It is therefore an example of a *deep* rule (expressing deep knowledge).

The distinction between deep and shallow rules should not be confused with the distinction between *high level* and *low level* rules. Low level rules are those that depend on low level facts. Rule 3.8 is a low level rule since it is dependent on a transducer reading. High level rules make use of more abstract information, such as rule 3.3 which relates the occurrence of a steam outlet blockage to a recommendation to replace a pipe. Higher level rules are those which are closest to providing a solution to a problem, while lower level rules represent the first stages towards reaching a conclusion.

3.3 Rule examination and rule firing

In section 3.2, a rule base for boiler control was described without mention of how the rules would be applied. The task of interpreting and applying the rules belongs to the inference engine (see chapter 1). The application of rules can be broken down as follows:

i   selecting rules to examine - these are the *available rules*;
ii   determining which of these are applicable - these form the *conflict set*; and
iii selecting a rule to *fire* (described below).

The distinction between examination and firing of rules is best explained by example. Suppose the rule-based system has access to the transducer output and to the temperature readings. A sensible set of rules to *examine* would be 3.2, 3.7 and 3.8, as these rules are conditional on the boiler temperature and transducer output. If the transducer level is found to be low, then rule 3.8 is applicable. If it is selected and used to make the deduction "`water level low`", then the rule is said to have *fired*. If the rule is examined but cannot fire (because the transducer reading is not low), the rule is said to *fail*.

The condition part of rule 3.2 can only be satisfied if rule 3.8 has been fired. It therefore makes sense to examine rule 3.8 before rule 3.2. If rule 3.8 fails, then rule 3.2 need not be examined as it too will fail. The inter-dependence between rules is discussed further in sections 3.4 and 3.5.

The method for rule examination and firing described so far is a form of forward-chaining. This strategy and others are discussed in more detail in sections 3.6 to 3.9.

3.4 Maintaining consistency

As mentioned in section 3.1, one advantage of rule-based systems is their flexibility. New rules can be added at will, but only if each rule is written with care and without assuming the behavior of other rules. Consider rule 3.4:

```
/* Rule 3.4 */
IF release valve stuck THEN steam outlet blocked.
```

Given the current rule base, the fact "`release valve stuck`" could only be established by first firing rule 3.5:

```
/* Rule 3.5 */
IF pressure high AND release valve closed
THEN release valve stuck
```

Rule 3.5 is sensible, since the purpose of the release valve is to open itself automatically if the pressure becomes high, thereby releasing the excess pressure.   Rule 3.4, however, is less sensible.   The fact "release valve stuck" is not in itself sufficient evidence to deduce that the steam outlet is blocked. The other necessary evidence is that the pressure in the drum must be high. The reason that the rule base works in its current form is that in order for the system to believe the release valve to be stuck, the pressure *must* be high. Although the rule base works, it is not robust and is not tolerant of new knowledge being added.   Consider for instance the effect of adding the following rule:

```
/* Rule 3.11 */
IF pressure low AND release valve open THEN release valve stuck
```

This rule is in itself sensible.   However, the addition of the rule has an unwanted effect on Rule 3.4. Because of the unintended interaction between rules 3.4 and 3.11, low pressure in the drum and the observation that the release valve is open result in the erroneous conclusion that the steam outlet is blocked. Problems of this sort can be avoided by making each rule an accurate statement in its own right. Thus in our example, rule 3.4 should be written as:

```
/* Rule 3.4a */
IF pressure high AND release valve stuck
THEN steam outlet blocked.
```

A typical rule firing order, given that the drum pressure is high and the release valve closed, might be:

```
/* Rule 3.5 */
IF pressure high AND release valve closed
THEN release valve stuck
            ↓
/* Rule 3.4a */
IF pressure high AND release valve stuck
THEN steam outlet blocked
            ↓
/* Rule 3.3 */
IF steam outlet blocked THEN replace outlet pipe
```

The modification that has been introduced in rule 3.4a means that the conditions of both rules 3.5 and 3.4a involve checking to see whether the drum pressure is high. This source of inefficiency can be justified through the improved robustness of the rule base. In fact the Rete algorithm, described in section 3.7.2, allows rule conditions to be duplicated in this way with minimal loss of efficiency.

In general, rules can be considerably more complex than the ones we have considered so far. For instance, rules can contain combinations of conditions and conclusions, exemplified by combining rules 3.3, 3.4 and 3.6 to form a new rule:

```
/* Rule 3.12 */
IF (pressure high AND release valve stuck) OR steam escaping
THEN steam outlet blocked AND outlet pipe needs replacing.
```

3.5 The closed world assumption

If we do not know that a given proposition is true, then in many rule-based systems the proposition is assumed to be false. This assumption, known as the *closed world assumption*, simplifies the logic required as all propositions are either TRUE or FALSE. If the closed world assumption is not made, then a third category, namely UNKNOWN, has to be introduced. To illustrate the closed world assumption, let us return to the boiler control example. If "steam outlet blocked" is not known, then "NOT (steam outlet blocked)" is assumed to be true. Similarly if "water level low" is not known, then "NOT (water level low)" is assumed to be true. The latter example of the closed world assumption affects the interaction between rules 3.7 and 3.8:

```
/* Rule 3.7 */
IF temperature high AND NOT(water level low) THEN pressure high
```

```
/* Rule 3.8 */
IF transducer output low THEN water level low
```

Consider the case where the temperature reading is high and the transducer output is low. Whether or not the pressure is assumed to be high will depend upon the order in which the rules are selected for firing. If we fire rule 3.7 followed by 3.8, the following deductions will be made:

```
temperature high – TRUE
NOT(water level low) – TRUE by closed world assumption
Therefore pressure is high (rule 3.7)

transducer output low – TRUE
Therefore water level low (rule 3.8).
```

Alternatively, we could examine rule 3.8 first:

```
transducer output low - TRUE
Therefore water level low (rule 3.8)
```

```
temperature high - TRUE
NOT(water level low) - FALSE
```
Rule 3.7 fails

It is most likely that the second outcome was intended by the rule-writer. There are two measures that could be taken to avoid this ambiguity, namely to modify the rules or to modify the inference engine. The latter approach would aim to ensure that rule 3.8 is examined before 3.7, and a method for achieving this is described in section 3.10. The former solution could be achieved by altering the rules so that they do not contain any negative conditions, as shown below:

```
/* Rule 3.7a */
IF temperature high and water level not_low THEN pressure high
```

```
/* Rule 3.8 */
IF transducer output low THEN water level low
```

```
/* Rule 3.8a */
IF transducer output not_low THEN water level not_low
```

3.6 Use of variables within rules

The boiler shown in figure 3.1 was a simplified view of a real system, and the accompanying rule set much smaller than those associated with most real-world problems. In real-world systems, variables can be used to make rules more general, thereby reducing the number of rules needed and keeping the rule set manageable. The sort of rule that is often required is of the form:

```
For all X, IF condition about X THEN conclusion about X.
```

In order to illustrate this idea, let us imagine a more complex boiler. This boiler may, for instance, have many water supply pipes, each with its own control valve. For each pipe, the flow rate will be related to whether or not the control valve is open. So some possible rules might be of the form:

```
/* Rule 3.13 */
IF control valve 1 is open THEN flow rate in tube 1 is high
```

```
/* Rule 3.14 */
IF control valve 2 is open THEN flow rate in tube 2 is high
```

```
/* Rule 3.15 */
IF control valve 3 is open THEN flow rate in tube 3 is high

/* Rule 3.16 */
IF control valve 4 is open THEN flow rate in tube 4 is high

/* Rule 3.17 */
IF control valve 5 is open THEN flow rate in tube 5 is high
```

A much more compact, elegant and flexible representation of these rules would be:

```
/* Rule 3.18 */
IF control valve ?X is open THEN flow rate in tube ?X is high.
```

Here we have used a question mark ('?') to denote that X is a variable. Now if the sensors detect that any control valve is open, the identity of the control valve is substituted for X when the rule is fired. The variable X is said to be *instantiated* with a value, in this case an identity number. Thus if control valve 3 is open, X is instantiated with the value '3' and the deduction "flow rate in tube 3 is high" is made.

In this example the possible values of X were limited, and so the use of a variable was convenient rather than necessary. Where the possible values of a variable cannot be anticipated in advance, the use of variables becomes essential. This is the case when values are being looked up, perhaps from a database or from a sensor. As an example, consider the following rule:

```
/* Rule 3.19 */
IF (drum pressure is ?P) AND (?P > ?threshold) THEN
tube pressure is (?P/10)
```

Without the use of the variable name P, it would not be possible to generate a derived fact which states explicitly a pressure value. Suppose that the drum pressure sensor is reading a value of 300MPa and threshold is a variable currently set to 100MPa. Rule 3.19 can therefore be fired, and the derived fact "tube pressure is 30MPa" is generated. Note that in this example the value of the variable, P, has been manipulated (i.e., divided by 10). The more sophisticated rule-based systems allow values represented as variables to be manipulated in this way or passed as parameters to procedures and functions.

The association of a specific value (say 300MPa) with a variable name (such as P) is sometimes referred to as *unification*. The term applies not only to numerical examples but to any form of data. The word arises because, from the computer's perspective, the following are contradictory pieces of information:

```
pressure is P
pressure is 300MPa.
```

This conflict can be resolved by recognizing that one of the values is a variable name (because in our syntax it is preceded by a question mark) and by making the following assignment or unification:

```
P:=300MPa.
```

It should be noted that the use of variable names within rules is integral to the Prolog language (see section 2.6). In Prolog, rather than using '?', variables are distinguished from constants by having an underscore or upper case letter as their first character. Other languages (including AI languages) would require the user to program this facility or to purchase suitable software.

3.7 Forward chaining (a data-driven strategy)

As noted in section 3.3, the inference engine applies a strategy for deciding which rules to apply and when to apply them. Forward chaining is the name given to a data-driven strategy, i.e., rules are selected and applied in response to the current fact base. The fact base comprises all facts known by the system, whether derived by rules or supplied directly (see section 3.1).

A schematic representation of the cyclic selection, examination and firing of rules is shown in figure 3.2. The cycle of events shown in figure 3.2 is just one version of forward-chaining, and variations in the strategy are possible. The key points to notice about the scheme shown in figure 3.2 are:

• rules are examined and fired on the basis of the current fact base, independently of any predetermined goals;

• the set of rules available for examination may comprise *all* of the rules or a subset;

• of the available rules, those whose conditions are satisfied comprise the *conflict set*, and the method of selecting a rule from the conflict set is called *conflict resolution* (see section 3.8);

• although the conflict set may contain many rules, only one rule is fired on a given cycle. (This is because once a rule has fired, the stored deductions have potentially changed, and so it cannot be guaranteed that the other rules in the conflict set still have their condition parts satisfied.)

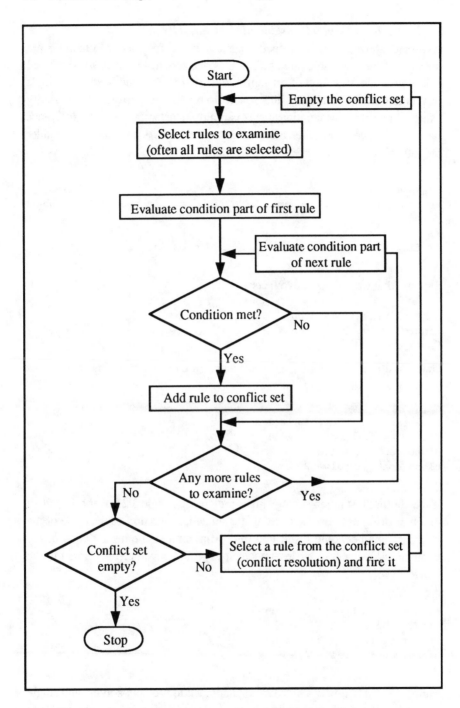

Figure 3.2 Forward chaining.

3.7.1 *Single and multiple instantiation of variables*

As noted above, variations on the basic scheme for forward chaining are possible. Where variables are used in rules, the conclusions may be performed using just the first set of instantiations that are found - this is single instantiation. Alternatively, the conclusions may be performed repeatedly using all possible instantiations - this is multiple instantiation. The difference between the two approaches is shown in figure 3.3. As an example, consider the following pair of rules:

```
/* Rule 3.20 */
IF control valve ?X is open THEN flow rate in tube ?X is high

/* Rule 3.21 */
IF flow rate in tube ?X is high THEN close control valve ?X.
```

Suppose that we start with two facts:

```
control valve 1 is open
control valve 2 is open.
```

Under multiple instantiation, each rule would fire once, generating conclusions in the order:

```
flow rate in tube 1 is high
flow rate in tube 2 is high
close control valve 1
close control valve 2
```

If the conflict resolution strategy gives preference to rule 3.21 over rule 3.20, a different firing order would occur under single instantiation. Each cycle of the inference engine would result in a rule firing on a single instantiation of the variable, *X*. After four cycles, conclusions would have been generated in the order:

```
flow rate in tube 1 is high
close control valve 1
flow rate in tube 2 is high
close control valve 2.
```

Multiple instantiation is a breadth-first approach to problem-solving and single instantiation is depth-first approach, as illustrated in figure 3.4. The practical implications of the two approaches are discussed in chapters 7 and 10.

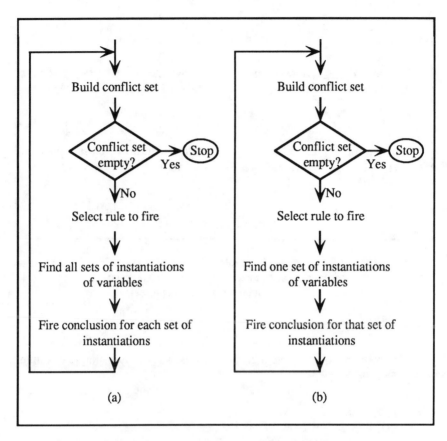

Figure 3.3 Alternative forms of forward chaining:
(a) multiple instantiation of variables;
(b) single instantiation of variables.

3.7.2 Rete algorithm
The scheme for forward chaining shown in figure 3.2 contains at least one source of inefficiency. Once a rule has been selected from the conflict set and fired, the conflict set is thrown away and the process starts all over again. This is because firing a rule alters the fact base, so that a different set of rules may qualify for the conflict set. A new conflict set is therefore drawn up by re-examining the condition parts of all of the available rules. In most applications, the firing of a single rule makes only slight changes to the fact base and hence to the membership of the conflict set. Therefore, a more efficient approach would be to examine only those rules whose condition is affected by changes made to the facts base on the previous cycle. The Rete (pronounced "ree-tee") algorithm [1, 2] is one way of achieving this.

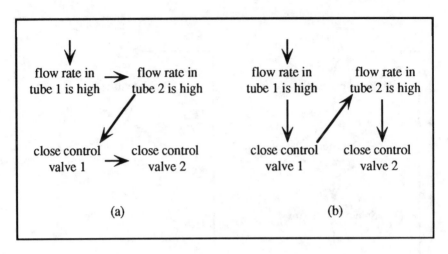

Figure 3.4 Applying rules 3.20 and 3.21:
(a) multiple instantiation is a breadth-first process;
(b) single instantiation is a depth-first process.

The principle of the Rete algorithm can be shown by a simple example, using the following rule:

```
/* Rule 3.22*/
IF ?P is a pipe of bore ?B AND ?V is a valve of bore ?B
THEN ?P and ?V are compatible.
```

Prior to running the system, the condition parts of all of the rules are assembled into a *Rete network*, where each node represents an atomic condition, i.e., one that contains a simple test. There are two types of node - alpha nodes can be satisfied by a single fact, whereas beta nodes can only be satisfied by a pair of facts. The condition part of rule 3.22 would be broken down into two alpha nodes and one beta node:

```
α1:     find a pipe
α2:     find a valve
β1:     the bore of each must be equal.
```

The Rete network for this example is shown in figure 3.5. Suppose that initially the only relevant fact is:

```
p1 is a pipe of bore 100mm.
```

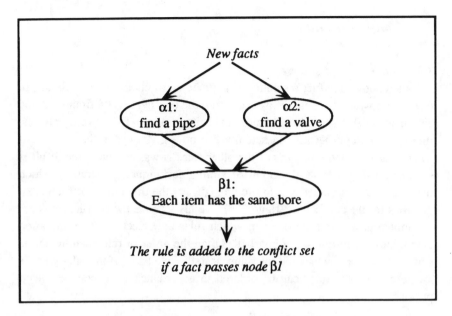

Figure 3.5 A Rete network for rule 3.22.

Node $\alpha 1$ would be satisfied, and so the fact would be passed on to node $\beta 1$. However, node $\beta 1$ would not be satisfied as it has received no information from node $\alpha 2$. The fact that there is a pipe of bore 100mm would remain stored at node $\beta 1$. Imagine now that, as a result of firing other rules, the following fact is derived:

```
v1 is a valve of bore 100mm.
```

This fact satisfies node $\alpha 2$, and is passed on to node $\beta 1$. Node $\beta 1$ is satisfied by the combination of the new fact and the one that was already stored there. Thus rule 3.22 can be added to the conflict set without having to find a pipe again (the task of node $\alpha 1$).

A full Rete network would contain nodes representing the subconditions of all the rules in the rule base. Every time a rule is fired, the altered facts would be fed into the network and the changes to the conflict set generated. Where rules contain identical subconditions, nodes can be shared, thereby avoiding duplicated testing of the conditions. In an evaluation of some commercially available AI toolkits that use forward chaining, those that incorporated the Rete algorithm were found to offer substantial improvements in performance [3].

3.8   Conflict resolution

3.8.1   First come, first served

As noted above, conflict resolution is the method of choosing one rule to fire from those which are able to fire, i.e., from the conflict set. In figure 3.2, the complete conflict set is found before choosing a rule to fire. Since only one rule from the conflict set can actually fire on a given cycle, the time spent evaluating the condition parts of the other rules is wasted unless the result is saved by using a Rete algorithm or similar technique. A strategy which overcomes this inefficiency is to fire immediately the first rule to be found that qualifies for the conflict set (figure 3.6). In this scheme, the conflict set is not assembled at all, and the order in which rules are selected for examination determines the resolution of conflict. Often the order of rule examination is simply the order in which the rules appear in the rule base. If the rule-writer is aware of this, the rules can be ordered in accordance with their perceived priority.

3.8.2   Priority values

Rather than relying on rule ordering as a means of determining rule priorities, rules can be written such that each has an explicitly stated priority value. Where more than one rule is able to fire, the one chosen is the one having the highest priority. The two rules below would be available for firing if the water level had been found to be low (i.e., rule 3.8 had fired) and if the temperature were high:

```
/* Rule 3.1a */
IF water level low THEN open control valve PRIORITY 4.0

/* Rule 3.2a */
IF temperature high and water level low THEN
open control valve AND shut down boiler tubes PRIORITY 9.0
```

In the scheme shown here, rule 3.2a would be selected for firing as it has the higher priority value. This scheme arbitrarily uses a scale of priorities from 1 to 10.

As the examination of rules which are not fired represents wasted effort, an efficient use of priorities would be to select rules for examination in order of their priority. Once a rule has been found which is fireable, it could be fired immediately. This scheme is identical to the "first come, first served" strategy (figure 3.6), except that rules are selected for examination according to their priority value rather than their position in the rule base.

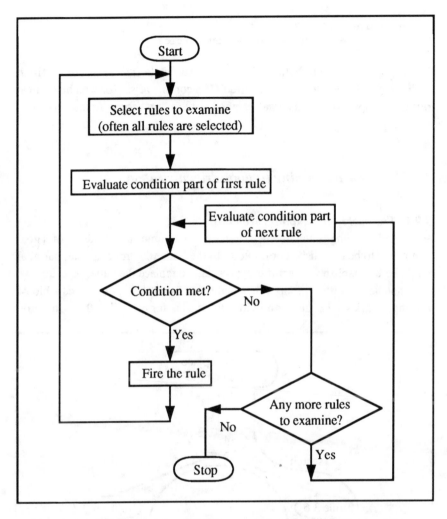

Figure 3.6 Forward chaining with "first come, first served" conflict resolution.

3.8.3 *Meta-rules*
Meta-rules are rules which are not specifically concerned with knowledge about the application at hand, but rather with knowledge about how that knowledge should be applied. Meta-rules are therefore "rules about rules" (or more generally, "rules about knowledge"). Some examples of meta-rules might be:

```
/* Meta-rule 3.23 */
PREFER rules about shut-down TO rules about control valves
```

```
/* Meta-rule 3.24 */
PREFER high level rules TO low level rules.
```

If rules 3.1 and 3.2 are both in the conflict set, meta-rule 3.23 will be fired, with the result that rule 3.2 is then fired. If a conflict arises for which no meta-rule can be applied, then a default method such as "first come, first served" can be used.

3.9 Backward chaining (a goal-driven strategy)

3.9.1 The backward chaining mechanism
Backward chaining is an inference strategy that assumes the existence of a goal that needs to be established or refuted. In the boiler control example, our goal might be to establish whether it is appropriate to replace the outlet pipe, and we may not be interested in any other deductions that the system is capable of making. Backward chaining provides the means for achieving this. Initially,

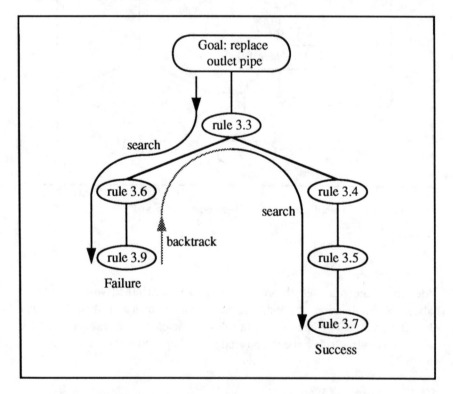

Figure 3.7   Backward chaining applied to the boiler control rules.
The search for rules proceeds in a depth-first manner.

only those rules which can lead directly to the fulfillment of the goal are selected for examination. In our case the only rule which can achieve the goal is rule 3.3, since it is the only rule whose conclusion is "`replace outlet pipe`". The condition part of rule 3.3 is examined, but as there is no information about a steam outlet blockage in the fact base, rule 3.3 cannot be fired yet. A new goal is then produced, namely "`steam outlet blocked`", corresponding to the condition part of rule 3.3. Two rules, 3.4 and 3.6, are capable of fulfilling this goal, and are therefore *antecedents* of rule 3.3. What happens next depends on whether a depth-first or breadth-first search strategy is used. These two methods for exploring a search tree were introduced in chapter 1, but now the nodes of the search tree are *rules*.

For the moment we will assume the use of a depth-first search strategy, as this is normally adopted. The use of a breadth-first search is discussed in section 3.9.3. One of the two relevant rules (3.4 or 3.6) is selected for examination. Let us suppose that rule 3.6 is chosen. Rule 3.6 can only fire if steam is escaping from the drum. This information is not in the fact base, so "`steam escaping`" becomes the new goal. The system searches the rule base for a rule which can satisfy this goal. Rule 3.9 can satisfy the goal, if its condition is met. The condition part of rule 3.9 relies only on the status of the release valve. If the valve were found to be open, then 3.9 would be able to fire, the goal "`steam escaping`" could be satisfied, rule 3.6 would be fireable and the original goal thus fulfilled.

Let us suppose, on the other hand, that the release valve is found to be closed. Rule 3.9 therefore fails, with the result that rule 3.6 also fails. The system *backtracks* to the last place where a choice between possible rules was made, and will try an alternative, as shown in figure 3.7. In the example shown here, this means that rule 3.4 is examined next. It can only fire if the release valve is stuck, but as this information is not yet known, it becomes the new goal. This process continues until a goal is satisfied by the information in the fact base. When this happens, the original goal is fulfilled, and the chosen path through the rules is the solution. If all possible ways of achieving the overall goal have been explored and failed, then the overall goal fails.

The backward chaining mechanism described so far has assumed a depth-first search for rules. This means that whenever a choice between rules exists, just one is selected, the others only being examined if backtracking occurs.

The inference mechanism built into Prolog (see section 2.6) is a depth-first backward chainer, like that described here. As with Prolog, there are two sets of circumstances under which backtracking takes place:

i   when a goal cannot be satisfied by the set of rules currently under consideration; or

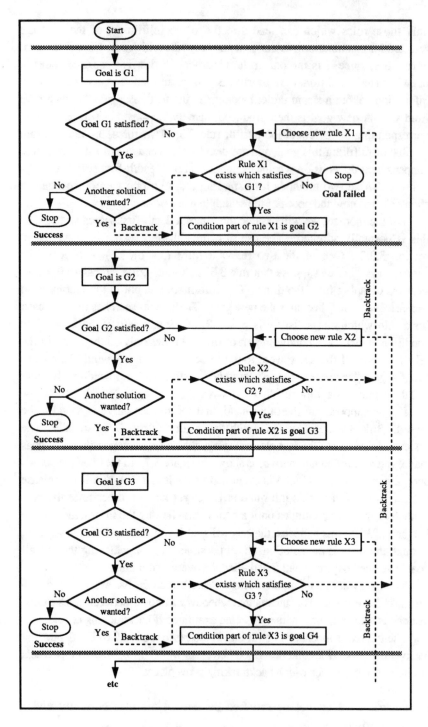

Figure 3.8 A flowchart for backward chaining.

ii   when a goal has been satisfied and the user wants to investigate other ways of achieving the goal (i.e., to find other solutions).

3.9.2 Implementation of backward chaining

Figure 3.8 shows a generalized flowchart for backward chaining from a goal G1. In order to simplify the chart, it has been assumed that each rule has only one condition, so that the satisfaction of a condition can be represented as a single goal. In general, rules can have more than one condition. The flowchart is an attempt to represent backward chaining as an iterative process. This is difficult to achieve, as the length of the chain of rules cannot be predetermined. The flowchart has therefore, of necessity, been left incomplete. The flowchart

```
define function backwardchain(G);
   /* returns a boolean (i.e., true/false) value */
   /* G is the goal being validated */
variable S, X, C;
   result:= false;
   /* ':=' represents assignment of a value to a variable */
   S:= set of rules whose conclusion part matches goal G;
   if S is empty then
       result:= false;
   else
       while (result=false) and (S is not empty) do
           X:= rule selected from S;
           S:= S with X removed;
           C:= condition part of X;
           if C is true then
               result:=true
           elseif C is false then
               result:=false
           elseif (backwardchain(C)=true) then
               result:=true;
           /* note the recursive call of 'backwardchain' */
           /* C is the new goal */
           endif;
       endwhile;
   endif;
return result;
   /* 'result' is the value returned by the function */
   /* 'backwardchain' */
enddefine;
```

Box 3.1 A recursive definition of backward chaining.

contains repeating sections which are identical except for the variable names, an indication that while it is difficult to represent the process iteratively, it can be elegantly represented *recursively*. A recursive definition of a function is one that includes the function itself. Recursion is an important aspect of the AI languages (Lisp, Prolog and Pop-11) discussed in chapter 2, as well as many other computer languages. Box 3.1 shows a recursive definition of backward chaining, where it has again been assumed that rules have only one condition. It is not always necessary to write such a function for yourself as backward chaining forms an integral part of Prolog, and most expert system shells and AI toolkits (see chapter 2) already include such facilities.

3.9.3 *Variations of backward chaining*

There are a number of possible variations to the idea of backward chaining. Some of these are:

i   depth-first or breadth-first search for rules;

ii whether or not to pursue other solutions (i.e., other means of achieving the goal) once a solution has been found;

iii different ways of choosing between branches to explore (depth-first search only);

iv deciding upon the order in which to examine rules (breadth-first search only); or

v   having found a succession of enabling rules whose lowest level conditions are satisfied, whether or not to fire the sequence of rules, or simply to conclude that the goal is proven.

Breadth-first backward chaining is identical to depth-first, except for the mechanism for deciding between alternative rules to examine. In the example described in section 3.9.1 (and in figure 3.7), instead of choosing to explore either 3.4 or 3.6, both rules would be examined. Then the preconditions of each (i.e., rule 3.5 and 3.9) would be examined. If either branch fails, then the system will not need to backtrack, as it will simply carry on down those branches which still have the potential to fulfil the goal. The process is illustrated in figure 3.9. The first solution to be found will be the one with the shortest (or joint shortest) chain of rules. A disadvantage with the breadth-first approach is that large amounts of computer memory may be required, as the system needs to keep a record of progress along all branches of the search tree, rather than just one branch.

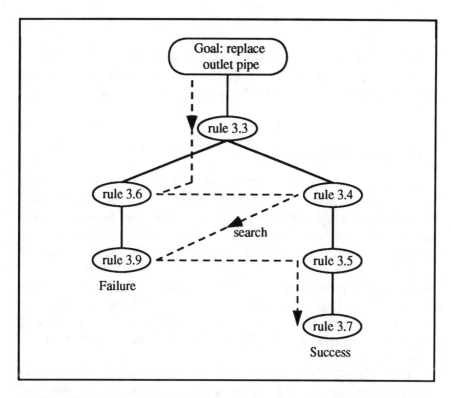

Figure 3.9   A variation of backward chaining applied to the boiler control rules;
here the search for rules proceeds in a breadth-first manner.

The last item (v) in the above list of variations of backward chaining is
important but subtle. So far our discussion of backward chaining has made
limited reference to rule firing. If a goal is capable of being satisfied by a
succession of rules, the first of which is fireable, then the goal is assumed to be
true and *no rules are actually fired*. If all that is required is validation of a
goal, then this approach is adequate. However, by actually firing the rules, all
of the intermediate deductions such as "water level low" are recorded in the
fact base and may be used by other rules, thereby eliminating the need to re-
establish them. Therefore in some implementations of backward chaining,
once the path to a goal has been established, rules are fired until the original
goal is fulfilled. In more complex rule-based systems, rules may call up and
run a procedurally coded module as part of their conclusion. In such systems,
the firing of the rules is essential for the role of the procedural code to be
realized.

Finally, it should be noted that in some backward chaining systems the
rule syntax is reversed compared with the examples that we have discussed so
far. A possible syntax would be:

```
DEDUCE <conclusion> IF <condition>.
```

The placing of the conclusion before the condition reflects the fact that in backward chaining systems it is the conclusion part of a rule that is assessed first, and only if the conclusion is relevant is the condition examined.

3.10 A hybrid strategy

A system called ARBS (described in section 7.6) makes use of an inference engine which can be thought of as part forward chaining and part backward chaining [4]. Conventional backward chaining involves initial examination of the rule which achieves the goal. If that cannot fire, its antecedent rules are recursively examined, until rules can be fired and progress made towards the goal. In all problems involving data interpretation (such as the boiler control example), the high level rules concerning the goal itself can never fire until lower level rules for data manipulation have been fired. The standard mechanisms for forward or backward chaining therefore involve a great deal of redundant rule examination. The hybrid strategy is a means of eliminating this source of inefficiency.

Under the hybrid strategy, a network of rule dependencies is built *prior to running the system.* For each rule, the network shows which other rules may enable it (i.e., its antecedents) and which rules it may enable. The rule dependencies for the boiler control knowledge base are shown in figure 3.10. In its data-driven mode, the hybrid strategy achieves improved efficiency by using the dependence network to select rules for examination. Low level rules concerning the sensor data are initially selected for examination. As shown in figure 3.10, only rules 3.8, 3.9 and 3.10 need be examined initially. Then higher level rules, leading towards a solution, are selected depending on which rules have actually fired. So, if rules 3.8 and 3.9 fire successfully, the new set of rules to be examined becomes 3.1, 3.2, and 3.6. The technique is an effective way of carrying out the instruction marked "select rules to examine" in the flowchart for forward chaining (figure 3.2).

The same mechanism can easily be adapted to provide an efficient goal-driven strategy. Given a particular goal, the control mechanism can select the branch of the dependence network leading to that goal and then forward chain through the selected rules.

For a given rule base, the dependence network only needs to be generated once, and is then available to the system at run time. The ordering of rules in the rule base does not affect the system, since the application of rules is dictated by their position in the dependence network rather than in the rule set.

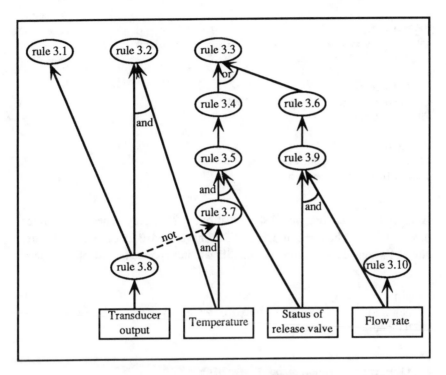

Figure 3.10 A rule dependence network.

Rule 3.7 has a "negative dependency" on rule 3.8, meaning that rule 3.7 is fireable if rule 3.8 fails to fire:

```
/* Rule 3.7 */
IF temperature high AND NOT(water level low) THEN pressure high

/* Rule 3.8 */
IF transducer output low THEN water level low.
```

As discussed in section 3.5, the closed world assumption will lead to "NOT(water level low)" being assumed true unless rule 3.8 is successfully fired. Therefore, for rule 3.7 to behave as intended, rule 3.8 must be examined (and either fire or fail) before rule 3.7 is examined. Using the dependence network to direct rule examination and firing is one way of ensuring this order of events.

The use of dependence networks is more complicated when variables are used within rules because the dependencies between rules are less certain. Consider, for example, the following set of rules which do *not* use variables:

```
/* Rule 3.25 */
IF control valve 1 is open AND pipe 1 is blocked
THEN open release valve
```

```
/* Rule 3.26 */
IF flow rate through pipe 1 is high
THEN control valve 1 is open
```

```
/* Rule 3.27 */
IF pressure in pipe 1 is high
THEN pipe 1 is blocked
```

A dependence network would show that rule 3.25 is only dependent on rules 3.26 and 3.27. Therefore, if 3.26 and 3.27 have fired, 3.25 can definitely fire. Now let's consider the same rules modified to incorporate the use of variables:

```
/* Rule 3.25a */
IF control valve ?X open AND pipe ?X blocked
THEN open release valve
```

```
/* Rule 3.26a */
IF flow rate through pipe ?X is high
THEN control valve ?X open
```

```
/* Rule 3.27a */
IF pressure in pipe ?X is high
THEN pipe ?X is blocked
```

Rule 3.25a is dependent on rules 3.26a and 3.27a. However, it is possible for rules 3.26a and 3.27a to have fired, but for rule 3.25a to fail. This is because the condition of rule 3.25a requires the valve and pipe numbers (represented by X) to be identical, whereas rules 3.26a and 3.27a could each use a different value for X. Thus when rules contain variables, a dependence network shows which rules have the *potential* to enable others to fire. Whether or not the dependent rules will actually fire cannot be determined until run-time. The dependence network shows us that rule 3.25a should be examined if rules 3.26a and 3.27a have fired, but otherwise it can be ignored.

A similar situation arises when there is a negative dependence between rules containing variables, for example:

```
/* Rule 3.25b */
IF NOT(control valve ?X open) AND pipe ?X blocked
THEN open release valve
```

```
/* Rule 3.26b */
IF flow rate through pipe ?X is high
THEN control valve ?X open

/* Rule 3.27b */
IF pressure in pipe ?X is high
THEN pipe ?X is blocked
```

Here 3.25b has a negative dependence on 3.26b and a normal (positive) dependence on 3.27b. Under these circumstances, 3.25b should be examined after both:

i   3.27b has fired; *and*
ii   3.26b has been examined, *whether it fired or not.*

The condition "NOT(control valve ?X open)" will certainly be true if rule 3.26b fails. However, because there is a constraint on the value of X (i.e., the value of X must be the same throughout the condition part of rule 3.25b), rule 3.25b may be fireable even if rule 3.26b has fired.

3.11 Explanation facilities

One of the claims frequently made in support of expert systems is that they are able to explain their reasoning, and that this gives users of such systems confidence in the accuracy or wisdom of the system's decisions. However, as noted in chapter 1, the explanations offered by many systems are little more than a trace of the firing of rules. While this is an important facility, tracing the flow of a computer program is standard practice and not a particularly special capability.

Explanation facilities can be divided into two categories:

- *how* a conclusion has been derived; and
- *why* a particular line of reasoning is being followed.

The first type of explanation would normally be applied when the system has completed its reasoning, whereas the second type is applicable while the system is carrying out its reasoning process. The latter type of explanation is particularly appropriate in an interactive expert system, which involves a dialogue between a user and the computer. During such a dialogue the user will often want to establish why particular questions are being asked. If either type of explanation is incorrect or impenetrable, the user is likely to distrust or ignore the system's findings.

   Returning once more to our rule set for boiler control (section 3.2), the following would be a typical explanation for a recommendation to replace the outlet pipe:

```
Replace outlet pipe
BECAUSE (rule 3.3) steam outlet blocked

steam outlet blocked
BECAUSE (rule 3.4) release valve stuck

release valve stuck
BECAUSE (rule 3.5) pressure high AND release valve closed

pressure high
BECAUSE (rule 3.7) temperature high AND NOT(water level low)

NOT(water level low)
BECAUSE (rule 3.8) NOT(transducer output low)

        release valve closed  ⎤
             temperature high  ⎬  are supplied facts.
    NOT(transducer output low) ⎦
```

Explanation facilities are desirable for increasing user confidence in the system, as a teaching aid, and as an aid to debugging. However, a simple trace like the one shown is likely to be of little use except for debugging. Explanation facilities might be made more relevant by supplying the user with a level of detail tailored to his or her needs.

3.12 Summary

Rules are an effective way of representing knowledge in many application domains. They are most versatile when variables are used within rules and they can be particularly useful in cooperation with procedural algorithms or object-oriented systems (chapter 5). The role of interpreting, selecting and applying rules is fulfilled by the inference engine. Rule-writing should ideally be independent of the details of the inference engine, apart from fulfilling its syntax requirements. In practice, the rule-writer needs to be aware of the strategy for applying rules and any assumptions that are made by the inference engine. For instance, under the closed world assumption, any facts that have not been supplied or derived are assumed to be false. Forward and backward chaining are two distinct strategies for applying rules, but many variations of these strategies are also possible.

References

1. Forgy, C., "Rete: a fast algorithm for the many-pattern/many-object-pattern match problem", *Artificial Intelligence*, **19**, p17 (1982).
2. Graham, P., "Using the Rete algorithm", *AI Expert*, p46 (December 1990).
3. Mettrey, W., "A comparative evaluation of expert system tools", *IEEE Computer*, **24**, (2), p19 (February 1991).
4. Hopgood, A. A., Woodcock, N. and Hallam, N. J., "On-line knowledge-based interpretation of industrial ultrasonic images", in *Pop-11 comes of age: the advancement of an AI programming language*, Anderson, J. A. D. W. (ed.), Ellis Horwood (1989).

Further reading

- Hayes-Roth, F., Waterman, D. and Lenat, D. (ed.), *Building expert systems*, Addison-Wesley (1984).
- Jackson, P., *Introduction to expert systems - 2nd edition*, Addison-Wesley (1990).

chapter four

Dealing with uncertainty

4.1 Sources of uncertainty

Our discussion of rule-based systems in chapter 3 assumed that we live in a clear-cut world, where every hypothesis is either true, false or unknown. Furthermore, we pointed out that many systems make use of the *closed world assumption*, whereby any hypothesis that is unknown is assumed to be false. We were then left with a binary system, where everything is either true or false. While this model of reality is very useful in many applications, real reasoning processes are rarely so clear-cut. Referring to the example of the control of a power station boiler, we made use of the following rule:

```
IF transducer output is low THEN water level is low.
```

There are three distinct forms of uncertainty that might be associated with this rule:

Uncertainty in the rule itself
A low level of water in the drum is not the only possible explanation for a low transducer output. Another possible cause could be that the float attached to the transducer is stuck. What we really mean by this rule is that if the transducer output is low then the water level is *probably* low.

Uncertainty in the evidence
The evidence upon which the rule is based may be uncertain. There are two possible reasons for this uncertainty. Firstly the evidence may come from a source which is not totally reliable. For instance, we may not be absolutely certain that the transducer output is low, as this information relies upon a meter to measure the voltage. Alternatively the evidence itself may have been derived by a rule whose conclusion was probable rather than certain.

Use of vague language

The above rule is based around the notion of a "low" transducer output. Assuming that the output is a voltage, we must consider whether "low" corresponds to 1mV, 1V or 1kV.

It is important to distinguish between these sources of uncertainty, as they need to be handled differently. There are some situations in nature which are truly random and whose outcome, while uncertain, can be anticipated on a statistical basis. For instance, we can anticipate that on average one out of six throws of a die will result in a score of '4'. Some of the techniques that we will be discussing are based upon probability theory. These assume that a statistical approach can be adopted, although this assumption will be only an approximation to the real circumstances unless the problem is truly random.

In this chapter we will review some of the commonly used techniques for reasoning with uncertainty. The first technique that we will consider is Bayesian updating, which has a rigorous derivation based upon probability theory, but whose underlying assumptions may not be true in practical situations (such as the statistical independence of multiple pieces of evidence). Most of the other techniques that are discussed here do not have a rigorous mathematical basis, but have been devised as practical ways of overcoming the limitations of Bayesian updating. The heuristic nature of these techniques has meant that reasoning under uncertainty remains a controversial issue.

4.2 Bayesian updating

4.2.1 Representing uncertainty by probability

Bayesian updating assumes that it is possible to ascribe a probability to every hypothesis or assertion, and that these probabilities can be updated in the light of evidence for or against the hypothesis or assertion. The derivation of the updating formulae from Bayes' rule of dependent probabilities is shown in section 4.2.4. The rest of section 4.2 will only be concerned with how the technique can be used. One of the earliest successful applications of Bayesian updating to expert systems was PROSPECTOR, a system which assisted mineral prospecting by interpreting geological data [1, 2].

Let's start our discussion by returning to our rule set for control of the power station boiler (see section 3.2), which included the following two rules:

```
/* Rule 3.4 */
IF release valve stuck THEN steam outlet blocked
```

```
/* Rule 3.6 */
IF steam escaping THEN steam outlet blocked.
```

We are going to consider the hypothesis that there is a steam outlet blockage. Previously, under the closed world assumption, we asserted that in the absence of any evidence about a hypothesis, the hypothesis could be treated as false. The Bayesian approach is to ascribe an *a priori* probability (sometimes simply called the *prior* probability) to the hypothesis that the steam outlet is blocked. This is the probability that the steam outlet is blocked, in the absence of any evidence that it is or is not blocked. Bayesian updating is a technique for updating this probability in the light of evidence for or against the hypothesis. So, whereas we had previously assumed that "steam escaping" led to the deduction "steam outlet blockage" with absolute certainty, now we can only say that it supports that deduction. Bayesian updating is cumulative, so that if the probability of a hypothesis has been updated in the light of one piece of evidence, the new probability can then be updated further by a second piece of evidence.

4.2.2 Updating probabilities with supporting evidence

Suppose that the prior probability of "steam outlet blockage" is 0.01 (blockages only rarely occur). Our modified version of rule 3.6 might look like this:

```
IF steam escaping
THEN steam outlet blockage IS X times more likely.
```

With this new rule, if steam is escaping we can update the probability of a steam outlet blockage provided we have an expression for X. A value for X can be expressed most easily if the hypothesis "steam outlet blockage" is expressed as odds rather than a probability. The odds, O(H), of a given hypothesis (or assertion), H, are related to its probability, P(H), by the relations:

$$O(H) = \frac{P(H)}{P(\sim H)} = \frac{P(H)}{1 - P(H)} \tag{4.1}$$

and

$$P(H) = \frac{O(H)}{O(H) + 1} \tag{4.2}$$

where ~H means "not H". Thus a hypothesis with a probability of 0.2 has odds of 0.25 (or "4 to 1 against"). Similarly a hypothesis with a probability of 0.8 has odds of 4 (or "4 to 1 on"). An assertion that is absolutely certain, i.e., has a probability of 1, has infinite odds. In practice, limits are often set on odds values so that, for example, if O(H)>1000 then H is true, and if O(H)<0.001 then H is false. These limits are arbitrary.

The standard formula (derived in section 4.2.4) for updating the odds of a hypothesis H, given that evidence E is observed, is:

$$O(H|E) = A \times O(H) \tag{4.3}$$

where O(H|E) is the odds of H, given the presence of evidence E, and A is the *affirms* weight of E. The definition of A is:

$$A = \frac{P(E|H)}{P(E|{\sim}H)} \tag{4.4}$$

Formula 4.3 gives us a simple way of updating our confidence in hypothesis H in the light of new evidence E, assuming that we have a value for A and the current odds of H, O(H). O(H) will be at its *a priori* value if it has not previously been updated by other pieces of evidence. In the case of rule 3.6, H refers to the hypothesis "steam outlet blockage" and E refers to the evidence "steam escaping".

Given the definition of A in equation 4.4, the right-hand side of equation 4.3 might appear more formidable than the expression we are hoping to derive, namely O(H|E). However, the expression for A is couched in terms of the probability of evidence, given a hypothesis, rather than the reverse. In the case of diagnosis problems, this information is usually more readily available (at least in an informal way) than the probability of a hypothesis, given the evidence. So in our example an expert may have some idea of how often steam is observed escaping when there is an outlet blockage, but is less likely to know how often a steam escape is due to an outlet blockage. This premise is one of the justifications for using Bayesian updating. However, even if this premise is not satisfied in a given application, Bayesian updating can still be useful if a heuristic value can be attached to A.

4.2.3 Updating probabilities with opposing evidence

In many cases, the absence of a piece of supporting evidence may reduce the likelihood of a certain hypothesis. In other words, the absence of supporting evidence is equivalent to the presence of opposing evidence. The absence of evidence is distinct from not knowing whether or not the evidence is present, and can be used to reduce the probability (or odds) of the hypothesis by an appropriate amount. The standard formula for updating the odds of a hypothesis H given that the evidence E is absent is:

$$O(H|{\sim}E) = D \times O(H) \tag{4.5}$$

where O(H|~E) is the odds of H, given the absence of evidence E; and D is the *denies* weight of E:

$$D = \frac{P({\sim}E|H)}{P({\sim}E|{\sim}H)}$$

or (4.6)

$$D = \frac{1 - P(E|H)}{1 - P(E|{\sim}H)}$$

If a given piece of evidence E has an *affirms* weight A which is greater than 1, then its *denies* weight must be less than 1, and vice versa:

$A > 1$ implies $D < 1$,
$A < 1$ implies $D > 1$.

If $A < 1$ and $D > 1$, then the absence of evidence is supportive of a hypothesis. Rule 3.7 provides an example of this, where "NOT(water level low)" supports the hypothesis "pressure high" and "water level low" opposes the hypothesis:

```
/* Rule 3.7 */
IF temperature high AND NOT(water level low)
THEN pressure high.
```

A Bayesian version of this rule might be:

```
/* Rule 4.1 */
IF temperature high (AFFIRMS 18.0; DENIES 0.11)
AND water level low (AFFIRMS 0.10; DENIES 1.90)
THEN pressure high
```

4.2.4 Derivation of the Bayesian updating formulae

In this section we will derive the Bayesian updating formulae (equations 4.3 to 4.6). The derivation is included for completeness, but is not needed in order to understand the use of the updating formulae as described in sections 4.2.5-4.2.10. The technique of Bayesian updating is based upon the application of Bayes' theorem, which provides an expression for the probability, P(H|E), of a hypothesis H given some evidence E, in terms of the probability, P(E|H), of E given H:

$$P(H|E) = \frac{P(H)\,P(E|H)}{P(E)} \,.$$

(4.7)

The theorem is easily proved by looking at the definition of dependent probabilities. Of an expected population of events in which E is observed, $P(H|E)$ is the fraction in which H is also observed. Thus:

$$P(H|E) = \frac{P(H\&E)}{P(E)} \,.$$

(4.8)

Similarly,

$$P(E|H) = \frac{P(H\&E)}{P(H)} \,.$$

(4.9)

Combining equations 4.8 and 4.9 yields equation 4.7.

For the purpose of updating probabilities in a rule-based system, it is more convenient to rewrite equation 4.7 in terms of odds values. We firstly consider the hypothesis "not H", or ~H, in equation 4.7:

$$P(\sim H|E) = \frac{P(\sim H)\,P(E|\sim H)}{P(E)} \,.$$

(4.10)

By dividing equation 4.7 by equation 4.10:

$$\frac{P(H|E)}{P(\sim H|E)} = \frac{P(E|H)\,P(H)}{P(E|\sim H)\,P(\sim H)} \,.$$

(4.11)

By definition, the odds value of H, $O(H)$, is given by

$$O(H) = \frac{P(H)}{P(\sim H)}$$

(4.1)

and similarly

$$O(H|E) = \frac{P(H|E)}{P(\sim H|E)} \,.$$

Substituting these two expressions into equation 4.11 yields:

$$O(H|E) = A \times O(H)$$

(4.3)

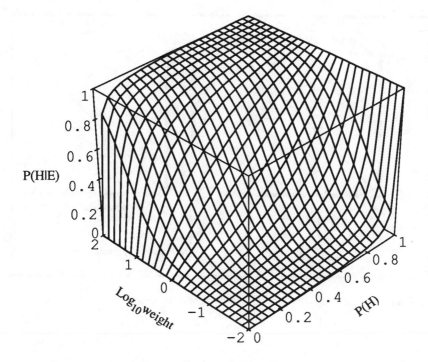

Figure 4.1 The Bayesian updating function.

where:

$$A = \frac{P(E|H)}{P(E|{\sim}H)} .$$ (4.4)

By considering the absence of evidence, i.e ~E, we obtain:

$$O(H|{\sim}E) = D \times O(H)$$ (4.5)

where:

$$D = \frac{P({\sim}E|H)}{P({\sim}E|{\sim}H)} .$$ (4.6)

A and D are the *affirms* and *denies* weights of evidence E respectively. The function represented by equations 4.3 and 4.5 is shown in figure 4.1. Rather than displaying odds values, probabilities have been shown as these have a finite range (0 - 1). The weight (A or D) has been shown on a logarithmic scale over the range 0.01 to 100.

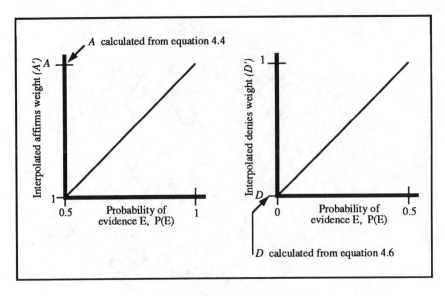

Figure 4.2 Linear interpolation of affirms and denies weights when the evidence is uncertain.

4.2.5 Dealing with uncertain evidence

So far we have assumed that evidence is either definitely present (i.e., has a probability of 1) or definitely absent (i.e., has a probability of 0). If the probability of the evidence lies between these extremes, then the confidence in the conclusion must be scaled appropriately. There are two reasons why the evidence may be uncertain:

- the evidence could be an assertion generated by another uncertain rule, and which therefore has a probability associated with it; or

- the evidence may be in the form of data which are not totally reliable, such as the output from a sensor.

In terms of probabilities, we wish to calculate $P(H|E)$, where E is uncertain. We can handle this problem by assuming that E was asserted by another rule whose evidence was B, where B is certain (has probability 1). Given the evidence B, the probability of E is $P(E|B)$. Our problem then becomes one of calculating $P(H|B)$. This task is not straightforward, although an expression for $P(H|B)$ has been derived by Duda et al. [3]:

$$P(H|B) = P(H|E) \times P(E|B) + P(H|\sim E) \times [1 - P(E|B)]. \tag{4.12}$$

As the terms on the right-hand side of equation 4.12 might be considered too difficult to evaluate or estimate, a shortcut is often sought. One such technique is to modify the *affirms* and *denies* weights in equations 4.3 and 4.5 in order to reflect the uncertainty in E. A possible means of achieving this is to interpolate the weights linearly as the probability of E varies between 1 and 0. Figure 4.2 illustrates this scaling process, where the interpolated *affirms* and *denies* weights are given the symbols A' and D' respectively. While P(E) is greater than 0.5, the *affirms* weight is used, and when P(E) is less than 0.5 the *denies* weight is used. Over the range of values for P(E), A' and D' vary between 1 (neutral weighting) and A and D respectively. The interpolation process achieves the right sort of result, but has no rigorous basis. The expressions used to calculate the interpolated values are:

$$A' = [2(A-1) \times P(E)] + 2 - A \tag{4.13}$$

$$D' = [2(1-D) \times P(E)] + D. \tag{4.14}$$

4.2.6 Combining evidence

Much of the controversy concerning the use of Bayesian updating is centered on the issue of how to combine several pieces of evidence that support the same hypothesis. If n pieces of evidence are found which support a hypothesis H, then the formal restatement of the updating equation is straightforward:

$$O(H|E_1 \& E_2 \& E_3 ..... E_n) = A \times O(H)$$

where

$$A = \frac{P(E_1 \& E_2 \& E_3 ..... E_n \mid H)}{P(E_1 \& E_2 \& E_3 ..... E_n \mid \sim H)}.$$

However, the usefulness of this pair of equations is doubtful, since we do not know in advance which pieces of evidence will be available to support the hypothesis H. We would therefore have to write expressions for A covering all possible pieces of evidence E_i, as well as all combinations of the pairs $E_i \& E_j$, of the triples $E_i \& E_j \& E_k$, of quadruples $E_i \& E_j \& E_k \& E_m$, and so on. As this is clearly an unrealistic requirement, especially where the number of possible pieces of evidence (or symptoms) is large, a simplification is normally sought. The problem becomes much more manageable if it is assumed that all pieces of evidence are *statistically independent*. It is this assumption that is one of the

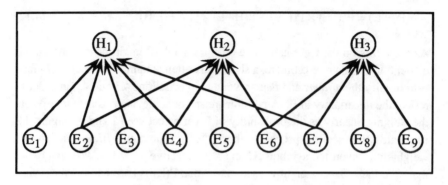

Figure 4.3 A shallow Bayesian inference network (E_i = evidence, H_i = hypothesis).

most controversial aspects of the use of Bayesian updating in knowledge-based systems, since the assumption is rarely accurate. Statistical independence of two pieces of evidence (E_1 and E_2) means that the probability of observing E_1 given that E_2 has been observed is identical to the probability of observing E_1 given no information about E_2. Stating this more formally, the statistical independence of E_1 and E_2 is defined as:

$$P(E_1|E_2) = P(E_1)$$

and

$$P(E_2|E_1) = P(E_2).$$

If the independence assumption is made, then the rule-writer need only worry about supplying weightings of the form:

$$A_i = \frac{P(E_i|H)}{P(E_i|{\sim}H)}$$

and

$$D_i = \frac{P({\sim}E_i|H)}{P({\sim}E_i|{\sim}H)}$$

for each piece of evidence E_i that has the potential to update H. If, in a given run of the system, *n* pieces of evidence are found that support or oppose H, then the updating equations are simply:

$$O(H|E_1 \& E_2 \& E_3 .... E_n) = A_1 \times A_2 \times A_3 \times .... \times A_n \times O(H)$$

and

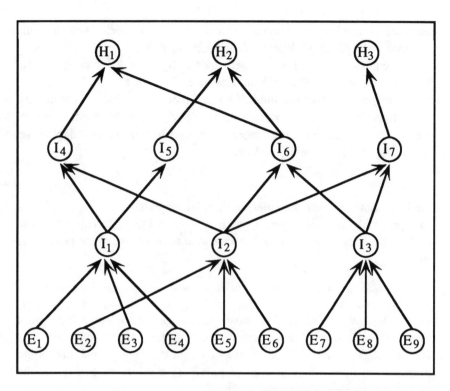

Figure 4.4 A deeper Bayesian inference network
(E_i = evidence, H_i = hypothesis, I_i = intermediate hypothesis).

$$O(H|\sim E_1 \& \sim E_2 \& \sim E_3 .... \sim E_n) = D_1 \times D_2 \times D_3 \times .... \times D_n \times O(H)$$

Problems arising from the interdependence of pieces of evidence can be avoided if the rule base is properly structured. Where pieces of evidence are known to be interdependent, they should not be combined in a single rule. Instead assertions (and the rules that generate them) should be arranged in a hierarchy from low level input data to high level conclusions, with many levels of hypotheses between. This does not limit the amount of evidence that is considered in reaching a conclusion, but controls the interactions between the pieces of evidence. Inference networks are a convenient means of representing the levels of assertions from input data, through intermediate deductions to final conclusions. Figures 4.3 and 4.4 show two possible inference networks. Each node represents either a hypothesis or a piece of evidence, and has an associated probability (not shown). In figure 4.3 the rule-writer has attempted to draw all the evidence that is relevant to particular conclusions together in a single rule for each conclusion. This produces a shallow network, with no intermediate levels between input data and conclusions. Such a system would be prone to the effects of dependence between input data.

In contrast, the inference network in figure 4.4 includes several intermediate steps. The probabilities at each node are modified as the reasoning process proceeds, until they reach their final values. Note that the rules in the boiler control example made use of several intermediate nodes, which helped to make the rules more understandable and avoided duplication of tests for specific pieces of evidence.

4.2.7 Combining Bayesian rules with production rules

In a practical rule-based system, we may wish to mix uncertain rules with production rules. For instance, we may wish to make use of the production rule:

```
IF release valve is stuck THEN release valve needs cleaning
```

even though the assertion "`release valve is stuck`" may have been established with a probability less than 1. In this case the hypothesis "`release valve needs cleaning`" can be asserted with the same probability as the evidence. This avoids the issue of providing a prior probability for the hypothesis or a weighting for the evidence.

Where two pieces of evidence are conjoined (i.e., they are joined by "AND"), the resulting hypothesis can be drawn with the same probability as the least probable piece of evidence. This can be expressed most clearly by example:

```
IF evidence1 AND evidence2 THEN hypothesis3.
```

The probability of hypothesis3 is given by:

$$P(\text{hypothesis3}) = \min[P(\text{evidence1}), P(\text{evidence2})].$$

Where items of evidence are disjoined (i.e., joined by "OR"), the probability of the most likely piece of evidence is propagated through to the hypothesis. So given the rule:

```
IF evidence1 OR evidence2 THEN hypothesis3,
```

the probability of hypothesis3 is given by:

$$P(\text{hypothesis3}) = \max[P(\text{evidence1}), P(\text{evidence2})].$$

H	E	P(H)	O(H)	P(E|H)	P(E|~H)	A	D
release valve needs cleaning	release valve is stuck	——	——	——	——	——	——
release valve is stuck	warning light is on	0.02	0.02	0.88	0.4	2.20	0.20
release valve is stuck	pressure is high	0.02	0.02	0.85	0.01	85.0	0.15
pressure is high	temperature is high	0.1	0.11	0.90	0.05	18.0	0.11
pressure is high	water level is low	0.1	0.11	0.05	0.5	0.10	1.90

Table 4.1 Values used in the worked example of Bayesian updating.

These expressions for conjoining and disjoining evidence in a production rule have been taken from Zadeh's possibility theory (see section 4.4).

4.2.8 A worked example of Bayesian updating
We will consider the same example that was introduced in chapter 3, namely control of a power station boiler. Let us start with just four rules:

```
/* Rule 4.1a */
IF release valve is stuck THEN release valve needs cleaning

/* Rule 4.2a */
IF warning light is on THEN release valve is stuck

/* Rule 4.3a */
IF pressure is high THEN release valve is stuck

/* Rule 4.4a */
IF temperature is high AND NOT(water level is low)
THEN pressure is high
```

The conclusion of each of these rules is expressed as an assertion. The four rules contain four assertions (or hypotheses) and three pieces of evidence which are independent of the rules, namely the temperature, the status of the warning light (on or off), and the water level. The various probability estimates for these, and their associated *affirms* and *denies* weights are shown in table 4.1.

Having calculated the *affirms* and *denies* weights, we can now rewrite our production rules as probabilistic rules. We will leave rule 4.1a unaltered in order to illustrate the interaction between production rules and probabilistic rules. Our new rule set is therefore as follows:

```
/* Rule 4.1b */
IF release valve is stuck THEN release valve needs cleaning

/* Rule 4.2b */
IF warning light is on        (AFFIRMS 2.20; DENIES 0.20)
THEN release valve is stuck

/* Rule 4.3b */
IF pressure is high           (AFFIRMS 85.0; DENIES 0.15)
THEN release valve is stuck

/* Rule 4.4b */
IF temperature is high        (AFFIRMS 18.0; DENIES 0.11)
AND water level is low        (AFFIRMS 0.10; DENIES 1.90)
THEN pressure is high
```

Rule 4.4b makes use of two pieces of evidence, and it no longer needs a negative condition, as this has been accommodated by the *affirms* and *denies* weights. The requirement that "NOT (water level is low)" be supportive evidence is expressed by the *denies* weight of "water level is low" being greater than 1 while the *affirms* weight is less than 1.

To illustrate how the various weights are used, let's consider how a Bayesian inference engine would use the following set of input data:

- NOT(water level is low);
- warning light is on;
- temperature is high.

We will assume that the rules fire in the order:

Rule 4.4b → Rule 4.3b → Rule 4.2b → Rule 4.1b

The resultant rule trace might then appear as follows:

```
Rule 4.4b
H = pressure is high;              O(H) = 0.11
E₁ = temperature is high;          A₁ = 18.0
E₂ = water level is low;           D₂ = 1.90
O(H|(E₁&~E₂)) = O(H) × A₁ × D₂ = 3.76
/* Updated odds of pressure is high are 3.76 */
```

```
Rule 4.3b
H = release valve is stuck;          O(H) = 0.02
E = pressure is high;                  A = 85.0
Because E is not certain (O(E) = 3.76, P(E) = 0.79), the
inference engine must calculate an interpolated value A' for
the affirms weight of E (see section 4.2.5).
A'= [2(A-1) × P(E)] + 2 - A = 49.7
O(H|(E)) = O(H) × A' = 0.99
/* Updated odds of release valve is stuck are 0.99, */
/* corresponding to a probability of approximately 0.5 */
```

```
Rule 4.2b
H = release valve is stuck;          O(H) = 0.99
E = warning light is on;               A = 2.20
O(H|(E)) = O(H) × A = 2.18
/* Updated odds of release valve is stuck are 2.18 */
```

```
Rule 4.1b
H = release valve needs cleaning
E = release valve is stuck;
This is a production rule, so the conclusion is asserted with
same probability as the evidence. O(E)= 2.18 implies O(H)= 2.18
/* Updated odds of release valve needs cleaning are 2.18 */
```

4.2.9 Discussion of the worked example

The above example serves to illustrate a number of features of Bayesian updating. Our final conclusion that the release valve needs cleaning is reached with a certainty represented as:

```
O(release valve needs cleaning) = 2.18; or
P(release valve needs cleaning) = 0.69.
```

Thus there is a probability of 0.69 that the valve needs cleaning. In a real world situation, this is a more realistic outcome than concluding that the valve definitely needs cleaning, which would have been the conclusion had we used the original set of production rules.

The initial three items of evidence were all stated with complete certainty - "NOT(water level is low)"; "warning light is on"; and "temperature is high". In other words, P(E)=1 for each of these. Consider the evidence "warning light is on". A probability of less than 1 might be associated with this evidence if it were generated as an assertion by another probabilistic rule, or if it were supplied as an input to the system but the user's view of the light was impaired. If P(warning light is on) is 0.8, an interpolated value of the *affirms* weight would be used in rule 4.2b. Equation 4.13 yields an interpolated value of 1.72 for the *affirms* weight.

However, if P(warning light is on) were less than 0.5, then an interpolated *denies* weighting would be used. If P(warning light is on) were 0.3, an interpolated *denies* weighting of 0.68 is yielded by equation 4.14.

If P(warning light is on) = 0.5, then the warning light is just as likely to be on as it is to be off. If we try to interpolate either the *affirms* or *denies* weight, a value of 1 will be found. Thus if each item of evidence for a particular rule has a probability of 0.5, then the rule has no effect whatsoever.

Assuming that the prior probability of a hypothesis is less than 1 and greater than 0 (a value of 1 or 0 cannot be updated using the techniques described here), then the hypothesis can never be confirmed or refuted with complete certainty.

While Bayesian updating is a mathematically rigorous technique for updating probabilities, it is important to remember that the results obtained can only be valid if the data supplied are valid. This is the key issue to consider when assessing the virtues of the technique. The probabilities shown in table 4.1 have not been measured from a series of trials, but instead they are an expert's "best guesses". Given that the values upon which the *affirms* and *denies* weights are based are only guesses, then a reasonable alternative to calculating them is to simply take an educated guess at the appropriate weightings. Such an approach is just as valid as calculating values from unreliable data. If a rule-writer takes such an ad hoc approach, the provision of both an *affirms* and *denies* weighting becomes optional. If an *affirms* weight is provided for a piece of evidence E, but not a *denies* weight, then that rule can be ignored when P(E) < 0.5.

As well as relying on the rule-writer's weightings, Bayesian updating is also critically dependent on the values of the prior probabilities. Obtaining accurate estimates for these is also problematic.

Even if we assume that all of the data supplied in the above worked example are accurate, the validity of the final conclusion relies upon the statistical independence from each other of the supporting pieces of evidence. In our example, as with very many real problems, this assumption is dubious. For example, "pressure is high" and "warning light is on" were used as independent pieces of evidence, when in reality there is a cause and effect relationship between the two.

4.2.10 Advantages and disadvantages of Bayesian updating

Bayesian updating is a means of handling uncertainty by updating the probability of an assertion when evidence for or against the assertion is provided.

The principal *advantages* of Bayesian updating are:

i   The technique is based upon a proven statistical theorem.

ii   Likelihood is expressed as a probability (or odds), which has a clearly defined and familiar meaning.

iii   Weightings are based upon the probability of evidence (the symptoms) given a hypothesis (the cause). These are therefore deductive probabilities rather than abductive ones (see chapter 1) and as such are easier to estimate.

iv   Weightings and prior probabilities can be replaced by sensible guesses. (This is at the expense of advantages 1 and 2, as the probabilities subsequently calculated cannot be interpreted literally, but rather as an imprecise measure of likelihood).

v   Evidence for and against a hypothesis (or the presence and absence of evidence) can be combined in a single rule by using *affirms* and *denies* weights.

vi   Linear interpolation can be used to take account of any uncertainty in the evidence (i.e., uncertainty about whether the condition part of the rule is satisfied), though this is an ad hoc solution.

vii   The probability of a hypothesis can be updated in response to more than one piece of evidence.

The principal *disadvantages* of Bayesian updating are:

i   The prior probability of an assertion must be known or guessed at.

ii   Dependent probabilities must be measured or estimated in order to calculate the *affirms* and *denies* weights, or failing that a guess must be taken at suitable weightings. The dependent probabilities are often easier to judge than the prior probability, but nonetheless are a considerable source of errors. Often estimates of likelihood are clouded by a subjective view of the importance or utility of a piece of information [4].

iii   The single probability value for the truth of an assertion tells us nothing about its precision.

iv   Because evidence for and against an assertion are lumped together, no record is kept of how much there is of each.

v   The addition of a new rule which asserts a new hypothesis often requires alterations to the prior probabilities and weightings of several other rules. This contravenes one of the main advantages of knowledge-based systems.

vi   The assumption that pieces of evidence are independent is often unfounded. The only alternatives are to calculate *affirms* and *denies* weights for all possible combinations of dependent evidence, or to restructure the rule base so as to minimize these interactions.

vii The linear interpolation technique for dealing with uncertain evidence is
not mathematically justified.

4.3 Certainty theory

4.3.1 Introduction
Certainty theory [5] is an adaptation of Bayesian updating which is
incorporated in the EMYCIN expert system shell. EMYCIN is based upon
MYCIN [6], an expert system that assists in the diagnosis of infectious
diseases. The name EMYCIN is derived from "essential MYCIN", reflecting
the fact that it is not specific to medical diagnosis and that its handling of
uncertainty is simplified. Certainty theory represents an attempt to overcome
some of the shortcomings of Bayesian updating, although the mathematical
rigour of Bayesian updating is lost. As this rigour is rarely justified by the
quality of the data, this is not really a problem.

4.3.2 Making uncertain hypotheses
Instead of using probabilities, each assertion in EMYCIN has a certainty value
associated with it. Certainty values can range between 1 and –1.
For a given hypothesis H, its certainty value C(H) is given by:

$C(H) = 1.0$ if H is known to be true;
$C(H) = 0.0$ if H is unknown;
$C(H) = -1.0$ if H is known to be false.

There is a similarity between certainty values and probabilities, such that:

$C(H) = 1.0$ corresponds to $P(H)=1.0$;
$C(H) = 0.0$ corresponds to $P(H)$ being at its a priori value;
$C(H) = -1.0$ corresponds to $P(H)=0.0$.

Rules also have a certainty associated with them (i.e., their certainty factor),
serving a similar role to the *affirms* and *denies* weightings in Bayesian systems:

```
IF <evidence> THEN <hypothesis> WITH certainty factor CF.
```

Part of the simplicity of certainty theory stems from the fact that identical
measures of certainty are attached to rules and to hypotheses. A rule can be
applied if the certainty of the evidence, C(E), is greater than 0, i.e., the

evidence is more likely to be present than not.[*] The certainty factor of a rule is modified to reflect the level of certainty of the evidence, such that the modified certainty factor (CF ') is given by:

$$CF' = CF \times C(E). \tag{4.15}$$

If the evidence is known to be present, i.e., $C(E) = 1$, then equation 4.15 yields $CF' = CF$.

The technique for updating the certainty of hypothesis H, in the light of evidence E, involves the application of the following composite function:

if $C(H) \geq 0$ and $CF' \geq 0$:
$$C(H|E) = C(H) + [CF' \times (1 - C(H))] \tag{4.16}$$

if $C(H) \leq 0$ and $CF' \leq 0$:
$$C(H|E) = C(H) + [CF' \times (1 + C(H))] \tag{4.17}$$

if $C(H)$ and CF' have opposite sign:
$$C(H|E) = \frac{C(H) + CF'}{1 - \min(|C(H)|, |CF|)} \tag{4.18}$$

where
$C(H|E)$ = certainty of H updated in the light of evidence E;
$C(H)$ = initial certainty of H;
($C(H)=0$ unless it has been updated by the previous application of a rule).

It can be seen from the above equations that the updating procedure consists of *adding* a positive or negative value to the current certainty of a hypothesis. This contrasts with Bayesian updating, where the odds of a hypothesis are always *multiplied* by the appropriate weighting. The composite function represented by equations 4.16 to 4.18 is plotted in figure 4.5, and can be seen to have a broadly similar shape to the Bayesian updating equation (plotted in figure 4.1). Although there is no theoretical justification for the function for updating certainty values, it does have a number of desirable properties:

i   the function is continuous and has no singularities or steps;

ii   the updated certainty, $C(H|E)$, always lies within the bounds -1 and $+1$;

---

[*] EMYCIN requires that $C(E)>0.2$ (rather than $C(E)>0.0$) for a rule to be considered applicable. The justification for this heuristic is that it saves computational power and makes explanations clearer, as marginally effective rules are suppressed.

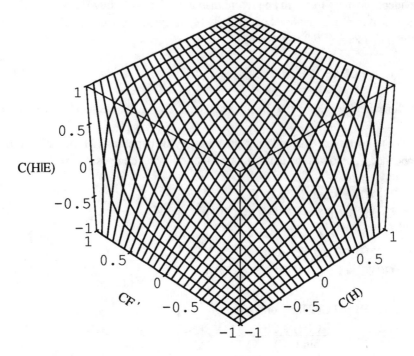

Figure 4.5 Formulae 4.16 - 4.18 for updating certainties.

iii   if either C(H) or CF ' is +1 (i.e., definitely true) then C(H|E) is also +1;

iv   if either C(H) or CF ' is –1 (i.e., definitely false) then C(H|E) is also –1;

v   when contradictory conclusions are combined, they tend to cancel each other out, i.e., if C(H) = –CF ' then C(H|E) = 0;

vi   several pieces of independent evidence can be combined by repeated application of the function, and the outcome is independent of the order in which the pieces of evidence are applied;

vii if C(H)=0 (i.e., the certainty of H is at its a priori value) then C(H|E) = CF ';

viii if the evidence is certain (i.e., C(E) = 1) then CF ' = CF.

4.3.3   *Logical combinations of evidence*

In Bayesian updating systems, each piece of evidence that contributes towards a hypothesis is assumed to be independent and is given its own *affirms* and *denies* weights. In systems based upon certainty theory, the certainty factor is associated with the rule as a whole, rather than with individual pieces of evidence. For this reason, certainty theory provides a simple algorithm for determining the value of the certainty factor that should be applied when more than one item of evidence is included in a single rule. The dependence between pieces of evidence is made explicit by the use of "AND" and "OR", while independent pieces of evidence that contribute towards a single hypothesis must be placed in separate rules. The algorithm is the same as that used when production rules are used within a Bayesian updating system, and is borrowed from Zadeh's possibility theory (section 4.4). The algorithm covers the cases where evidence is conjoined (i.e., joined by AND), disjoined (i.e., joined by OR), and negated.

Conjunction
Consider a rule of the form:

```
IF <evidence E1> AND <evidence E2> THEN <hypothesis>
   WITH certainty factor CF
```

The certainty of the combined evidence is given by $C(E_1 \text{ AND } E_2)$, where:

$$C(E_1 \text{ AND } E_2) = \min[C(E_1), C(E_2)] \tag{4.19}$$

Disjunction
Consider a rule of the form:

```
IF <evidence E1> OR <evidence E2> THEN <hypothesis>
   WITH certainty factor CF
```

The certainty of the combined evidence is given by $C(E_1 \text{ OR } E_2)$, where:

$$C(E_1 \text{ OR } E_2) = \max[C(E_1), C(E_2)] \tag{4.20}$$

Negation
Consider a rule of the form:

```
IF NOT <evidence E> THEN <hypothesis> WITH certainty factor CF
```

The certainty of the negated evidence, $C(E)$, is given by $C(\sim E)$ where:

$$C(\sim E) = -C(E). \tag{4.21}$$

4.3.4 A worked example of certainty theory
In order to illustrate the application of certainty theory, we can rework the example that was used to illustrate Bayesian updating. Four rules were used,

which together could determine whether the release valve of a power station boiler needs cleaning (see sections 4.2.8 - 4.2.9). Each of the four rules can be rewritten with an associated certainty factor, which is estimated by the rule-writer:

```
/* Rule 4.1c */
IF release valve is stuck THEN release valve needs cleaning
WITH CERTAINTY FACTOR 1
```

```
/* Rule 4.2c */
IF warning light is on THEN release valve is stuck
WITH CERTAINTY FACTOR 0.2
```

```
/* Rule 4.3c */
IF pressure is high THEN release valve is stuck
WITH CERTAINTY FACTOR 0.9
```

```
/* Rule 4.4c */
IF temperature is high AND NOT(water level is low)
THEN pressure is high
WITH CERTAINTY FACTOR 0.5
```

Although the process of providing certainty factors might appear ad hoc compared with Bayesian updating, it may be no less reliable than estimating the probabilities upon which Bayesian updating relies. In the Bayesian example, the production rule 4.1b had to be treated as a special case. In a system based upon uncertainty theory, rule 4.1c can be made to behave like a production rule simply by giving it a certainty factor of 1.

As before, the following set of input data will be considered:

- NOT(water level is low);
- warning light is on;
- temperature is high.

We will assume that the rules fire in the order:

Rule 4.4c $\rightarrow$ Rule 4.3c $\rightarrow$ Rule 4.2c $\rightarrow$ Rule 4.1c

The resultant rule trace might then appear as follows:

```
Rule 4.4c                               CF = 0.5
H = pressure is high;                   C(H) = 0
E₁ = temperature is high;               C(E₁) = 1
E₂ = water level is low;C(E₂) = -1, C(~E₂) = 1
C(E₁&~E₂) = min[C(E₁),C(~E₂)] = 1
```

```
CF' = CF × C(E₁&~E₂) = CF
C(H|(E₁&~E₂)) = CF' = 0.5
/* Updated certainty of pressure is high is 0.5 */
```

$$CF' = CF \times C(E_1 \& \sim E_2) = CF$$
$$C(H|(E_1 \& \sim E_2)) = CF' = 0.5$$
/* Updated certainty of *pressure is high* is 0.5 */

```
Rule 4.3c                          CF = 0.9
H = release valve is stuck;         C(H) = 0
E = pressure is high;              C(E) = 0.5
CF' = CF × C(E) = 0.45
C(H|(E)) = CF' = 0.45
/* Updated certainty of release valve is stuck is 0.45 */
```

```
Rule 4.2c                          CF = 0.2
H = release valve is stuck;       C(H) = 0.45
E = warning light is on;            C(E) = 1
CF' = CF × C(E) = CF
C(H|(E)) = C(H) + [CF' × (1−C(H)] = 0.56
/* Updated certainty of release valve is stuck is 0.56 */
```

```
Rule 4.1c                            CF = 1
H = release valve needs cleaning     C(H) = 0
E = release valve is stuck;        C(E) = 0.56
CF' = CF × C(E) = 0.56
C(H|(E)) = CF' = 0.56
/* Updated certainty of release valve needs cleaning is 0.56 */
```

4.3.5 Discussion of the worked example

Given the certainty factors shown, the example yielded the result "`release valve needs cleaning`" with a similar level of confidence as the Bayesian updating example.

Under Bayesian updating, rules 4.2b and 4.3b could be combined into a single rule without changing their effect:

```
/* Rule 4.5b */
IF warning light is on      (AFFIRMS 2.20; DENIES 0.20)
AND pressure is high        (AFFIRMS 85.0; DENIES 0.15)
THEN release valve is stuck
```

With certainty theory, the weightings apply not to the individual pieces of evidence (as with Bayesian updating) but to the rule itself. If rules 4.2c and 4.3c were combined in one rule, a single certainty factor would need to be chosen to replace the two used previously. Thus a combined rule might look like:

```
/* Rule 4.5c */
IF warning light is on AND pressure is high
THEN release valve stuck WITH CERTAINTY FACTOR 0.95.
```

In the combined rule, the two items of evidence are no longer being treated independently and the certainty factor is the adjudged weighting if *both* items of evidence are present. If our worked example had contained this combined rule (4.5c) instead of rules 4.2c and 4.3c, then the rule trace would contain the following:

```
Rule 4.5c                              CF = 0.95
H = release valve is stuck;             C(H) = 0
E₁ = warning light is on;              C(E₁) = 1
E₂ = pressure is high;                 C(E₂) = 0.5
C(E₁ & E₂) = min[C(E₁),C(E₂)] = 0.5
CF' = CF × C(E₁ & E₂) = 0.48
C(H|(E₁ & E₂)) = CF' = 0.48
/* Updated certainty of release valve is stuck is 0.48 */
```

With the certainty factors used in the example, the combined rule yields a lower confidence in the hypothesis "release valve stuck" than rules 4.2c and 4.3c used separately. As a knock-on result, rule 4.1c would yield the conclusion "release valve needs cleaning" with a diminished certainty of 0.48.

4.3.6 Relating certainty factors to probabilities
It has already been noted that there is a similarity between the certainty factors that are attached to hypotheses and the probabilities of those hypotheses, such that:

$C(H) = 1.0$ corresponds to $P(H)=1.0$;
$C(H) = 0.0$ corresponds to $P(H)$ being at its a priori value;
$C(H) = -1.0$ corresponds to $P(H)=0.0$.

Additionally, a formal relationship exists between the certainty factor associated with a rule and the conditional probability, $P(H|E)$, of a hypothesis (H) given some evidence (E). This is only of passing interest as certainty factors are not normally calculated in this way, but instead are simply estimated or chosen so as to give the right sort of results. The formal relationships are as follows.

If evidence E supports hypothesis H, i.e., $P(H|E)$ is greater than $P(H)$, then:

$$\left. \begin{array}{ll} CF = \dfrac{P(H|E) - P(H)}{1 - P(H)} & \text{if } P(H) \neq 1 \\ CF = 1.0 & \text{if } P(H) = 1 \end{array} \right\} \qquad (4.22)$$

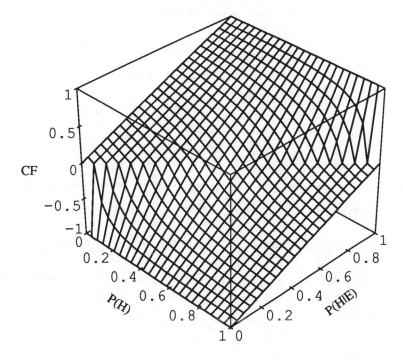

Figure 4.6 The relationship between certainty factors and probability.

If evidence E opposes hypothesis H, i.e., P(H|E) is less than P(H), then:

$$\left.\begin{array}{ll} CF = \dfrac{P(H|E) - P(H)}{P(H)} & \text{if } P(H) \neq 0 \\[2mm] CF = -1 & \text{if } P(H) = 0 \end{array}\right\} \qquad (4.23)$$

The shape of equations 4.22 and 4.23 is shown in figure 4.6.

4.4 Possibility theory - fuzzy sets and fuzzy logic

Bayesian updating and certainty theory are techniques for handling the uncertainty that arises (or is assumed to arise) from statistical variations or randomness. Possibility theory addresses a different source of uncertainty, namely vagueness in the use of language. Possibility theory, or fuzzy logic, was developed by Zadeh [7, 8, 9] and builds upon his theory of fuzzy sets [10]. Zadeh asserts that while probability theory may be appropriate for measuring

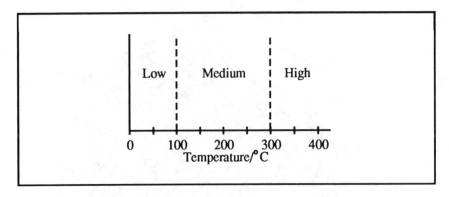

Figure 4.7 Conventional "crisp" sets applied to temperature.

the likelihood of a hypothesis, it says nothing about the *meaning* of the hypothesis.

The rules shown in this chapter and the previous one contain a number of examples of vague language where fuzzy sets might be applied, such as the following phrases:

```
water level is low
temperature is high
pressure is high.
```

In conventional set theory, the sets "high", "medium" and "low", applied to a variable such as temperature, would be mutually exclusive. If a given temperature (say 400°C) is "high", then it is neither "medium" nor "low". Such sets are said to be crisp or non-fuzzy (figure 4.7). If the boundary between medium and high is set at 300°C, then a temperature of 301°C is considered "high", while 299°C is considered "medium". This distinction is rather artificial, and means that a tiny difference in temperature can completely change the rule-firing, while a rise in temperature from 301°C to 1000°C has no effect at all.

Fuzzy sets are a means of smoothing out the boundaries between categories. The theory of fuzzy sets expresses imprecision quantitatively by introducing characteristic membership functions that can assume values between 0 and 1 corresponding to degrees of membership from "not a member" through to "a full member". If F is a fuzzy set, then the membership function $\mu_F(e)$ measures the degree to which e belongs to F. This degree of membership is the *possibility* that e is described by F.

Conversely, consider that we are given the imprecise statement "temperature is low". If *LT* is the fuzzy set of low temperatures, then we might define the membership function μ_{LT} such that:

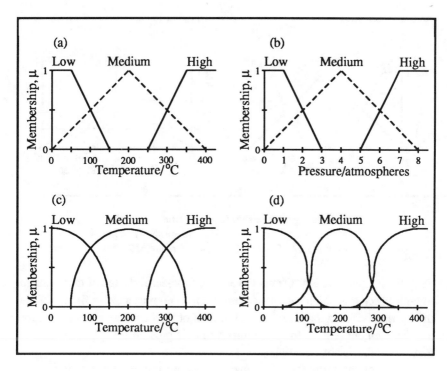

Figure 4.8 A variety of membership functions.

$\mu_{LT}(200°C) = 0.0$
$\mu_{LT}(150°C) = 0.0$
$\mu_{LT}(125°C) = 0.25$
$\mu_{LT}(100°C) = 0.5$
$\mu_{LT}(75°C) = 0.75$
$\mu_{LT}(50°C) = 1.0$
$\mu_{LT}(0°C) = 1.0$

These values correspond with a linear membership function (figure 4.8a), which is convenient in many applications. The most suitable shape of the membership function depends on the particular application, and figures 4.8c and 4.8d show some alternatives.

The key differences between fuzzy and crisp sets are that:

- an element has a degree of membership (0 - 1) of a fuzzy set; and
- membership of one fuzzy set does not preclude membership of another.

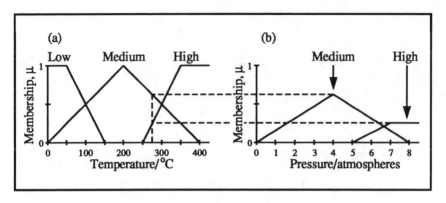

Figure 4.9   Calculating membership functions from fuzzy rules.
Membership functions for pressure are shown, derived
from rules 4.6f and 4.7f, for a temperature of 275°C.

Thus the temperature 300°C may have some (non-zero) degree of membership
to both fuzzy sets "high" and "medium". This is represented in figure 4.8 by
the overlap between the fuzzy sets. The total of the membership functions for
a given element (e.g., a specific temperature or pressure) can be arranged to
total 1, but this is not essential.

Some of the terminology of fuzzy sets may require clarification. The
statement "temperature is low" is an example of a *fuzzy statement*, involving
the *fuzzy set* "low temperature" and a *fuzzy variable* "temperature". A fuzzy
variable is one that can take any value from a global set (e.g., the set of all
temperatures), where each value can have a degree of membership of a fuzzy
set (e.g., "low temperature") associated with it.

Now let us consider what happens when we fire some fuzzy rules.
Suppose that our rule base contains the following fuzzy rules:

```
/* Rule 4.6f */
IF temperature is high THEN pressure is high

/* Rule 4.7f */
IF temperature is medium THEN pressure is medium

/* Rule 4.8f */
IF temperature is low THEN pressure is low
```

Suppose that the measured temperature is 275°C. As this is a member of both
fuzzy sets "high" and "medium", both rules 4.6f and 4.7f will fire. The
pressure, we conclude, will be somewhat high and somewhat medium.
Suppose that the membership functions for temperature are as shown in figure
4.9a. The possibility that the temperature is high, μ_{TH}, is 0.25 and the

possibility that the temperature is medium, μ_{TM}, is 0.625. These values can be passed on to other rules that might have "pressure is high" or "pressure is medium" in their condition clauses.

Suppose that we wish to interpret these membership values in terms of numerical values of pressure (although this is not necessary if we only wish to pass on the possibilities through another rule). This can be achieved if we have previously defined membership functions for "high", "medium" and "low" pressure (figure 4.8b). When rule 4.6f fires, the conclusion is drawn that the pressure is high, but the membership function μ_{PH} must be compressed to reflect the fact that μ_{TH} is less than 1 (figure 4.9b). The same also applies to rule 4.7f, in order to derive the membership function for "pressure is medium", μ_{PM}. If we wish to know the possibility associated with a particular amount of pressure, we might use the union of the membership functions μ_{PH} and μ_{PM}. Thus the membership functions can be interpreted as follows:

For any value of pressure, P1, the possibility of the actual pressure being P1 is max{$\mu_F(P1)$}, for all fuzzy sets F for which P1 is a member (PH and PM in this case).

This is a useful heuristic rather than a rigorous treatment, but possibility theory, like certainty theory, is non-rigorous anyway. If a rule has a control action as its conclusion, then the conclusion must be *defuzzified* in order to determine a precise action. This is discussed in section 10.6.

In figure 4.9, the membership functions for "pressure is high" and "pressure is medium" were compressed because the condition parts of the fuzzy rules 4.6f and 4.7f were only partially satisfied. This ensures a linear correlation between the degree of satisfaction of the condition and the defuzzified conclusion. Rather than compressing the membership functions, they can be truncated as shown in figure 4.10. This technique results in a nonlinear relationship between the degree of satisfaction of the condition and the defuzzified conclusion [11, 12].

The rules 4.6f, 4.7f and 4.8f contained only simple conditions. Possibility theory provides a recipe for computing the possibilities of compound conditions. The formulae for conjunction, disjunction and negation are similar to those used in certainty theory (section 4.3):

$$\left.\begin{array}{l} \mu(X \text{ AND } Y) = \min[\mu(X), \mu(Y)] \\ \mu(X \text{ OR } Y) \ = \max[\mu(X), \mu(Y)] \\ \mu(\text{NOT } X) \ \ \ = (1 - \mu(X)) \end{array}\right\} \qquad (4.24)$$

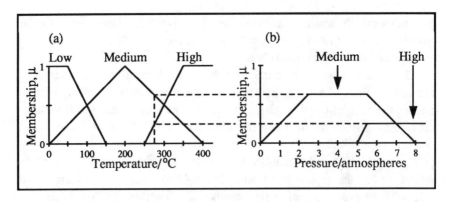

Figure 4.10 An alternative way of calculating membership functions from fuzzy rules. The membership functions for pressure have been truncated rather than compressed.

Although this discussion of possibility theory has concentrated on continuous variables such as temperature and pressure, the same ideas can also be applied to discrete variables, such as a count of the number of cracks in a steel plate. Note also that while the examples above have used only three fuzzy sets (high, medium and low), several more could be used.

4.5 Other techniques

Possibility theory occupies a distinct position among the many strategies for handling uncertainty, as it is the only established one that is concerned specifically with uncertainty arising from imprecise use of language. Techniques have been developed for dealing with other specific sources of uncertainty. For example, plausibility theory [13] addresses the problems arising from unreliable or contradictory sources of information.   Other techniques have been developed in order to overcome some of the perceived shortcomings of Bayesian updating and certainty theory. Notable among these are the Dempster-Shafer theory of evidence and Quinlan's Inferno, which are briefly reviewed here.

None of the more sophisticated techniques for handling uncertainty overcome the most difficult problem, namely obtaining accurate estimates of the likelihood of events and combinations of events. For this reason, their use is rarely justified in practical knowledge-based systems.

4.5.1 Dempster-Shafer theory of evidence

The theory of evidence [14] is a generalization of probability theory that was created by Dempster and developed by Shafer [15]. It addresses two specific deficiencies of probability theory that have already been highlighted, namely:

- the single probability value for the truth of a hypothesis tells us nothing about its precision; and

- because evidence for and against a hypothesis are lumped together, we have no record of how much there is of each.

Rather than representing the probability of an hypothesis H by a single value P(H), Dempster and Shafer's technique binds the probability to a subinterval [L(H), U(H)] of the interval [0, 1]. Although the exact probability P(H) may not be known, L(H) and U(H) represent lower and upper bounds on the probability, such that:

$$L(H) \leq P(H) \leq U(H). \tag{4.25}$$

The precision of our knowledge about H is characterized by the difference U(H) – L(H). If this is small, our knowledge about H is fairly precise, but if it is large we know relatively little about H. A clear distinction is therefore made between uncertainty and ignorance, where uncertainty is expressed by the limits on the value of P(H), and ignorance is represented by the size of the interval defined by those limits. According to [4], Dempster and Shafer have pointed out that the Bayesian agony of assigning prior probabilities to hypotheses is often due to ignorance of the correct values, and this ignorance can make any particular choice arbitrary and unjustifiable.

The above ordering (4.25) can be interpreted as two assertions:

- the probability of H is at least L(H); and

- the probability of ~H is at least 1.0 – U(H).

Thus a separate record is kept of degree of belief and disbelief in H. Like Bayesian updating, the theory of evidence benefits from the solid basis of probability theory for the interpretation of L(H) and U(H). When L(H) = U(H), the theory of evidence reduces to the Bayesian updating method. It is therefore not surprising that the theory of evidence also suffers from many of the same difficulties.

4.5.2 Inferno

The conclusions that can be reached by the Dempster-Shafer theory of evidence are of necessity weaker than those that can be arrived at by Bayesian updating. If the available knowledge does not justify stronger solutions, then drawing weaker solutions is desirable. This theme is developed further in Inferno [16], a technique that its creator, Quinlan, has subtitled "a cautious approach to uncertain inference". Although Inferno is based upon probability theory, it avoids assumptions about the dependence or independence of pieces of evidence and hypotheses. As a result, the correctness of any inferences can be guaranteed, given the available knowledge. Thus Inferno deliberately errs on the side of caution.

The three key motivations for the development of Inferno were as follows:

i   Other systems often make unjustified assumptions about the dependence or independence of pieces of evidence or hypotheses. Inferno allows users to state any such relationships when they are known, but it makes no assumptions.

ii Other systems take a measure of belief (e.g., probability or certainty) in a piece of evidence, and calculate from it a measure of belief in a hypothesis or conclusion. In terms of an inference network (figures 4.3 and 4.4), probabilities or certainty values are always propagated in one direction, namely from the bottom (evidence) to the top (conclusions). Inferno allows users to enter values for any node on the network, and to observe the effects on values at all other nodes.

iii Inferno informs the user of inconsistencies that might be present in the information presented to it, and can make suggestions of ways to restore consistency.

Quinlan [16] gives a detailed account of how these aims are achieved, and provides a comprehensive set of expressions for propagating probabilities throughout the nodes of an inference network.

4.6 Summary

A number of different schemes exist for assigning numerical values to assertions in order to represent levels of confidence in them, and for updating the confidence levels in the light of supporting or opposing evidence. The greatest difficulty lies in obtaining accurate values of likelihood, whether measured as a probability or by some other means. The certainty factors that are associated with rules in certainty theory, and the *affirms* and *denies* weightings in Bayesian updating, can be derived from probability estimates. However, a more pragmatic approach is frequently adopted, namely to choose values which produce the right sort of results, even though the values cannot be theoretically justified. As the more sophisticated techniques (e.g., Dempster-Shafer theory of evidence and Inferno) also depend upon probability estimates that are often dubious, their use is rarely justified.

Bayesian updating is soundly based on probability theory, whereas many of the alternative techniques are ad hoc. In practice, Bayesian updating is also an ad hoc technique because:

- linear interpolation of the *affirms* and *denies* weighting is frequently used as a convenient means of compensating for uncertainty in the evidence;

- the weightings (or the probabilities from which they are derived) and prior probabilities are often based on estimates rather than statistical analysis;

- separate items of evidence which support a single assertion are assumed to be statistically independent, although this may not be the case in reality.

Neural networks (see chapter 6) represent an alternative approach that avoids the difficulties in obtaining reliable probability estimates. Neural networks can be used to "train" a computer system, using many examples, so that it can draw conclusions weighted according to the evidence supplied. Of course, given a large enough set of examples, it would also be possible to calculate accurately the prior probabilities and weightings needed in order to make Bayesian updating or one of its derivatives work effectively.

References

1. Hart, P. E., Duda, R. O. and Einaudi, M. T., "PROSPECTOR; a computer-based consultation system for mineral exploration", *Math Geology*, **10**, p589 (1978).
2. Duda, R., Gashnig, J. and Hart, P., "Model design in the PROSPECTOR consultant system for mineral exploration", in *Expert systems in the micro-electronic age*, Michie, D. (ed.), Edinburgh University Press (1979).
3. Duda, R. O., Hart, P. E. and Nilsson, N. J., "Subjective Bayesian methods for rule-based inference systems", in *Proc. National Computer Conference (AFIPS, vol 45)* (1976).

4. Buchanan, B. G. and Duda, R. O., "Principles of rule-based expert systems", in *Advances in computers - vol 22*, Yovits, M. C. (ed.), Academic Press (1983).

5. Shortliffe, E. H. and Buchanan, B. G., "A model of inexact reasoning in medicine", *Mathematical Biosciences*, **23**, p351 (1975).

6. Shortliffe, E. H., *Computer-based medical consultations: MYCIN*, American Elsevier (1976).

7. Zadeh, L. A., "Fuzzy logic and approximate reasoning", *Synthese*, **30**, p407 (1975).

8. Zadeh, L. A., "Commonsense knowledge representation based on fuzzy logic", *Computer*, **16**, p61 (1983).

9. Zadeh, L. A., "The role of fuzzy logic in the management of uncertainty in expert systems", *Fuzzy Sets and Systems*, **11**, p199 (1983).

10. Zadeh, L. A., "Fuzzy sets", *Information and Control*, **8**, p338 (1965).

11. Lee, C. C., "Fuzzy Logic in Control Systems: Fuzzy Logic Controller - Part I", *IEEE Transactions on Systems, Man and Cybernetics*, **20**, p404 (1990).

12. Lee, C. C., "Fuzzy Logic in Control Systems: Fuzzy Logic Controller - Part II", *IEEE Transactions on Systems, Man and Cybernetics*, **20**, p419 (1990).

13. Rescher, N., *Plausible reasoning*, Van Gorcum (1976).

14. Barnett, J. A., "Computational methods for a mathematical theory of evidence", in *7th Int Joint Conf on Artificial Intelligence (IJCAI'81)*, Vancouver (1981).

15. Shafer, G., *A mathematical theory of evidence*, Princeton University Press (1976).

16. Quinlan, J. R., "Inferno: a cautious approach to uncertain inference", *The Computer Journal*, **26**, p255 (1983).

Further reading

- Bacchus, F., *Representing and reasoning with probabilistic knowledge*, MIT Press (1991).
- Buchanan, B. G. and Shortliffe, E. H. (ed.), *Rule-based expert systems: the MYCIN experiments of the Stanford Heuristic Programming Project*, Addison-Wesley (1984).
- Hajek, P., Havranek, T. and Jirousek, R., *Uncertain information processing in expert systems*, CRC Press (1992).
- Kandel, A., *Fuzzy expert systems*, CRC Press (1991).

chapter five

Object-oriented systems

5.1 Introduction

Programming often involves breaking down complex problems into simpler constituents. Object-oriented programming, or OOP, achieves this in a particular manner, as we will see. Decomposing a problem using OOP assists in the design of software, and makes the resultant software more maintainable, adaptable and recyclable. It is therefore a technique that has found a large range of applications, including many in knowledge-based systems.

As well as these purely practical advantages, OOP is also a natural way of representing many real world problems within the confines of a computer. Programs of interest to engineers and scientists normally perform calculations or make decisions about physical entities. Such programs must contain a model of those entities, and OOP is a convenient way to carry out this modeling. Every entity can be represented by a self-contained "object", where an object contains data and the code that can be performed on those data. Thus a system for simulating ultrasonic imaging of steel components might include an ultrasonic pulse, which is reflected between features in a component. The pulse, the features and the component itself can all be represented by objects.

Modeling with objects is not restricted to physical things, but extends to include entities within the programming environment such as windows, icons, clocks and just about anything that you can think of. OOP is a powerful technique in its own right, and is by no means restricted to knowledge-based systems. However, OOP does have a critical role in many knowledge-based systems, as it offers a way of representing the things that are being reasoned about, their properties, and the relationships between them.

There are many languages and programming environments that offer object-orientation, some of which are supplied as extensions to existing languages. Three of the most widely used OOP languages are C++, Smalltalk, and CLOS (Common Lisp Object System). Smalltalk is a language in its own right, whereas C++ and CLOS are extensions of C and Lisp respectively. Smalltalk is a programming environment rather than just a language. It

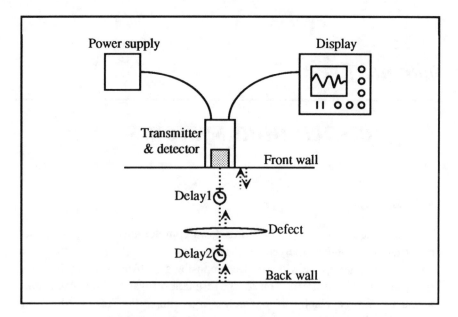

Figure 5.1 Detection of defects using ultrasonics.
Delays simulate the depth of the defect and the back wall.

includes a number of menus, windows, browsers (see section 5.4.5) and built-in classes (see section 5.3.1).

According to Pascoe [1], an OOP language offers at least the following facilities, which are discussed in sections 5.3-5.6:

- data abstraction;
- inheritance;
- encapsulation (or information hiding); and
- dynamic (late) binding.

Section 5.2 introduces an example of a problem that has been successfully tackled using OOP. This example will be used during the remainder of this chapter in order to illustrate the features of OOP and the resultant benefits.

5.2   An illustrative example

We will illustrate the features of object-oriented programming by considering a small simulation of ultrasonic imaging. The physical arrangement that is to be simulated is shown in figure 5.1. It comprises an ultrasonic probe, containing a detector and a transmitter, which sits on the surface of a component under test.

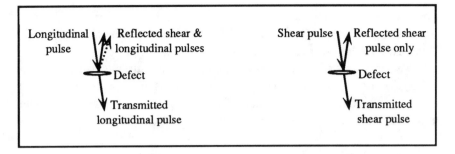

Figure 5.2 Reflection of longitudinal and shear pulses at a defect.

The probe emits a single pulse, which is strongly reflected by the front and back walls of the component and weakly reflected by defects within the component. The intensity and time of arrival of reflected pulses reaching the detector are plotted on an oscilloscope. Ultrasonic pulses may be longitudinal or shear. The emitted pulse is always longitudinal, but reflections may generate both a longitudinal and a shear pulse (figure 5.2).

This system, like so many others, lends itself to modeling with objects. Each of the components of the system can be treated as an independent object, containing data and code that defines its own particular behavior. Thus there will be objects representing each pulse, the transmitter, the detector, the component, the front wall, the back wall, the defects, and the oscilloscope. The following sections describe how the features of data abstraction, inheritance and dynamic binding relate to this model and the advantages that they confer.

5.3 Data abstraction

5.3.1 Classes

The ultrasonic example involves several different *types* of object. Shear pulses are objects of the same type as each other, but of a different type from the detector. Data abstraction allows us to define these types and the functions that go with them. These object types are called *classes*, and they form templates for the objects themselves. Objects which represent the same idea or concept are grouped together as a class.

Most computer languages include some built-in data types, such as "integer" or "real". An object-oriented language allows us to define additional data types (i.e., classes) which are treated identically (or nearly so) to the built-in types. The user-defined classes may be quite abstract (such as shear pulse, circle, polymer) and are therefore sometimes called *abstract data types*. The same name is also applied to user-defined classes which are not so abstract, such as "big integer". The words "type" and "class" are generally equivalent, although some languages draw a distinction between them.

The definition of a class contains the class name, attribute names (section 5.3.3), functions (section 5.3.4) and the relationships to other classes (sections 5.4 and 5.9). C++ and some other OOP languages require that the attribute types and the visibility from other classes also be specified.

5.3.2 Instances

It was stated in section 5.3.1 above that classes form templates for "the objects themselves", meaning object instances. Once a class has been defined, one or more instances of that class can be created, which have the properties defined for the class. For example, pulse#259 might be an ultrasonic pulse whose location at a given moment is (x=112.mm, y=294mm, z= 3.5mm). We would represent pulse#259 as an instance of the class longitudinal_pulse. As a more tangible example, my car is an instance of the class of car. The class specifies the characteristics and behavior of its instances. A class can therefore be thought of as the blueprint from which instances are built. The terms "object" and "instance" can be used interchangeably, the latter often being used to stress the distinction from a class.

This is just an extension of the concepts of data types and variables that exist in conventional programming languages. For instance, most languages include a built-in definition of the type "integer". However, we can only draw upon the properties of an integer by creating an instance, i.e., an integer variable. In C, this would look like this:

```
int x;                    /* create an instance, x, of type int */
x = x+1;                              /* manipulate x */
```

Similarly, having defined a class in an object-oriented language, its properties can only be used by creating one or more instances. Consider the class longitudinal_pulse. One instance of this class is generated by the transmitter object (which is itself an instance of the class transmitter). This instance represents one specific pulse, which has a position, amplitude, phase, speed and direction. When this pulse interacts with a defect (another instance), a new instance of longitudinal_pulse must be created, since there will be both a transmitted and a reflected pulse (see figure 5.2). The new pulse will have the same attributes as the old one since they are both derived from the same class, but some of these attributes will have different values associated with them (e.g., the amplitude and direction will be different).

5.3.3 Attributes (or data members)

A class definition includes attribute names and function specifications. The attributes are particular quantities that describe instances of that class. Thus the class shear_pulse might have attributes such as amplitude, position, speed and direction. The class acts as a template, so that when a new shear pulse is created, it will contain the names of these attributes, but their values will need to be supplied (although a default value may be provided in the class definition). The attributes are sometimes described as *slots* into which values are inserted. The values can be of any type, including abstract data types (i.e., classes). Some languages, such as C++, require that the class definition defines the types in advance (see section 5.5). Amplitude and speed might be of type "float", whereas position and direction would be of type "vector".

If the language permits, default values for attributes can be supplied in the class definition. Any new instances would then carry those default values unless specifically over-written. Most OOP languages distinguish between *class attributes* (or class variables) and *instance attributes* (or instance variables). The value of a class attribute is the same for all instances of that class. In contrast, each instance contains its own copy of each instance attribute, and the associated values vary from one instance to another. Thus in the above example, speed might be a class attribute for shear_pulse, since the speed will be the same for all shear pulses in a given material. On the other hand, amplitude and position are properties of each individual pulse, and are therefore represented as instance variables.

In C++, attributes are called data members. All data members are assumed to be instance attributes unless they are declared "static". Static data members reside at the same place for every instance of a class, and there is only one copy, regardless of how many instances there might be. Static data members are therefore equivalent to class attributes.

5.3.4 Methods (or member functions)

Each object has access to a set of functions which describe operations that can be carried out on that object. Thus a shear_pulse object may contain the function move. This function might take as its parameters the amount and direction of movement, and return a new value for its position attribute. In some OOP languages, functions attached to objects are called *methods* (or operators). In C++ they are called *member functions*. Methods or member functions are defined for a class, and can then be used by all instances of that class. It may also be possible for instances of other classes to access these functions (see section 5.4 on inheritance).

5.3.5 Memory management

Creating a new instance requires the computer to set aside some of its memory for storing the instance. Given a class definition, Myclass, the creation of new instances is similar in Smalltalk and in C++. In Smalltalk we might write:

```
Myinstance := Myclass new.    "Myinstance is a global variable"
```

The words in quotes are a comment and are ignored by the compiler. The equivalent in C++ would be:

```
myclass* myinstance;
        // declare a pointer to objects of type myclass
myinstance = new myclass;
        // pointer now points to a new instance
```

Here the '//' symbol indicates a comment. The C++ version can be abbreviated to:

```
myclass* myinstance = new myclass;
        // new pointer points to a new instance.
```

Large numbers of instances may be created while running a typical object-oriented system. An important consideration, therefore, is the release of memory that is no longer required. In the example of the ultrasonic simulation, new pulse instances are generated through reflections, but they must be removed when they reach the detector. The memory which is occupied by these unwanted instances must be released again if we are to avoid building a system with an insatiable appetite for computer memory. In the Smalltalk example above, Myinstance is a global variable, indicated by the capitalization of the first letter of the name. Global variables are accessible from any part of the program and are retained in the programming environment until explicitly deleted. It is more common to attach instances to temporary variables:

```
|myinstance|    "myinstance is declared as a temporary variable"
myinstance := Myclass new.
```

Temporary variables only exist within the method in which they are declared, and their lifetime is that of the method activation. When execution of the method has finished, these variables (and deleted global variables) leave behind an area of "unowned" memory. The Smalltalk system automatically reclaims this memory - a process known as *garbage collection*. Depending on the particular implementation, garbage collection may cause the program to momentarily "freeze" while the system carries out its memory management.

Garbage collection is a feature of Smalltalk, CLOS and other OOP languages. Some implementations allow the programmer to influence the timing of garbage collection, while in other implementations garbage collection is an unnoticed background process.

In C++ the responsibility for memory management rests with the programmer. Objects which are created as described above must be explicitly destroyed when they are no longer needed:

```
delete myinstance;
```

This operation releases the corresponding memory. C++ also allows an alternative method of object creation and deletion which relies on the *scope* of objects. A new instance, myinstance, may be created within a block of code in the following way:

```
myclass myinstance;
```

The instance only exists within that particular block of code, which is its scope. When the flow of execution enters the block of code, the object is automatically created. Similarly, it is deleted as soon as soon as the flow of execution leaves the block.

C++ gives the programmer the option to define special functions to be performed when a new instance is created or deleted. These are known respectively as the constructor and the destructor. The constructor is a member function whose name is identical to the name of the class, and is typically used to set the values of some attributes. The destructor is defined in a similar way to the constructor, and its name is that of the class preceded by a tilde, '~'. As an example, consider the definition for sonic_pulse:

```
// class definition:
class sonic_pulse
{
   float amplitude;
public:
   sonic_pulse(float initial_amplitude);   // optional constructor
   ~sonic_pulse();                          // optional destructor
};

// constructor definition:
sonic_pulse::sonic_pulse(float initial_amplitude)
{
   amplitude=initial_amplitude;            // set up initial value
}
```

```
// destructor definition:
sonic_pulse::~sonic_pulse()
{
     // perform any tidying up that may be necessary before
     // deleting the object
}
```

The class has a single attribute, amplitude, and this is set to an initial value by the constructor. Whenever a new instance of sonic_pulse is created, the constructor is called immediately after creation. Thus to create a new sonic pulse whose initial amplitude is 131.4 units, we would write either:

```
sonic_pulse* myinstance = new sonic_pulse(131.4);  //technique 1
```

or

```
sonic_pulse myinstance(131.4);                            //technique 2
```

If a destructor has been defined for a class, it is called whenever an instance is deleted. If the instance was created by technique 1, it must be explicitly deleted by the programmer. If it was created by technique 2, it is automatically deleted when it becomes out of scope.

5.4 Inheritance

5.4.1 Single inheritance

Returning again to our example of the ultrasonic simulation, note that there are two classes of sonic pulse, namely longitudinal_pulse and shear_pulse. While there are some differences between the two classes, there are also many similarities. It would be most unwieldy if all of this common information had to be specified twice. This problem can be avoided by the use of *inheritance*. A class sonic_pulse is defined which encompasses both types of pulse. All of the attributes and methods that are common can be defined here. The classes longitudinal_pulse and shear_pulse are then designated as subclasses of sonic_pulse. Conversely, sonic_pulse is said to be the superclass of the other two classes. The sub/super class relationship can be thought of as "is-a-kind-of", since:

```
shear_pulse "is-a-kind-of" sonic_pulse.
```

The following expressions, commonly used to describe the "is-a-kind-of" relationship, are all equivalent:

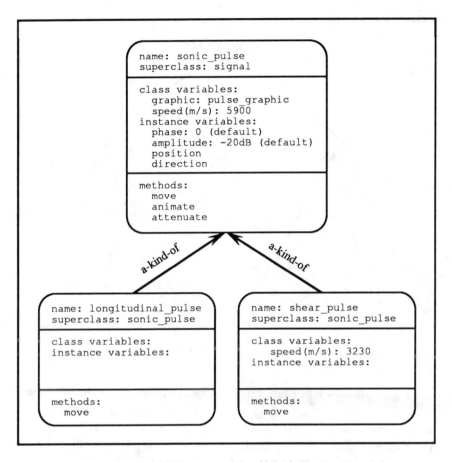

Figure 5.3 An example of inheritance.

```
<subclass>         is-a-kind-of  <superclass>
<offspring>        is-a-kind-of  <parent>
<derived class>    is-a-kind-of  <base class>.
```

In defining a derived class, it is only necessary to specify the name of the base class and the *differences* from the base class. Attributes (and their values where supplied) and methods are inherited by the derived class. Any attributes or methods that are redefined in the derived class are said to be specialized, and the derived class is said to be a specialization of the base class. Another form of specialization is the introduction of extra attributes and methods in the derived class. C++ gives the user some control over which methods and attributes are inheritable and which are not (section 5.5). Many other OOP languages assume that *all* attributes and methods of the base class are inherited by the derived class, apart from those that are explicitly specialized.

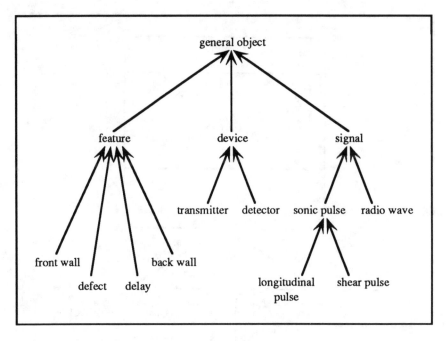

Figure 5.4 Single inheritance defines a class hierarchy.

Figure 5.3 shows the class definitions for `sonic_pulse` and its subclasses
`shear_pulse` and `longitudinal_pulse`. The attributes `graphic`, `speed`,
`phase`, `amplitude`, `position` and `direction` are all declared within the
parent class and are inherited by the offspring. The class variable `graphic`,
which determines the screen representation of an instance, is assigned a value
at the parent level and this value, as well as the declaration of the attribute, is
inherited by the offsprings. The class variable `speed` is redeclared for the
`shear_pulse` class, and has a different value from that inherited by
`longitudinal_pulse`. Default values for the instance variables `amplitude`
and `phase` are defined at the parent level. If permitted by the OOP language,
these default values may be overridden either when an instance is created or
subsequently.

Methods are inherited as well as attributes. Therefore instances of
`shear_pulse` and `longitudinal_pulse` have access to the methods `animate`,
`move` and `attenuate`, which are defined for the class `sonic_pulse`.

Figure 5.4 shows the inheritance between other objects in the ultrasonic
simulation. Note that the "is-a-kind-of" relationship is *transitive*, that is:

```
IF (x "is-a-kind-of" y) AND (y "is-a-kind-of" z)
    THEN (x "is-a-kind-of" z).
```

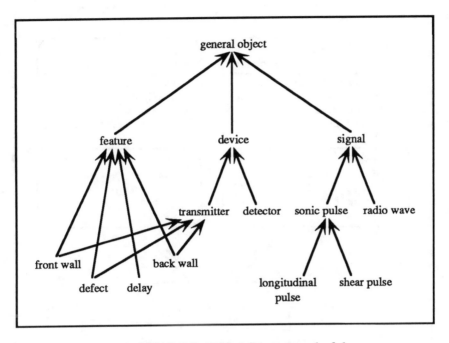

Figure 5.5 Multiple inheritance defines a network of classes.

Therefore the class defect, for example, inherits information that is defined at the feature level and at the general object level (figure 5.4).

5.4.2 Multiple inheritance
In the example shown in figure 5.4, each offspring has only one parent. The network of "is-a-kind-of" relationships therefore forms a hierarchy. Some OOP languages insist upon hierarchical inheritance. Others, however, allow an offspring to inherit from more than one parent. This is known as multiple inheritance. Where multiple inheritance occurs, the "is-a-kind-of" relationships between classes define a network rather than a hierarchy.

Figure 5.5 shows how multiple inheritance might be applied to the ultrasonic simulation. The parts of the component that interact with sonic pulses all inherit from the class feature. Three of the classes derived from feature are required to simulate partial reflection of pulses. This is done by generating one or more reflected pulses, while the existing pulse is re-transmitted in the forward direction with diminished amplitude. Code for generating pulses is contained within the class definition for transmitter. Multiple inheritance allows those features that need to generate pulses (front_wall, b ack_wall and defect) to inherit this capability from transmitter, while inheriting other functions and attributes from feature.

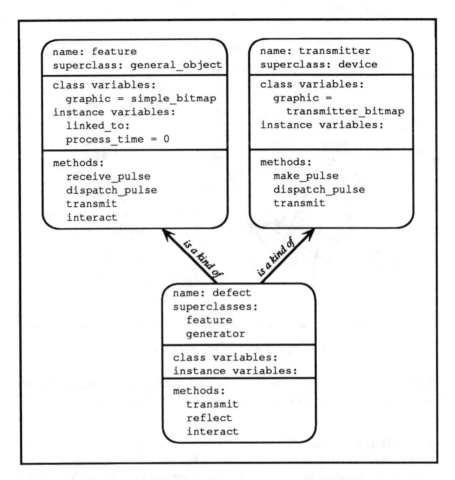

Figure 5.6 Conflicts arising from multiple multiple inheritance.
(Each parent has a different value for `graphic` and for `dispatch_pulse`.)

While multiple inheritance is useful, it can cause ambiguities. This is
illustrated in figure 5.6, where `defect` inherits the graphic `simple_bitmap`
from `feature` and at the same time inherits the graphic `transmitter_bitmap`
from `transmitter`. This raises two questions. Firstly, do the two attributes with
the same name refer to the same attribute? If so, the class `defect` can have
only one value corresponding to the attribute `graphic`, so which value should
be selected? Similarly, `defect` inherits conflicting definitions for the method
`dispatch_pulse`. There is no conflict over `transmit` since `defect` has its
own local definition. The most reliable way to resolve such conflicts is to have
them detected by the language compiler, so that the programmer can then state
explicitly the intended meaning. Some OOP environments allow the user to
set a default strategy for resolving conflicts. Examples might be to give

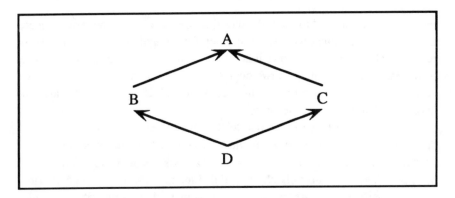

Figure 5.7 Repeated inheritance.

preference to the parent class which is closest to the root of the inheritance tree, or furthest away, or to consider the class names to be significant in some way, or to prefer the most recently defined "is-a-kind-of" relationship.

A further problem is that one class may find itself indirectly inheriting from another via more than one route, as shown in figure 5.7. This is known as

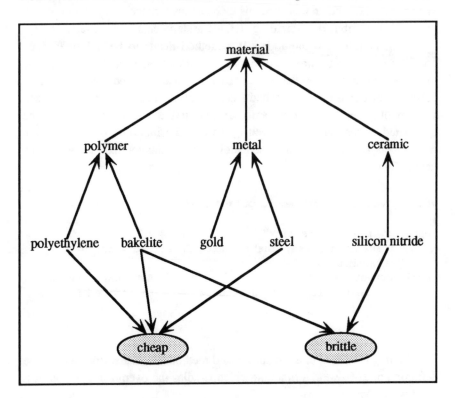

Figure 5.8 An example of the use of mixins.

repeated inheritance. Although the meaning may be clear to the programmer, an OOP language must have some strategy for recognizing and dealing with repeated inheritance, if it allows it at all. C++ offers the programmer a choice of two strategies. D can have two copies of A, one for each inheritance route. Alternatively it can have just a single copy, if both B and C are declared to have class A as a *virtual* base class.

Multiple inheritance gives rise to the idea of *mixins*, which are classes designed solely to help organize the inheritance structure. Instances of mixins cannot be created. Consider, for example, a class hierarchy for engineering materials. The materials polyethylene, Bakelite, gold, steel, and silicon nitride can be classified as polymers, metals or ceramics. Single inheritance would allow us to construct these hierarchical relationships. Under multiple inheritance we can categorize the materials in a variety of ways at the same time. Figure 5.8 shows the use of the mixins cheap and brittle for this purpose.

5.4.3 Specialization of methods

We have already shown that specialization can involve the introduction of new methods or attributes, overriding default assignments to attributes, or re-definition of inherited methods. If a method needs to be redefined (i.e., specialized), it is not always necessary to rewrite it from scratch. Consider the methods interact, transmit and reflect which are defined for a defect. A definition of transmit is inherited from the class feature. The specialized version of transmit is the same, except that the sonic pulse must be attenuated. This can be achieved by calling the inherited definition from within the specialized one, and then adding the attenuation instruction, shown here in C++:

```
void defect::transmit(sonic_pulse* inst1)
{
feature::transmit(inst1);
    // Transmit a pulse, inst1, using inherited version of
    // 'transmit'
inst1->attenuate(0.5);                       // Attenuate the pulse.
    // The member function 'attenuate' must be defined for the
    // class 'sonic_pulse'.
}
```

We might wish to call the specialized method transmit from within the definition of interact, a function which handles the overall interaction of a pulse with a defect:

```
void defect::interact(sonic_pulse* inst1)
{
transmit(inst1);
    // Transmit a pulse, inst1, using the locally defined member
    // function.
reflect(inst1);
    // Generate a new pulse and send it in the opposite
    // direction
}
```

5.4.4 Browsers

Many OOP systems provide not only a language, but an environment in which to program. The environment may include tools that make OOP easier, and one of the most important of these tools is a class-browser. A class-browser shows inheritance relationships, often in the form of a tree like those in figures 5.4 and 5.5. If the programmer wants to alter a class or to specialize it to form a new one, he or she simply chooses the class from the browser (with a mouse) and then selects the type of change from a pop-up menu. Incidentally, browsers themselves are invariably built using OOP. Thus the class-browser may be an instance of a class called class_browser, which may be a specialization of browser, itself a specialization of window. The class class_browser could be further specialized to provide different display or editing facilities.

5.5 Encapsulation

Encapsulation, or information-hiding, is a term used to express the notion that the instance attributes and the methods that define an object belong to that object and to no other. The methods and attributes are therefore private, and are said to be encapsulated within the object . The interface to each object reveals as little as possible of the inner workings of the object. The object has control over its own data, and those data cannot be directly altered by other objects. Class attributes are an exception, as these are not encapsulated within any one instance, but instead are shared between all instances of the same class.

In general, Smalltalk adheres to the principle of encapsulation, whereas C++ adopts a more liberal approach. In Smalltalk, object A can only influence object B by sending it a message telling B to call one of its methods (see section 5.8). Apart from this mechanism, secrecy is maintained between objects. The method on B can access and change its own data, but it cannot access the data of any other objects.

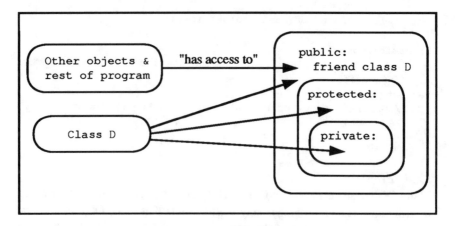

Figure 5.9   Access control in C++.

C++ offers flexibility in its enforcement of encapsulation through access controls. All data members and member functions (collectively known as "members") are allocated one of four access levels:

- private: access from member functions of this class only (the default);
- protected: access from member functions of this class and of derived classes;
- public: access from any part of the program;
- friend: access from member functions of nominated classes.

Access controls are illustrated in figure 5.9. C++ allows two types of derivation (i.e., inheritance), public and private. In private derivation, protected and public members in the base class become private members of the derived class. In public derivation, the access level of members in the derived class is unchanged from the base class. In neither case does the derived class have access to private members of the base class. The two types of derivation are shown in figure 5.10.

5.6 Dynamic (or late) binding

Three necessary features of an OOP language, as defined in section 5.1, are data abstraction, inheritance and encapsulation, as we have seen. The fourth and final necessary feature is *dynamic binding* (or *late binding*). Although the parent classes of objects may be known at compilation time, the actual (derived) classes may not be. The actual class is not bound to an object name at compilation time, but instead the binding is postponed until run time. This is known as dynamic binding and its significance is best shown by example.

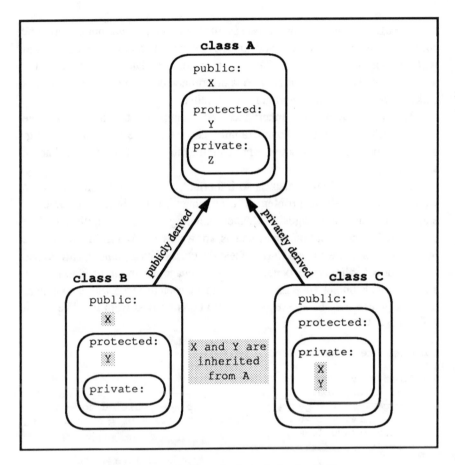

Figure 5.10 Public and private derivation in C++.

Suppose that we have a method, transmit, defined for the class, feature:

```
void feature::transmit(sonic_pulse* p)
{
float x, y;
x = getx(); y = gety();    // calculate new position for pulse, p
p->move(x,y);              // move pulse p to its new position
}
```

Suppose also that sp1 and 1p1 are instances of shear_pulse and longitudinal_pulse respectively. When the program is run, transmission of sp1 and 1p1 by a feature is achieved by calls to transmit, with pointers to each pulse passed as parameters. The parameter types are correct, since sp1 is an instance of shear_pulse, which is derived from sonic_pulse. Similarly 1p1 is an instance of longitudinal_pulse, which is also derived from sonic_pulse. The method transmit calls the method move, but this may be specialized differently for sp1 and for lp1. Nonetheless the correct definition will be chosen in each case. This is an example of late binding, since the actual method move that will be used is determined each time that transmit is called, rather than when the program is compiled.

The combined effect of inheritance and dynamic binding is that the same function call (move in the above example) can have more than one meaning, and the actual meaning is not interpreted until run time. This effect is known as *polymorphism.**

To see why polymorphism is so important, we should consider how we would tackle the above problem in a language where binding is static (or early). In such languages the exact meaning of each function call is determined at compilation time, and is known as monomorphism. In the method transmit, we would have to test the class of its argument, and invoke a behavior accordingly. Depending on the language, we might need to include a class variable on sonic_pulse, in order to tag each instance with the name of its class (which may be sonic_pulse or a class derived from it). We might then use a CASE statement:

```
void feature::transmit(sonic_pulse* p)
{
    float x, y;
    char class_label;
    x = getx(); y = gety();// calculate new position for pulse p
    class_label = p->tag;// identify the class of p from its tag
    switch (class_label) {
    case 's':
        ....;                           // code to move a shear_pulse
        break;
    case 'l':
        ....;                           // code to move a longitudinal_pulse
        break;
    default:
        ....;                           // print an error message
    }
}
```

---

* C++ distinguishes between those member functions (i.e., methods) that can be re-defined polymorphically in a derived class, and those that cannot. Functions that can be re-defined polymorphically are called virtual functions. In this example, move must be a virtual function if it is to be polymorphic. A pure virtual function is one that is declared in the base class, but no definition is supplied there. (The declaration merely states the existence of a function; the definition is the chunk of code that makes up the function). A definition must therefore appear in one or more of the derived classes. Any class containing one or more pure virtual functions is termed an abstract base class. Instances of an abstract base class are not allowed, since an instance (if it were allowed) would "know" that it had access to a virtual function but would not have a definition for it.

Two drawbacks are immediately apparent. Firstly, the code which uses monomorphism is much longer, and is likely to include considerable duplication since the code for moving a `shear_pulse` will be similar to the code for moving a `longitudinal_pulse`. In contrast, polymorphism avoids duplication and allows the commonality between classes to be made explicit. Secondly, the code is more difficult to maintain than the polymorphic code, because subsequent addition of a new class of pulse would require changes to the method `transmit` in the class `feature`. This runs against the philosophy of encapsulation, since addition of a class should not require changes to existing classes.

The effect of polymorphism is that the language will always select the sensible meaning for a function call. Thus, once its importance has been understood, polymorphism need not vex the programmer.

5.7 *Type checking*

Smalltalk and C++ both offer the key features of OOP, namely data abstraction, inheritance, encapsulation and dynamic binding. There are, however, some significant differences between the languages, as well as their obvious differences in syntax. An important difference is that C++ uses static type checking whereas Smalltalk uses dynamic type checking. Thus a C++ programmer must explicitly state the type (or class) of all variables, and the compiler checks for consistency. The Smalltalk programmer does not need to specify the classes of variables, and no checks are made during compilation. Static type checking is sometimes called *strong* type checking, and the variables are said to be *manifestly* typed. Conversely, dynamic type checking is sometimes called *weak* type checking, and the variables are said to be *latently* typed. The words *strong* and *weak* are perhaps misleading, since they might alternatively indicate the strictness or level of detail of static type checking.

Static type checking describes the ability of the compiler to check that objects of the right class are supplied to all functions and operators. In C++, the programmer must explicitly state the class of all objects (including built-in types such as `int` or `float`). Whenever assignments are made, the compiler checks that types are compatible. Assignments can be made directly by a statement like:

```
x = "a string";
```

or indirectly by passing an object as a parameter to a function. Consider again our definition of the method `transmit` (in C++):

```
void feature::transmit(sonic_pulse* p)
{
float x, y;
x = getx(); y = gety();
                        // calculate new position for sonic_pulse p
p->move(x,y);           // move sonic_pulse p to its new position
}
```

Let us now create some object instances:

```
sonic_pulse* p1 = new shear_pulse();
shear_pulse* p2 = new shear_pulse();
defect* d1 = new defect();
defect* d2 = new defect();
```

If we pass as a parameter to t ransmit any object whose type is not sonic_pulse and is not derived from sonic_pulse, we will get an error at compilation time:

```
d1->transmit(p1);       // OK because p1 is of type sonic_pulse.
d1->transmit(p2);                 // OK because p2's type is
                                  // derived from sonic_pulse.
d1->transmit(d2);            // ERROR: d2 is not a sonic_pulse.
```

Contrast this with the Smalltalk equivalent. The method transmit may be defined as follows for the class feature:

```
transmit: aSonicpulse
| x y |
x:= self getx.
y:= self gety.
aSonicpulse move: x and: y.
```

Now we create some instances as before, and try passing them as parameters to transmit. The following would be typed into a temporary workspace, selected, and the "Do It" command invoked:

```
|p1 p2 d1 d2|
p1 := Sonicpulse new.
p2 := Shearpulse new.
d1 := Defect new.
d2 := Defect new.

d1 transmit: p1.    "OK because method move is defined for p1"
d1 transmit: p2.    "OK because method move is defined for p2"
d1 transmit: d2.     "Compiles OK but causes a run-time error"
```

All of this code will compile, but the last line will cause an error at run time, producing a message similar to:

```
"Message not understood - move:and:"
```

The type of the argument to transmit is neither specified nor checked, and therefore the compiler allows us to supply anything. In our definition of transmit, the argument was given the name aSonicpulse. This helps us to recognize the appropriate argument type, but the name has no significance to the compiler. When we passed d2 (an instance of defect) as the parameter, a run-time error came about because Smalltalk tried to find the method move:and: for d2, when this method was only defined for the class Sonicpulse and its derivatives.

The difference between static and dynamic typing represents a difference in programming philosophy. C++ insists that all types are stated, and checks them all at compilation time to ensure that there are no incompatibilities. This means extra work for the programmer, especially if he or she is only performing a quick experiment. On the other hand it leads to clearly defined interactions between objects, thereby helping to document the program and making error detection easier. Static typing therefore tends to be preferred for building large software systems, possibly involving more than one programmer. Dynamically typed languages such as Smalltalk (and Lisp, Prolog and Pop-11) are ideal for trying out ideas and building prototypes, but they are more likely to contain latent bugs which may show up unpredictably at run time. CLOS offers a compromise between static and dynamic typing by allowing the programmer to make type declarations and giving the option to enforce or ignore them.

5.8 Message passing and function calls

In C++, member functions (equivalent to methods) are accessed in a similar way to any other function, except that we need to distinguish the object to which the member function belongs. We have already seen some examples of accessing member functions in C++:

```
result = somefunc(parameter);
    // call a conventional function, defined elsewhere.

defect* d1 = new defect();  // make a new instance d1 of defect.
sonic_pulse* p1 = new shear_pulse();
shear_pulse* p2 = new shear_pulse();
            // make two new instances of pulses, p1 and p2.
```

```
d1->transmit(p1);
    // call member function, 'transmit', with parameter p1.

defect d2;                          // make a new instance d2 of defect.
d2.transmit(p2);
    // call member function, 'transmit', with parameter p2.
```

In Smalltalk and other OOP languages, methods are invoked by passing *messages*. This terminology emphasizes the concept of encapsulation. Each object is independent, and is in charge of its own methods. Nonetheless, objects can interact. One object can stimulate another to fire up a method by sending a message to it. An example of message passing in Smalltalk that we have already seen is:

```
d1 transmit: p1.
```

This is interpreted as:

   send to the instance d1 *the message* transmit:, *with parameter p1.*

The Smalltalk syntax becomes a little more confusing where there are many parameters:

```
p1 move: x and: y.
```

The arguments are interspersed with the method name, making the message read rather like English. This example means:

   send to the instance p1 the message move:and:, *with parameters x and y.*

Upon receiving a message, an object calls up the corresponding method using the supplied parameters.

5.8.1 Pseudovariables
Smalltalk (and other OOP languages) has a shorthand form for "this object" and "the parent class of this object", which avoids the need to name classes explicitly. In Smalltalk, the shorthand words are self and super, and these are known as *pseudovariables*. They differ from normal variables because they cannot be assigned a value directly by the programmer. In order to illustrate the use of super, consider the example of specializing the method transmit, which was shown in section 5.4.3 using C++. Here is a Smalltalk equivalent, defined for the class defect:

```
transmit: inst1
    super transmit: inst1.
"Transmit a pulse, inst1, using inherited version of transmit"
```

```
inst1 attenuate: 0.5.                    "Attenuate the pulse."
"The method 'attenuate' must be defined for the class of inst1"
```

The version of transmit defined for the parent class, feature, is firstly called. Then the inst1 is sent the message attenuate:, which instructs it to apply the method attenuate:, thereby reducing its amplitude. It is assumed that inst1 is a sonic pulse.

Similarly, the method interact that is described for the class defect describes the overall interaction between a pulse and the defect. This method includes calls to the locally defined versions of reflect and transmit:

```
interact: inst1
    self transmit: inst1.
"Transmit a pulse, inst1, using the locally defined method."

    self reflect: inst1.
"Generate a new pulse and send it in the opposite direction"
```

C++ includes the pseudovariable this, which is equivalent to Smalltalk's self. Because of the differences in the nature of the two languages, this is needed less often in C++ than self in Smalltalk.

5.8.2 Metaclasses

It was emphasized in section 5.3 that a class defines the characteristics (methods and attributes) that are available to instances. Methods can therefore only be used by instances, and not by the class itself. This is a sensible constraint, since it is clearly appropriate that methods such as move, transmit, reflect, etc., should be performed by instances in the ultrasonics example. However, a problem arises with the creation of new instances. In Smalltalk, new instances are created by sending the message new. This message cannot be sent to an instance, as we have not yet created one. Instead it is sent to the class. This apparent paradox is overcome by imagining that each class is an instance of a metaclass, which is a class of classes (figure 5.11). Thus the method new is defined within one or more metaclasses, and made available to each class. The notion of metaclasses goes some way to solving a philosophical problem, but for most practical purposes it is sufficient to remember that messages are always sent to instances, except for the message new, which is sent to a class.

Metaclasses also provide a means by which class variables can be implemented. In some OOP languages, though not in Smalltalk, class variables are simply instance variables that are declared at the metaclass level. However, these implementation details are rarely of concern to the

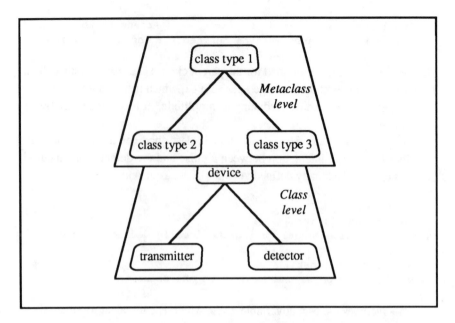

Figure 5.11 Classes and metaclasses.
Each class can be treated as an instance of a metaclass.

programmer. Although C++ does not explicitly include metaclasses, it supports class variables in the form of static data members. C++ also provides static member functions. Unlike ordinary member functions which are encapsulated within each instance, there is only one copy of a static member function for a class. The single copy is shared by all instances of the class and is not associated with any particular instance. A static member function is therefore equivalent to a method (like new) that is defined within a metaclass.

5.9 Class and instance relationships

We have already come across two types of relationships involving classes and instances, namely:

- specialization; and
- instantiation.

Specialization describes the class/superclass or "is-a-kind-of" relationship between classes, and involves the inheritance of common information. Instantiation describes the relation between a class and an instance of that

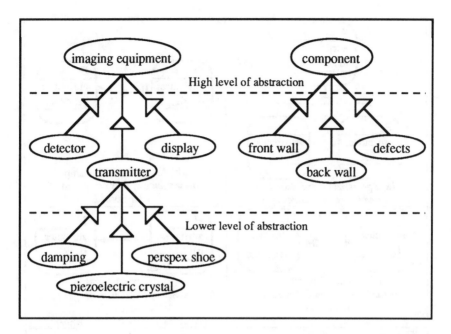

Figure 5.12 The assembly relationship allows problems to be viewed on different levels of abstraction.

class. An instance of a class and a subclass of a class are both said to be *clients* of that class, since they both derive information from it, but in different ways.

We will now consider three more types of relationship:

- assembly (or "containing");
- utility (or "using" or "message connection"); and
- instance connection.

An *assembly* relationship exists when an object can be viewed as being composed of several sub-objects (e.g., a car comprises an engine, chassis, wheels etc.). The relationship can be defined at either the instance or the class level. At the instance level, we can say that one particular engine is part of one particular car, such as mine. At the class level, we can state that all cars have an engine. Returning to our ultrasonic example, we can create a class of component, which is made up of front and back walls and defects. Figure 5.12 shows that assembly relationships allow the simulation to be viewed at different levels of abstraction.

The *utility* relationship exists where one object makes use of another by sending messages to it (or, in the case of C++, calling its member functions or accessing its data members). Like the assembly relationship, the utility

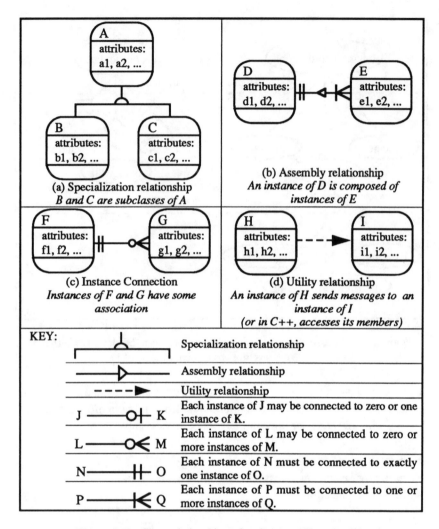

Figure 5.13   Class relationships, after Coad and Yourdon [2].

relationship has a different meaning when viewed at the class and at the instance level. At the class level we might recognize that pulses send the message receive_pulse to features. At the instance level, we might note that the instance delay1 sends the method dispatch_pulse to the instance defect1. The senders of messages are termed *actors*, and the recipients are *servers*. Objects that both send and receive messages are termed *agents*.

Instance connections are associations between instances.   Such associations can be used for a variety of purposes, but may typically be used to represent the spatial layout of instances.   Thus in the ultrasonic simulation example shown in figure 5.1, instance connections would be used to represent the path between the front wall and delay1, and between delay1 and the defect, and so on. These relationships can be implemented by naming the related instance as an instance attribute. The utility and assembly relationships between instances (but not between classes) are types of instance connection.

Coad and Yourdon's *object-oriented analysis (OOA)* [2] includes a diagrammatic representation for the relationships between classes (figure 5.13). The diagrams also give information about the instance connections that can exist between instances of those classes.

5.10 Further aspects of OOP

This section examines some further issues that may arise in object-oriented programming. The features described here may be available in some OOP languages, but unlike those described in sections 5.3-5.6, they are not essential according to our definition of an OOP language (section 5.1).

5.10.1 Persistence
We have already discussed the creation and deletion of objects. The lifetime of an object is the time between its creation and deletion. So far our discussion has implicitly assumed that instances are created and destroyed in a time frame corresponding to:

- the evaluation of a single expression;
- running a method or other block of code;
- specific creation and deletion events during the running of a program, or
- the duration of the program.

However, object instances can outlive the run of the program in which they were created. A program can create an object and then store it. That object is said to be persistent across time (because it is stored) and space (because it can be moved elsewhere). Persistent objects are particularly important in database applications. For example, a payroll system might store instances of the class employee. Such applications require careful design, since the stored instances are required not only between different executions of the program, but also between different versions of the program.

5.10.2 Concurrency
Each object acts independently, on the basis of messages that it receives. Objects can therefore perform their own individual tasks concurrently. This

makes them strong candidates for implementation on parallel processing computers. Returning once more to our object-oriented ultrasonic simulation, a pulse could arrive at one feature (say the front wall) at the same time as another arrives at a different feature (say a defect), and both require to be processed by the respective features. Although this could be achieved on a parallel machine, the actual implementation was on a serial computer, where concurrency was simulated. A clock (implemented as an object) marked simulated time. Thus if two pulses arrived at different features at the same time (t), it would not matter which was processed first, as according to the simulation clock, they would both be processed at time t.

5.10.3 Overloading

Most high level languages provide "in-line" operators such as +, -, *, / which are placed between the arguments to which they refer, for example:

```
a:=b+c;
```

This roughly equivalent to calling the function "plus" with the arguments b and c and assigning the result to a:

```
a:=plus(b,c);
```

It is only roughly equivalent since the use of an operator may be more efficient than a function call. From the perspective of the compiler, the operator '+' has to fulfill a different task depending on whether its arguments are integers or floats. However, it is convenient from the programmer's perspective for the operator to be called '+' irrespective of whether integer or float addition is required. The compiler "knows" which meaning of '+' is intended by examining the type of the arguments. This is termed operator *overloading* - the same operator has a different meaning depending on the type and number of its arguments. This is similar to polymorphism (section 5.6), except that in this case the meaning of an operator is determined at compile time rather than at run time. Some languages, such as C++, allow operator overloading to be extended to classes as well as to built in data types. A common example of this is to define the class "complex", describing complex numbers. The class definition might include a definition for '+' such that it would carry out complex number addition.

Consider now the expression:

```
pulse1 + pulse2
```

where `pulse1` and `pulse2` are instances of `shear_pulse`. This could have a sensible meaning if we defined '+' within the definition of class `shear_pulse` so that it performed constructive interference where the two pulses were in phase and destructive interference where they were out of phase. This is another example of operator overloading.

Overloading is not just restricted to operators, but can apply to function names as well (depending on the language). In C++, functions can be overloaded independent of whether they are member functions (functions defined as part of a class definition) or other functions. For instance, we might have separate functions called `print` for printing an integer, a character, or a string. In C++ this would look like this:

```
void print(int x)
{
/* code for printing an integer */
}

void print(char x)
{
/* code for printing a character */
}

void print(char* x)
{
/* code for printing a string */
}
```

```
print(74);                    // uses 1st definition of print
print('A');                   // uses 2nd definition of print
print("have a nice day");     // uses 3rd definition of print
```

Overloading is a convenient feature of some object-oriented and conventional languages. It is not, however, essential that an OOP language should have this facility.

5.10.4 Active values and daemons

So far we have considered programs in which methods are explicitly called and where these methods may involve reading or altering data attached to object attributes. Control is therefore achieved through function (method) calls and data is accessed as a side effect. Active values and daemons allow us to achieve the opposite effect, namely function calls are made as a side-effect of accessing data. Attributes that can trigger function calls in this way are said to be active, and their data are active values. The functions that are attached to the data are called daemons. A daemon can be thought of as a piece of code

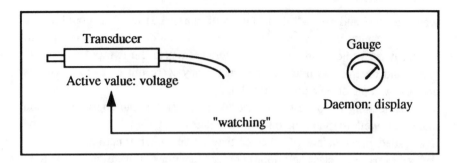

Figure 5.14 Using a daemon to monitor an active value.

that lies dormant, watching an active value, and which springs to life as soon as the active value is accessed.

Daemons can pose some problems for the flow of control in a program. Suppose that a method M accesses an active value which is monitored by daemon D. If D were to fire immediately, before M has finished, then D might disrupt some control variables that M relies upon. The safer solution is to have M run to completion before D fires.

Active values need not be confined to attributes (data members), but may also include methods (member functions). Thus a daemon may be set to fire when one or more of the following occurs:

- an attribute is read;
- an attribute is set; or
- a method is called.

An example of the use of daemons is in the construction of gauges in graphical user interfaces (figure 5.14). A gauge object may be created to monitor some attribute of an object in a physical model, such as the voltage across a transducer. As soon as the voltage value is altered, the gauge should update its display, regardless of what caused the change in voltage. The voltage attribute on the object transducer is active, and the display method on the object gauge is a daemon.

5.11 Frame-based systems

Frame-based systems are closely allied to object-oriented systems. Frame-based systems evolved from artificial intelligence research, whereas OOP has been developed as "a better way to program". Frames were conceived as a versatile and expressive way of representing and organizing information.

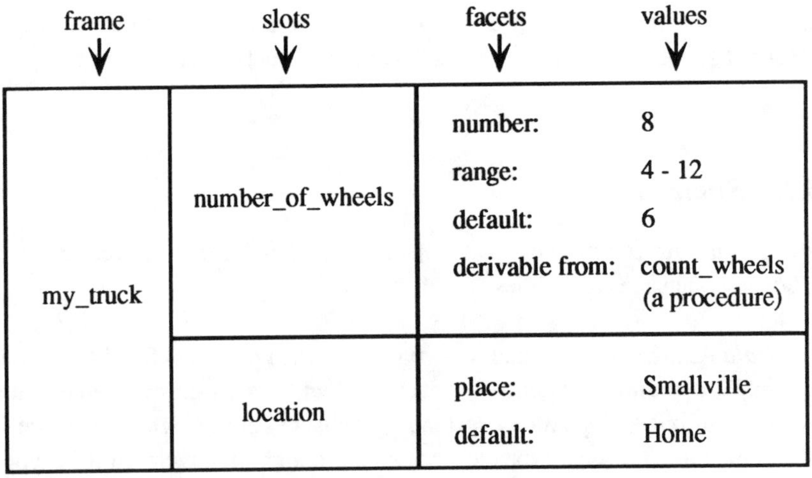

frame	slots	facets	values
my_truck	number_of_wheels	number: range: default: derivable from:	8 4 - 12 6 count_wheels (a procedure)
	location	place: default:	Smallville Home

Figure 5.15 An example of a frame-based representation.

The frame-based view is that an item, such as my truck, can be represented by a data structure, i.e., a frame, such as my_truck. Onto this frame we can hang extra information such as the number of wheels on my truck. Thus number_of_wheels would be a slot associated with the frame my_truck. The frame-based representation allows us to do more than just place a single value in a slot. For instance, we may wish to specify limits on the number of wheels, or provide a default. We might even want to supply a procedure (count_wheels) which calculates the number of wheels when a value is not previously known. These are all things that we might want to say about the slot, and are known as *facets* of that slot. Each facet can have a value associated with it, as shown in figure 5.15. A value might be a number, a description, a number range, a procedure, another frame, or practically anything.

Frames may be related to other frames, thereby modeling physical or abstract connections. Just as instances are derived from classes, so frames can be derived from class frames, taking advantage of inheritance. The term "frame" has been used here to mean a framework onto which information can be hung. However, frames are also analogous to the frames of a movie film or video tape. In associating values with the slots of a frame we are taking a snapshot of the world at a given instant. At one moment the slot location on my_truck might contain the value Smallville, while sometime later it might contain the value Largetown.

We have seen how frames can be applied to things. The things may be physical, such as a_truck, or abstract, such as a_plan or a_design. A special kind of frame, known as a script can be used to describe actions or sequences of actions. For instance, in a system for fixing plumbing faults we might construct scripts called `changing_a_washer` or `unblocking_a_pipe`.

5.12 Summary

We began with the premise that object-oriented programming requires the following language capabilities:

- *Data Abstraction*, in which new types (classes) can be defined and a full set of operations provided for each, so that the new classes behave like built-in ones. Operator overloading enhances this perception, since it allows the new data types to be used as though they were built-in types such as "int" and "float".

- *Inheritance*. Class definitions can be treated as specializations of other (parent) classes. This ability maximizes code reuse and minimizes duplication. OOP therefore helps us to build a world model which maps directly onto the real world. This model is expressed in terms of the classes of objects that the world manipulates, and OOP helps us to successively refine our understanding of these classes.

- *Encapsulation*. Data and code are bundled together into objects and are hidden from other objects. This simplifies program maintenance, helps to ensure that interactions between objects are clearly defined and predictable, and provides a realistic world model.

- *Dynamic (late) binding*. The object (and hence its class) that is associated with a given variable is not determined until run time. Although the parent class may be specified and checked at compile time (depending on the language), the instance used at run time could legitimately belong to a subclass of that parent. Therefore, it cannot be known at compile time whether the object will use methods defined within the parent class or specialized versions of them. Different objects can therefore respond to a single command in a way that is appropriate for those objects, and which may be different from the response of other objects. This property is known as polymorphism.

Stroustrup [3] has pointed out that although it is *possible* to build these capabilities in many computer languages, a language can only be described as object-oriented if it *supports* these features, i.e., it makes these features convenient for the programmer.

Class definitions act as templates from which multiple instances (i.e., objects) can be created. Classes and instances are easily inspected, modified, and reused. All of these capabilities assist in the construction of large complex software systems by breaking the system down into smaller, independent, manageable chunks. The problem representation is also more natural, allowing more time to spent designing a system and less on coding, testing and integration.

References

1. Pascoe, G. A., "Elements of object-oriented programming", *Byte*, p139 (August 1986).
2. Coad, P. and Yourdon, E., *Object-oriented analysis*, Prentice-Hall (1990).
3. Stroustrup, B., "What is object-oriented programming?", *IEEE Software*, p10 (May 1988).

Further reading

- Booch, G., *Object-oriented design with applications*, Benjamin/Cummings (1991).
- Budd, T., *An introduction to object-oriented programming*, Addison-Wesley (1991).
- Cox, B. and Novobilski, A., *Object-oriented programming: an evolutionary approach - 2nd edition*, Addison-Wesley (1991).
- Goldberg, A., *Smalltalk-80: the language*, Addison-Wesley (1989).
- Keene, S., *Object-oriented programming in Common Lisp: a programmer's guide to CLOS*, Addison-Wesley (1989).
- LaLonde, W. R. and Pugh, J. R., *Inside Smalltalk - volume I*, Prentice Hall (1990).
- LaLonde, W. R. and Pugh, J. R., *Inside Smalltalk - volume II*, Prentice Hall (1991).
- Meyer, B., *Object-oriented software construction*, Prentice Hall (1988).
- Mullin, M., *Object-oriented program design, with examples in C++*, Addison-Wesley (1989).
- Stroustrop, B., *The C++ programming language - 2nd edition*, Addison-Wesley (1991).

- Touretzky, D. S., *The mathematics of inheritance systems*, Pitman/Morgan Kaufmann (1986).

chapter six

Machine learning

6.1 Introduction

The preceding chapters have discussed ways of representing knowledge and drawing inferences. It was assumed that the knowledge itself was readily available and could be expressed explicitly. However, there are many circumstances where this is not the case, such as those listed below.

- The software engineer may need to obtain the knowledge from a domain expert. This task of knowledge acquisition has been extensively discussed in the literature, mainly as an exercise in psychology.

- The rules that describe a particular domain may not be known.

- The problem may not be expressible explicitly in terms of rules, facts or relationships. This category includes *skills*, such as welding or painting.

One way around these difficulties is to have the system learn for itself from a set of example solutions. Two approaches can be broadly recognized - symbolic learning and numerical learning. Symbolic learning covers the formulation and modification of explicit rules, facts and relationships. Numerical learning applies where the system can be numerically modeled, and learning in this context refers to techniques for optimizing numerical parameters. Numerical learning includes artificial neural networks, genetic algorithms, simulated annealing, and other more conventional optimization techniques.

As numerical techniques do not generate an explicit knowledge base, perhaps they do not belong in a book on knowledge-based systems. They are nonetheless covered here for three reasons: to give a more complete picture; because the techniques can be mixed with knowledge-based systems; and because of the great interest that they have generated in the artificial intelligence community.

A learning system is normally given some feedback on its performance. The source of this feedback is called the *teacher* (or the oracle), and often the teacher role is fulfilled by the environment within which the knowledge-based system is working (i.e., the reaction of the environment to a decision is sufficient to indicate whether the decision was right or wrong). Learning with a teacher is sometimes called *supervised* learning. Learning can be classified as follows, where each category involves a different level of supervision:

i   *Rote learning*

The system receives confirmation of correct decisions. When it produces an incorrect decision it is "spoon-fed" with the correct rule or relationship that it should have used. Rote learning can provide an interactive means for a human expert to supply the knowledge base.

ii   *Learning from advice*

Rather than being given a specific rule that should apply in a given circumstance, the system is given a piece of general advice, such as "gas is more likely to escape from a valve than from a pipe". The system must sort out for itself how to move from this high level abstract advice to an immediately usable rule.

iii   *Learning by induction*

The system is presented with sets of example data and is told the correct conclusions that it should draw from each. The system continually refines its rules and relations so as to correctly handle each new example.

iv   *Learning by analogy*

The system is told the correct response to a similar, but not identical task. The system must adapt the previous response to generate a new rule applicable to the new circumstances.

v   *Explanation-based learning (EBL)*

The system analyzes a set of example solutions (and their outcomes) in order to determine *why* each one was successful or otherwise. Thus explanations are generated, which are used to guide future problem-solving. EBL is incorporated into PRODIGY, a general-purpose problem-solver [1].

vi   *Case-based reasoning*

Any case about which the system has reasoned is filed away, together with the outcome, whether it be successful or otherwise. Whenever a new case is encountered, the system adapts its stored behavior to fit the new circumstances. Case-based reasoning is discussed in further detail in chapter 7, in the context of problems of diagnosis.

vii *Explorative or unsupervised learning*
Rather than having an explicit goal, an explorative system continuously searches for patterns and relationships in the input data, perhaps marking some patterns as interesting and warranting further investigation. Examples of the use of unsupervised learning include clustering data as a means of compressing it, and learning to recognize fundamental features, such as edges, from pixel images.

In the first two categories, the sophistication lies in the ability of the teacher rather than the learning system. As noted above, the teacher in these circumstances is often the human expert, and the learning system represents an interactive way of extracting the expert's knowledge. Reasoning by analogy is similar to case-based reasoning, which is discussed in section 7.4. Explorative learning may have applications to engineering design, where innovation is a desirable characteristic. However, most of the interest in symbolic learning has focussed on the third category, learning by induction, which is discussed below. Many of the problems and solutions associated with inductive learning apply to the other categories of symbolic learning as well.

6.2 Symbolic learning by induction

6.2.1 Overview
Rule induction involves generating a general rule of the type:

```
IF <general circumstance> THEN <general conclusion>
```

from specific examples. Since it is based on trial-and-error, induction can be said to be an empirical approach. We can never be certain of the accuracy of an induced rule, since it may be shown to be invalid by an example that we have not yet encountered. The aim of induction is to build rules which are successful as often as possible, and to quickly modify them when they are found to be wrong. In other words, the rules, relationships or whatever is being learnt, should match the positive examples but not the negative ones.
    Rule modifications can be classified as either strengthening or weakening. The condition is made stronger (or specialized) by restricting the circumstances to which it applies, and conversely it is made weaker (or generalized) by

increasing its applicability. A rule needs to be generalized if it fails to fire for a given set of data, but where we are told by the teacher that it should have done. Conversely, a rule needs to be specialized if it fires when it should not.

Assume for the moment that we are dealing with a rule that needs to be generalized. The first task is to spot where the condition is deficient. This is easy using pattern matching, provided that we have a suitable representation. Consider the following rule:

```
IF ?X is open AND ?X is a gas_valve
THEN flow rate through ?X is high
```

This rule would fire given the scenario:

```
valve_1 is open
valve_1 is a gas_valve.
```

The rule is able to fire because "`valve_1 is open`" matches "`?X is open`" and "`valve_1 is a gas_valve`" matches "`?X is a gas_valve`". The conclusion "`flow rate through valve_1 is high`" would be drawn.

Now consider the following scenario:

```
valve_2 is open
valve_2 is a water_valve.
```

The rule would not fire. However, the teacher may tell us that the conclusion "`flow rate through valve_2 is high`" should have been drawn. We now look for matches as before and find that "`valve_1 is open`" matches "`?X is open`". However, there is no match to "`?X is a gas_valve`", so this part of the condition needs to be generalized to embrace the circumstance "`?X is a water_valve`".

Thus we can recognize where a rule is deficient by pattern-matching between the condition part of the rule and the scenario description. This is analogous to means-ends analysis, which is used in systems for planning (see chapter 9). In means-ends analysis, pattern matching is used to determine which rules can move the world from its current state to a goal state.

6.2.2 *Learning viewed as a search problem*
The task of generalizing or specializing a rule is not straightforward, as there are many alternative ways in which a rule can be altered. Finding the correct rule is a search problem, where the search field can be enormous. Figure 6.1 shows a possible form of the search tree, where each branch represents a generalization or specialization that would correctly handle the most recently encountered input. Subsequent inputs may reveal an incorrect choice

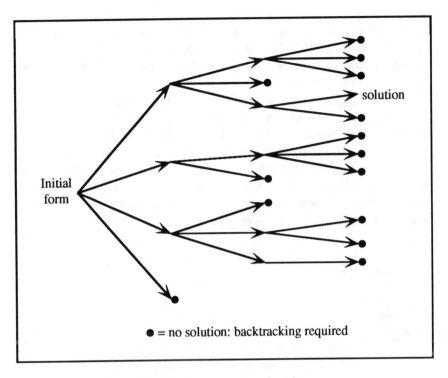

Figure 6.1 A search tree for rules.

(indicated by a dot at the end of a branch). The system must keep track of its current position in the search tree, as it must backtrack whenever an unsuitable choice is found to have been made.

Recording all of the valid options (or branches) that make up a search tree is likely to be unwieldy as there are such a large number of them. The Lex system [2] offers a neat solution to this problem. Rather than keeping track of all the possible solutions, it just records the most general and the most specific representations that fit the examples. These boundaries define the range of acceptable solutions. The boundaries move as further examples are encountered, converging on a smaller and smaller choice of rules, and ideally settling on a single rule.

There are other difficulties associated with the search problem. Suppose that a rule-based system is controlling a boiler. It makes a series of adjustments, but ultimately the boiler overheats, i.e., the control objective has not been achieved. In this case the feedback of the temperature reading to the learning system serves as the teacher. The system is faced with the difficulty of knowing where it went wrong, i.e., which of its decisions were good and which ones were at fault. This is the *credit assignment problem*. Credit assignment applies not only to negative examples such as this (which could be termed "blame assignment") but also to cases where the overall series of decisions was successful. For example, a boiler controller which succeeds in keeping the temperature within the specified range might do so because some good decisions compensate for some poorer ones.

Yet another issue is the *frame problem* (or *situation-identification problem*), which also affects other areas of artificial intelligence such as planning (see section 9.2). The problem is to determine which aspects of a given example situation are relevant to the new rule. A system for control of a boiler will have access to a wide range of information. Suppose that it comes across a set of circumstances where it is told by the teacher that it should shut off valve_2. The current world state perceived by the system is determined by stored data and sensor values, for example:

```
valve_1:                          shut
valve_2:                          open
gas_flow_rate                     high
gas_temperature:                  300°C
water_temperature (pressurized):  150°C
fuel oil stored:                  100 gallons
preferred supplier of fuel oil:   ACME inc.
```

In order to derive a rule condition such as:

```
IF gas_flow_rate is high AND valve_2 is open THEN shut valve_2
```

the system must be capable of deducing which parts of its world model to ignore (such as the information about fuel oil) and which to include. The ability to distinguish the relevant information from the rest places a requirement that the system must already have some knowledge about the domain.

6.2.3 Techniques for generalization and specialization
We can identify at least five methods of generalizing (or specializing through the inverse operation):

i   universalization;
ii replacing constants with variables;
iii using disjuncts (generalization) and conjuncts (specialization);
iv moving up a hierarchy (generalization) or down it (specialization); and
v   chunking.

Universalization

Universalization involves inferring a new general rule from a set of specific cases. Consider the following series of separate scenarios:

```
valve_1 is open AND flow rate for valve_1 is high
valve_2 is open AND flow rate for valve_2 is high
valve_3 is open AND flow rate for valve_3 is high.
```

From these we might induce the following general rule:

```
/* Rule 6.1 */
IF ?X is open THEN flow rate for ?X is high.
```

Thus we have generalized from a few specific cases to a general rule. This rule turns out to be *too* general as it does not specify that X must be a valve. However, this could be fixed through subsequent specialization based on some negative examples.

Replacing constants with variables

Universalization showed how we might induce a rule from a set of example scenarios. Similarly, general rules can be generated from more specific ones by replacing constants with variables (see section 3.6). Consider, for example, the following specific rules:

```
IF gas_valve_1 is open THEN flow rate for gas_valve_1 is high
IF gas_valve_2 is open THEN flow rate for gas_valve_2 is high
IF gas_valve_3 is open THEN flow rate for gas_valve_3 is high
IF gas_valve_4 is open THEN flow rate for gas_valve_4 is high
IF gas_valve_5 is open THEN flow rate for gas_valve_5 is high
```

From these specific rules we might induce the more general rule:

```
/* Rule 6.1 */
IF ?X is open THEN flow rate for ?X is high.
```

However, even this apparently simple change requires a certain amount of meta-knowledge (knowledge about knowledge). The system must "know" to favour rule 6.1 rather than, say:

```
/* Rule 6.2 */
IF ?X is open THEN flow rate for ?Y is high
```

or

```
/* Rule 6.3 */
IF ?X is open THEN ?Y for ?X is high.
```

Rule 6.2 implies that if any valve is open (we'll assume for now that we are only dealing with valves) then the flow rate through all valves is high. Rule 6.3 implies that if a valve is open then everything associated with that valve (e.g., cost and temperature) is high.

Using disjuncts and conjuncts

Rules can be made more specific by adding conjuncts to the condition and more general by adding disjuncts. Suppose that rule 6.1 is applied when the world state includes the information `office_door is open`. We will draw the nonsensical conclusion that `flow rate through office_door is high`. The rule clearly needs to be modified by strengthening the condition. One way to achieve this is by use of a conjunction:

```
/* Rule 6.4 */
IF ?X is open AND ?X is a gas_valve THEN flow rate for ?X is
high
```

We are relying on the teacher to tell us that `flow rate through office_door is high` is not an accurate conclusion. We have already noted that there may be several alternative ways in which variables might be introduced. The number of alternatives greatly increases when compound conditions are used. Here are some examples:

```
IF valve_1 is open and valve_1 is a gas_valve THEN ...
IF valve_1 is open and ?X is a gas_valve THEN ...
IF ?X is open and valve_1 is a gas_valve THEN ...
IF ?X is open AND ?X is a gas_valve THEN ...
IF ?X is open AND ?Y is a gas_valve THEN ...
```

The existence of these alternatives is another illustration that learning by rule induction is a search process in which the system searches for the correct rule.

Suppose now that we wish to extend rule 6.4 so that it includes water valves as well as gas valves. One way of doing this is to add a disjunction ("OR") to the condition part of the rule:

```
/* Rule 6.5 */
IF ?X is open AND (?X is a gas_valve OR ?X is a water_valve)
THEN flow rate for ?X is high.
```

This is an example of generalization by use of disjuncts. The use of disjuncts in this way is a "cautious generalization", as it caters for the latest example, but

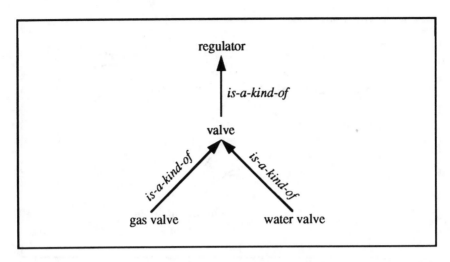

Figure 6.2 Class hierarchy for valves.

does not embrace any novel situations. The other techniques risk over-generalization, but the risky approach is necessary if we want the system to learn to handle data that it may not have seen previously. Overgeneralization can be fixed by specialization at a later stage when negative examples have come to light. However, the use of disjunctions should not be avoided altogether, as there are cases where a disjunctive condition is correct. This dilemma between the cautious and risky approach to generalization is called the *disjunctive-concept* problem. A reasonable approach is to look for an alternative form of generalization, only resorting to the use of disjunctions if no other form can be found that fits the examples.

Moving up or down a hierarchy
Rule 6.5 showed a cautious way of adapting rule 6.4 to include both water valves and gas valves. Another approach would be to modify rule 6.4 so that it dealt with valves of any description:

```
/* Rule 6.6 */
IF ?X is open AND ?X is a valve THEN flow rate for ?X is high
```

Here we have made use of an *"is-a-kind-of"* generalization (see chapter 5). In the class hierarchy for valves, water_valves and gas_valves are both specializations of the class of valves, as shown in figure 6.2.

Chunking
Chunking is a mechanism for organizing and storing experiences automatically. It has been adapted for use in SOAR [3, 4] as a technique for

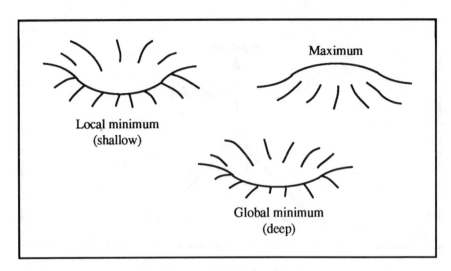

Figure 6.3 Local and global minima.

automatic learning. SOAR works on the premise that, given an overall task, every problem encountered along the way can be regarded as a subgoal. For example, an automatic boiler controller might decide that it needs to close one valve and open another. However, the controller may have no knowledge of which action should be performed first, and so a decision on the ordering of the actions becomes a subgoal. Whichever decision is taken, the outcome is used to form a preference (positive, negative or indifferent) for applying that decision to that subgoal. A rule is then formed by storing together ("chunking") the subgoal, a description of the circumstances in which the subgoal arose, the chosen solution and the resultant preference. For example we might generate the rule:

```
IF subgoal is (decide order of "open valve1" & "close valve2")
AND temperature is high
AND pressure is low
THEN (first action is "open valve1") has a positive preference.
```

Whenever the same subgoal arises in similar circumstances, a fixed procedure is used to interpret the accumulated preferences and to select the most appropriate action.

6.3 *Optimization algorithms*

We have already seen that symbolic learning by induction is a search process, where the search for the correct rule, relationship or statement is steered by the examples that are encountered. Numerical learning systems can be viewed in the same light. An initial model is set up, and its parameters are progressively refined in the light of experience. The goal is invariably to determine the maximum or minimum value of some function of one or more variables. This is the process of *optimization*. To remain consistent with convention, we will consider the problem to be one of determining a minimum, and the function that is being minimized is referred to as a *cost function*. If a maximum value of a function is actually required, the cost function is simply taken to be the negation of that function. Often the cost function is the difference, or *error*, between a desired output and the actual output.

Determining a minimum value for a multivariable function is not straightforward. The techniques described here (6.3.1 - 6.3.4) are all based upon the idea of choosing a starting point, and then altering one or more variables in an attempt to reduce the value of the cost function. However, it is easy to fall into a local minimum which is not the global minimum for the function. This is illustrated in figure 6.3. In this context, the search space is the allowed range of values for the variables.

6.3.1 Gradient descent

Gradient descent is the simplest of the optimization procedures described here, and it offers no protection against finding a local minimum rather than the global one. From a given starting point (i.e., a trial solution), the direction of steepest descent is determined. A point lying a small distance along this direction is then taken as the new trial solution. The process is repeated until it is no longer possible to descend, at which point it is assumed that the optimum has been reached. A common way of guarding against the trap of detecting a local minimum is to repeat the process many times with different starting points.

6.3.2 Conjugate gradient descent

Conjugate gradient descent is a simple attempt at avoiding the problem of falling into local minima. From a given starting point, the direction of steepest descent is initially chosen. New trial solutions are then taken by stepping along this direction, with the same direction being retained until the slope begins to curve uphill. When this happens, an alternative direction having a downhill gradient is chosen. When the direction which has been followed curves uphill, and all of the alternative directions are also uphill, it is assumed that the optimum has been reached. As the method does not continually hunt for the sharpest descent, it may be more successful than the gradient descent method in finding the global minimum. However, the technique will never cause a gradient to be climbed, even though this is often necessary in order to reach the global minimum.

6.3.3 Simulated annealing

Simulated annealing owes its name to its similarity to the problem of atoms re-arranging themselves in a cooling metal. In the cooling metal, atoms move to form a near perfect crystal lattice, even though they may have to pass through locally disordered states in order to do so. The function being minimized in this physical system is energy (E), which is related to disorder (entropy, S) and temperature (T) through the relation:

$$\Delta E = -T \, \Delta S. \tag{6.1}$$

In simulated annealing, a trial solution is chosen and the effects of taking a small random step from this position are tested. If the step results in a reduction in the cost function, it replaces the previous solution as the current trial solution. If it does not result in a cost saving, the solution has a probability (P) of being accepted as the new trial solution, typically given by:

$$P = \exp(-E/kT), \tag{6.2}$$

where k is Boltzmann's constant, T is temperature and E is energy. The energy, E, corresponds to the cost function. Temperature, T, is a numerical value which determines the stability of a trial solution. If T is high, new trial solutions will be generated continually; if T is low then a trial solution will remain fixed in a local or global minimum. The value of T is initially set high and is periodically decremented. While T is high, the optimization routine is free to accept many varied solutions, but as it drops, this freedom diminishes until the search has effectively ceased. If the optimization is successful, the final solution will be the global minimum. The success of the technique is dependent upon values chosen for starting temperature, the size and frequency of the temperature decrement, and the size of perturbations applied to the trial solutions.

Simulated annealing has been successfully applied to partitioning circuits into electronic chips, positioning chips on printed circuit boards, and circuit layout within chips [5]. All of these are mathematically "clean", though complex, design problems where an optimum arrangement does exist.

6.3.4 Genetic algorithms

Genetic algorithms have been inspired by natural evolution, the process by which successive generations of animals and plants are modified so as to approach an optimum form. Each offspring has some different features from its parents, i.e., it is not a perfect copy. If the new characteristics are favorable, the offspring is more likely to flourish and pass its characteristics to the next generation. However, an offspring with unfavorable characteristics is likely to die out.

These ideas have been applied to mathematical optimization [6]. The technique requires the maintenance of a pool of solutions, and allocating a measure of fitness to each solution. The possible solutions are represented as *chromosomes*, which are sequences of *genes*. Each gene has a value. If the values are restricted to binary digits, they are known as *alleles*. Chromosomes are made to reproduce according to their fitness, with the less fit ones dying off. Any point in the search space can be represented as a chromosome. So, for example, if we are trying to find the minimum value of a function $f(x,y)$, all possible solutions can be represented by a chromosome containing two genes (assuming that the genes can hold all of the alternative values for x and y):

The chromosome can be made as long as necessary for problems involving many variables. Rather than obtaining new trial solutions by taking a small step in a chosen direction (as in the previous three techniques), new alternatives (i.e., new chromosomes) are produced from old ones in three different ways, described below.

Crossover

Here child chromosomes are produced by aligning two parents, picking a random position along their length, and swapping the two parts. An example for an eight gene chromosome, where the mother and father genes are represented by m_i and f_i respectively, would be:

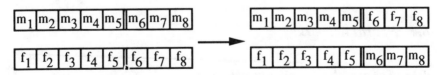

This is known as single-point crossover, as there is only one division between the swapped and unswapped genes. Multipoint crossover is also possible, for instance two-point crossover:

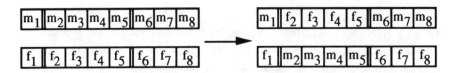

Note that crossover does not lead to any new values being generated, but simply rearranges existing values.

Inversion

Crossover and "survival of the fittest" are aimed at selecting combinations of genes that perform well together. However, if a beneficial combination is reached, further crossover tends to break up the cooperating genes. Inversion is a technique for keeping cooperative genes close together within the chromosome. The process of inversion consists of reversing the order of a short section of genes within a chromosome, for example:

$$g_1 \; g_2 \; g_3 \; g_4 \; g_5 \; g_6 \; g_7 \; g_8 \longrightarrow g_1 \; g_2 \; g_5 \; g_4 \; g_3 \; g_6 \; g_7 \; g_8$$

Mutation

Unlike crossover and inversion, mutation involves altering the values of one or more genes. This creates new possibilities for gene combinations that can be generated by crossover and inversion. Randomly selected alleles may be toggled (i.e., 1 becomes 0 and 0 becomes 1) or replaced by a randomly generated binary digit.

The examples shown here assumed that chromosomes were of fixed length, although some researchers have experimented with variable length chromosomes. The main problem in applying genetic algorithms to real optimization problems lies in finding a chromosome representation that remains valid after each generation. Nonetheless, the technique has been successfully employed in the automatic scheduling of machining operations [7, 8] and designing communications networks [9].

6.4 Neural networks

6.4.1 The appeal of neural networks

Artificial neural networks are another family of numerical learning techniques. They consist of many nonlinear computational elements which form the network nodes, linked by weighted interconnections. They are therefore analogous in structure to the neurological system in animals, which is made up from *real* rather than *artificial* neural networks. Practical artificial neural networks are much simpler than biological ones, so it is unrealistic to expect them to produce the sophisticated behavior of humans or animals. Nonetheless, they can perform certain tasks, particularly classification, most effectively. Throughout the rest of this book we will use the expression "neural network" to mean an artificial neural network. The technique of using neural networks is described as *connectionism*.

Each node in a neural network performs a simple computation, independently of the other nodes (though some groups of nodes may be required to operate after other groups). Thus neural networks have a highly parallel structure, allowing them to explore many competing hypotheses simultaneously. This parallelism allows neural networks to take advantage of parallel processing computers. They can also run on conventional serial computers - they just take longer to run that way.

The weights on the node interconnections (together with the overall topology) define the output that is derived from a given input. The weights do not need to be known in advance, but can be learned automatically. In the case of supervised learning, the weights are derived by presenting the network with a set of exemplars. In the case of unsupervised learning, the weights evolve with use and there are no exemplars.

Part of the appeal of neural networks is that when presented with noisy or incomplete data, they will produce an approximate answer rather than one that is incorrect. In the jargon, their performance is said to degrade gracefully. Similarly, when presented with unfamiliar data that lies within the range of its exemplars, the net will generally produce an output that is a reasonable interpolation between the exemplar outputs. Neural networks are, however, unable to extrapolate reliably beyond the range of the exemplars. Interpolation and graceful degradation are also properties of fuzzy logic (see section 4.4). Thus neural networks and fuzzy logic often represent alternative solutions to a particular engineering problem.

6.4.2 Neural network applications

Neural nets can be applied to a diversity of tasks. In general, the net associates a given set of input data $(x_1, x_2...x_n)$ with a particular output $(y_1, y_2...y_m)$, although the function linking the two may be unknown and may be highly nonlinear*. The input and output data are one-dimensional arrays, i.e., *vectors*. Neural nets thus provide a useful technique for determining the values of

---

* Here, a linear function is one that can be represented as $f(x) = mx + c$, where m and c are constants. A nonlinear function may include higher order terms and trigonometric or logarithmic functions.

crucial variables that cannot be easily measured, but which are known to depend in some complex way on other more accessible variables. We will call this use *nonlinear estimation*.

Often the output from the net is used to represent one of a set of possible outcomes, i.e., the neural net acts as a *classifier*. Three types of classification tasks can be identified, and the differences between the first two (categorization and content-addressable memory) will be shown by anticipating an example that will be discussed in detail in chapter 7. In this example, neural networks are used to determine whether a feature in an ultrasonic image is a critical defect (i.e., a crack) or a noncritical defect such as a pore. The characteristics of one crack would be similar, but not identical, to another.   However, they would be substantially different from the characteristics of a pore.

Categorization
The net is initially trained using a set of exemplars, where each exemplar consists of a numerical description of the image features (the input) and a numerical code to identify the corresponding defect type (the output). When it is subsequently presented with a new input vector, the net selects the code for the defect type that offers the closest match.   Categorization using non-connectionist techniques would not be straightforward, as the input data rarely correspond exactly to any one exemplar.

Content-addressable memory
This classification task also involves supervised learning, but it is different from categorization. Although the net is trained on a numerical description of each exemplar, the exemplars are not identified with any particular meaning. Each exemplar is therefore a single vector, rather than a pair of vectors. During training, each exemplar vector becomes stored in a dispersed form through the network. A new input vector (such as a defect description) is treated as though it were an incomplete or error-ridden version of one of the exemplars. When the new input vector is presented to the network, the net will progressively regenerate the exemplar that most closely resembles it.

Clustering
Clustering has no distinct training phase and no teacher is necessary, i.e., learning can be unsupervised. As successive input vectors are presented, they are clustered into N groups, where the integer N may be prespecified or may be allowed to grow according to the diversity of the data. This technique may be useful for data compression.

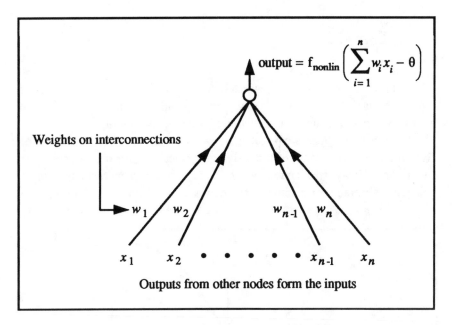

Figure 6.4 A single node and its connections.

6.4.3 Nodes and interconnections

Each node in a neural net is a simple computing element having an input side and an output side. Each node may have connections to many other nodes at both its input and output sides. Typically, the node's role is to sum each of its inputs, subtract a bias term, θ, and pass the result through a nonlinear function, f_{nonlin}, known as the *activation function*. The output is then sent to each of its output connections. The interconnections have an input end and an output end, and they too perform a simple arithmetic function. Each interconnection has a weighting (w_i) associated with it, so that for an input, x_i, its output is $w_i x_i$. Figure 6.4 shows the function of a node and its interconnections.

The behavior of a neural network depends on its topology, the interconnection weights, the bias terms, and the activation function. The weights and biases can be learnt, and the learning behavior of a net depends on the chosen algorithm. Typically a sigmoid function is used as the activation function, as shown in figure 6.5(a). The sigmoid function is given by:

$$f_{nonlin}(x) = \frac{1}{1 + e^{-x}}.$$

For a network node, x is given by:

$$x = \sum_{i=1}^{n} w_i x_i - \theta$$

where θ is a bias term, defined separately for each node, and n is the number of inputs. Figures 6.5(b) and (c) show the ramp and step functions, which are alternative nonlinear functions sometimes used as activation functions.

Many net topologies are possible, but we will concentrate on a selection of five which illustrate some of the different applications for neural nets. The first is the multilayer perceptron, which can be used for categorization or, more generally, for nonlinear mapping. The others are the Hopfield net for use as a

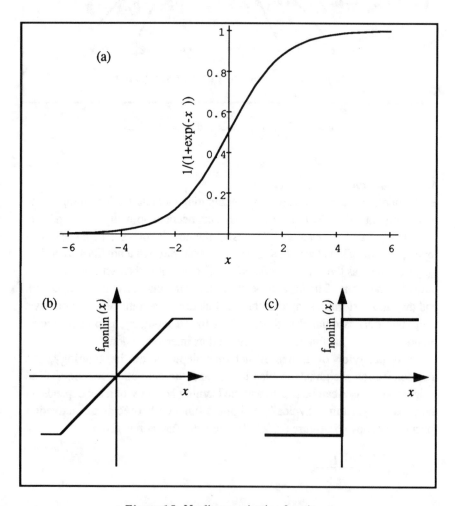

Figure 6.5 Nonlinear activation functions:
(a) A sigmoid function; (b) A ramp function; (c) A step function.

content-addressable memory; the MAXNET for selecting the maximum among its inputs; and the ART1 net and Kohonen's self-organizing net, both used for clustering.

6.4.4 The multilayer perceptron

The topology of a multilayer perceptron is shown in figure 6.6. These networks are also called *feedforward networks*, although the latter term could be applied more generally to any network where the direction of data flow is always "forwards", i.e., towards the output. Perceptrons may be used either for classification or as nonlinear estimators. The number of nodes in each layer and the number of layers are determined by the net builder, often on a trial-and-error basis. There is always an input layer and an output layer. The number of nodes in each is determined by the number of inputs and outputs being considered. There may be any number of layers (including none) between these layers. Unlike the input and output layers, the layers between often have no obvious meaning associated with them, and they are known as *hidden layers*. The net shown in figure 6.6 has three input nodes, two hidden layers with four nodes each and an output layer of two nodes. It can therefore be described as a 3-4-4-2 net.

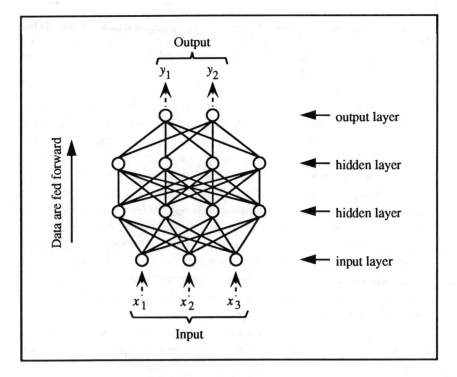

Figure 6.6 A 3-4-4-2 perceptron.

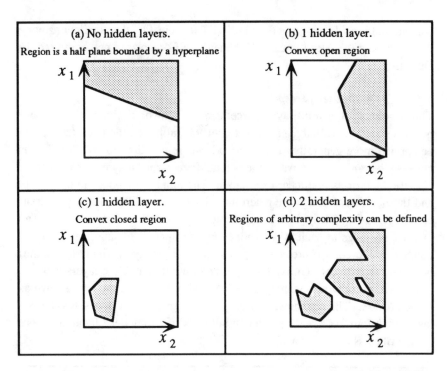

Figure 6.7 Regions in state space distinguished by a perceptron (adapted from [11]). The regions shown can be generated by a perceptron with a step nonlinearity (figure 6.5(c)). A convex region has the property that a line joining points on the boundary passes only through that region.

There is some inconsistency in the literature over the counting of layers. We will describe the network in figure 6.6 as a four-layer network. The input nodes do not perform any processing, but simply feed the input data into the nodes above. For this reason, some authors would describe this as a three-layer network, or as a four-layer network with three processing layers. Thus the so-called "single-layer perceptron" would be a two-layer perceptron in our terminology. It is generally accepted that only one hidden layer is necessary in a perceptron that uses a sigmoid activation function and that no more than two are necessary if a step function is used [10]. However, the ability to learn from a set of examples cannot be guaranteed and therefore the detailed topology of a network inevitably involves a certain amount of trial and error. A pragmatic approach to network design is to start with a small network and expand the number of nodes or layers as necessary.

A perceptron operates by feeding data forwards along the interconnections from the input layer, through the hidden layers, to the output layer. With the exception of the nodes in the input layer, the input to each node is the weighted output from each node in the previous layer. At each node, the weighted data are summed and passed through the activation function associated with the node.

In general, networks are designed so that there is one input node for each element of the input vector and one output node for each element of the output vector. Thus in a categorization application, each output node would represent a particular category. A typical representation for a category would be for a value close to '1' to appear at the corresponding output node, with the remaining output nodes generating a value close to zero. A simple decision rule is needed in conjunction with the perceptron, namely that the node with the highest output corresponds to the selected category (so-called "winner takes all"). If the input vector falls between two categories, two output nodes might have values substantially above zero.

More compact representations are also possible. Hallam et al. [12] have used just two output nodes to represent four categories. This was achieved by treating both outputs together, so that the four possibilities corresponding to four classes are (0,0), (0,1), (1,0) and (1,1). A drawback of this approach is that it is more difficult to interpret an output which does not closely match one of these possibilities (e.g., what would an output of (0.5, 0.5) represent?).

Let us now return to the more normal case where each output node represents a distinct category. If the input vector has two elements, it can be represented as a point in two-dimensional state space. The process of categorization is then one of drawing dividing lines between regions. Figure 6.7 shows the different sorts of boundaries that can be drawn as the number of hidden layers in a perceptron is increased from zero to two. Within the limitations shown, the boundaries can be made more complex by increasing the number of nodes in the hidden layers. More generally, regions in multi-dimensional state space are divided by hyperplanes, rather than by lines in a plane.

6.4.5 Training a perceptron

The use of a perceptron as described so far is quite straightforward, assuming that we know the values of the interconnection weights and the bias terms. Appropriate values are learnt from a set of examples comprising input vectors and the correct corresponding output vectors. An input vector is applied to the input layer and the output that is generated is compared with the correct output, the difference in each vector element being the *error*. The sum of the squares of the errors is minimized by altering the weights and bias terms, which may take many passes through the training data. When the total squared error has become acceptably low for each example vector, the network is said to have *converged* and the weights and bias are terms are retained for application of the net to new input data.

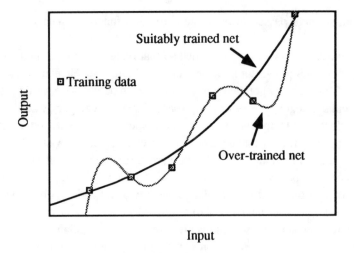

Figure 6.8 The effect of over-training.

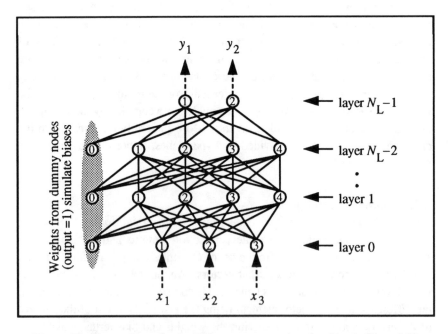

Figure 6.9 Nomenclature for the back-error propagation algorithm in figure 6.10.
   N_L = number of layers (4 in this example);
   w_{Aij} = weight between node i on level A-1 and node j on level A ($N_L \geq A \geq 1$);
   O_{Aj} = output from node j on level A;
   δ_{Aj} = an error term associated with node j on level A.

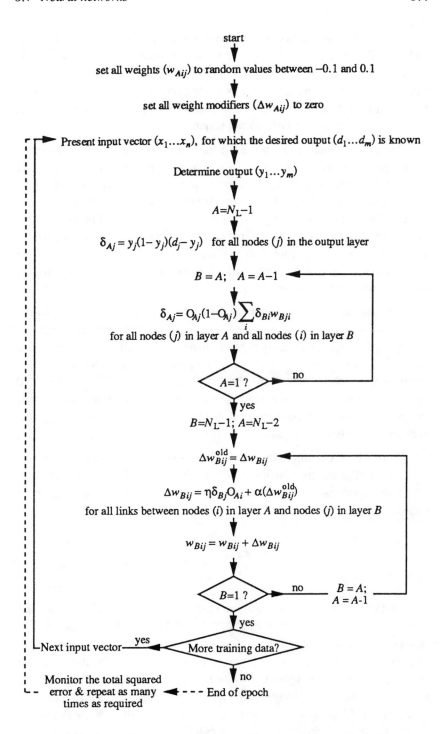

start

set all weights (w_{Aij}) to random values between -0.1 and 0.1

set all weight modifiers (Δw_{Aij}) to zero

Present input vector $(x_1...x_n)$, for which the desired output $(d_1...d_m)$ is known

Determine output $(y_1...y_m)$

$A=N_L-1$

$\delta_{Aj} = y_j(1-y_j)(d_j-y_j)$ for all nodes (j) in the output layer

$B = A;$ $A = A-1$

$\delta_{Aj}= O_{Aj}(1-O_{Aj})\sum_i \delta_{Bi}w_{Bji}$
for all nodes (j) in layer A and all nodes (i) in layer B

$A=1$?   no

yes

$B=N_L-1; A=N_L-2$

$\Delta w_{Bij}^{old} = \Delta w_{Bij}$

$\Delta w_{Bij} = \eta\delta_{Bj}O_{Ai} + \alpha(\Delta w_{Bij}^{old})$
for all links between nodes (i) in layer A and nodes (j) in layer B

$w_{Bij} = w_{Bij} + \Delta w_{Bij}$

$B=1$?   no $B = A;$
                          $A = A-1$

yes

Next input vector —— yes —— More training data?

Monitor the total squared   no
error & repeat as many ◄--- End of epoch
times as required

Figure 6.10 The back-error propagation algorithm (derived from [11] and [15]).

Sometimes it is appropriate to stop the training process before the point where no further reductions in the error are possible. This is because it is possible to over-train the network, so that it becomes expert at giving the correct output for the training data, but less expert at dealing with new data. The effect of over-training is shown in figure 6.8, for the case where there is only one input variable and one output variable.

One of the most commonly used training algorithms is the back-error propagation algorithm [13, 14]. This is a gradient descent technique (see section 6.3.1), and it relies upon the activation function being continuous and differentiable. The sigmoid function (figure 6.5(a)) is therefore normally chosen. The task of optimizing weights and bias terms is simplified by treating the biases as weights on the interconnections from dummy nodes, whose output is always '1' (figure 6.9). A flowchart describing the back-error propagation algorithm is presented in figure 6.10, and the key to the nomenclature is shown in figure 6.9.

Gradient descent techniques can be inefficient, especially close to the minima. Therefore a "momentum" term is usually incorporated into the algorithm, the effect of which is to force changes in weight to be dependent on previous weight changes. The amount of momentum is defined by the coefficient, α, whose value must be in the range 0-1, where a value of 0 signifies no momentum. Knight [15] suggests that α be set to zero for the first few training passes and then increased to 0.9. He also suggests a learning rate, η, of about 0.35 (see figure 6.10).

Many other training algorithms have been successfully applied to perceptrons. For instance, Willis et al. [16] favour the chemotaxis algorithm, which incorporates a random statistical element in a similar fashion to statistical annealing (section 6.3.3).

6.4.6 The Hopfield net

The Hopfield net has only one layer, and the nodes are used for both input and output. The net topology is shown in figure 6.11. The net can be used in various ways, but is typically used as a content-addressable memory with binary input (for example, values may be either +1 or -1). By using the step nonlinearity shown in figure 6.5(b) as the activation function, f_{nonlin}, the output can be forced to remain binary too. If the net has N_n nodes, then each exemplar would consist of a vector of N_n binary digits. If there are N_e exemplars, the network weights are set according to the following equation:

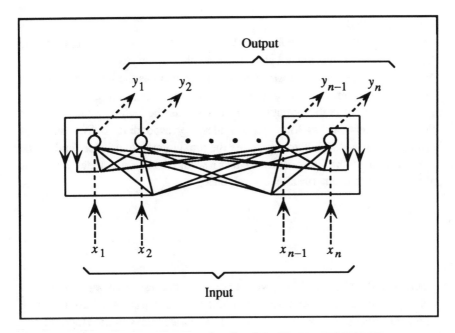

Figure 6.11 The topology of the Hopfield Net and the MAXNET.

$$w_{ij} = \begin{cases} \sum\limits_{k=1}^{N_e} x_{ik}\, x_{jk} & \text{if } i \neq j \\[2ex] 0 & \text{if } i = j \end{cases} \tag{6.3}$$

where w_{ij} is the weighting on the connection from node i to node j, and x_{ik} is the ith digit of exemplar k.

Setting weights in this way constitutes the learning phase, and results in the exemplars being stored in a distributed fashion in the network. If a new pattern is subsequently presented as the input, then this pattern is initially the output too, as nodes are used for both input and output. The node function (figure 6.4) is then performed on each node in parallel. If this is repeated many times, the output will be progressively modified and will converge on the exemplar pattern which most closely resembles the unknown pattern. In order to achieve this effect reliably, the number of exemplars (N_e) should not exceed approximately $0.15 N_n$ [11].

If the network is to be used as for categorization, a further stage is needed in which the result is compared with the exemplars in order to pick out the one that matches.

6.4.7 MAXNET

The MAXNET has an identical topology to the Hopfield net, except that the 'circular' weights, w_{ii}, are not always zero as they are in the Hopfield net. The MAXNET is used to recognize which of its inputs has the highest value. In this role it is often used in conjunction with other nets, such as a multilayer perceptron, to select the output node that generates the highest value. Suppose that the perceptron has four output nodes, corresponding to four different categories. A MAXNET to determine the maximum output value (and hence the solution to the categorization task) would have four nodes and four alternative output patterns after convergence:

        X 0 0 0
        0 X 0 0
        0 0 X 0
        0 0 0 X,

where $X > 0$. The MAXNET would adjust its highest input value to X, and reduce the others to 0. Note that the MAXNET is constructed to have the same number of nodes (N_n) as exemplars (N_e). Contrast this with the Hopfield net, which needs approximately seven times as many nodes as there are exemplars.

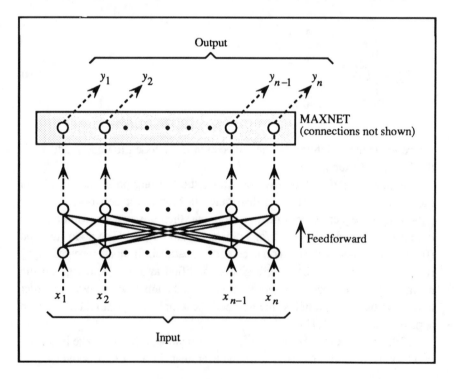

Figure 6.12 The Hamming Net.

Using the same notation as equation 6.3, interconnection weights are set as follows:

$$w_{ij} = \begin{cases} 1 & \text{if } i \neq j \\ -\varepsilon & \text{if } i = j \quad \left(\text{where } \varepsilon < \dfrac{1}{N_n} \right) \end{cases} \tag{6.4}$$

The *Hamming net* has two parts - a twin layered feedforward network and a MAXNET, as shown in figure 6.12. The feedforward network is used to compare the input vector with each of the exemplars, awarding a matching score to each exemplar. The MAXNET is then used to pick out the exemplar that has attained the highest score. Thus the overall effect is that the net can categorize its input vector.

6.4.8 *Adaptive Resonance Theory (ART) nets*

The Adaptive Resonance Theory nets (ART1 and ART2) of Carpenter and

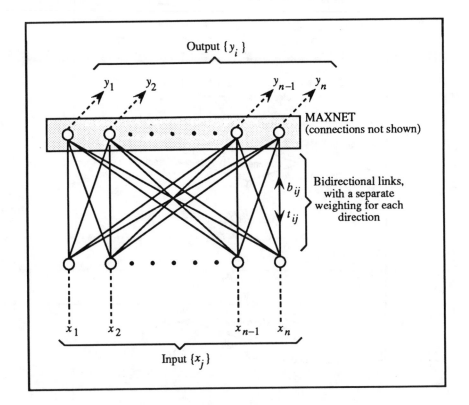

Figure 6.13 The ART1 Net.

Grossberg [17] are worthy of mention because they are examples of networks that learn without supervision. The ART1 network topology comprises bidirectional interconnections between a set of input nodes and a MAXNET, as shown in figure 6.13. The network classifies the incoming data into clusters, a process which may have an important role in data compression, as noted in section 6.4.2.

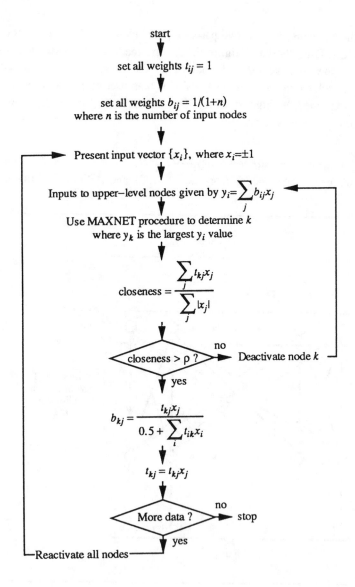

Figure 6.14 Unsupervised learning in ART1.

When the first input vector is presented to the net, this becomes stored as an exemplar. The second input vector is then compared with the exemplar and is either considered sufficiently similar to belong to the same cluster, or is stored as a new exemplar. If a vector is considered to belong to a previously defined cluster, the exemplar for that cluster is modified to take account of the new member. The performance of the net is dependent on the way in which the differences are measured, and the threshold (or *vigilance*, ρ) beyond which a new exemplar is stored. As each new vector is presented, it is compared with all of the current exemplars in parallel. The number of exemplars grows as the net is used, i.e., the net learns new patterns. The operation of the ART1 net, which takes binary inputs, is summarized in figure 6.14. ART2 is similar but takes continuously varying inputs.

6.4.9 Kohonen self-organizing nets

Kohonen's self-organizing nets provide another example of nets that can learn without supervision. The output nodes can be imagined to be arranged in a 2-dimensional array, with interconnections between all nodes. There is also a separate one-dimensional array of input nodes, where each input node is connected to each output node via a weighted interconnection. Suppose that the input vector has two elements, which are passed to two input nodes, as shown in figure 6.15. When suitably trained, the network has the property that the distribution of the output values corresponds with the Cartesian coordinates represented by the input vector. Thus, if the input elements fall in the range -1 to +1, then an input vector of (-0.9, 0.9) will cause an output node close to the

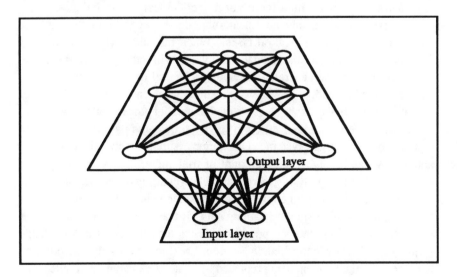

Figure 6.15 A Kohonen self-organizing net.

top left of the array to produce a value of approximately 1, while other output nodes will produce an output of approximately 0. The learning mechanism, described in [18, 19, 20, 11], involves competition between the nodes to respond to a particular input vector. The "winner" has its interconnection weightings set so as to generate an output of '1', and the "losers" have their weightings set so as to generate an output of '0'.

6.5 *Summary*

Systems which can learn offer a way around the so-called "knowledge acquisition bottleneck". In cases where it is difficult or impossible to extract accurate knowledge about a specific domain, it is clearly an attractive proposition for a computer system to derive from examples its own representation of the knowledge. We have distinguished between two categories of learning systems - symbolic and numerical. A large research effort has been devoted to symbolic learning systems, but their application in real engineering situations has been limited and numerical learning systems have gained wider acceptance. Numerical learning is based upon adapting numerical parameters so as to achieve a close match between a desired output and the actual output. The process is therefore one of optimization. Most optimization techniques are based upon minimizing a particular quantity, described as a cost function. Often the cost function is the error between the output and the desired output, or some function of the error.

Neural networks form a family of numerical learning techniques. They can be used to model any nonlinear mapping between variables, and are frequently used in classification tasks. When presented with data that lies between previously encountered data, many nets will interpolate to produce an output between those generated previously. Neural nets may therefore be a substitute for fuzzy logic in some applications. The enormous parallelism of neural networks makes them ideally suited to parallel processing computers.

A neural network may be used to solve a problem in its own right, or as a component of a larger system. Designing a suitable network for a given application can involve a large amount of trial-and-error. Whether or not a network will converge (i.e., "learn" suitable weightings) will depend on the topology, the activation function of the nodes, the values of the parameters in the learning algorithm, and the training data. It may even depend on the order in which the training data are presented. Thus the difficulties in knowledge acquisition that are described in section 1.6 (the "knowledge acquisition bottleneck") might end up being replaced by a "network parameter bottleneck"

[21]. There is some interest in the possible use of other numerical optimization techniques, such as genetic algorithms, to derive the network parameters.

A drawback of neural networks is that their reasoning is opaque. The various learned weightings can rarely be understood in a meaningful way. Thus the neural net is often regarded as a "black box" which simply generates an output from a given input. However, by confining the use of the neural net to subtasks within an overall problem, the problem-solving strategy can remain clear.

References

1. Minton, S., Carbonell, J. G., Knoblock, C. A., Kuokka, D. R., Etzioni, O. and Gil, Y., "Explanation-based learning: a problem-solving perspective", *Artificial Intelligence*, **40**, p63 (1989).

2. Mitchell, T. M., Utgoff, P. E. and Banerji, R., "Learning by experimentation: acquiring and refining problem-solving heuristics", in *Machine learning: an artificial intelligence approach, volume 1*, Michalski, R., Carbonell, J. G. and Mitchell, T. M. (ed.), Springer-Verlag (1983).

3. Laird, J. E., Rosenbloom, P. S. and Newell, A., "Chunking in SOAR: the anatomy of a general learning mechanism", *Machine Learning*, **1**, p11 (1986).

4. Laird, J. E., Newell, A. and Rosenbloom, P. S., "SOAR: an architecture for general intelligence", *Artificial Intelligence*, **33**, p1 (1987).

5. Kirkpatrick, S., Gelatt, C. D. and Vecchi, M. P., "Optimization by simulated annealing: quantitative studies", *Science*, **220**, p671 (1983).

6. Holland, J. H., *Adaptation in natural and artificial systems*, University of Michigan Press, Ann Arbor (1975).

7. Husbands, P., Mill, F. and Warrington, S., "Generating optimal process plans from first principles", in *Expert Systems for Management and Engineering*, Balagurasamy, E. and Howe, J. (ed.), Ellis Horwood (1990).

8. Husbands, P. and Mill, F., "Simulated co-evolution as the mechanism for emergent planning and scheduling", in *4th Int. Conf. on Genetic Algorithms*, Belew, R. and Booker, L. (ed.), Morgan Kaufmann, p264 (1991).

9. Davis, L. and Coombs, S., "Optimizing network link sizes with genetic algorithms", in *Modelling and Simulation Methodology: Knowledge Systems Paradigms*, Elzas, M. S., Oren, T. I. and Zeigler, B. P. (ed.), North Holland Publishing Co. (1987).

10. Picton, P. D., Hallam, N. J. and Woodcock, N., "Are three- layers enough? A review of Kolmogorov's existence theorem", to be published in *Systems and Cybernetics* (1992).

11. Lippmann, R. P., "An introduction to computing with neural nets", *IEEE ASSP Magazine*, p4 (April 1987).

12. Hallam, N. J., Hopgood, A. A. and Woodcock, N., "Defect classification in welds using a feedforward network within a blackboard system", in *International Neural Network Conference*, Paris (1990).

13. Rumelhart, D. E., Hinton, G. E. and Williams, R. J., "Learning internal representations by error propagation", in *Parallel Distributed Processing: Explorations in the Microstructures of Cognition*, Rumelhart, D. E. and McClelland, J. L. (ed.), MIT Press (1986).

14. Rumelhart, D. E., Hinton, G. E. and Williams, R. J., "Learning representations by back-propagating errors", *Nature*, 323, p533 (1986).

15. Knight, K., "Connectionist ideas and algorithms", *Communications of the ACM*, 33, p59 (1990).

16. Willis, M. J., Di Massimo, C., Montague, G. A., Tham, M. T. and Morris, A. J., "Artificial neural networks in process engineering", *IEE Proceedings-D*, 138, p256 (1991).

17. Carpenter, G. A. and Grossberg, S., "ART2: Self-organization of stable category recognition codes for analog input patterns", *Applied Optics*, 26, p4919 (1987).

18. Kohonen, T., "Adaptive, associative, and self-organizing functions in neural computing", *Applied Optics*, 26, p4910 (1987).

19. Kohonen, T., *Self-organization and associative memory, second edition*, Springer-Verlag (1988).

20. Hecht-Nielson, R., *Neurocomputing*, Addison-Wesley (1990).

21. Woodcock, N., Hallam, N. J., Picton, P. and Hopgood, A. A., "Interpretation of ultrasonic images of weld defects using a hybrid system", in *Neural Networks and their applications*, Nimes, France (1991).

Further reading

• Beale, R. and Jackson, T., *Neural computing: an introduction*, Adam Hilger (1990).

• Carbonell, J. (ed.), *Machine learning: paradigms and methods*, MIT Press (1990)

• Davis, L. (ed.), *Genetic algorithms and simulated annealing*, Pitman/Morgan Kaufmann (1987).

- Davis, L. (ed.), *Handbook of genetic algorithms*, Van Nostrand Reinhold (1991).
- Goldberg, D.E., *Genetic algorithms in search, optimization and machine learning*, Addison-Wesley (1989)
- Hecht-Nielson, R., *Neurocomputing*, Addison-Wesley (1990).
- Michalski, R. S., Carbonell, J. G. and Mitchell, T. M. (ed.), *Machine learning: an artificial intelligence approach, volume 1*, Springer-Verlag (1983).
- Michalski, R. S., Carbonell, J. G. and Mitchell, T. M. (ed.), *Machine learning: an artificial intelligence approach, volume 2*, Morgan Kaufmann (1986).
- Pao, Y.-H., *Adaptive pattern recognition and neural networks*, Addison-Wesley (1989).

chapter seven

Systems for interpretation and diagnosis

7.1 Introduction

Diagnosis is the process of determining the nature of a fault or malfunction, based on a set of symptoms. Input data (the symptoms) are interpreted and the underlying cause of these symptoms is the output. Diagnosis is therefore a special case of the more general problem of interpretation. There are many circumstances in which we may wish to interpret data, other than diagnosing problems. Examples include the interpretation of images (e.g., optical, x-ray, ultrasonic, electron microscopic), meters, gauges, and statistical data (e.g., from surveys of people or from counts registered by a radiation counter). This chapter will examine some of the techniques that are used in knowledge-based systems for diagnosis and for more general interpretation problems. The diagnosis of faults in a refrigerator will be used as an illustrative example, and the interpretation of ultrasonic images from welds in steel plates will be used as a detailed case study.

Since the inception of expert systems in the late 1960s and early 1970s, diagnosis and interpretation have been favorite application areas. Some of these early expert systems were quite successful, and became "classics". Three examples of these early successes are outlined below.

MYCIN
This was a medical system for diagnosing infectious diseases and for selecting an antibiotic drug treatment. It is frequently referenced because of its novel (at the time) use of certainty theory (see section 4.3).

PROSPECTOR
This system interpreted geological data, and made recommendations of suitable sites for mineral prospecting. The system made use of Bayesian updating as a means of handling uncertainty (see section 4.2).

DENDRAL

This system interpreted mass-spectrometry data, and was notable for its use of a three phase approach to the problem:

i *Plan*

(Suggest molecular substructures that may be present, as a guide to phase ii).
↓

ii *Generate hypotheses*

(Generate all plausible molecular structures).
↓

iii *Test*

(For each structure generated in phase ii, compare predicted data with the actual data. Reject poorly matching structures and place the remainder in rank order).

More recently, a vast number of expert systems have been produced that tackle a wide range of diagnosis and interpretation problems in engineering. Diagnostic systems include applications to electronic circuits [1], manufacturing plant [2], furnaces [3], and batteries in the Hubble space telescope [4]. Systems for the more general problem of interpretation have been applied to drawings [5], seismic data [6], and ultrasonic images [7, 8]. The latter is described in a detailed case study in section 7.6.

7.2 *Deduction and abduction for diagnosis*

Given some information about the state of the world, we can often infer additional information. If this inference is logically correct (i.e., is guaranteed to be true given that the starting information is true), then this process is termed *deduction*. Deduction is used to predict an effect from a given cause (see section 1.4). Consider, for instance, a domestic refrigerator (figure 7.1). If a refrigerator is unplugged from the mains electricity, we can confidently predict that after a few hours the ice in the ice box will melt and the food in the main compartment will no longer be chilled. The new assertion (that the ice melts) follows logically from the given facts and assertions (that the power is disconnected). Imagine that we have an object representation of a refrigerator, with an attribute `state` which is a list describing the current state of the fridge. If my refrigerator is represented by the object instance `my_fridge`, then a simple deductive rule might be (using the convention of section 3.6):

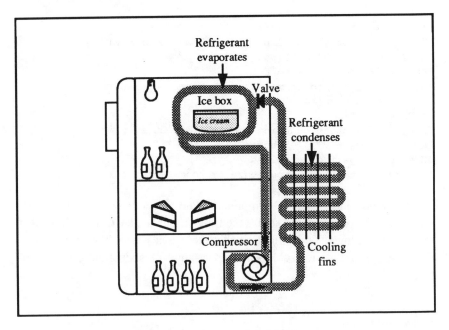

Figure 7.1 A domestic refrigerator.

```
/* Rule 7.1 */
IF my_fridge.state contains "unplugged at time ?T"
AND (time_now - ?T) > 5 hours
THEN my_fridge.ice := melted
AND  my_fridge.food_temperature := room_temperature.
```

While deductive rules have an important role to play, they are inadequate on their own for the problems of diagnosis and interpretation. Instead of determining an effect given a cause, diagnosis and interpretation involve finding a cause given an effect. This problem is termed *abduction*, and involves drawing a plausible inference rather than a certain one. Thus, if we observe that the ice in our ice box has melted and the food has warmed to room temperature, we could infer from rule 7.1 that our fridge is unplugged. However this is clearly an unsound inference as there may be several other reasons for the observed effects. For instance, by reference to rules 7.2 and 7.3 below, we might infer that the fuse has blown or that there is a power blackout respectively:

```
/* Rule 7.2 */
IF my_fridge.state contains "fuse blown at time ?T"
AND (time_now - ?T) > 5 hours
THEN my_fridge.ice := melted
AND  my_fridge.food_temperature := room_temperature.

/* Rule 7.3 */
IF my_fridge.state contains "power blackout at time ?T"
AND (time_now - ?T) > 5 hours
THEN my_fridge.ice := melted
AND  my_fridge.food_temperature := room_temperature.
```

So, given the observed symptoms about the temperature within the refrigerator, the cause might be that the fridge is unplugged, or it might be that the fuse has blown, or it might be that there is a power blackout. Three different approaches to tackling the uncertainty of abduction are outlined below.

Exhaustive testing

We could use rules whose condition parts exhaustively test for every eventuality. Rules are therefore required of the form:

```
IF my_fridge.state contains "unplugged at time ?T"
AND (time_now - ?T) > 5 hours
AND NOT(a power blackout)
AND NOT(fuse blown)
AND .....
AND .....
THEN my_fridge.ice := melted
AND  my_fridge.food_temperature := room_temperature.
```

This is not a practical solution except for trivially simple domains, and the resulting rule base would be difficult to modify or maintain. In the RESCU system [9], those rules which *can* be used with confidence for both deduction and abduction are labeled as "reversible". Such rules describe a one-to-one mapping between cause and effect, such that no other causes can lead to the same effect.

Explicit modeling of uncertainty

The uncertainty can be explicitly represented using techniques like those described in chapter 4. This is the approach that was adopted in MYCIN and PROSPECTOR. As noted in chapter 4, many of the techniques for representing uncertainty are founded on dubious assumptions.

Hypothesize-and-test

A tentative hypothesis can be put forward for further investigation. The hypothesis may be subsequently confirmed or abandoned. This hypothesize-and-test approach, which was used in DENDRAL, avoids the pitfalls of finding a valid means of representing and propagating uncertainty.

There may be additional sources of uncertainty, as well as the intrinsic uncertainty associated with abduction. For instance the evidence itself may be uncertain (e.g., we may not be sure that the food isn't cool), or vague (e.g., just what does "cool" or "chilled" mean precisely?).

The production of a hypothesis which may be subsequently accepted, refined or rejected is similar, but not identical, to *nonmonotonic logic*. Under nonmonotonic logic, an earlier conclusion may be withdrawn in the light of new evidence. Conclusions which can be withdrawn in this way are termed *defeasible*, and a defeasible conclusion is assumed to be valid until such time as it is withdrawn.

In contrast, the hypothesize-and-test approach involves an active search for supporting evidence once a hypothesis has been drawn. If sufficient evidence is found, the hypothesis becomes held as a conclusion. If contrary evidence is found then the hypothesis is rejected. If insufficient evidence is found, the hypothesis remains unconfirmed.

This distinction between nonmonotonic logic and the hypothesize-and-test approach can be illustrated by considering the case of a refrigerator that is not working. Suppose that the refrigerator is plugged into the mains, the compressor is silent, and the light does not come on when the door is opened. Using the hypothesize-and-test approach, we might produce the hypothesis that there is a power blackout. We would then look for supporting evidence by testing whether another appliance is also inoperable. If this supporting evidence were found, the hypothesis would be confirmed. If other appliances were found to be working, the hypothesis would be withdrawn. Under nonmonotonic logic, reasoning would continue based on the assumption of a power blackout until the conclusion is defeated (if it is defeated at all). Confirmation is neither required nor sought in the case of nonmonotonic reasoning. Implicitly, the following default assumption is made:

```
IF an electrical appliance is "dead",
AND there is no proof that there is not a power failure
THEN by default, we can infer that there is a power failure.
```

The term *default reasoning* describes this kind of implicit rule in nonmonotonic logic.

7.3 Depth of knowledge

7.3.1 Shallow knowledge

The early successes of diagnostic expert systems are largely attributable to the use of shallow knowledge, expressed as rules. This is the knowledge that a human expert might acquire by experience, without regard to the underlying reasons. For instance, a mechanic looking at a broken refrigerator, might "know" that if the fridge makes a humming noise but does not get cold then it has lost coolant. While he or she may also know the details of the workings of a refrigerator, this detailed knowledge need not be used. Shallow knowledge can be easily represented:

```
/* Rule 7.4 */
IF fridge makes humming sound
AND fridge does not get cold
THEN hypothesize loss of coolant.
```

Note that we are using the hypothesize-and-test approach to dealing with uncertainty in this example. With the coolant as its focus of attention, an expert system may then progress by seeking further evidence in support of its hypothesis (e.g., the presence of a leak in the pipes). Shallow knowledge is given a variety of names in the literature, including *heuristic, experiential, empirical, compiled, surface,* and *low-road.*

Expert systems built upon shallow knowledge may look impressive since they can rapidly move from a set of input data (the symptoms) to some plausible conclusions with a minimal number of intermediate steps, just as a human expert might. However, the limitations of such an expert system are easily exposed by presenting it with a situation which is outside its narrow area of expertise. When it is confronted with a set of data about which it has no explicit rules, the system cannot respond, or worse still, may give wrong answers.

There is a second important deficiency of shallow-reasoning expert systems. Because the knowledge bypasses the causal links between an observation and a deduction, the system has no understanding of its knowledge. Therefore it is unable to give helpful explanations of its reasoning. The best it can do is to regurgitate the chain of heuristic rules that lead from the observations to the conclusions.

7.3.2 Deep knowledge
Deep knowledge is the fundamental building block of understanding. A number of deep rules might make up the causal links underlying a shallow rule.

For instance the effect of the shallow rule 7.4 (above) may be achieved by the following deep rules:

```
/* Rule 7.5 */
IF current flows in the windings of the compressor
THEN there is an induced rotational force on the windings

/* Rule 7.6 */
IF motor windings are rotating
AND axle is attached to windings and compressor vanes
THEN compressor axle and vanes are rotating

/* Rule 7.7 */
IF a part is moving
THEN it may vibrate or rub against its mounting

/* Rule 7.8 */
IF two surfaces are vibrating or rubbing against each other
THEN mechanical energy is converted to heat and sound.

/* Rule 7.9 */
IF compressor vanes rotate
AND coolant is present as a gas at the compressor inlet
THEN coolant is drawn through the compressor and pressurized

/* Rule 7.10 */
IF pressure on a gas exceeds its vapor pressure
THEN the gas will condense to form a liquid

/* Rule 7.11 */
IF a gas is condensing
THEN it will release its latent heat of vaporization.
```

Figure 7.2 shows how these deep rules might be used to draw the same hypothesis as the shallow rule 7.4.

There is no clear distinction between deep and shallow knowledge, but rather some rules are deeper than others. Thus while rule 7.5 is deep relative to the shallow rule 7.4, it could be considered shallow compared with knowledge of the flow of electrons in a magnetic field and the origins of the electromotive force that gives rise to the movement of the windings. In recognition of this, Fink and Lusth [10] distinguish fundamental knowledge, which is the deepest knowledge that has relevance to the domain. Thus, "unsupported items fall to the ground" may be considered a fundamental rule in a domain where details of Newton's laws of gravitation are irrelevant. Similarly Kirchoff's first law (which states that the sum of the input current is equal to the sum of the output current at any point in a circuit) would be considered a deep rule for most

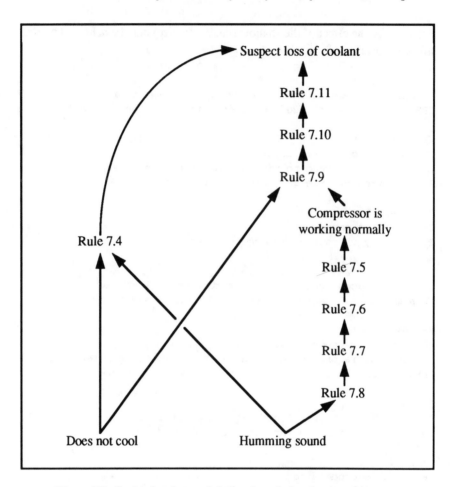

Figure 7.2 Comparing deep and shallow knowledge about a refrigerator.

electrical or electronic diagnosis problems, but is nonetheless rather shallow compared with detailed knowledge of the behavior of electrons under the influence of an electric field. Thus Kirchoff's first law is not fundamental in the broad domain of physics, since it can be derived from deeper knowledge. However, it may be treated as fundamental for most practical problems.

7.3.3 Combining shallow and deep knowledge

There are merits and disadvantages to both deep and shallow knowledge. A system based on shallow knowledge can be very efficient, but it possesses no understanding and therefore has no ability to explain its reasoning. It will also fail dismally when confronted with a problem that lies beyond its expertise. The use of deep knowledge can alleviate these limitations, but the knowledge base will be much larger and less efficient. There is therefore a trade-off between the two approaches.

IDM [10] is a system that attempts to integrate deep and shallow knowledge. Knowledge is partitioned into deep and shallow knowledge bases, either one of which is in control at any one time. The controlling knowledge base decides which data to gather, either directly or through dialogue with the user. However, the other knowledge base remains active and is still able to make deductions. For instance, if the shallow knowledge base is in control and has determined that the light comes on when the refrigerator door is opened (as it should), the deep knowledge base can be used to deduce that the power supply is working, that the fuses are OK, that wires from power supply to bulb are OK, and that the bulb is OK. All of this knowledge then becomes available to both knowledge bases.

In IDM, the shallow knowledge base is given control first, and it passes control to the deep knowledge base if it fails to find a solution. The rationale for this is that a quick solution is worth trying first. The shallow knowledge base can be much more efficient at obtaining a solution, but it is more limited in the range of problems that it can handle. If it fails, the information that has been gathered is still of use to the deep knowledge base.

A shallow knowledge base in IDM can be expanded through experience in two ways:

i   each solved case can be stored, and used to assist in solving similar cases - this is the basis of case-based reasoning (section 7.4);

ii   if a common pattern between symptom and conclusions has emerged over a large number of cases, then a new shallow rule can be created - this is an example of rule induction (section 6.2).

7.4 Case-based reasoning

The design of knowledge-based systems is often inspired by attempts to emulate the characteristics of human intelligence. One such characteristic is the ability to recall previous experience whenever a similar problem arises. This is the essence of case-based reasoning. Let us return to our example of a faulty refrigerator. If an expert system has made a successful diagnosis of the fault, given a set of symptoms, it may file away this information for future use. If the system later faces a faulty refrigerator which displays exactly the same symptoms in exactly the same circumstances, then the diagnosis can be completed simply by recalling the previous solution. However, a full description of the symptoms and the environment would be very detailed, and the chances of it ever being exactly reproduced are remote. What we need is the ability to identify a previous case whose solution can be modified to reflect the slightly altered circumstances. Thus case-based reasoning involves two difficult problems:

- determining which cases constitute a similar problem to the current one; and
- adapting a case to the current circumstances.

7.4.1 Classifying case histories
An effective way of representing the relevance of cases is by storing the cases as objects. Riesbeck and Schank [11] have defined a number of types of links between classes and instances in order to assist in locating relevant cases. These links are described below and examples of their use are shown in figure 7.3a and 7.3b.

Instance-of links
Each case is an instance of a specific class of cases (see chapter 5 for a discussion of object classes and instances). Thus each case has an *instance-of* relation with its parent class.

Abstraction links and index links
The classes may form a structured hierarchy, in which the different levels correspond to the level of detail of the description. Links between classes and their specializations are called abstraction links. Riesbeck and Schank [11] distinguish abstraction links from index links. An index link is a subclass / superclass relation, where the subclass has an attribute value that is different from the default defined in its superclass. For instance, the class `refrigerator fault` might have an index link to the class `electrical fault`, where the default appliance type might be a vacuum cleaner.

Suppose that we wish to save an instance of fixing a refrigerator, where the refrigerator exhibited the following symptoms:
- failed to chill food;
- made no noise; and
- the light would not come on.

This case might be stored as an instance of the class `refrigerator faults`, which, as already noted, has an index link to the class `electrical faults`.

Scene links
These are used to link an historical event to its subevents. For example, removing the outer casing of the compressor is a subevent of the "changing

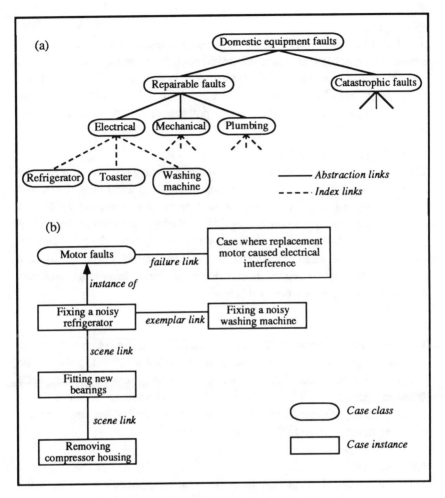

Figure 7.3 Classifying case histories:
(a) abstraction links and index links between classes;
(b) links between instances.

compressor bearings" event. Both the event and subevent are stored as case instances, with a scene link between them.

Exemplar links
These are used to link instances to other similar instances. Suppose that a refrigerator motor fault was diagnosed by referring to a previous case involving a failed washing machine motor. This new case could have an exemplar link to the case from which it was adapted.

Failure links
A failure link is a special type of class-instance relation, where the instance represents a specific case where things did not turn out as expected. This is a convenient way of storing cases that form exceptions to their general category. For example, the class `motor faults` might have a failure link to a case in which a replacement motor created a new problem, such as radio interference.

7.4.2 Adapting case histories
There are two distinct categories of techniques for adapting a case history to suit a new situation, namely structural and derivational adaptation. Structural adaptation describes techniques which use a previous solution as a guide, and adapt it to the new circumstances. Derivational adaptation involves looking at the *way* in which the previous solution was derived, rather than the solution itself. The same reasoning processes are then applied to the set of data describing the new circumstances. Four structural techniques and one derivational technique are outlined below:

Null adaptation
This is the simplest approach and, as the name implies, involves no adaptation at all of the previous solution. Instead, the previous solution is given as the solution to the new case. Suppose that the case history selector decides that a failed refrigerator is similar to the case of a failed washing machine. If the washing machine failure was found to be due to a severed power lead, then this is offered as the solution to the refrigerator problem.

Parameterization
This is a structural adaptation technique that is applicable when both the symptoms and the solution have an associated magnitude or extent. The previous solution can then be scaled up or down in accordance with the severity of the symptoms. Suppose, for example, that a case history was as follows:

symptom: fridge cabinet temperature is 15°C, which is too warm;
solution: reduce thermostat setting by 11°C.

If our new scenario involves a fridge whose cabinet temperature is 10°C, which is still warmer than it should be, the new solution would be to turn down the thermostat, but by a modified amount (say 6°C).

Reasoning by analogy
This is another structural adaptation technique. If a case history cannot be

found in the most appropriate class, then analogous case histories are considered. Given a hierarchically organized database of case histories, the search for analogous cases is relatively straightforward. The search begins by looking at siblings, and then cousins, in a class hierarchy like the one shown in figure 7.3a. Some parts of the historical solution may not applicable, as the solution belongs to a different class. Under such circumstances, the inapplicable parts are replaced by referring back to the class of the current problem.

As an example, consider a refrigerator that is found to be excessively noisy. There may not be a case in the database that refers to noisy refrigerators, but there may be a case that describes a noisy washing machine. The solution in that case may have been that the bearings on the washer's drum were worn and needed replacing. This solution is not directly applicable to the refrigerator, as a refrigerator does not have a drum. However, the refrigerator has bearings on the compressor, and so it is concluded that the compressor bearings are worn and are in need of replacement.

Critics
The use of critics has stemmed from work on a planning system called HACKER [12], which can rearrange its planned actions if they are found to be incorrectly ordered (see section 9.6.1). The ideas are also applicable to other problems, including diagnosis. Critics are modules which can look at a nearly correct solution and determine what flaws it has, if any, and suggest modifications. In the planning domain, critics would look for unnecessary actions, or actions that make subsequent actions more difficult. Adapting these ideas to diagnosis, critics can be used to "fine-tune" a previous solution so that it fits the current circumstances. For instance, a case-based reasoner might diagnose that the compressor bearings in a refrigerator need replacing. Critics might notice that most compressors have two sets of bearings, and that in a particular refrigerator one set is fairly new. The modified solution would then be to replace only the oldest set of bearings.

Reinstantiation
The above adaptation techniques are all structural, that is they modify a previous solution. Reinstantiation is a derivational technique, because it involves replaying the derivation of the previous solution using the new data. Previously used names, numbers, structures and components are reinstantiated to the corresponding new ones. Suppose that a case history concerning a central heating system contained the following abduction to explain why a room felt cold:

```
IF thermostat is set too low
THEN boiler will not switch on

IF boiler is not switched on
THEN radiators stay at ambient temperature

IF radiators are at ambient temperature
THEN room will not warm up.

<Abductive conclusion: thermostat is set too low>
```

By suitable reinstantiation, this case history can be adapted to diagnose why food in a refrigerator is not chilled:

```
IF thermostat is set too high
THEN compressor will not switch on

IF compressor is not switched on
THEN cabinet stays at ambient temperature

IF cabinet is at ambient temperature
THEN food will not be chilled.

<Abductive conclusion: thermostat is set too high>
```

7.4.3   Dealing with mistaken conclusions

Suppose that a system has diagnosed that a particular component is faulty, and that this has caused the failure of an electronic circuit. If it is then discovered that there was in fact nothing wrong with the component after all, or that replacing it made no difference, then the diagnosis needs *repair*. Repair is conceptually very similar to adaptation, and similar techniques can be applied so as to modify the incorrect diagnosis to reach a correct one. If this fails, then a completely new solution must be sought. In either case, it is important that the failed diagnosis be recorded in the database of case histories with a link to the correct diagnosis. If the case is subsequently retrieved in a new scenario, the system will be aware of a possible failure and of a possible way around that failure.

7.5   Model-based reasoning

7.5.1   The limitations of rules

The amount of knowledge about a device that can be represented in rules alone is somewhat limited. A deep understanding of how a device works (and hence what can go wrong with it) is facilitated by a physical model of the device being examined. Fulton and Pepe [13] have highlighted three major inadequacies of a purely rule-based diagnostic system:

i Building a complete rule set is a massive task. For every possible failure, the rule-writer must predict a complete set of symptoms. In many cases this information may not even be available, because the failure may never have happened before. It may be possible to overcome the latter hurdle by deliberately causing a fault and observing the sensors. However, this is inappropriate in some circumstances, such as an overheated core in a nuclear power station.

ii Symptoms are often in the form of sensor readings, and a large number of rules are needed solely to verify the sensor data [14]. Before an alarm signal can be believed at face value, related sensors must be checked to see whether they are consistent with the alarm. Without this measure, there is no reason to assume that a physical failure has occurred rather than a sensor failure.

iii Even supposing that a complete rule set could be built, it would rapidly become obsolete. As there is frequently an interdependence between rules, updating the rule base may require more thought than simply adding new rules.

These difficulties can be circumvented by means of a model of the physical system. Rather than storing a huge collection of symptom-cause pairs in the form of rules, these pairs can be *generated* by applying physical principles to the model.

7.5.2 Modeling function, structure and state
Practically all physical devices are made up of fundamental components such as tubes, wires, batteries and valves. As each of these performs a fairly simple role, it also has a simple failure mode. For example, a wire may break and fail to conduct electricity, a tube can spring a leak, a battery can lose its charge and a valve may be blocked. Given a model of how these components operate and interact to form a device, faults can be diagnosed by determining the effects of local malfunctions on the global view (i.e., on the overall device). Reasoning through consideration of the behavior of the components is sometimes termed reasoning from *second principles*. "First principles" are the basic laws of physics which determine component behavior.

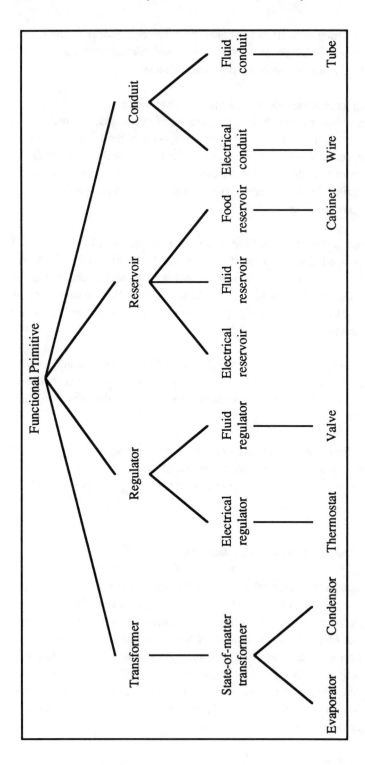

Figure 7.4 Functional hierarchy for some components of a refrigerator.

Numerous different techniques and representations have been devised for modeling physical devices. Examples include the Integrated Diagnostic Model (IDM) [10]; Knowledge Engineer's Assistant (KEATS) [15]; DEDALE [16]; and FLAME [17]. All of these representations are object-oriented (see chapter 5). The device is made up of a number of components, each of which is represented as an instance of a class of component. The *function* of each component is defined within its class definition. The *structure* of a device is defined by links between the instances of components that make up the device. The device may be in one of several *states*, for example a refrigerator door may be open or closed, and the thermostat may have switched the compressor on or off. These states are defined by setting the values of instance variables.

Object-oriented programming is particularly suited to device modeling because of this clear separation of function, structure and state. These three aspects of a device are fundamental to understanding its operation and possible malfunctions. A contrast can be drawn with mathematical modeling, where a device can often be modeled more easily by considering its overall activity than by analyzing the component processes.

Function

The function of a component is defined by the methods and attributes of its class. Fink and Lusth [10] define four functional primitives, which are classes of components. All components are considered to be specializations of one of these four classes, although Fink and Lusth hint at the possible need to add further functional primitives in some applications. The four functional primitives are:

- *transformer* - transforms one substance into another;
- *regulator* - alters the output of substance B, based upon changes in the input of substance A;
- *reservoir* - stores a substance for later output; and
- *conduit* - transports substances between other functional primitives.

A fifth class, *sensor*, may be added to this list. A sensor object simply displays the value of its input.

It should be noted that the word "substance" is intended to be interpreted loosely. Thus water or electricity would both be treated as substances. The scheme was not intended to be completely general purpose, and Fink and Lusth acknowledge that it would need modifications in different domains. However, such modifications may be impractical in many domains, where specialized modeling may be more appropriate. As an illustration of the kind of modification required, Fink and Lusth point out that the behavior of an electrical conduit (a wire) is very different from a water conduit (a pipe), since a break in a wire will stop the flow of electricity, while a broken pipe will cause an out-gush of water. These differences can be recognized by making pipes and wires specializations of the class conduit in an object-oriented representation. The pipe class requires that a substance be pushed through the conduit, whereas the wire class requires that a substance (i.e., electricity) be both pushed and pulled through the conduit. Gas pipes and water pipes would then be two of many possible specializations of the class pipe. Figure 7.4 shows a functional hierarchy of classes for some of the components of a refrigerator.

Structure
Links between component instances can be used to represent their physical associations, thereby defining the structure of a device. For example, two resistors connected in series might be represented as two instances of the class resistor and one instance of the class wire. Each instance of resistor would have a link to the instance of wire, to represent the electrical contact between them.

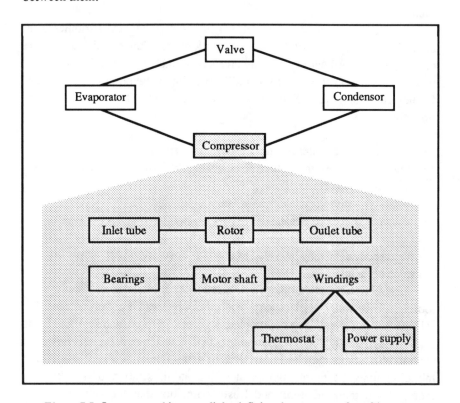

Figure 7.5 Instances and instance links defining the structure of a refrigerator.

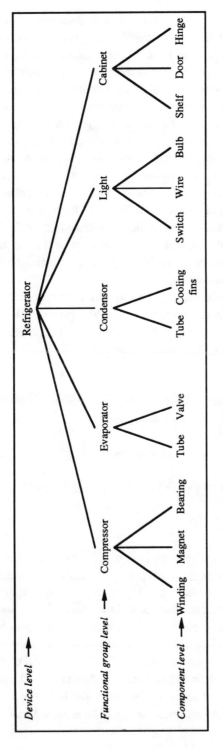

Figure 7.6 Structural hierarchy for some components of a refrigerator.

Figure 7.5 shows the instances and links that define some of the structure of a refrigerator. This figure illustrates that a compressor can either be regarded as a device made up from several components, or it can be regarded as a component of a refrigerator. It is therefore an example of a *functional group*. The compressor forms a distinct module in the physical system. However, functional groups in general need not be modular in the physical sense. Thus the evaporation section of the refrigerator may be regarded as a functional group even though it is not physically separate from the condensation section, and the light system forms a functional group even though the switch is physically removed from the bulb.

Many device-modeling systems can produce a graphical display of the structural layout of a device (similar to figure 7.5), given a definition of the instances and the links between them. Some systems (e.g., KEATS and IDM) allow the reverse process as well. With these systems, the user draws a structural diagram like figure 7.5 on the computer screen, and the instances and links are generated automatically.

In devices where functional groups exist, the device structure is hierarchical. The hierarchical relationship can be represented by means of the assembly relationship between objects (see section 5.9). It is often adequate to consider just three levels of the structural hierarchy:

Figure 7.6 illustrates the application of a three-level hierarchy to the structure of a refrigerator.

State

As already noted, a device may be in one of many alternative states. For example, a refrigerator door may be open or closed, and the compressor may be running or stopped. A state can be represented by setting appropriate instance variables on the components or functional groups, and transitions between states can be represented on a state map [18] as shown in figures 7.7 and 7.8.

The state of some components and functional groups will be dependent on other functional groups or on external factors. Let us consider a refrigerator that is working correctly. The compressor will only be in the state *running* if the thermostat is in the state *closed circuit*. The state of the thermostat will

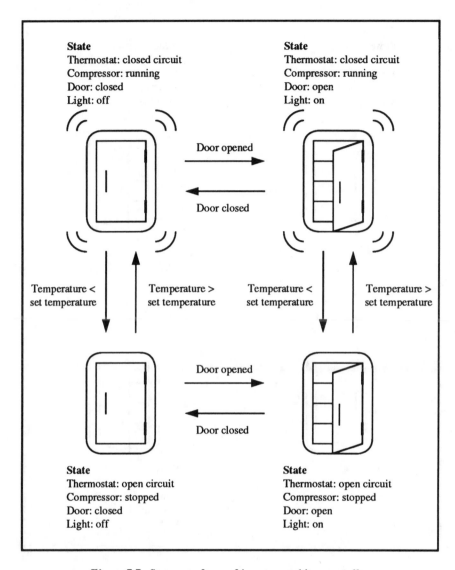

State
Thermostat: closed circuit
Compressor: running
Door: closed
Light: off

State
Thermostat: closed circuit
Compressor: running
Door: open
Light: on

Door opened

Door closed

Temperature <
set temperature

Temperature >
set temperature

Temperature <
set temperature

Temperature >
set temperature

Door opened

Door closed

State
Thermostat: open circuit
Compressor: stopped
Door: closed
Light: off

State
Thermostat: open circuit
Compressor: stopped
Door: open
Light: on

Figure 7.7 State map for a refrigerator working normally.

alter according to the cabinet temperature. The cabinet temperature is partially dependent on an external factor, namely the room temperature, particularly if the door to the refrigerator is open.

The thermostat behavior can be modeled by making the attribute temperature of the cabinet object an active value (see section 5.10.4). The thermostat object is updated every time that the registered temperature alters by more than some amount (say 0.5°C). A method attached to the thermostat would toggle its state between *open circuit* and *closed circuit* depending on a

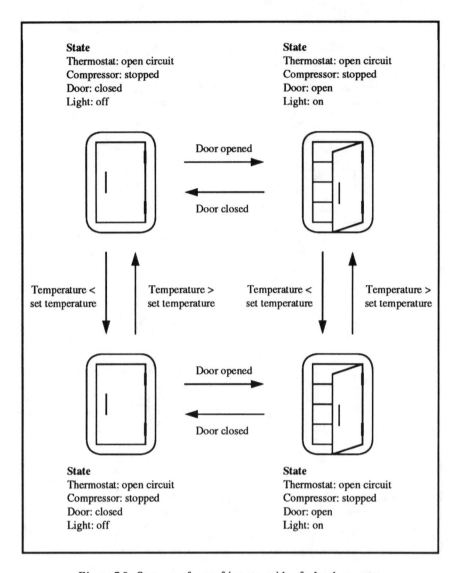

Figure 7.8   State map for a refrigerator with a faulty thermostat.

comparison between the registered temperature and the set temperature. If the thermostat changes its state, it would send a message to the compressor, which in turn would change its state.

A map of possible states can be drawn up, with links indicating the ways in which one state can be changed into another. A simple state map for a correctly functioning refrigerator is shown in figure 7.7. A faulty refrigerator will have a different state map. Figure 7.8 shows the case of a thermostat that is stuck in the "open circuit" position.

Price and Hunt [19] have modeled various mechanical devices using object-oriented programming techniques. They created an instance of the class device_state for every state of a given device. In their system, each device_state instance is made up of instance variables (recording, for example, external factors like temperature) and links to components and functional groups that make up the device. This is sufficient information to completely restore a state. Price and Hunt found advantages in the ability to treat a device state as an object in its own right. In particular, the process of manipulating a state was simplified and kept separate from the other objects in the system. They were thus able to construct state maps like that shown in figure 7.7 and 7.8, where each state was an instance of device_state. Instance links were used to represent transitions (such as opening the door) which could take one state to another.

7.5.3 Using the model

The details of how a model can assist the diagnostic task vary according to the specific device and the method of modeling it. In general, three potential uses can be identified:

- monitoring the device to check for malfunctions;
- finding a suspect component, thereby forming a tentative diagnosis; and
- confirming or refuting the tentative diagnosis by simulation.

The diagnostic task is to determine which nonstandard component behavior in the model could make the output values of the model match those of the physical system. An overall strategy is shown in figure 7.9. A modification of this strategy is to place a weighting on the forward links between evidence and hypotheses. As more evidence is gathered, the weightings can be updated using the techniques described in chapter 4 for handling uncertainty. The hypothesis with the highest weighting is tried first, and if it fails the next highest is considered, and so on. The weighting may be based solely on perceived likelihood, or it may include factors like the cost or difficulty of fixing the fault. It is often worth trying a quick and cheap repair before resorting to a more expensive solution.

When a malfunction has been detected, the *single point of failure* assumption is often made. This is the assumption that the malfunction has only one root cause. Such an approach is justified by Fulton and Pepe [13] on the basis that no two failures are truly simultaneous. They argue that one failure will always follow the other either independently or as a direct knock-on.

A model can assist a diagnostic system that is confronted with a problem that lies outside its expertise. Since the function of a component is contained

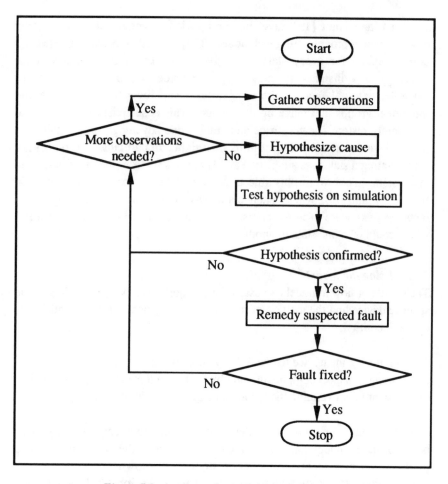

Figure 7.9 A strategy for model-based diagnosis.

within the class definition, its behavior in novel circumstances may be predicted. If details of a specific type of component are lacking, comparisons can be drawn with sibling components in the class hierarchy.

7.5.4 Monitoring

A model can be used to simulate the behavior of a device. The output (e.g., data, a substance, or a signal) from one component forms the input to another component. If we alter one input to a component, the corresponding output may change, which may alter another input and so on, resulting in a new set of sensor readings being recorded. Comparison with real world sensors provides a monitoring facility.

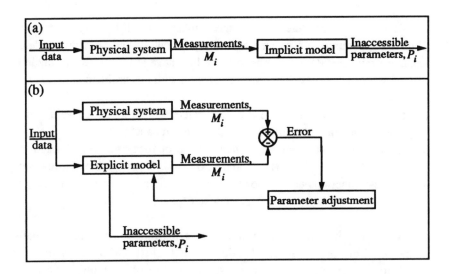

Figure 7.10 Monitoring inaccessible parameters by process modeling,
(a) using an implicit model; (b) using an explicit model; (adapted from [9]).

The RESCU system [9] uses model-based reasoning for monitoring
inaccessible plant parameters. In a chemical plant, for instance, a critical
parameter to monitor might be the temperature within the reaction chamber.
However, it may not be possible to measure the temperature directly, as no
type of thermometer would be able to survive the highly corrosive
environment. Therefore the temperature has to be inferred from temperature
measurements at the chamber walls, and from gas pressure and flow
measurements.

Rules or algorithms that can translate the available measurements (M_i) into
the inaccessible parameters (P_i) are described by Leitch et al. [9] as an *implicit
model* (figure 7.10a). Obtaining a reliable implicit model is often difficult, and
model-based reasoning normally refers to the use of *explicit models* like those
described in section 7.5.2. The real system and the explicit model are operated
in parallel, the model generating values for both the available measurements
(M_i) and the inaccessible parameters (P_i). The model parameters (possibly
including the parameters P_i) are adjusted in order to minimize the difference
between the values of M_i generated by the model and the real system. This
difference is called the *error*. By modifying the model in response to the error
we have provided a feedback mechanism (figure 7.10b), discussed further in
section 10.2.3. This mechanism ensures that the model accurately mimics the
behavior of the physical system. If a critical parameter P_i in the model
deviates from its expected value, it is assumed that the same has occurred in
the physical system and an alarm is triggered.

Analogue devices (electrical or mechanical) can fail by varying degrees. Thus when comparing a parameter in the physical system with the modeled value, we must decide how far apart the values have to be before we conclude that a discrepancy exists. Two ways of dealing with this problem are:

i to apply a tolerance to the expected value, so that an actual value lying beyond the tolerance limit is treated as a discrepancy; or

ii to give the value a degree of membership of fuzzy sets (e.g. "much too high", "too high", "just right", and "too low"). The degree of membership of these functions determines the extent of the response needed. This is the essence of fuzzy control (section 10.6).

It is sometimes possible to anticipate a malfunction before it actually happens. This is the approach adopted in EXPRES [20], a system for anticipating faults in the customer distribution part of a telephone network. The network is routinely subjected to electrical tests which measure characteristics such as resistance, capacitance and inductance between particular points. A failed circuit would show up as a very high resistance. Failures can be anticipated and avoided by monitoring changes in the electrical characteristics with reference to the fault histories of the specific components under test and of similar components.

7.5.5 Tentative diagnosis

The strategy for diagnosis shown in figure 7.9 requires the generation of a hypothesis, i.e., a tentative diagnosis. The method of forming a tentative diagnosis depends on the nature of the available data. In some circumstances a complete set of symptoms and sensor measurements is immediately available, and the problem is one of interpreting them. More commonly in diagnosis, a few symptoms are immediately known and additional measurements must be taken as part of the diagnostic process. The tentative diagnosis is a best guess, or hypothesis, of the actual cause of the observed symptoms. We will now consider three ways of generating a tentative diagnosis.

The shotgun approach

Fulton and Pepe [13] advocate collecting a list of all objects that are upstream of the unexpected sensor reading. All of these objects are initially under suspicion. If several sensors have recorded unexpected measurements, only one need be considered as it is assumed that there is only one cause of the problem. The process initially involves diagnosis at the functional grouping level. Having identified the faulty functional group, it may be sufficient to stop the diagnosis and simply replace the functional group in the real system.

Alternatively the process may be repeated by examining individual components within the failed functional group to locate the failed component.

Structural isolation

KEATS [15] has been used for diagnosing faults in analogue electronic circuits, and makes use of the *binary chop* or *structural isolation* strategy of Milne [21]. Initially the electrical signal is sampled in the middle of the signal chain and compared with the value predicted by the model. If the two values correspond, then the fault must be downstream of the sampling point, and a measurement is then taken half-way downstream. Conversely, if there is a discrepancy between the expected and actual values, the measurement is taken half-way upstream. This process is repeated until the defective functional grouping has been isolated. If the circuit layout permits, the process can be repeated within the functional grouping in order to isolate a specific component. Motta et al. [15] found in their experiments that the structural isolation strategy closely resembles the approach that is adopted by human experts. They have also pointed out that the technique can be made more sophisticated by modifying the "examine midpoint" rule to reflect heuristics concerning the most likely location of the fault.

The heuristic approach

Either of the above two strategies can be refined by the application of shallow (heuristic) knowledge. As noted in section 7.3.3, IDM [10] has two knowledge bases, containing deep and shallow knowledge. If the shallow knowledge base has failed to find a quick solution, the deep knowledge base seeks a tentative solution using a set of five guiding heuristics:

i   if an output from a functional unit is unknown, find out its value by testing or by interaction with a human operator;

ii   if an output from a functional unit appears incorrect, check its input;

iii   if an input to a functional unit appears incorrect, check the source of the input;

iv   if the input to a functional unit appears correct but the output is not, assume that the functional unit is faulty; and

v   examine components that are *nodes* before those that are *conduits*, as the former are more likely to fail in service.

7.5.6 Fault simulation

Both the correct and the malfunctioning behavior of a device can be simulated using a model. The correct behavior is simulated during the monitoring of a device (section 7.5.4). Simulation of a malfunction is used to confirm or refute a tentative diagnosis. A model allows the effects of changes in a device or in its input data to be tested. Thus a diagnosis can be tested by changing the behavior of the suspected component within the model and checking that the model produces the symptoms that are observed in the real system. Such tests cannot be conclusive, as other faults might also be capable of producing the same symptoms, as noted in section 7.2. Suppose that a real refrigerator is not working, and makes no noise. If the thermostat on the refrigerator is suspected of being permanently open-circuit, this malfunction can be incorporated into the model and the effects noted. The model would show the same symptoms that are observed in the real system. The hypothesis is then confirmed as the most likely diagnosis.

Most device simulations proceed in a step-by-step manner, where the output of one component (component A) becomes the input of another (component B). Component A can be thought of as being "upstream" of component B. An input is initially supplied to the components that are furthest upstream. For instance, the thermostat is given a cabinet temperature, and the power cord is given (simulated) mains electricity. These components produce outputs, which become the inputs to other components, and so on. This sort of simulation can run into difficulties if the model includes a feedback loop. In these circumstances, a defective component not only produces an unexpected output, but also has an unexpected input. The output can only be predicted if the input is known, and the input can only be predicted if the output is known. One approach to this problem is to supply initially all of the components with their correct input values. If the defective behavior of the feedback component is modeled, its output and input values would be expected to converge on a failure value after a number of iterations. Fink and Lusth [10] found that convergence was achieved in all of their tests, but they acknowledge that there might be cases where this does not happen.

7.5.7 Fault repair

Once a fault has been diagnosed, the next step is normally to fix the fault. Most fault diagnosis systems offer some advice on how a fault should be fixed. In many cases this recommendation is trivial, given the diagnosis. For example the diagnosis "worn bearings" might be accompanied by the recommendation "replace worn bearings", while the diagnosis "leaking pipe" might lead to the recommendation "fix leak". A successful repair provides definite confirmation of a diagnosis. If a repair fails to cure a problem, then the diagnostic process must commence again. A failed repair may not mean that a diagnosis was incorrect. It is possible that the fault which has now been fixed had caused a second fault which also needs to be diagnosed and repaired.

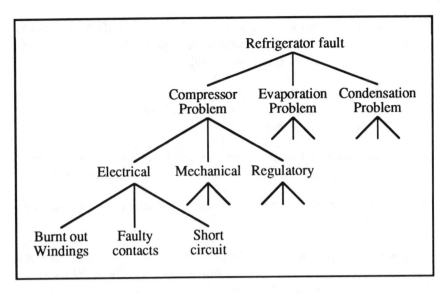

Figure 7.11   A problem tree for a refrigerator.

7.5.8 Using problem trees

Some researchers [3, 22] favour the explicit modeling of faults, rather than inferring faults from a model of the physical system. Dash [3] builds a hierarchical tree of possible faults (a problem tree - figure 7.11), similar to those used for classifying case histories (figure 7.3a). Unlike case-based reasoning, problem trees cover all anticipated faults, whether or not they have occurred previously. By applying deep or shallow rules to the observed symptoms, progress can be made from the root (a general problem description) to the leaves of the tree (a specific diagnosis). The tree is therefore used as a means of steering the search for a diagnosis. An advantage of this approach is that a partial solution is formed at each stage in the reasoning process. Thus a partial solution is generated even if there is insufficient knowledge or data to produce a complete diagnosis.

7.5.9 Summary of model-based reasoning

Some of the advantages of model-based reasoning are listed below.

- A model is less cumbersome to maintain than a rule-base. Real-world changes are easily reflected in changes in the model.

- The model need not waste effort looking for sensor verification. Sensors are treated identically to other components, and therefore a faulty sensor is as likely to be detected as any other fault.

- Unusual failures are just as easy to diagnose as common ones. This is not the case in a rule-based system, which is likely to be most comprehensive in the case of common faults.

- The separation of function, structure and state may help a diagnostic system to reason about a problem that is outside of its area of expertise.

- The model can simulate a physical system, for the purpose of monitoring or for verifying a hypothesis.

Model-based reasoning only works well in situations where there is a complete and accurate model. It is therefore inappropriate for physical systems that are too complex to model properly, such as medical diagnosis or weather forecasting.

An ideal would be to build a model for monitoring and diagnosis directly from CAD data generated during the design stage. The model would then be available as soon as a device entered service.

7.6 Case-study: a blackboard system for interpreting ultrasonic images

One of the aims of this book is to demonstrate that there is a wide variety of computing techniques (both knowledge-based and conventional) that can be applied to particular problems. The more complicated problems have many facets, where each facet may be best suited to a different technique. This is so for the interpretation of ultrasonic images, which will be discussed as a case study in the remainder of this chapter. A *blackboard system*, described below, has been used to tackle this complex interpretation problem. Blackboard systems allow a problem to be divided into subtasks, each of which can be tackled using the most suitable technique.

An image interpretation system attempts to understand the processed image and hence to describe the world represented by it. This requires symbolic reasoning (using rules, objects, relationships, list-processing or other techniques) as well as signal processing [23]. ARBS (Algorithmic and Rule-based Blackboard System) is a system that has been designed to incorporate both processes. Numerically intensive signal processing, which may involve a large amount of raw data, is performed by conventional routines. Facts, causal

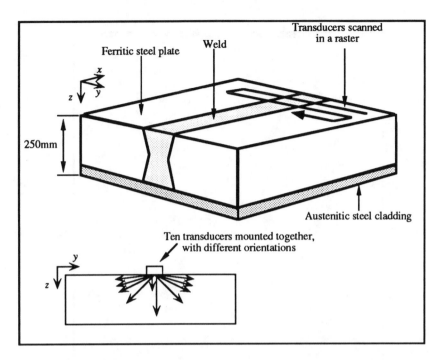

Figure 7.12 Gathering ultrasonic b-scan images (adapted from [8]).

relationships and strategic knowledge are symbolically encoded in one or more knowledge bases. This explicit representation allows encoded domain knowledge to be modified or extended easily. Signal processing routines are used to transform the raw data into a description of its key features (i.e., into a symbolic image) and knowledge-based techniques are used to interpret this image.

The architecture allows signal interpretation to proceed under the control of knowledge in such a way that, at any one time, only the subset of the data which might contribute to a solution is considered. When a particular set of rules needs access to a chunk of raw data, it can have it. No attempt has been made to write rules that look at the whole of the raw data, as the preprocessing stage avoids the need for this. Unlike many diagnostic systems, ARBS does not interact with a human when running, but produces a log of its actions and decisions.

7.6.1 Ultrasonic imaging
Ultrasonic imaging is widely used for the detection and characterization of features, particularly defects, in manufactured components. The technique belongs to a family of nondestructive testing methods, which are distinguished

Figure 7.13 A typical b-scan image.

by the ability to examine components without causing any damage. Various arrangements can be used for producing ultrasonic images. Typically a transmitter and receiver of ultrasound (i.e., high frequency sound at approximately 1-10MHz), are situated within a single probe which makes contact with the surface of the component. The probe emits a short pulse of ultrasound and then detects waves returning as a result of interactions with the features within the specimen. If the detected waves are assumed to have been produced by single reflections, then the time of arrival can be readily converted to the depth *(z)* of these features. By moving the probe in one dimension *(y)*, an image can be plotted of *y* versus *z*, with intensity represented by color or gray scale. This image is called a b-scan, and it approximates to a cross section through a component. It is common to perform such scans with several probes pointing at different angles into the specimen, and to collect several b-scans by moving the probes in a raster (figure 7.12).

A typical b-scan image is shown in figure 7.13. A threshold has been applied, so that only received signals of intensity greater than -30 db are displayed, and these appear as dots on the image. Ten probes were used, pointing into the specimen at five different angles. Because ultrasonic beams are not collimated, a point defect is detected over a range of y values, giving rise to a characteristic arc on the b-scan image. Arcs produced by a single probe generally lie parallel to each other, and normal to the probe direction. The point of intersection of arcs produced by different probes is a good estimate of the location of the defect that caused them.

The problems of interpreting a b-scan are different from those of other forms of image interpretation. The key reason for this is that a b-scan is not a direct representation of the inside of a component, but rather it represents a set of wave interactions (reflection, refraction, diffraction, interference and mode conversion) which can be used to *infer* some of the internal structure of the component.

7.6.2 Blackboard systems

ARBS is based on a structure, illustrated in figure 7.14, that is described as a *blackboard model* or *blackboard architecture*. Systems having this kind of structure are termed *blackboard systems*. Arguably the first such system was Hearsay-II, for computerized understanding of natural speech [24].

In a blackboard system, knowledge of the application domain is divided into modules, referred to as *knowledge sources* (or KSs), each of which contains knowledge relating to a particular task. KSs are independent and may communicate only by reading from or writing to the *blackboard*, a globally accessible working memory where the current state of understanding is represented. Many systems allow knowledge sources to delete unwanted information from the blackboard as well as adding information.

Knowledge sources can make use of the most appropriate form of knowledge representation and control for their specialization, and their modularity is helpful when making changes. Some knowledge sources may be conventional procedural routines, some may be object-oriented (chapter 5), some may be rule-based (chapter 3), and some may be connectionist (chapter 6). Each rule-based knowledge source can use a suitable reasoning strategy for its particular task (e.g., backward or forward chaining), and can be thought of as a rule-based system in its own right.

A blackboard system is analogous to a team of experts who communicate their ideas via a physical blackboard, by adding or deleting items in response to the information that they find there. Each knowledge source represents such an expert having a specialized area of knowledge. Knowledge sources are applied in response to information on the blackboard, when they have some contribution to make. This leads to increased efficiency since the detailed knowledge within a knowledge source is only applied when that knowledge source becomes relevant.

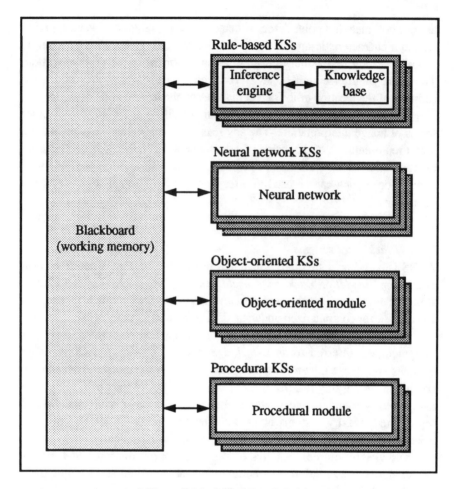

Figure 7.14 A blackboard model.

In the idealized blackboard system, the KSs would be completely *opportunistic*, activating themselves whenever they can contribute to the global solution. This is, however, difficult to achieve in practice. One approach is to use a control module which determines the order of KS activation, on the basis of applicability and past activation records of the KSs. As an extension of this idea, a separate control blackboard might be used, where the system can reason about which control strategy to use, using explicit rule-based knowledge of the different strategies. This level of sophistication may, however, result in a slow response. In ARBS, control of KS activation is contained within the KSs themselves, though separate from any domain knowledge. Each KS contains a set of preconditions stating when that KS should be activated. A separate control module uses a *first come, first served* strategy (see section 3.8.1) for the testing the KS preconditions.

In the interests of efficiency and clarity some degree of structure is usually imposed on the blackboard. Typically the blackboard is divided into various layers corresponding to different levels of analysis of the problem, since problems of interpretation usually involve progress from detailed information to more abstract concepts. For example, in the Hearsay-II speech-understanding system the levels of analysis include that of syllable, word and phrase [24]. In ultrasonic interpretation, progress is made from raw data, via a description of the significant image features, to a description of the defects in the component.

The key advantages of the blackboard architecture, adapted from Feigenbaum [25] can be summarized as follows:

i   Many and varied sources of knowledge can participate in the development of a solution to a problem.

ii   Since each knowledge source has access to the blackboard, each can be applied as soon as it becomes appropriate. This is known as opportunism, i.e., application of the right knowledge at the right time.

iii For many types of problem, especially those involving large amounts of numerical processing, the characteristic style of incremental solution development is particularly efficient.

iv   Different types of reasoning strategy (e.g., data- and goal-driven) can be mixed as appropriate in order to reach a solution.

v   Hypotheses can be posted onto the blackboard for testing by other knowledge sources. A complete test solution does not have to be built before deciding to modify or abandon the underlying hypothesis.

vi   In the event that the system is unable to arrive at a complete solution to a problem, the partial solutions appearing on the blackboard are available and may be of some value.

7.6.3 Knowledge sources in ARBS

Each knowledge source in ARBS is contained in a record. Records are data structures consisting of different data types, and are provided in most modern computer languages. Unlike lists, the format of a record has to be defined before values can be assigned to any of its various parts (or *fields*). The record structure that is used to define an ARBS knowledge source is shown in figure 7.15. There is a set of preconditions, in the preconditions field, which must be satisfied before the KS can be activated. The preconditions are expressed using the same syntax as the rules described in section 7.6.4 below. ARBS has a control module which examines each KS in turn, testing the preconditions

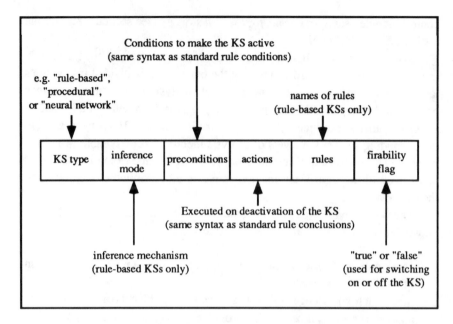

Figure 7.15 A knowledge source in ARBS is stored as a record.

and activating the KS if the preconditions are satisfied. This is the simplest strategy, akin to forward chaining within a rule-based system. More sophisticated strategies can be applied to the selection of knowledge sources, just as more complex inference engines can be applied to rules.

When a KS is activated, it applies its knowledge to the current state of the blackboard, adding to it or modifying it. The entry in the KS type field states whether the KS is procedural, rule-based or contains a neural network. If a KS is rule-based then it is essentially a rule-based system in its own right. The rules field contains the names of the rules to be used and the inference mode field contains the name of the inference engine. When the rules are exhausted, the KS is deactivated and any actions in the actions field of the KS are performed. These actions usually involve reports to the user or the addition of control information to the blackboard. If the KS is procedural or contains a neural network then the required code is simply included in the actions field and the inference mode and rules fields are not used.

ARBS includes provisions for five different types of knowledge source. One is procedural, one is connectionist, and the other three are all rule-based, but with different types of inference mechanism. We have already met two of the inference mechanisms, namely multiple and single instantiation of variables (see section 3.7.1) with a hybrid inference engine (see section 3.10). The third type of rule-based knowledge source is used for generating hypotheses. Such hypotheses can then be tested and thereby supported, confirmed, weakened or refuted. ARBS uses this hypothesize-and-test approach (see section 7.2) to handle the uncertainty that is inherent in problems of abduction, and the uncertainty that arises from sparse or noisy data.

The blackboard architecture is able to bring together the most appropriate tools for handling specific tasks. Procedural tasks are not entirely confined to procedural knowledge sources, since rules within a rule-based knowledge source can access procedural code from either their condition or conclusion parts (see section 7.6.4 below). In the case of ultrasonic image interpretation, we can use procedural KSs (written in C) for fast numerically intensive data-processing, and rule-based KSs to represent specialist knowledge. In addition, neural network KSs may be used for judgmental tasks, involving the weighing of evidence from various sources. Judgmental ability is often difficult to express in rules, and neural networks were incorporated into ARBS as a response to this difficulty. The different types of knowledge source in ARBS are summarized below.

Procedural KS
When activated, a procedural KS simply runs its associated procedure and is then deactivated. An example is the procedure that preprocesses the image, using the Hough Transform to detect lines of indications (or dots).

Rule-based KS with a hybrid inference engine
When activated, this type of KS behaves like a conventional rule based system. A rule's conditions are examined and, if they are satisfied by a statement on the blackboard, then the rule fires and the actions dictated by its conclusion are carried out. Single or multiple instantiation of variables can be selected.

Rule-based hypothesis-generating KS
This KS initiates a "hypothesize-and-test" cycle. The inference engine selects a rule and asserts its conclusion as a hypothesis. Its conditions are now referred to as *expectations* and placed in a list on the blackboard. Other KSs may then be selected to test whether the expectations are confirmed by the image data. The hypothesis-generating rules use a different syntax from other rules as they are are used in a different way. The hypothesize-and-test method reduces the solution search space by focusing attention on those KSs relevant to the current hypothesis.

Neural Network KS
This type of KS is used, for example, in small-scale classification tasks, where domain knowledge is difficult to express in rule form. The use of neural networks is described in more detail in section 7.6.7 below.

```
rule::=          [rule_no condition implies conclusion]

rule_no::=       <constant>

condition::=     [condition and condition],
                 [condition or condition],
                 [present statement partition],
                 [absent statement partition],
                 [run [<procedure_name> [input_parameters]] output_parameter],
                 [compare [operand operator operand] nil]

conclusion::=    [conclusion conclusion conclusion ...]
                 [add statement partition],
                 [remove statement partition],
                 [report statement nil],
                 [run [<procedure_name> [input_parameters]] output_parameter]

partition::=     <list_name>          /* a partition of the blackboard */

statement::=     ~<variable_name>,    /* uses the value of the variable */
                 ?<variable_name>,    /* matches a value to the variable */
                 ~~<list_name>,       /* as ~ but separates the list elements */
                 ??<list_name>,       /* as ? but separates the list elements */
                 <string>,
                 <constant>
                 ~[run [<procedure_name> [input_parameters]] output_parameter],
                 <a list containing any of the above>

operand::=       ~[run [<procedure_name> [input_parameters]] output_parameter],
                 ~<variable_name>,
                 ?<variable_name>,
                 <constant>

operator::=      eq,   /* equal */
                 lt,   /* less than */
                 gt,   /* greater than */
                 le,   /* less than or equal */
                 ge,   /* greater than or equal */
                 ne    /* not equal */
```

Box 7.1 ARBS rule syntax.
For clarity, some details of the syntax have been omitted or altered.
A different syntax is used for hypothesis generation.

7.6.4 Rules in ARBS

Rules are used in ARBS in two contexts:

- to express domain knowledge within a rule-based knowledge source; and
- to express the applicability of a knowledge source.

Just as knowledge sources are activated in response to information on the blackboard, so too are individual rules within a rule-based knowledge source. The main functions of ARBS rules are to look up information on the blackboard, to draw inferences from that information, and to post new information on the blackboard. Rules can access procedural code for performing such tasks as numerical calculations or database lookup.

In this section we will only be concerned with deductive rules, rather than the hypothesis-generating rules described in section 7.6.3 above. The rules are implemented as lists in the Pop-11 language (see section 2.7). Each rule is a list comprising 4 elements: a number to identify the rule, a condition part, the word "implies" and a conclusion part. A rule is therefore defined as follows:

rule :: [number *condition* **implies** *conclusion*].

The double colon (::) means "takes the form of". The word "implies" is shown in bold type as it is recognized as a key word in the ARBS syntax. The words in italics have their own formal syntax description. The condition may comprise subconditions joined with boolean operators AND and OR, while the conclusion can contain several action statements. There is no explicit limit on the number of subconditions or subconclusions that can be combined in this way.

In the syntax description shown in box 7.1, many items have several alternative forms. Where square brackets are shown, these delimit lists. Notice that both *condition* and *conclusion* are defined recursively, thereby allowing any number of subconditions or subconclusions. It can also be seen that where multiple subconditions are used, they are always combined in pairs. This avoids any ambiguity over the order of precedence of the Boolean combinations.

Statements on the blackboard are recognized using the Pop-11 pattern-matching facilities (see section 2.7). Thus the '?' is used to make assignments to variables in rules. The use of '~' symbols is, however, peculiar to ARBS. The '~' symbols serve a similar function to the '^' symbols in the Pop-11 language, i.e., the name of the variable that follows is replaced by its assigned value. However, whereas any variables preceded by '^' are replaced by their value as soon as the rules are loaded, variables preceded by '~' are replaced by their value only when that part of a rule is being evaluated. Blackboard information which has been assigned to variables can thereby be used within a rule.

Rules are interpreted by sending them to a parser, i.e., a piece of software which breaks down a rule into its constituent parts and interprets them. This is achieved by pattern-matching between rules and templates which describe the rule syntax. The ARBS rule parser firstly extracts the condition statement and evaluates it, using recursion if there are embedded subconditions. If a rule is selected for firing and its overall condition is found to be true, all of the conclusion statements are interpreted and carried out.

Atomic conditions (i.e., conditions that contain no subconditions) can be evaluated in any of the following ways:

- test for the presence of information on blackboard, and look up the information if it is present;
- call algorithms or external procedures which return Boolean or numerical results; or
- numerical comparison of variables, constants or algorithm results.

The conclusions, or subconclusions, can comprise any of the following:

- add or remove information to or from the blackboard;
- call an algorithm or external procedure, and optionally add the results to the blackboard; or
- report actions to the operator.

In ARBS, the blackboard, like the rules, is made up from lists. The retrieval of information from the blackboard by pattern-matching is best demonstrated by considering a rule:

```
[7.12   ;;; the rule number
  [
    [present [the size of ?rect is ?size] line_info]
    and
    [compare [~size ge 200] nil]
  ]
  implies
  [
    [add [the rectangle ~rect covers a LARGE AREA] line_info]
    [add [FEATURE ~rect | PROPERTY AreaSize | DEGREE large]
        property_info]
    [report [the rectangle ~rect covers a LARGE AREA] nil]
    [run [show_area [~rect]] nil]
  ]
]
```

This rule examines the partition of the blackboard called `line_info`. Like all the blackboard partitions, `line_info` is a list. Supposing that `line_info` contains the sublist:

```
[the size of rectangle_B is 243],
```

then the first condition of the rule is true, and the local variables `rect` and `size` would become bound to `rectangle_B` and `243` respectively. This simple subcondition has thus checked for the presence of information on the blackboard and retrieved information. The second subcondition checks to see whether the value of `size` is ≥200. Notice the use of the '~' symbol, which instructs the ARBS parser to replace the word `size` with its current value. As both subconditions are true, the actions described in the conclusions part of the rule are carried out. The first two conclusions involve adding information to the blackboard. The other two conclusions are for the purposes of logging the system's actions. A message reporting the deduction that `rectangle_B` covers a large area is sent to the user, and the rectangle is displayed on the processed image.

Procedures can be directly accessed from within the condition or conclusion parts of any rules. This is achieved by use of the ARBS key word `run`. The rule parser knows that the word immediately following `run` is the procedure name, and that its parameters, if any, are in the accompanying list. The following subconclusion is taken form a KS in the ultrasonic interpretation system:

```
[add [~[run [group_intersections [~coord_list]] result]
       are the GROUPS of points of intersection] line_info]
```

When the rule is fired, the function `group_intersections` is called with the value of `coord_list` as its parameter. The value returned is added to the blackboard as part of the sentence:

```
... are the GROUPS of points of intersection].
```

The syntax shown in box 7.1 has evolved to meet the requirements of the ultrasonic interpretation problem, and could be extended further if necessary.

7.6.5 Inference engines in ARBS
The strategy for applying rules is a key decision in the design of a system. In many types of rule-based system, this decision is irrevocable, committing the rule-writer to either a forward or backward chaining system. However, the blackboard architecture allows much greater flexibility, as each rule-based

knowledge source can use whichever inference mechanism is most appropriate. ARBS makes use of the hybrid inference mechanism described in section 3.10, which it can use with either single or multiple instantiation of variables (see section 3.7.1).

The hybrid mechanism requires the construction of a network representing the dependencies between the rules. A separate dependence network is built for each rule-based knowledge source by a specialized ARBS module, prior to running the system. The networks are saved and only need to be regenerated if the rules are altered. The code to generate the networks is simplified by the fact that the only interaction between rules is via the blackboard. For rule A to enable rule B to fire, rule A must either add something to the blackboard that rule B needs to find, or remove something that rule B requires to be absent. When a rule-based knowledge source is activated, the rules within the knowledge source are selected for examination in the order dictated by the dependence network.

Several rules in the ultrasonic interpretation rule base need to be fired for each occurrence of a particular feature in the image. As an example, rule 7.12 is used to look at rectangular areas that have been identified as areas of interest on an image, and to pick out those that cover a large area. The condition clause is:

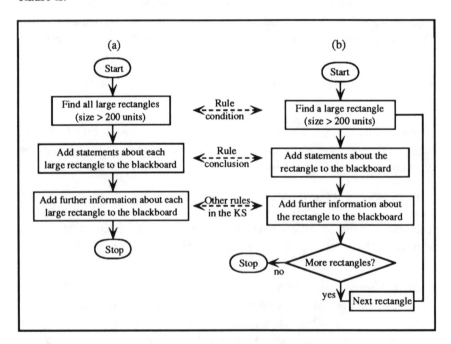

Figure 7.16   Firing rule 7.12 using:
(a) multiple instantiation of variables; and (b) single instantiation of variables.

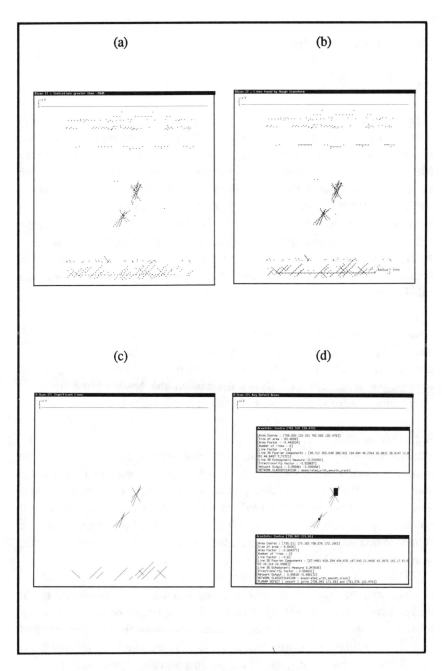

Figure 7.17 The stages of interpretation of a b-scan image:
(a) before interpretation;
(b) with lines found by a Hough transform;
(c) significant lines; and
(d) conclusion - a crack runs between the two marked areas.

```
[
    [present [the size of ?rect is ?size] line_info]
    and
    [compare [~size ge 200] nil]
]
```

A list matching [the size of ?rect is ?size] is sought in the portion of
the blackboard called line_info, and appropriate assignments are made to the
variables rect and size. However, rather than just finding one match to the
list template, we actually require all matches. In other words, we wish to find
all rectangles and check the size of them all. This can be achieved by either
single or multiple instantiation. The resultant order in which the image areas
are processed in shown in figure 7.16. In this example, there is no strong
reason to prefer one strategy over the other, although multiple instantiation in
ARBS is more efficient. In spite of the reduced efficiency, it is shown in
section 10.5.3 that single instantiation may be preferable in problems where a
solution must be found within a limited time frame.

7.6.6 The stages of image interpretation

The problem of ultrasonic image interpretation can be divided into three
distinct stages: arc detection, gathering information about the regions of
intersecting arcs, and classifying defects on the basis of the gathered
information. These stages are now described in more detail.

Arc detection using the Hough Transform

The first step towards defect characterization is to place on the blackboard the
important features of the image. This is achieved by a procedural knowledge
source which fits arcs to the data points (figure 7.17b). In order to produce
these arcs, a Hough transform [26] was used to determine the groupings of
points. The transformation was modified so that isolated points some distance
from the remainder would not be included [7]. The actual positions of the arcs
were determined by least squares fitting.

This preprocessing phase is desirable in order to reduce the sheer volume
of data and to convert it into a form suitable for knowledge-based
interpretation. Thus, knowledge-based processing begins on data concerning
thirty or so linear arcs rather than on data concerning four or five hundred
points. No information is lost permanently. If in the course of its operations
ARBS judges that more data concerning a particular line would help the
interpretation then it retrieves from file the information about the individual
points that comprise that line and represents these point data on the blackboard.
It is natural, moreover, to work with lines rather than points in the initial stages
of interpretation. Arcs of indications are produced by all defect types, and

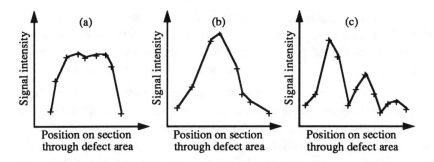

Figure 7.18 Echodynamics across (a) a crack face;
(b) a crack tip, pore, or inclusion;
(c) an area of porosity.

therefore much of the knowledge used to identify flaws is readily couched in terms of the properties of lines and the relations between them.

Gathering the evidence

Once a description of the lines has been recorded on the blackboard, a rule-based KS picks out those lines that are considered significant according to criteria such as intensity, number of points and length. Rules are also used to recognize the back wall echo and lines that are due to probe reverberation. Both are considered "insignificant" for the time being. Key areas in the image are generated by finding points of intersection between significant lines and then grouping them together. Figure 7.17d shows the key areas found by applying this method to the lines shown in figure 7.17c. For large smooth cracks, each of the crack tips is associated with a distinct area. Other defects are entirely contained in their respective areas.

Rule-based KSs are used to gather evidence about each of the key areas. The evidence includes:

- the size of the area;
- the number of arcs passing through it;
- the shape of the echodynamic (defined below);
- the intensity of indications; and
- the sensitivity of the intensity to the angle of the probe.

The *echodynamic* associated with a defect is the profile of the signal intensity along one of the "significant" lines. This is of considerable importance in defect classification as different profiles are associated with different types of defect. In particular, the echodynamics for a smooth crack face, a spheroidal defect (e.g., a single pore or an inclusion) or crack tip, and for a series of gas pores are expected to be similar to those in figure 7.18 [27]. In ARBS, pattern classification of the echodynamic is performed using a Fast Fourier Transform and a set of rules to analyze the features of the transformed signal. A neural network has also been used for the same task (section 7.6.7).

The sensitivity of the defect to the angle of the probe is another critical indicator of the nature of the defect in question. Roughly spherical flaws, such as individual gas pores, have much the same appearance when viewed from different angles. Smooth cracks on the other hand have a much more markedly "directional" character - a small difference in the direction of the probe may result in a considerable reduction (or increase) in the intensity of indications. The "directionality factor" of an area of intersection is a measure of this sensitivity and is represented in ARBS as a number between −1 and 1.

Defect classification

Quantitative evidence about key areas in an image is derived by rule-based knowledge sources, as described above. Each piece of evidence gives some clues as to the nature of the defect associated with the key area. For instance, the indications from smooth cracks tend to be sensitive to the angle of the probe, and the echodynamic tends to be plateau-shaped. In contrast, indications from a small round defect (e.g., an inclusion) tend to be insensitive to probe direction and have a cusp-shaped echodynamic. There are several factors like these that need to be taken into account when producing a classification, and each must be weighted appropriately.

Two techniques for classifying defects based upon the evidence have been tried out using ARBS: a rule-based hypothesize-and-test approach, and a neural network. In the former approach, hypotheses concerning defects are added to the blackboard. These hypotheses relate to smooth or rough cracks, porosity, or inclusions. They are tested by deriving from them *predictions* (or *expectations*) relating to other features of the image. On the basis of the correspondence between the predictions and the image, ARBS arrives at a conclusion about the nature of a defect, or, where this is not possible with any degree of certainty, it alerts the user to a particular problem case.

Writing rules to verify the defect classification is a difficult task, and in practice the rules needed continual refinement and adjustment in the light of experience [8]. The use of neural networks to combine the evidence and produce a classification provides a means of circumventing this difficulty since they only need a representative training set of examples, instead of the formulation of explicit rules.

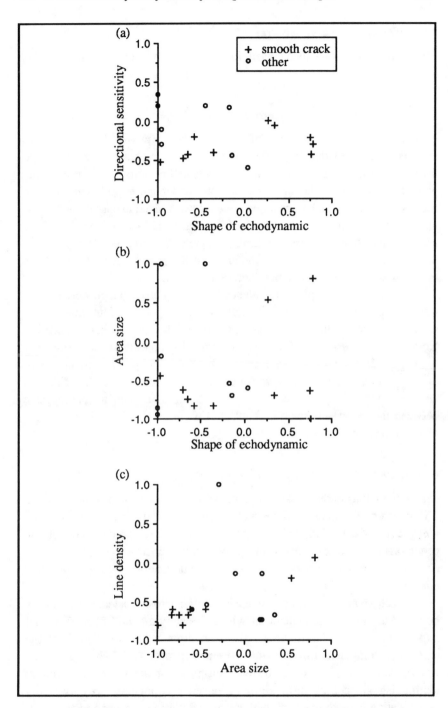

Figure 7.19 Evidence for the classification of 18 suspected defect areas
(adapted from [8]).

7.6.7 The use of neural networks

Neural networks have been used in ARBS for two quite distinct tasks, described below.

Defect classification using a neural network

Neural networks can perform defect classification provided that there are sufficient training examples and the evidence can be presented in numerical form. There was insufficient data to train a neural network to perform a four-way classification of defect types, as done under the hypothesize-and-test method. Instead, a backpropagation network was trained to classify defects as either critical or noncritical on the basis of four local factors - the size of the area, the number of arcs passing through it, the shape of the echodynamic, and the sensitivity of the intensity to the angle of the probe. Each of these local factors was expressed as a number between -1 and 1.

Figure 7.19 shows plots of evidence for the 18 defects which were used to train and test a neural network. The data are in fact points in four-dimensional space, where each dimension represents one of the four factors considered. Notice that the clusters of critical and noncritical samples might not be linearly separable. This means that traditional numerical techniques for finding linear discriminators [28] are not powerful enough to produce good classification. However, a multilayer perceptron (see chapter 6) is able to discriminate between the two cases, since it is able to find the three-dimensional surface required to separate them.

Echodynamic classification using a neural network

One of the inputs to the classification network requires a value between -1 and 1 to represent the shape of the echodynamic. This value can be obtained by using a rule-based KS which examines the Fourier components of the echodynamic and uses heuristics to provide a numerical value for the shape. An alternative approach is to use another neural network to generate this number.

An echodynamic is a signal intensity profile across a defect area, and can be classified as a cusp, plateau, or wiggle. Ideally a neural network would make a three-way classification, given an input vector derived from the amplitude components of the first n Fourier coefficients, where $2n$ is the echodynamic sample rate. However, cusps and plateaux are difficult to distinguish since they have similar Fourier components, so a two-way classification is more practical, with cusps and plateaux grouped together. A multilayer perceptron has been used for this purpose.

Combining the two applications of neural networks

The use of two separate neural networks in distinct KSs for the classification of echodynamics and of the potential defect areas might seem unnecessary. Since the output of the former feeds (via the blackboard) into the input layer of the latter, they could be combined into one large neural network. This would remove the need for a preclassified training set of echodynamics. However, such an approach would lead to a loss of modularity and explanation facilities. Furthermore, it may be easier to train several small neural networks separately on subtasks of the whole classification problem than to attempt the whole problem at once with a single large network. These are important

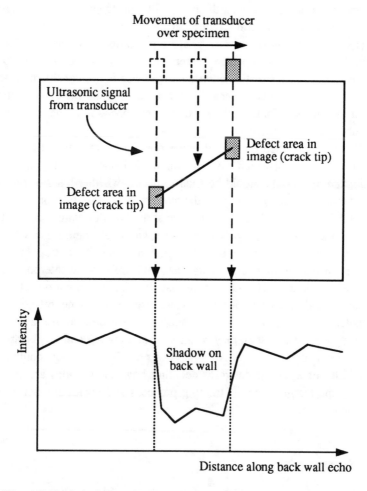

Figure 7.20 A shadow on the back wall can confirm the presence of a crack
(adapted from [8]).

considerations when there are many subtasks amenable to connectionist treatment.

7.6.8 Mixing rules and neural networks

Defect classification, whether performed by the hypothesize-and-test method or by neural networks, has so far been discussed purely in terms of evidence gathered from the region of the image that is under scrutiny. However, there are other features in the image which can be brought to bear on the problem. Knowledge of these features can be expressed easily in rule form and can be used to *verify* the classification. For example, an easily identifiable feature of a b-scan image is the line of indications due to the back wall echo. A defect in the sample, particularly a smooth crack, will tend to cast a "shadow" on the back wall directly beneath it (figure 7.20). The presence of a shadow in the expected position can be used to verify the location and classification of a defect. Such checks are considered essential in safety-critical systems [29, 30]. In ARBS, the absence of this additional evidence is not considered a strong enough reason to reject a defect classification. Instead, the classification in such cases is marked for the attention of a human operator, as there are grounds for doubt over its accuracy.

We have described the use of either rules or neural networks for defect classification, each of which has some merit. Johnson et al. [30] suggest that an *adjudicator* module should be used to decide whether a set of rules or a neural network is likely to provide the more reliable classification for a given test example. The adjudicator would have access to information relating to the extent of the neural network's training set and could determine whether a neural network would have to interpolate between, or extrapolate from, examples in the training set. Neural networks are good at interpolation but poor at extrapolation. The adjudicator may therefore call upon rules to handle the exceptional cases which would otherwise require a neural network to extrapolate from its training data. If heuristic rules are also available for the less exceptional cases, then they could be used to provide an explanation for the neural network's findings. A supervisory rule-based module could dictate the training of a neural network, deciding how many nodes are required, adjusting the learning rate as training proceeds and deciding when training should terminate.

7.7 Summary

This chapter has introduced some of the techniques that can be used to tackle the problems of automated interpretation and diagnosis. Diagnosis is considered to be a specialized case of the more general problem of interpretation. It has been shown that a key part of diagnosis and interpretation is abduction, the process of determining a cause, given a set of observations. There is uncertainty associated with abduction, since causes other than the selected one might give rise to the same set of observations. Two possible approaches to dealing with this uncertainty are to explicitly represent the uncertainty using the techniques described in chapter 4, or to *hypothesize-and-test*. As the name implies, the latter technique involves generating a hypothesis (or best guess), and either confirming or refuting the hypothesis depending on whether it is found to be consistent with the observations.

Several different forms of knowledge can contribute to a solution. We have paid specific attention to rules, case histories, and physical models. We have also shown that neural networks and conventional "number-crunching" can play an important role when included as part of a blackboard system. Rules can be used to represent both shallow (heuristic) and deep knowledge. They can also be used for the generation and verification of hypotheses. Case-based reasoning involves comparison of a given scenario with previous examples and their solutions. Model-based reasoning relies on the existence of a model of the physical system which can be used for monitoring, generation of hypotheses, and verification of hypotheses by simulation.

Blackboard systems have been introduced as part of a case study into the interpretation of ultrasonic images. These systems allow various different forms of knowledge representation to come together in one system. They are therefore well suited to problems which can be broken down into subtasks, where the most suitable form of knowledge representation for different subtasks is not necessarily the same. Each module of knowledge within a blackboard system is called a knowledge source (KS).

A neural network knowledge source was shown to be effective for combining evidence generated by other KSs and for categorizing the shape of an echodynamic. This approach can be contrasted with the use of a neural network alone for interpreting images. The blackboard architecture avoids the need to abandon rules in favour of neural networks or vice versa, since the advantages of both can be incorporated into a single system. Rules can represent knowledge explicitly, whereas neural networks can be used where explicit knowledge is hard to obtain. Although neural networks can be rather impenetrable to the user and are unable to explain their reasoning, these deficiencies can be reduced by using them for small-scale localized tasks with reports generated in between.

The blackboard architecture may be regarded as a generalization of some of the tools dealt with previously. If the system contained a solitary rule-based knowledge source, and no algorithms were accessed, then it would reduce to a production rule system (see chapter 3). If, on the other hand, the system contained just a single procedural knowledge source, then the blackboard system would become a conventional program.

References

1. Dague, P., Jehl, O., Deves, P., Luciani, P. and Taillibert, P., "When oscillators stop oscillating", in *International Joint Conference on Artificial Intelligence (IJCAI-91)*, Sydney, p1109 (1991).
2. Rowen, R., "Diagnostic systems for manufacturing", *AI Expert*, (April 1990), p28 (1990).
3. Dash, E., "Diagnosing furnace problems with an expert system", *SPIE-Applications of Artificial Intelligence VIII*, **1293**, p966 (1990).
4. Bykat, A., "Nicbes-2, a nickel-cadmium battery expert system", *Applied Artificial Intelligence*, **4**, p133 (1990).
5. Maderlechner, G., Egeli, E. and Klein, F., "Model guided interpretation based on structurally related image primitives", in *Knowledge-based expert systems in industry*, Kriz, J. (ed.), Ellis Horwood (1987).
6. Zhang, Z. and Simaan, M., "A rule-based interpretation system for segmentation of seismic images", *Pattern Recognition*, **20**, (1987).
7. Hallam, N. J., Woodcock, N. and Hopgood, A. A., "A knowledge based system for defect detection and characterization", in *Applications of artificial intelligence in engineering V - vol 2*, Rzevski, G. (ed.), Computational Mechanics Publications / Springer-Verlag, p155 (1990).
8. Woodcock, N., Hallam, N. J., Picton, P. D. and Hopgood, A. A., "Interpretation of ultrasonic images of weld defects using a hybrid system", in *Neural Networks and their Applications*, Nimes, France (1991).
9. Leitch, R., Kraft, R. and Luntz, R., "RESCU: a real-time knowledge based system for process control", *IEE Proceedings-D*, **138**, p217 (1991).
10. Fink, P. K. and Lusth, J. C., "Expert systems and diagnostic expertise in the mechanical and electrical domains", *IEEE Transactions on Systems, Man, and Cybernetics*, **17**, p340 (1987).
11. Riesbeck, C. K. and Schank, R. C., *Inside case-based reasoning*, Lawrence Erlbaum Associates (1989).
12. Sussman, G. J., *A computer model of skill acquisition*, American Elsevier (1975).
13. Fulton, S. L. and Pepe, C. O., "An introduction to model-based reasoning", *AI Expert*, (January 1990), p48 (1990).

14. Scarl, E. A., Jamieson, J. R. and Delaune, C. I., "Diagnosis and sensor validation through knowledge of structure and function", *IEEE Transactions on Systems, Man, and Cybernetics*, 17, p360 (1987).

15. Motta, E., Eisenstadt, M., Pitman, K. and West, M., "Support for knowledge acquisition in the Knowledge Engineer's Assistant (KEATS)", *Expert Systems*, 5, p6 (1988).

16. Dague, P., Deves, P., Zein, Z. and Adam, J. P., "DEDALE: an expert system in VM/Prolog", in *Knowledge-based expert systems in industry*, Kriz, J. (ed.), Ellis Horwood (1987).

17. Price, C. J. and Hunt, J. E., "Automating FMEA through multiple models", in *Research and development in expert systems VIII*, Graham, I. and Milne, R. (ed.), Cambridge University Press (1991).

18. Harel, D., "On visual formalisms", *Communications of the ACM*, 31, p514 (1988).

19. Price, C. J. and Hunt, J., "Simulating mechanical devices", in *Pop-11 comes of age: the advancement of an AI programming language*, Anderson, J. A. D. W. (ed.), Ellis Horwood (1989).

20. Jennings, A. J., "Artificial intelligence: a tool for productivity", in *Institution of Engineers (Australia) National Conference*, Perth, Australia (1989).

21. Milne, R., "Strategies for diagnosis", *IEEE Transactions on Systems, Man, and Cybernetics*, 17, p333 (1987).

22. Steels, L., "Diagnosis with a function-fault model", *Applied Artificial Intelligence*, 3, p129 (1989).

23. Walker, N. and Fox, J., "Knowledge-based interpretation of images: a biomedical perspective", *Knowledge Engineering Review*, 2, p249 (1987).

24. Erman, L. D., Hayes-Roth, F., Lesser, V. R. and Reddy, D. R., "The Hearsay-II speech understanding system: integrating knowledge to resolve uncertainty", *ACM Computing Surveys*, 12, p213 (1980).

25. Feigenbaum, E. A., in *Blackboard systems*, Englemore, R. S. and Morgan, A. J. (ed.), Addison-Wesley (1988).

26. Duda, R. O. and Hart, P. E., "Use of the Hough transform to detect lines and curves in pictures", *Communications of the ACM*, 15, p11 (1972).

27. Halmshaw, R., *Non-destructive testing*, Edward Arnold (1987).

28. Duda, R. O. and Hart, P. E., *Pattern classification and scene analysis*, Wiley (1973).

29. Picton, P. D., Johnson, J. H. and Hallam, N. J., "Neural Networks in Safety Critical Systems", in *3rd International Congress on Condition Monitoring and Diagnostic Engineering Management*, Southampton, UK (1991).

30. Johnson, J. H., Hallam, N. J. and Picton, P. D., "Safety critical neurocomputing: explanation and verification in knowledge augmented neural networks", in *Colloquium on Human-Computer Interaction*, IEE, London (1990).

Further reading

• Englemore, R. S. and Morgan, A. J. (ed.), *Blackboard systems*, Addison-Wesley (1988).

chapter eight

Systems for design and selection

8.1 The design process

Before discussing how knowledge-based systems can be applied to design, it is firstly important to understand what we mean by the word "design". Traditionally, design has been broken down into engineering design and industrial design:

"Engineering design is the use of scientific principles, technical information, and imagination in the definition of a mechanical structure, machine or system to perform specified functions with the maximum economy and efficiency." [1]

"Industrial design seeks to rectify the omissions of engineering, a conscious attempt to bring form and visual order to engineering hardware where technology does not of itself provide these features." [1]

We will take a more catholic view of design, in which no distinction is drawn between the technical needs of engineering design and the aesthetic approach of industrial design. Thus our working definition of design will be the one used by Sriram et al.:

"(Design is) the process of specifying a description of an artefact that satisfies constraints arising from a number of sources by using diverse sources of knowledge." [2]

Some of the constraints must be predetermined, and these constitute the *product design specification (PDS)*. Other constraints may evolve as a result of decisions made during the design process. The PDS is an expression of the *requirements* of a product, rather than a specification of the product itself. The latter, which emerges during the design process, is the design. The design can

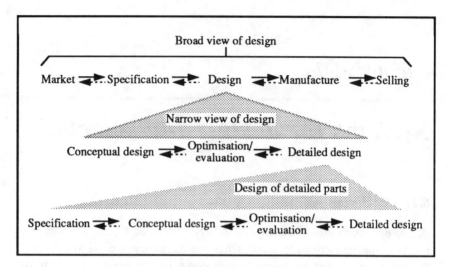

Figure 8.1 The principal phases of design.

be interpreted for manufacture or construction, and it allows predictions about the performance of the product to be drawn.

Different authors have chosen to analyze the design process in different ways. An approximate consensus is that the broadest view of the design process comprises the following phases:

market - specification - core of design - manufacture - selling.

It is the core of the design process, leading from a product design specification to the manufacturing stage, that fulfills the more common narrow view of design. The design core may be subdivided into conceptual design, analysis, and detailed design (figure 8.1). The purpose of each phase is as follows:

i   *Market.* This phase is concerned with determining the need for a product. A problem is identified, resources allocated, and end-users are targeted.

ii   *Specification.* A product design specification (PDS) is drawn up, which describes the requirements and performance specifications of the product. The PDS for a motorcar might specify a product which can transport up to four people in comfort, traveling at up to 70 miles per hour on tarmac roads.

iii *Conceptual design.* Preliminary design decisions are made at this stage, with the aim of satisfying a few key constraints. Several alternatives would normally be considered. Decisions taken at the conceptual design stage determine the general form of the product, and so have enormous implications for the remainder of the design process. The conceptual design for a motorcar has altered little since the Ford Model T was unveiled in 1908. It describes a steel body with doors and windows, a wheel at each corner, two seats at the front (one of which has access to the controls), two seats at the back, and so on.

iv *Optimization/evaluation*. The conceptual design is refined, for instance by placing values on numerical attributes such as length and thickness. The performance of the conceptual design is tested for its response to external effects and its consistency with the product design specification. The optimization and evaluation stage for a motorcar might include an assessment of the relationship between the shape of the body and its drag coefficient. If the conceptual design cannot be made to meet the requirements, a new one is needed.

v *Detailed design*. The design of the product and its components are refined so that all constraints are satisfied. Decisions taken at this stage might include the layout of a car's transmission system, the position of the ashtray, the covering for the seats, and the total design of a door latch. The latter example illustrates that the complete design process for a component may be embedded in the detailed design phase of the whole assembly (figure 8.1).

vi *Manufacture*. A product should not be designed without consideration of how it is to be manufactured, as it is all too easy to design a product which is uneconomical or impossible to produce. For a product which is to be mass-produced, the manufacturing plant needs to be designed just as rigorously as the product itself. Different constraints apply to a one-off product, as this can be individually crafted but mass-production techniques such as injection moulding are not feasible.

vii *Selling*. The chief constraint for most products is that they should be sold at a profit. The broad view of design therefore takes into account not only how a product can be made, but also how it is to be sold.

Although the design process has been portrayed as a chronological series of events, in fact there is considerable interaction between the phases, both forwards and backwards, as constraints become modified by the design decisions that are made. For instance, a decision to manufacture one component from polyethylene rather than steel has ramifications for the design of other components, and implications for the manufacturing process. It may also alter the PDS, as the polymer component may offer a product which is cheaper but less structurally rigid. Similarly, sales of a product can affect the market, thus linking the last design phase with the first.

In our description of both conceptual design and detailed design, we have made reference to the choice of materials from which to manufacture the product. Materials selection is one of the key aspects of the design process, and one where considerable effort has been placed in the application of knowledge-based systems. The process of materials selection is discussed in detail in section 8.8. Selection is also the key to other aspects of the design process, as attempts are made to select the most appropriate solution to the problem.

The description of the design process that has been proposed is largely independent of the nature of the product. The product may be a single component (such as a turbine blade) or a complex assembly (such as a jet engine); it may be a one-off product or one that will be produced in large numbers. Many designs do not involve manufacture at all in the conventional sense. An example that will be introduced in section 8.4 is the design of a communications network. This is a high-level design, which is not concerned with the layout of wires or optical fibers, but rather with the overall configuration of the network. The product is a *service* rather than a physical thing. Although selection is again one of the key tasks, materials selection is not applicable in this case.

In summary, we can categorize products according to whether they are:

- service-based or physical products;
- single component products or assemblies of many components;
- one-off products or mass-produced products.

Products in each category will have different requirements, leading to a different PDS. However, these differences do not necessarily alter the design process.

Three case studies will be introduced in this chapter. The specification of a communications network is used to illustrate the importance and potential complexity of the product design specification. The processes of conceptual design, optimization and evaluation, and detailed design are illustrated with reference to the floor of a passenger aircraft. This case study will introduce some aspects of the materials selection problem, and these are further illustrated by the third case study, which concerns the design of a kettle.

8.2 Design as a search problem

Design can be viewed as a search problem, as it involves searching for an optimum or adequate design solution. Alternative solutions may be known in advance (derivation problems), or they may be generated automatically (formulation problems). Designs may be tested as they are found in order to check whether they are feasible and meet the design requirements. This is the *generate and test* method. In application areas like diagnosis it may be sufficient to terminate the search as soon as a solution is found. In design there are likely to be many solutions, and we would like to find "the best". The search may therefore continue in order to find many feasible designs from which a selection can be made.

Search becomes impractical when large numbers of unreasonable designs are included. Consider, for example, the design of a house. In order to generate solutions automatically, we might write a computer program which generated every conceivable combination of shapes and sizes of rooms, walls, roofs and foundations. Of this massive number of alternatives, only a small proportion would be feasible designs. In order to make the search problem manageable, some means of eliminating the unfeasible designs is needed. Better still would be a means of eliminating whole *families* of ill-conceived designs before the individual variants have been produced. Thus the design-generator could be modified by heuristics so that it only produced designs with the roof above the walls and with the walls above the foundations. This would have the effect of pruning the search space (figure 8.2). The search space can also be reduced by decomposing the problem into one of designing the rooms, roof and foundations separately.

The search problem is similar to the proposition that a monkey playing random notes on a grand piano will eventually play a Beethoven symphony. The fault in this proposition is that the search space of compositions is so immense that the monkey would not stumble across the symphony within a practical time-frame. Only a composer with knowledge of suitable musical arrangements could hope to generate the symphony, as he or she is able to prune the search space of compositions.

Even if we succeed in pruning the search space so that only feasible designs are considered, we will still be left with the problem of selecting between alternatives. The selection problem is discussed in section 8.8 with particular reference to materials selection for design. The same techniques can be applied to selection between design alternatives.

Although heuristic rules can limit the search space, they do not offer unique solutions. This is because abductive rather than deductive rules are required (section 1.4), as with diagnosis (chapter 7). Consider this simple deductive rule:

```
/* Rule 8.1 */
IF ?X is a room with a bath and a toilet THEN ?X is a bathroom.
```

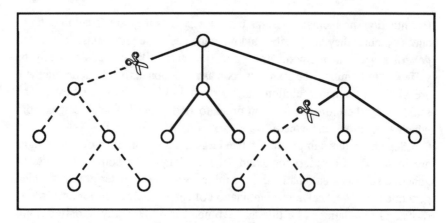

Figure 8.2 Pruning the search tree by eliminating classes of design that are unfeasible.

If a room fits the description provided by the condition part of the rule, we could use the rule to classify that room as a bathroom. The abductive interpretation of this rule is:

```
/* Rule 8.2 */
IF a room is to be a bathroom
THEN it must have a bath and a toilet.
```

The abductive rule poses two problems. Firstly, we have made the closed world assumption (see sections 1.4 and 3.5), and so the rule will never produce bathroom designs which have a shower and toilet but no bath. Secondly, the rule leads only to a partial design. It tells us that the bathroom will have a toilet and bath, but fails to tell us where these items should be placed or whether we need to add other items such as a basin or bidet.

8.3 Computer aided design

The expression "computer aided design", or CAD, is used to describe computing tools which can assist in the design process. However, most CAD systems are intended primarily to assist in drawing a design, rather than directly supporting the decision-making process. CAD systems of this type therefore carry out *computer aided drafting* rather than computer aided design. Typically, they allow the designer to draw on a computer screen using a mouse, graphics tablet or similar device. All dimensions are automatically calculated, and the design can be easily reshaped, resized, or otherwise modified. These systems have had an enormous impact on the design process since they remove much of the tedium and facilitate alterations. Furthermore, these CAD systems have altered the designers' working environment, as the traditional large flat drafting boards have been replaced by computer work-stations.

Traditional CAD systems of this type do not make decisions and they are not, in general, knowledge-based. They do, however, frequently make use of object-oriented programming techniques. Each line, box, circle, etc., that is created can be represented as an object instance. Rather than describing such systems in any more detail, this chapter will concentrate on the use of knowledge-based systems which can help designers to make design decisions.

8.4 The product design specification (PDS): a case study in telecommunications

8.4.1 Background

The product design specification (PDS) is a statement of the requirements of the product. In this section we will consider a case study concerning the problems of creating a PDS which can be accessed by a knowledge-based design system. In this case study, the "product" is not a material product but a service, namely the provision of a communications network. The model used to represent the PDS is called the Common Traffic Model (CTM) [3], so called because it is common to a variety of forms of communication traffic (e.g., analog voice, packetized data, or synchronous data).

The common traffic model allows different views of a communications network to be represented simultaneously. The simplest view is a set of requirements defined in terms of links between sites and the applications (e.g. fax or database access) to be used on these links. The more specialized views contain implementation details, including the associated costs. The model allows nontechnical users to specify a set of communications requirements, from which a knowledge-based system can design and cost a network, thereby creating a specialized view from a nonspecialized one. The model consists of object class definitions, and a PDS is represented as a set of instances of these classes.

8.4.2 Alternative views of a network

Suppose that a small retailer has a central headquarters, a warehouse and a retail store. The retailer may require various communications applications, including customer order by fax, customer order by phone, and stock reorder (where replacement stock is ordered from suppliers). The retailer therefore views the network in terms of the sites and the telecommunications applications that are carried between them. This is the simplest viewpoint, which defines the PDS. From a more technical viewpoint, the network can be broken down into voice and data components. For the voice section, each site has a fixed number of lines connecting it to the network via a private switching system, while the data section connects the head office to the other sites. The most detailed view of the network (the service-provider's viewpoint) includes a definition of the equipment and services used to implement the network. The detailed description is based on one of several possible implementations, while the less specialized views are valid regardless of the implementation.

There are therefore several possible views of the network, all of which are valid, and all of which can be represented by the Common Traffic Model. It is the translation from the customer view (defined in terms of the applications being used) to the service-provider's view (defined in terms of the equipment and services supplied) which determines the cost and efficiency of the communications network. This translation is the design task.

8.4.3 Implementation

The requirements of the network are represented as a set of object instances. For example, if the customer of the telecommunications company has an office in New York, that office is represented as an object with a name and position, and is an instance of the object class `customer_site`.

The Common Traffic Model has been designed using Coad & Yourdon's object-oriented analysis (OOA) [4], described in section 5.9. The model is implemented as a set of object classes which are templates for the object instances that are created when the system is used to represent a PDS. Various interclass relationships are employed. For example, a dispersion link is represented as a specialization of a communications link. Similarly, an assembly relationship is used to show that a network comprises several links. Instance connections are used to represent physical associations, such as the association between a communication link and the sites at its two ends.

The fact that instance connections are defined at the class level can be confusing. The common traffic model is defined entirely in terms of object classes, these being the templates for the instances that represent the user's communication needs. Although the common traffic model is only defined in terms of classes, it includes a specification of the instance connections that exist between instances *when they are created.*

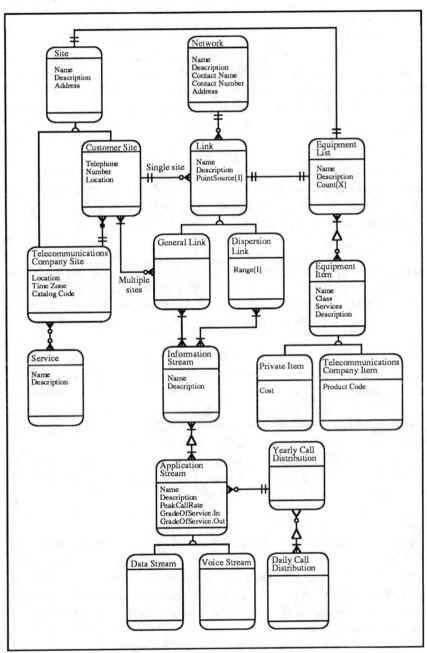

Figure 8.3 The main object classes and attributes in the Common Traffic Model. (Adapted from Hopgood, A. A. and Hopson, A. J., "The common traffic model: a universal model for communications networks", *IREECON'91*, Institution of Radio and Electronic Engineers, Sydney, p63 (1991). With permission.)

8.4.4 The classes

The classes that make up the Common Traffic Model and the relationships between those classes are shown in figure 8.3. A detailed understanding of figure 8.3 is not necessary for this case study. Instead it is hoped that the figure conveys the general idea of using object-oriented analysis for generating both the PDS and a detailed network description. The main classes of the Common Traffic Model are briefly described below.

Network

The network object contains the general information relating to the network, but is independent of the network requirements. It includes information such as contact people and their addresses. The specification of the network is constructed from a set of link objects (described below).

Link

A link identifies the path between customer sites along which an information stream (described below) occurs. Instance connections are used to associate links with appropriate customer sites, information streams, and equipment. Conceptually three types of link are defined:

- *Multipoint links*, where information is exchanged between a single nominated site and a number of other sites. The links are instances of the class general link, where an attribute (PointSource) indicates whether calls are initiated by the single site or by the multiple sites.
- *Point-to-point links*, which are treated like multipoint links, but where only one of the multiple sites is specified.
- *Dispersion links*, which carry application traffic that does not have a fixed destination site. This type of link applies to customers who want access to a public switched network.

Site

Two classifications of sites are defined, namely the customer's sites and the telecommunications company's sites. The latter specify sites which are part of the supplier's network, such as telephone exchanges. For most telecommunications services, the design and costing of a network is dependent on its spatial layout. For this reason, the Common Traffic Model has access to a geographical database.

Information stream

The information streams specify the traffic on a link in terms of a set of application streams. Two subclasses of application stream are defined, namely data stream and voice stream. The first specifies digital applications, while the second specifies analogue applications. Each application stream has a peak call rate and associated yearly and daily traffic profiles. Application streams can be broken down further into individual calls.

Equipment
An equipment list specifies a set of items which are present at a site or on a link. Two subclasses of equipment items are defined: those that are owned by the telecommunications company and those that are privately owned.

8.4.5 Summary of PDS case study
The common traffic model illustrates a formalized approach to creating a product design specification (PDS), showing that the PDS and its implementation need to be carefully thought out before a knowledge-based design system can be employed. The common traffic model has proved an effective tool for representing a set of communication requirements in a way that satisfies more than one viewpoint. Nontechnical users can specify the PDS in terms of the types of use that they have in mind for the network. The common traffic model can also be used to represent the detailed network design, which may be one of many that are technically possible.

8.5 Conceptual design

It has already been noted (section 8.1) that conceptual design is the stage where broad decisions about the overall form of a product are made. A distinction can be drawn between cases where the designer is free to innovate, and more routine cases where the designer is working within tightly bound constraints. An example of the former case would be the design of a can opener. Many designs have appeared in the past and the designer may call upon his or her experience of these. However, he or she is not bound by those earlier design decisions. In contrast, a designer might be tasked with arranging the layout of an electronic circuit on a VLSI (very large scale integration) chip. While this is undoubtedly a complex task, the conceptual design has already been carried out, and the designer's task is one which can be treated as a problem of mathematical optimization. We will call this *routine design*.

Brown and Chandrasekaran [5] subdivide the innovative design category between *inventions* (such as the first helicopter) and more modest *innovations* (such as the first twin-rotor helicopter). Both are characterized by the lack of any prescribed strategy for design, and rely on a spark of inspiration. The invention category makes use of new knowledge, whereas the second category involves the reworking of existing knowledge or existing designs. The three categories of design can be summarized as follows:

- invention;
- innovative use of existing knowledge or designs; and
- routine design.

Researchers have different opinions of how designers work, and it is therefore not surprising that markedly different software architectures have been produced. For instance, Sriram et al. [2] claim to have based their CYCLOPS system on the following set of observations about innovative design:

i   designers use multiple objectives and constraints to guide their decisions, but are not necessarily bound by them;
ii   as new design criteria emerge they are fed back into the PDS;
iii designers try to find an optimum solution rather than settling on a satisfactory one; and
iv   extensive use is made of past examples.

Demaid and Zucker [6] have no quarrel with observations (i), (ii) and (iv), but in contrast to observation (iii) they emphasize the importance of choosing "satisficing" (or adequate) materials for a product rather than trying to find an optimum choice.

The CYCLOPS [2] and FORLOG [7] systems assume that innovative design can be obtained by generating a variety of alternatives and choosing between them. CYCLOPS makes use of previous design histories, and attempts to adapt them to new domains. The success of this approach depends upon the ability to find diverse novel alternatives. In order to increase the number of past designs that might be considered, the design constraints are relaxed. Relaxation of constraints is discussed in section 8.8.5 as part of an overall discussion of techniques for selecting between alternatives. CYCLOPS also has provision for modification of the constraints in the light of past experience.

As well as selecting a preexisting design for use in a novel way, CYCLOPS allows adaptation of the design to the new circumstances. This is achieved through having a stored explanation of the precedent designs. The example cited by Sriram et al. [2] relates to houses in Thailand. Thai villagers put their houses on stilts to avoid flooding, and this forms a precedent design. The underlying explanation for the design, which is stored with it, is that stilts raise the structure. The association with flooding may not be stored at all, as this is not fundamental to the role of the stilts. CYCLOPS might then use this precedent to raise one end of a house which is being designed for construction on a slope.

Most work in knowledge-based systems for design relies on the application of a predetermined strategy. Dyer et al. [8] see this as a limitation on innovation and have therefore incorporated the idea of "brainstorming" in EDISON, a system for designing simple mechanical devices. Some of the key features of EDISON are:

- brainstorming by $\begin{cases} \text{mutation;} \\ \text{generalization;} \\ \text{analogy;} \end{cases}$
- problem-solving heuristics;
- class hierarchies of mechanical parts; and
- heuristics describing relationships between mechanical parts.

EDISON makes use of meta-rules to steer the design process between the various strategies that are provided. Brainstorming and problem-solving often work in tandem, as brainstorming tends to generate new problems. Brainstorming involves retrieving a previous design from memory, and applying *mutation, generalization* and *analogical reasoning* until a new functioning device is "invented". *Mutation* is achieved through a set of heuristics describing general modifications that can be applied to a variety of products. For example, slicing a door creates two slabs, each covering half a door frame. This operation results in a problem: the second slab is not connected to the frame. Two typical problem-solving heuristics might be:

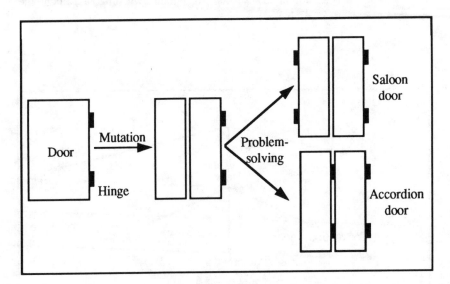

Figure 8.4 Inventing new types of door by mutation and problem-solving (after Dyer et al [8]).

```
Hinged joints allow rotation about pin;
Hinged joints prohibit motion in any other planes.
```

These rules provide information about the properties of hinges. Application of similar *problem-solving* rules might result in the free slab being connected either to the hinged slab, or to the opposite side of the frame. In one case we have invented the swinging saloon bar door; in the other case the accordion door (figure 8.4).

Generalization is the process of forming a generic description from a specific item. For instance, a door might be considered a sub-class of the general class of entrances (figure 8.5). Analogies can then be drawn (*analogical reasoning*) with another class of entrance, namely a cat flap, leading to the invention of a door which hangs from hinges mounted at the top. Generalization achieves the same goal as the deep explanations used in the adaptation mode of CYCLOPS, described above.

Murthy and Addanki [9] have built a system called PROMPT in which innovative structural designs are generated by reasoning from first principles, i.e., using the fundamental laws of physics. Fundamental laws can lead to unconventional designs that heuristics based on conventional wisdom might have failed to generate. Other authors [10, 11] have proposed a *systematic* approach to innovation which generates only feasible solutions, rather than large numbers of solutions from which the feasible ones must be extracted. In this approach, the goals are firstly determined and then the steps needed to satisfy these goals are found. These steps have their own subgoals, and so the processes proceeds recursively.

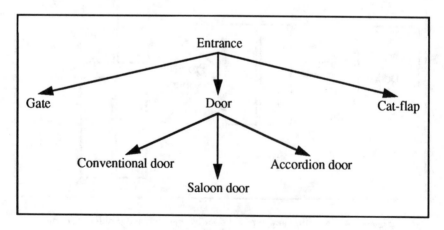

Figure 8.5 Hierarchical classification of types of entrance.

8.6 Constraint propagation and truth maintenance

The terms *constraint propagation* and *truth maintenance* are commonly used in the field of artificial intelligence to convey two separate but related ideas. They have particular relevance to design, as will be illustrated by means of some simple examples. Constraints are limitations or requirements that must be met when producing a solution to a problem (such as finding a viable design). Imagine that we are designing a product, and that we have already made some conceptual design decisions. Propagation of constraints refers to the problem of ensuring that new constraints arising from the decisions taken thus far are taken into account in any subsequent decisions. For instance, a decision to manufacture a car from steel rather than (say) fiberglass introduces a constraint on the design of the suspension, namely that it must be capable of supporting the mass of the steel body.

Suppose now that we wish to investigate two candidate solutions to a problem, such as a steel-bodied car and a fiberglass car. Truth maintenance refers to the problem of ensuring that more detailed investigations, carried out subsequently, are associated with the correct premise. For example, steps must be taken to ensure that a lightweight suspension design is only associated with the lightweight (fiberglass) design of car to which it is suited.

In order to illustrate these ideas in more detail, we have adapted the example provided by Dietterich and Ullman [7]. The problem is to place two batteries into a battery holder. There are four possible ways in which the batteries can be inserted, as shown in figure 8.6. This situation is described by the following Prolog clauses (section 2.6 gives an overview of the syntax and workings of Prolog):

```
terminal(X):- X=positive;X=negative.
    % battery terminal may be positive or negative


layout(T,B):- terminal(T),terminal(B).
    % layout defined by identifying top and bottom terminals
```

We can now query our Prolog system so that it will return all valid arrangements of the batteries:

```
prolog> ?layout(Top,Bottom).
    Nº1    Top = positive,  Bottom = positive
    Nº2    Top = positive,  Bottom = negative
    Nº3    Top = negative,  Bottom = positive
    Nº4    Top = negative,  Bottom = negative
    No more solutions
```

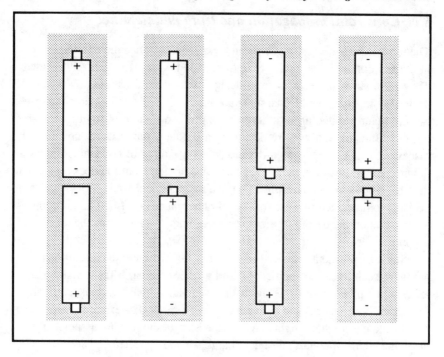

Figure 8.6 Four possible ways of inserting batteries into a holder.

Now let us introduce the constraint that the batteries must be arranged in series. This is achieved by adding a clause to specify that terminals at the top and bottom of the battery holder must be of opposite sign:

```
terminal(X) :- X=positive;X=negative.
```

```
layout(T,B) :- terminal(T),terminal(B),
not(T=B).              % top terminal not equal to bottom terminal
```

We can now query our Prolog system again:

```
prolog> ?layout(Top,Bottom).
   Nº1    Top = positive,  Bottom = negative
   Nº2    Top = negative,  Bottom = positive
   No more solutions
```

We will now introduce another constraint, namely that a positive terminal must appear at the top of the battery holder:

```
terminal(X) :- X=positive;X=negative.
```

```
layout (T,B) :- terminal (T) , terminal (B) ,
not (T=B) ,
T=positive.                    % positive terminal at top of holder
```

There is now only one arrangement of the batteries that meets the constraints:

```
prolog> ?layout (Top, Bottom) .
   Nº1    Top = positive,   Bottom = negative
   No more solutions
```

This is an example of constraint propagation, because it shows how a constraint affecting one part of the design (viz. the orientation of the battery at the top of the holder) is propagated to determine some other part of the design (viz. the orientation of the other battery). In this particular example, constraint propagation has been handled by the standard facilities of the Prolog language. Many workers, including Dietterich and Ullman [7], have found the need to devise their own means of constraint propagation in large design systems.

Truth maintenance becomes an important problem if we wish to consider more than one solution to a problem at a time, or to make use of nonmonotonic reasoning (see section 7.2). For instance, we might wish to develop several alternative designs, or to assume that a particular design is feasible until it is shown to be otherwise. In order to illustrate the concept of truth maintenance, we will stay with our example of arranging batteries in a holder. However, we will veer away from a Prolog representation of the problem, as standard Prolog can consider only one solution to a problem at a time.

Let us return to the case where we had specified that the two batteries must be in series, but we had not specified an orientation for either. There were therefore two possible arrangements:

```
   [Top = positive,   Bottom = neg]
or
   [Top = negative,   Bottom = positive].
```

It is not sufficient to simply store these four assertions together in memory:

```
   Top = positive
   Bottom = negative
   Top = negative
   Bottom = positive.
```

For these statements to exist concurrently, it would be concluded that the two terminals of a battery are identical (i.e., negative = positive). This is clearly not the intended meaning. A frequently used solution to this difficulty is to label each fact, rule, or assertion, such that those bearing the same label are recognized as interdependent and therefore "belonging together". This is the basis of deKleer's assumption-based truth maintenance system (ATMS) [12, 13, 14]. If we choose to label our two solutions as design1 and design2, then our four assertions might be stored as:

```
Top = positive          {design1}
Bottom = negative       {design1}
Top = negative          {design2}
Bottom = positive       {design2}.
```

Let us now make explicit the rule that the two terminals of a battery are different:

```
not (positive = negative)   {global}.
```

The English translation for these labels would be "if you believe the global assumptions, then you must believe not (positive = negative)". Similarly for design1, "if you believe design1, then you must also believe Top = negative and Bottom = positive". Any deductions made by the inference engine should be appropriately labeled. For instance the deduction:

```
negative = positive              {design1, design2}
```

is compatible with the sets of beliefs defined by design1 and design2. However, this deduction is incompatible with our global rule, and so a warning of the form:

```
INCOMPATIBLE                     {design1, design2, global}
```

should be produced. This tells us that we cannot believe design1, design2, and global simultaneously. It is however, all right to believe design1 and global alone or design2 and global. This is the behavior we want, as there are two separate designs, and the inference engine has simply found out that the two designs cannot be combined together.

8.7   Case study: the design of a lightweight beam

8.7.1   Conceptual design

To illustrate some of the ideas behind the application of knowledge-based systems to conceptual design, we will consider the design of a lightweight beam. The beam is intended to support a passenger seat in a commercial aircraft. The whole aircraft will have been designed, and we are concerned

with the design of one component of the whole assembly. The total design
process for the beam is part of the detailed design process for the aircraft. The
intended loading of the beam tends to cause it to bend, as shown in figure 8.7.
The objectives for the beam are:

i   to be stiff enough that the deflection *(D)* is kept small;
ii   to be strong enough to support the load without fracture; and
iii   to be as light as possible, so as to maximize the ratio of cargo weight to
      fuel consumption.

Together, these three objectives form the basis of the product design
specification (PDS). The PDS can be made more specific by placing limits on
the acceptable deflection *(D)* under the maximum design load *(F)*. A limit
could be placed on the mass of the beam too. However, a suitable mass limit is
difficult to judge, as it presupposes the form of the beam (i.e., its conceptual
design) and the materials used. For this reason, we will simply state that the
beam is required to be as light as possible within the constraints of fulfilling
the other two requirements. In practice, a number of additional constraints will
apply, such as materials costs, manufacturing costs and flammability.

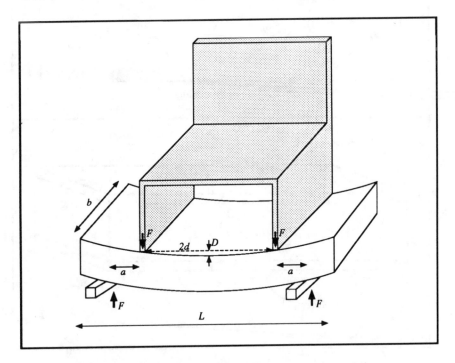

Figure 8.7 Four point loading of a beam supporting a chair.

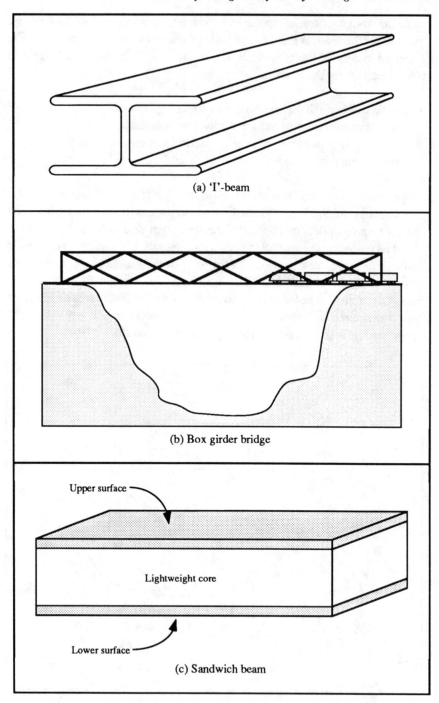

Figure 8.8 Some alternative conceptual designs for load-bearing beams.

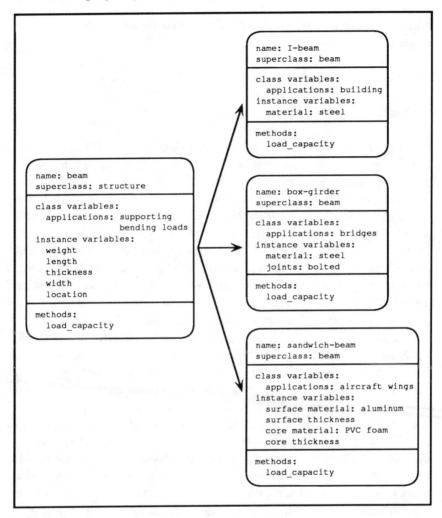

Figure 8.9 Hierarchical classification of beams.

Kim & Suh [15] propose that the design process in general can be based upon two axioms, which can be implemented as meta-rules:

```
axiom 1: maintain independence of functional requirements;
axiom 2: minimize information content.
```

Our statement of the PDS fulfills these two axioms since we have identified three concise and independent requirements.

Many knowledge-based systems for conceptual design attempt to make use of past designs (e.g., CYCLOPS, mentioned above), as indeed do human designers. Some past designs that are relevant to designing the beam shown in figure 8.8 are:

- "I-beams" used in the construction of buildings (figure 8.8a);
- box girder bridges (figure 8.8b); and
- sandwich structures used in aircraft wings (figure 8.8c).

All three structures have been designed to resist bending when loaded. For this knowledge to be useful, it must be accompanied by an explanation of the underlying principles of these designs, as well as their function. The principle underlying all three designs is that the strength and stiffness is provided by the top and bottom surfaces, while the remaining material keeps the two surfaces apart.   The heaviest parts of the beam are therefore concentrated at the surfaces, where they are most effective. This explanation could be expressed as a rule, or perhaps by hierarchical classification of the structural objects that share this property (figure 8.9). A set of conceptual design rules might seize upon the "beams" class as being appropriate for the current application because they maximize both *(stiffness/mass)* and *(strength/mass)* in bending.

At this stage in the design procedure three markedly different conceptual designs have been found which fulfill the requirements as laid down so far. A key difference between the alternatives is their shape. So a knowledge-based system for conceptual design might seek information about the shape requirements of the beam. If the beam is to be able to both support the seats and act as a floor that passengers can walk on, it should be flat, and able to fulfill the design requirements over a large area. Adding this criterion leaves only one suitable conceptual design, namely the sandwich beam. If the human who is interacting with the system is happy with this decision, the new application can be added to the `applications` attribute of the `sandwich beam` class so that this experience will be available in future designs (figure 8.9).

8.7.2 *Optimization and evaluation*
The optimization and evaluation stage of the design process involves performing calculations to optimize performance and to check whether specifications are being met. As this phase is primarily concerned with numerical problems, the tasks are mainly handled using procedural programming techniques. However, the numerical processes can be made more effective and efficient by the application of rules to steer the analysis. For instance, a design system may have access to a library of optimization procedures, the most appropriate for a specific task being chosen by a rule-based selection module.

Three important forms of numerical analysis are:

- mathematical optimization;
- finite-element analysis; and
- bespoke modeling.

Four techniques for mathematical optimization (gradient descent, conjugate gradient descent, simulated annealing and genetic algorithms) were described in section 6.3. Finite-element analysis is a general technique for modeling complex shapes. In order to analyze the performance of a three-dimensional physical product, a technique has to be devised for representing the product numerically within the computer. For regular geometric shapes, like a cube or sphere, this poses no great problem. But the shape of real products, such as a saucepan handle or a gas turbine blade, can be considerably more complex. Since the shape of an object is defined by its surfaces, or *boundaries*, the analysis of performance (e.g., the flow of air over a turbine blade) falls into the class of *boundary-value problems*. Finite-element analysis provides a powerful technique for obtaining approximate solutions to such problems. The technique is based upon the concept of breaking up an arbitrarily complex surface or volume into a network of simple interlocking shapes. The performance of the whole product is then taken to be the sum of the performances of each constituent part. There are many published texts which give a full treatment of finite-element analysis (e.g., [16, 17]).

Mathematical optimization or finite element analysis might be used in their own right or as subtasks within a customized model. If equations can be derived which describe the performance of some aspects of the product under design, then it is obviously sensible to make use of them. The rest of this section will therefore concentrate on the modeling of a physical system, with particular reference to the design of a sandwich beam.

In the case of the sandwich beam, expressions can be derived which relate the minimum mass of a beam that meets the stiffness and strength requirements to dimensions and material properties. Mass, stiffness and strength are examples of *performance variables*, as they quantify the performance of the final product. The thicknesses of the layers of the sandwich beam are *decision variables*, as the designer must choose values for these variables in order to achieve the required performance. Considering firstly the stiffness requirement, it can be shown [18, 19] that the mass of a beam that just meets the stiffness requirement is given by:

$$M \approx bL \left(\frac{2\rho_s fF a d^2}{DE_s b t_c^2} + \rho_c t_c \right) \tag{8.1}$$

where:

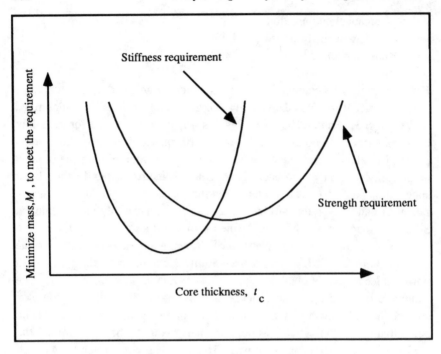

Figure 8.10 Mass of a sandwich beam that just meets stiffness and strength
requirements.

M = mass of beam
b, L, a, d = dimensions defined in figure 8.7
F = applied load
f = safety factor (f ≥ 1.0)
t_s, ρ_s, E_s= thickness, density and Young's modulus of surface material
t_c, ρ_c, E_c= thickness, density and Young's modulus of core material

Equation (8.1) is written in terms of the core thickness, t_c. For each value
of core thickness, there is a corresponding surface thickness, t_s, that is required
in order fulfill the stiffness requirement:

$$t_s \approx \frac{fF\,ad^2}{DE_s bt_c^2}. \tag{8.2}$$

Thus, given a choice of materials, the plan view dimensions (b, L, a and d), and
the maximum deflection *(D)* under load F, there is a unique pair of values of t_c
and t_s that correspond to the minimum mass beam that meets the requirement.

If this were the only requirement, the analysis would be complete. However, as well as being sufficiently stiff, the beam must be sufficiently strong, i.e., it must not break under the design load. A new pair of equations can be derived that describe the strength requirement:

$$M \approx bL\left(\frac{2\rho_s fFa}{\sigma_f bt_c} + \rho_c t_c\right) \tag{8.3}$$

$$t_s \approx \frac{fFa}{\sigma_f bt_c} \tag{8.4}$$

where σ_f = failure stress of the surface material.

Assuming a choice of core and surface materials, and given the plan dimensions and loading conditions, equations 8.1 and 8.3 can be plotted to show mass as a function of core thickness, as shown in figure 8.10. The position of the two curves in relation to each other depends upon the materials chosen. It should be noted that the minimum mass to fulfill the stiffness requirement may be insufficient to fulfill the strength requirement, or vice versa.

There are still two more complications to consider before the analysis of the beam is complete. Firstly the core material must not fail in shear. In order to achieve this, the following condition must be satisfied:

$$t_c \geq \frac{3fF}{2b\,\tau_c}. \tag{8.5}$$

where τ_c = critical shear stress for failure of the core material.

Finally, the upper surface, which is in compression, must not buckle. This condition is described by the following equation:

$$t_s \geq \frac{2fFa}{bt_c(E_sE_cG_c)^{1/3}} \tag{8.6}$$

where G_c is the shear modulus of the core material.

Armed with these numerical models, reasonable choices of layer thicknesses can be made. Without such models, a sensible choice would be fortuitous.

8.7.3 Detailed design

The detailed design phase allows the general view provided by the conceptual design phase to be refined. The optimization and evaluation phase provides the information needed in order to make these detailed design decisions. The decisions taken at this stage are unlikely to be innovative, as the design is constrained by decisions made during the conceptual design phase. In the case of the sandwich beam, the following decisions need to be made:

- choice of core material;
- choice of upper surface material;
- choice of lower surface material;
- choice of core thickness;
- choice of upper surface thickness;
- choice of lower surface thickness;
- method of joining the surfaces to the core.

There is clearly a strong interaction between these decisions. There is also an interaction with the optimization and evaluation process, as equations 8.1 - 8.6 need to be reevaluated for each combination of materials considered. The decisions will also need to take account of any assumptions or approximations which might be implicit in the analysis. For instance, equations 8.1 - 8.4 were derived under the assumption that the top and bottom surfaces were made from identical materials and each had the same thickness.

8.8 Design as a selection exercise

8.8.1 Overview

It should be noted that the crux of both conceptual and detailed design is the problem of selection. Some of the techniques available for making selection decisions are described in the following sections. In the case of a sandwich beam, the selection of the materials and glue involves making a choice from a very large but finite number of alternatives. Thickness, on the other hand, is a continuous variable and it is tempting to think that the "right" choice is yielded directly by the analysis phase. However, this is rarely the case. The requirements on, say, core thickness will be different depending on whether one is considering stiffness, surface strength, or core shear strength. The actual chosen thickness has to be a compromise. Furthermore, although thickness is a continuous variable, the designer may be constrained by the particular set of thicknesses that a supplier is willing to provide.

Some alternative approaches to materials selection using scoring techniques will now be discussed. In each case, candidate materials are given a score based upon their performance with respect to the requirements, and the highest scoring materials are chosen. We will start by showing a naive attempt at combining materials properties to come to an overall decision. We will then consider a more successful algorithm called AIM [20]. AIM will be illustrated by considering the selection of a polymer for the manufacture of a kettle.

For the purposes of this discussion, selection will be restricted to polymer materials. The full range of materials available to designers covers metals, composites, ceramics and polymers. Each of these categories is vast, and restricting the selection to polymers still leaves us with a very complex design decision.

8.8.2 Merit indices

The analysis of the sandwich beam yielded expressions for the mass of a beam that just meets the requirements. These expressions contained geometrical measurements and physical properties of the materials. Examination of equation 8.1 shows that the lightest beam that meets the stiffness requirement will have a low density core (ρ_c) and surfaces(ρ_s), and the surface material will have a high Young's modulus (E_s). However, this observation would not be sufficient to enable a choice between two materials where the first had a high value of E_s and ρ_s, and the second had a low value for each. Merit indices can help such decisions by enabling materials to be ranked according to *combinations* of properties. For instance, a merit index for the surface material of a sandwich beam would be E_s/ρ_s. This is because equation 8.1 reveals that the important combination of properties for the surface material is the ratio ρ_s/E_s. As the latter ratio is to be minimized, while merit indices are normally taken to be a quantity that is to be maximized, the merit index is the reciprocal

Minimum weight for given:	Merit index for surface material	Merit index for core material
stiffness	$\dfrac{E_s}{\rho_s}$	$\dfrac{1}{\rho_c}$
strength	$\dfrac{\sigma_f}{\rho_s}$	$\dfrac{\tau_c}{\rho_c}$
buckling resistance	$\dfrac{E_s^{1/3}}{\rho_s}$	$\dfrac{(E_c G_c)^{1/3}}{\rho_c}$

Table 8.1 Merit indices for a sandwich beam.

Mode of loading	Minimize mass for given	
	stiffness	ductile strength
Tie F, l specified r free 	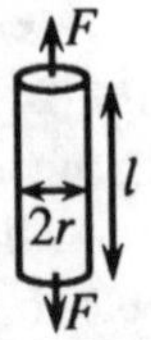 $\dfrac{E}{\rho}$	$\dfrac{\sigma_y}{\rho}$
Torsion bar T, l specified r free 	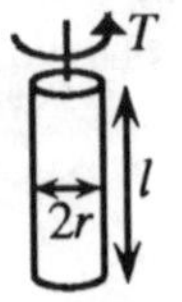 $\dfrac{G}{\rho}$	$\dfrac{\sigma_y}{\rho}$
Torsion tube T, l, r specified t free 	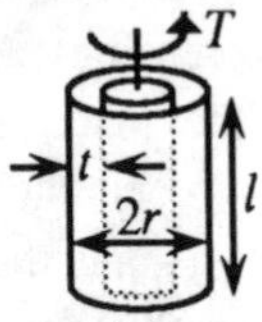 $\dfrac{G}{\rho}$	$\dfrac{\sigma_y}{\rho}$
Bending of rods and tubes F, l specified r or t free 	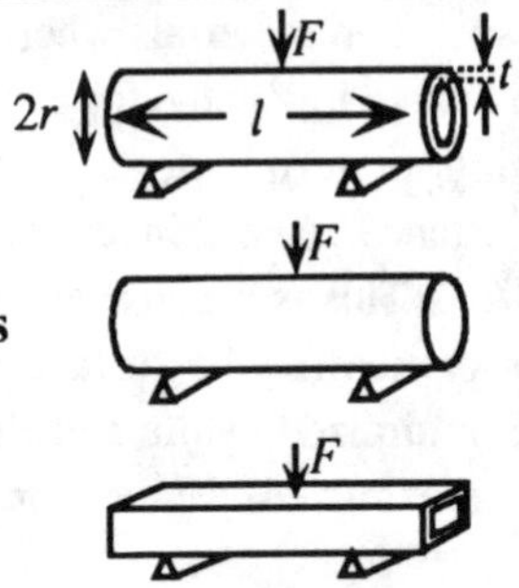 $\dfrac{E^{1/2}}{\rho}$	$\dfrac{\sigma_y^{2/3}}{\rho}$

Figure 8.11 Merit indices for minimum mass design (after Ashby [21]).
E=Young's modulus; G=shear modulus; ρ=density; σ_y=yield stress.

of this ratio. By considering equations 8.1 - 8.6, we can derive the merit indices shown in table 8.1.

Merit indices can be calculated for each candidate material. From these, tables showing the ranking order of the materials can be drawn up for each merit index. Thus merit indices go some way towards the problem of materials selection based on a combination of properties. However, if more than one merit index needs to be considered (as with the sandwich beam), the problem is not completely solved. Materials which perform well with respect to one merit index may not perform so well with respect to another. The designer then faces the problem of finding the materials which offer the best compromise. The scoring techniques described in sections 8.8.6 - 8.8.7 address this problem. Merit indices for minimum mass design of a range of mechanical structures are shown in figure 8.11.

8.8.3   *The polymer selection example*

With the huge number of polymers available, a human designer is unlikely to have sufficient knowledge to make the most appropriate choice of polymer for a specific application. Published data are often unreliable and are generally produced by polymer manufacturers, who have a vested interest in promoting their own products. Even when adequate data are available, the problem of applying them to the product design is likely to remain intractable unless the designer is an expert in polymer technology, or has on-line assistance. The selection system described here is intended to help the designer by making the best use of available polymer data. The quality of the recommendations made will be limited by the accuracy and completeness of these data. Use of a computerized materials selection system has the spin-off advantage of encouraging designers to consider and analyze their requirements of a material.

8.8.4   *Two-stage selection*

The selection system in this example is based upon the idea of ranking a shortlist of polymers by comparing their relative performance against a set of materials properties. The length of the shortlist can be reduced by the prior application of numerical specifications, such as a minimum acceptable impact strength. The selection process therefore comprises two stages, as shown in figure 8.12. Firstly, any polymers which fail to meet the user's numerical specifications are eliminated. These specifications are *constraints* on the materials, and can be used to limit the number of candidate polymers. Constraints of this sort are sometimes described as *primary constraints*, indicating that they are nonnegotiable. A facility to alter the specifications helps the user of a selection system to assess the sensitivity of the system to changes in the constraints.

The second stage of the selection process requires the system to weigh up the user's *objectives* to arrive at some balanced compromise solutions. The objectives are properties which are to be maximized or minimized as far as possible while satisfying constraints and other objectives. For instance, it may

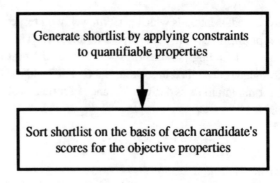

Figure 8.12 Two-stage selection.

be desirable to maximize impact strength while minimizing cost. Cost is treated as a polymer property in the same way as the other physical properties. Each objective has an importance rating (supplied by the user) associated with it. In the unlikely event of a polymer offering outstanding performance for each material objective, this polymer will appear at the top of the list of recommendations made by the selection system. More typically, the properties being optimized represent conflicting requirements for each polymer. For example, a polymer offering excellent impact resistance may not be easily injection moulded. For such problems there is not a single correct answer, but several answers offering different levels of suitability. Objectives may also be known as *preferences* or *secondary constraints*.

8.8.5   Constraint relaxation
Several authors (e.g., Demaid and Zucker [6], Navichandra and Marks [22] and Sriram et al. [2]) have stressed the dangers of applying numerical constraints too rigidly and so risking the elimination of candidates which would have been quite suitable. Hopgood [20] and Navichandra and Marks [22] overcome this problem by relaxing the constraints by some amount. In Hopgood's system the amount of constraint relaxation is described as a tolerance, which is specified by the user. Relaxation overcomes the artificial precision that is built into a specification. It could be that it is difficult to provide an accurately specified constraint, the property itself may be ill-defined, or the property definition may only approximate what we are really after. Application and relaxation of constraints can be illustrated by representing each candidate as a point on a graph where one property is plotted against another. A boundary is drawn between those materials which meet the constraints and those that do not, and relaxation of the constraints corresponds to sliding this boundary (figure 8.13).

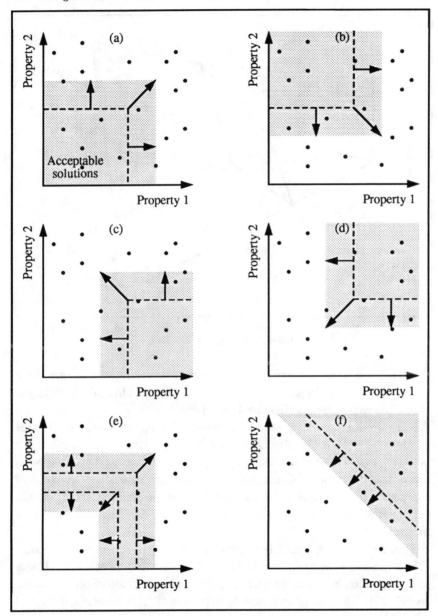

Figure 8.13 Relaxation of constraints:

(a) both constraints are maximum specifications;

(b) property 1 has a maximum specification; property 2 has a minimum specification;

(c) property 2 has a maximum specification; property 1 has a minimum specification;

(d) both constraints are minimum specifications;

(e) constraints are target values with associated tolerances;

(f) constraint is a trade-off between interdependent properties.

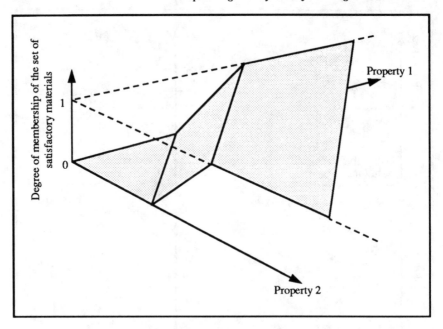

Figure 8.14 A fuzzy constraint.

If our specification represents a minimum value that must be attained for a single property (e.g., impact resistance must be at least 1kJ/m), the boundary is moved towards the origin (figure 8.13a). If one or both specifications are for a maximum value, then the boundary is moved in the opposite direction (figures 8.13b-d). Figure 8.13e illustrates the case where target specifications are provided, and constraint relaxation corresponds to increasing the tolerance on those specifications. Often the specifications cannot be considered independently, but instead some combination of properties defines the constraint boundary (figure 8.13f). In this case there is a trade-off between the properties.

An alternative approach is to treat the category of satisfactory materials (i.e., those that meet the constraints) as a fuzzy set (see section 4.4). Under such a scheme, those materials whose properties were comfortably within the specification would be given a membership value of '1', while those that failed miserably to reach the specification would be given a membership value of '0'. Materials close to the constraint boundary would be assigned a degree of membership between '0' and '1' (figure 8.14). The membership values for each material might then be taken into account in the next stage of the selection process, based on scoring each material.

Ashby [21] has plotted maps similar to those in figure 8.13 using logarithmic scales. These "Ashby maps" are a particularly effective means of

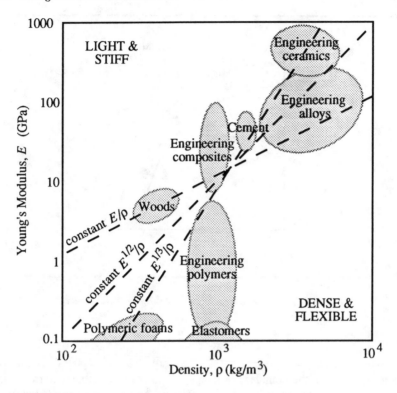

Figure 8.15 Ashby map for Young's modulus versus density [21].

representing a constraint on a merit index. Figure 8.15 shows the loci of points for which:

$$\frac{E}{\rho} = \text{constant},$$

$$\frac{E^{1/2}}{\rho} = \text{constant, and}$$

$$\frac{E^{1/3}}{\rho} = \text{constant.}$$

E/ρ is a suitable merit index for the surface material of a stiff lightweight sandwich beam, $E^{1/2}/\rho$ is a suitable merit index for the material of a stiff lightweight tube, and $E^{1/3}/\rho$ is a suitable merit index for the material of a stiff lightweight plate. In figure 8.15, the materials that meet the merit index specification most comfortably are those that are towards the top left side of the map.

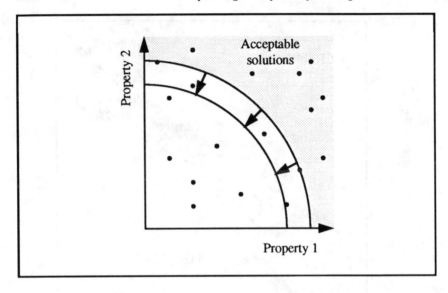

Figure 8.16 Constraint relaxation by sliding the Pareto surface.

When two desirable properties (such as strength and cheapness) are plotted against each other, the boundary of the population of acceptable materials may follow an arc, as shown in figure 8.16. This represents the trade-off between the properties. If more than two properties are considered, the boundary defines a surface in multidimensional space. Materials which lie on the boundary, known as the *Pareto surface*, are the best candidates. Selection could be restricted to these candidates alone, but constraint relaxation allows materials *close* to the boundary to be considered as well (figure 8.16). These same arguments apply to selection between design alternatives [2] as well as to selection between materials.

8.8.6 *A naive approach to scoring*

We shall now move on to the problem of sorting the shortlist into an order of preference. Let us assume the existence of a data file containing an array of performance values (ranging from 0 to 9) for each polymer against each of a number of different properties. The user can supply an importance weighting for each property of interest. A naive approach to determining a polymer's score is to multiply the two figures together for each property, and then to take the sum of the values obtained to be the overall score for that polymer. The polymers with the highest scores are recommended to the user. This scoring system is summarized below:

Total score for polymer $i = \sum_j [\text{performance}(i, j) \times \text{weight}(j)]$ (8.7)

where:
performance(i, j) = performance value of polymer i for property j;
weight(j) = user-supplied weighting for property j.

An implication of the use of a summation of scores is that even though a particular polymer may represent a totally inappropriate choice because of, for example, its poor impact resistance, it may still be highly placed in the ordered list of recommendations. An alternative to finding the arithmetic sum of all of the scores is to find their product:

Product of scores for polymer $i = \prod_j [\text{performance}(i, j) \times \text{weight}(j)]$ (8.8)

When combining by multiplication, a poor score for a given property is less readily compensated by the polymer performance for other properties. A polymer which scores particularly badly on a given criterion tends to be filtered out from the final list of recommendations. Thus, using the multiplication approach, good "all-round performers" are preferred to polymers offering performance which varies between extremes. This distinction between the two approaches is illustrated by the following simple example:

	Score 1	Score 2	Score 3	Combination by addition	Combination by multiplication
Polymer A	1	2	3	6	6
Polymer B	2	2	2	6	8

In this example polymer B offers a uniform mediocre rating across the three properties, while the rating of polymer A varies from poor (score 1) to good (score 3). Under an additive scheme the polymers are ranked equal, while under the multiplication scheme polymer B is favored.

A little reflection will show that both of these approaches offer an inadequate means of combining performance values with weightings. Where a property is considered important (i.e., has a high weighting), and a polymer performs well with respect to that property (i.e., has a high performance value), the contribution to the polymer score is large. However, where a property is considered less important (low weighting), and a polymer performs poorly with respect to that property (low performance value), this combination produces the smallest contribution to the polymer score. In fact, since the

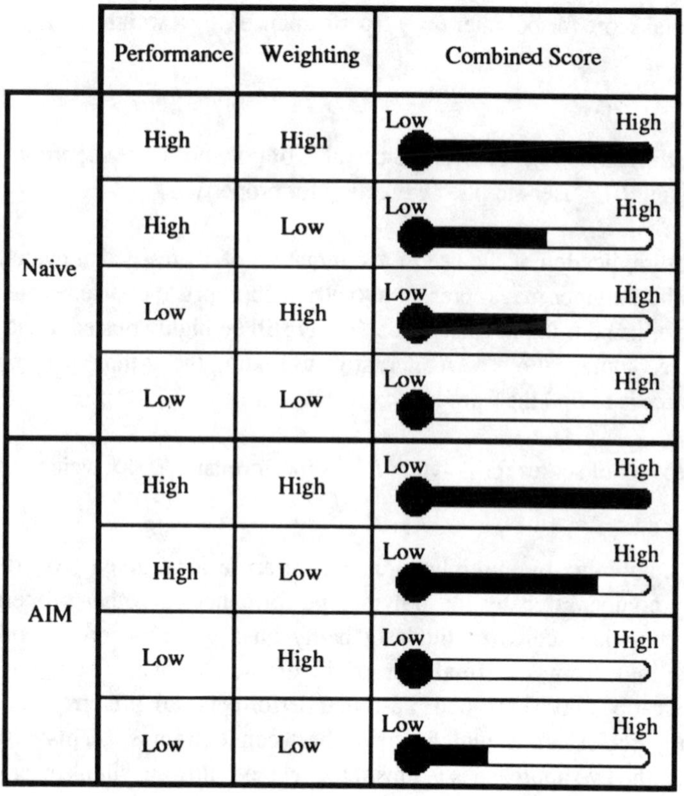

	Performance	Weighting	Combined Score
Naive	High	High	Low ▬▬▬▬▬▬▬ High
	High	Low	Low ▬▬▬ High
	Low	High	Low ▬▬▬ High
	Low	Low	Low ▬ High
AIM	High	High	Low ▬▬▬▬▬▬ High
	High	Low	Low ▬▬▬▬▬ High
	Low	High	Low ▬ High
	Low	Low	Low ▬▬ High

Figure 8.17 Comparison of naive and AIM scoring schemes.

property in question has a low importance rating, the selection of the polymer should be still favored. The AIM algorithm (section 8.8.7) was developed specifically to deal with this anomaly. The least appropriate polymer is actually one which has low performance values for properties with high importance weightings. Figure 8.17 contrasts the naive algorithms with AIM.

8.8.7 A better approach to scoring

The shortcomings of a naive approach to scoring have been noted above and used as a justification for the development of an improved algorithm, AIM. Using AIM, the score for each polymer is given by:

Total score for polymer i =

$$\prod_j \{[(weight(j)) \times (performance(i, j) - offset)] + scale\_shift\_term\} \qquad (8.9)$$

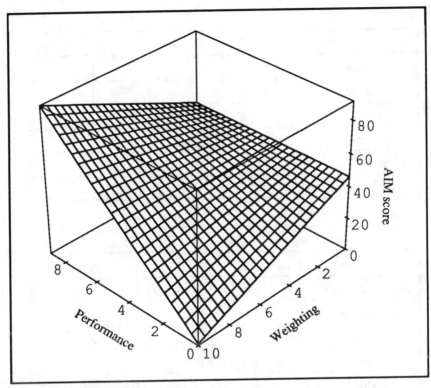

Figure 8.18 Combination of performance values with weightings for a single property, using AIM.

where *scale_shift_term* is the smallest number that will ensure that the combined weight and performance rating is positive. In an implemented system [20], the following parameters were selected:

polymer performance rating range	0 - 9
weighting range	0.0 - 10.0
offset	4.5
scale_shift_term	46.0

The AIM equation for a single property, with these parameters inserted, is shown in figure 8.18. Performance values lower than the offset value can be thought of as degrees of undesirability. On the weightings scale, zero means "I don't care".

Input:

Property	Constraint	Tolerance	Weighting
impact resistance			5
resistance to aqueous environments			8
maximum operating temperature	≥100°C	30°C	
glosssiness			3
cheapness			6
ease of injection molding			9

Output:

Recommended polymers	Normalized score
Polypropylene copolymer	4.05
ABS (acrylonitrile-butadiene-styrene copolymer)	3.59
Polypropylene homopolymer	3.29
Fire-retardant polypropylene	2.53
30% glass-fibre coupled polypropylene	2.40
TPX (poly-4-methyl pent-1-ene)	2.06
(114 others meet the contraints)	

Figure 8.19 Use of the AIM polymer selection system during the design of a kettle.

8.8.8 Case study: the design of a kettle

Figure 8.19 shows a possible set of inputs and outputs from a polymer selection system that uses AIM. After receiving a list of recommended polymers, the user may alter one or more previous inputs in order to test the effect on the system's recommendations. These "what if?" experiments are also useful for designers whose materials specifications were only vaguely formed when starting a consultation. In these circumstances, the system serves not only to make recommendations for the choice of polymer, but also to assist the designer in deciding upon the materials requirements. The interface contains gaps in places where an entry would be inappropriate. For instance, the user can indicate that "glossiness" is to be maximized, and supply a weighting. However, the user cannot supply a specification of the minimum acceptable glossiness, as only comparative data are available.

In the example shown in figure 8.19, the designer is trying to determine a suitable polymer for the manufacture of a kettle. The designer has decided that the kettle must be capable of withstanding boiling water for intermittent periods. In addition, a high level of importance has been placed upon the need for the polymer to be injection moldable. The designer has also chosen material cheapness as a desired property, independently of manufacturing costs. Additionally the glossiness and impact resistance of the polymer are to be maximized, within the constraints of attempting to optimize as many of the chosen properties as possible.

As we have already noted, care must be taken when entering any numerical specifications. In this example it has been specified that a maximum operating temperature of at least 100°C is required. A tolerance of 30°C has been placed on this value to compensate for the fact that the polymer will only be intermittently subjected to this temperature. A polymer whose maximum operating temperature is 69°C would therefore be eliminated from consideration. In the current example, the temperature requirement is clearly defined, although the tolerance is more subjective. The tolerance is equivalent to constraint relaxation.

The recommendations shown in the example are reasonable. The preferred polymer (polypropylene) is sometimes used in kettle manufacture. The second choice (ABS, or acrylonitrile-butadiene-styrene copolymer) is used for the handles of some brands of kettle. The most commonly used polymer in kettle manufacture is an acetal copolymer, which was missing from the selection system's database. This illustrates the importance of having access to adequate data.

8.8.9   Reducing the search space by classification

The selection system described above relies on the ability to calculate a score for every polymer in the system database. In this example, only 150 polymers are considered, and the data are complete (for a limited set of properties). However, even with the search constrained to polymer materials, there are in reality thousands of candidate polymers and grades of polymer. Countless more grades could be specified by slight variations in composition or processing. Clearly a system that relies on a complete and consistent set of data for each material cannot cope with the full range of available materials. Even if the data were available, calculating scores for every single one is unnecessary, and bears no relationship with the approach adopted by a human expert, who would use knowledge about *families* of materials.

In general, chemically similar materials tend to have similar properties, as shown by the Ashby map in figure 8.15. It would therefore be desirable to restructure the database so that polymers are hierarchically classified, with

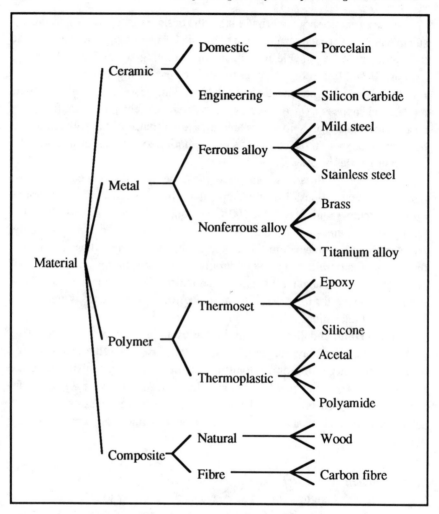

Figure 8.20   One of many possible ways to classify materials.

polymers of a given type grouped together. Thus, given only a vague specification, many categories could be eliminated from consideration early on. Within the category of materials called *polymers*, several subcategories, such as *acetals*, exist. The selection task is simplified enormously by using knowledge of the range of values for a given property that apply to a particular subcategory. The initial searches would then scan only polymer groups, based upon ranges of properties for polymers within that group.

Only when the search has settled on one or two such families is it necessary to consider individual grades of polymer within those groups. As such a classification of materials is hierarchical, it can be represented using

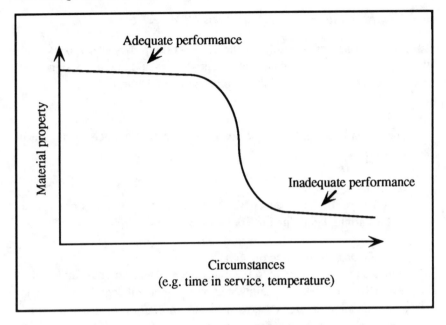

Figure 8.21 The "cliff edge" effect.

object classes joined by specialization relationships (chapter 5). One of many possible classification schemes is shown in figure 8.20.

Demaid and Zucker [23] make use of their own specialized object-oriented system to allow a full and detailed description of both real materials and also of the hypothetical "ideal" material for the job. They specifically aim to overcome the restrictions inherent in systems that rely on a single number to describe a complex property. The knowledge-based system incorporating AIM makes some attempt at this by using rules to modify data in certain circumstances [20]. However, the real problem is that a single value describing a material property, such as stiffness, can only be valid at one temperature, after a fixed duration, under a fixed load, and in a particular environment. So in order to choose a polymer that is sufficiently stiff to be suitable for a kettle body, we need more information than just its stiffness at room temperature. We also need to know its stiffness at 100°C and after (say) two years of daily use. To illustrate how acute the problems can be when dealing with polymers, figure 8.21 shows how a property like stiffness might vary with temperature or duration of exposure. The designer (or the intelligent selection system) needs to be aware that some polymers may have an adequate stiffness for many purposes at room temperature, but not necessarily after prolonged exposure to elevated temperatures.

8.9   Failure modes effects analysis (FMEA)

An important aspect of design is the consideration of what happens when
things go wrong. If any component of a product should fail, the designer will
want to consider the impact of that failure on the following:

- *Safety*
  For example, would an explosion occur? Would a machine run out of
  control?

- *Indication of failure*
  Will the user of the product notice that something is amiss? For example,
  will a warning light illuminate or an alarm sound?

- *Graceful or graceless degradation*
  Will the product continue to function after a component has failed, albeit
  less efficiently? This capability is known as graceful degradation, and has
  some advantages over designs in which the failure of a component is
  catastrophic. On the other hand, graceful degradation may require that the
  product contain more than the bare minimum of components, thereby
  increasing costs.

- *Knock-on damage*
  Will the failure of one component lead to damage of other components?
  Are these other components more or less vital to the function of the
  product? Is the knock-on damage more expensive to fix than the original
  damage?

The assessment of all possible effects from all possible failures is termed
failure modes effects analysis or *FMEA*. FMEA is not concerned with the
cause of failures (this is a diagnosis problem - see chapter 7) but the *effects* of
failures. FMEA comprises the following key stages:

- identifying the possible failure modes;
- generating the changes to the product caused by the failure;
- identifying the consequences of those changes; and
- evaluating the significance of the consequences.

The scoring technique discussed in section 8.8.7 could feasibly be adapted for
the fourth stage, i.e.,evaluating the *significance* of failure mode effects. Price
and Hunt's FLAME system [24] uses product models in order to automate the
first three stages of FMEA. Two modeling approaches have been used -

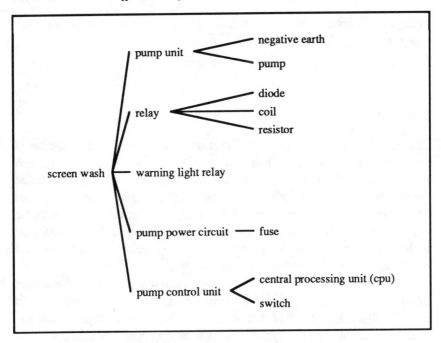

Figure 8.22 Functional decomposition of a screenwash system
(adapted from Price and Hunt [24]).

functional and structural modeling. Functional modeling involves the
breakdown of a system into subsystems, where each subsystem fulfills a
specific function. The subsystems may be further decomposed, leading to a
hierarchical breakdown based on functionality. The encapsulated nature of
each subsystem favors the use of object-oriented programming (see chapter 5).
In the case of the screen wash system of a car (figure 8.22), each subsystem is
modeled by its response to one of three standard electrical inputs - positive
voltage relative to earth, open circuit, or short-circuited to earth. The output
from a subsystem then forms the input to another.

Price and Hunt argue that functional modeling is only adequate when the
subsystems respond correctly to each of the modeled inputs. Under such
circumstances, each subsystem can be relied upon to generate one of a few
standard responses, which becomes the input to another subsystem. However,
if the behavior of a subsystem is altered by a failure mode, a response may be
generated which is not described in the functional model. If this response
forms the input to another subsystem, the functional model can no longer cope.
To model the functional response to *all* such inputs is impractical, as it would
require a complete FMEA in advance. FLAME [24] overcomes this problem
by augmenting the functional model with a structural model, i.e., a simulation

of the overall system, in order to analyze the inputs that are generated at each subsystem.

8.10   Summary

This chapter has addressed some of the issues in developing knowledge-based systems to support design decision-making. Design can be viewed as a search problem in which alternatives must be found or generated, and a selection made from among these. It is a particularly difficult task because it requires both creativity and a vast range of knowledge. Electrical and electronic engineering have been most amenable to the application of decision-support tools, as designs in these domains are often routine rather than innovative and can often be treated as optimization problems.

Selection between alternatives forms an integral part of the design problem. One important selection decision is the choice of materials, a problem that has been explored in some detail in this chapter. Similar techniques might be applied to other aspects of selection within design. Even within the apparently limited domain of materials selection, the range of relevant knowledge is so wide and the interactions so complex that current systems are rather inadequate.

We have seen by reference to the design of a telecommunication network that the design process can be applied to services as well as to manufactured products. This particular case study has also illustrated that producing a design specification can in itself be a complex task, and one that has to be formalized before computerized support tools can be considered. The concepts of constraint propagation and truth maintenance have been illustrated by considering the problem of arranging batteries in a battery holder Conceptual design, optimization, evaluation and detailed design have been illustrated by considering the design of an aircraft floor. This design exercise includes both geometric design and materials selection. The final case study, concerning the design of a kettle, was used to illustrate some additional ideas for materials selection.

Computer aided design packages have been mentioned briefly. These are useful tools, but are often limited to drafting rather than decision-making. The human designer remains at the center of the design process and a range of decision-support tools are being developed which will assist rather than replace him or her. To this end, it is likely that the coming years will bring a greater degree of integration of CAD tools with knowledge-based systems for decision support.

References

1. Open University, *PT610: Manufacture, Materials, Design - Unit 7*, Open University Press (1986).
2. Sriram, D., Stephanopoulos, G., Logcher, R., Gossard, D., Groleau, N., Serrano, D. and Navinchandra, D., "Knowledge-based system applications in engineering design: research at MIT", *AI Magazine*, p79 (Fall 1989).
3. Hopgood, A. A. and Hopson, A. J., "The common traffic model: a universal model for communications networks", in *Institution of Radio and Electronic Engineers Conference (IREECON'91)*, Sydney, p61 (1991).
4. Coad, P. and Yourdon, E., *OOA - object oriented analysis*, Prentice-Hall (1990).
5. Brown, D. and Chandrasekaran, B., "Expert systems for a class of mechanical design activity", in *Knowledge engineering in computer-aided design*, Gero, J. S. (ed.), North-Holland (1985).
6. Demaid, A. and Zucker, J., "A conceptual model for materials selection", *Metals and Materials*, p291 (May 1988).
7. Dietterich, T. G. and Ullman, D. G., "FORLOG: a logic-based architecture for design", in *Expert systems in computer-aided design*, Gero, J. S. (ed.), North-Holland (1987).
8. Dyer, M. G., Flowers, M. and Hodges, J., "Edison: an engineering design invention system operating naively", *International Journal for AI in Engineering*, 1, p36 (1986).
9. Murthy, S. S. and Addanki, S., "PROMPT: an innovative design tool", in *Expert systems in computer-aided design*, Gero, J. S. (ed.), North-Holland (1987).
10. Lirov, Y., "Systematic invention for knowledge engineering", *AI Expert*, p28 (July 1990).
11. Howe, A. E., Cohen, P. R., Dixon, J. R. and Simmons, M. K., "DOMINIC: a domain-independent program for mechanical engineering design", *International Journal for AI in Engineering*, 1, p23 (1986).
12. DeKleer, J., "An assumption-based TMS", *Artificial Intelligence*, 28, p127 (1986).
13. DeKleer, J., "Problem-solving with the ATMS", *Artificial Intelligence*, 28, p197 (1986).
14. DeKleer, J., "Extending the ATMS", *Artificial Intelligence*, 28, p163 (1986).
15. Kim, S. H. and Suh, N. P., "Formalizing decision rules for engineering design", in *Knowledge-based systems in manufacturing*, Kusiak, A. (ed.), Taylor and Francis (1989).

16. Oden, J. T. and Reddy, J. N., *An introduction to the mathematical theory of finite elements*, John Wiley and Sons (1976).
17. Astley, R. J., *Finite element methods in solids and structures*, Chapman & Hall (1992).
18. Reid, C. N. and Greenberg, J., "An exercise in materials selection", *Metals and Materials*, p385 (July 1980).
19. Greenberg, J. and Reid, C. N., "A simple design task (with the aid of a microcomputer)", in *2nd International Conference on Engineering Software*, Southampton, p926 (1981).
20. Hopgood, A. A., "An inference mechanism for selection, and its application to polymers", *AI in Engineering*, 4, p197 (1989).
21. Ashby, M. F., "On the engineering properties of materials", *Acta Metallurgica*, 37, p1273 (1989).
22. Navichandra, D. and Marks, D. H., "Design exploration through constraint relaxation", in *Expert systems in computer-aided design*, Gero (ed.), North-Holland (1987).
23. Demaid, A. and Zucker, J., "Prototype-oriented representation of engineering design knowledge", *AI in Engineering*, 7, p47 (1992).
24. Price, C. J. and Hunt, J. E., "Automating FMEA through multiple models", in *Research and development in expert systems VIII*, Graham, I. and Milne, R. (ed.), Cambridge University Press (1991).

Further reading

* *Computer Aided Design* journal.
* Coyne, R. D., Rosenman, M. A., Radford, A. D., Balachandran, M. and Gero, J. S., *Knowledge-based design systems*, Addison-Wesley (1990).
* Gero, J. S. (ed.), *Knowledge-engineering in computer-aided design*, North-Holland (1985).
* Gero, J. S. (ed.), *Expert systems in computer-aided design*, North-Holland (1987).
* Gero, J. S. (ed.), *Artificial intelligence in engineering: design*, Elsevier/Computational Mechanics (1988).
* Gero, J. S. (ed.), *Artificial intelligence in design*, Computational Mechanics/Springer Verlag (1989).
* Gero, J. S. (ed.), *Artificial intelligence in design '91*, Butterworth-Heinemann (1991).

chapter nine

Systems for planning

9.1 Introduction

The concept of planning is one that is familiar to all of us, as we constantly make and adjust plans that affect our lives. We may make long-term plans such as selecting a particular career path, or short-term plans such as what to eat for lunch. A reasonable definition of planning is the process of producing a *plan*, where:

a plan is a description of a set of actions or operations, in a prescribed order, which are intended to reach a desired goal.

Planning therefore concerns the analysis of actions that are to be performed in the future. It is a similar problem to designing (chapter 8), except that it includes the notion of time. Design is concerned with the detailed description of an artifact or service, without consideration of when any specific part should be implemented. In contrast, the timing of a series of actions, or at least the order in which they are to be carried out, is an essential aspect of planning. Planning is sometimes described as "reasoning about actions", which suggests that a key aspect to planning is the consideration of questions of the form "what would happen if ...?"

Charniak and McDermott [1] have drawn an analogy between planning and programming, as the process of drawing up a plan can be thought of as programming oneself. However, they have also highlighted some differences, in particular:

- programs are intended to be repeated many times, whereas plans are frequently intended to be used once only; and

- the environment for programs is predictable, whereas plans may need to be adjusted in the light of unanticipated changes in circumstances.

The need for computer systems that can plan, or assist in planning, is widespread. Potential applications include management decisions, factory configuration, organization of manufacturing processes, business planning and forecasting, and strategic military decision-making. Some complex software systems may feature *internal planning*, i.e., planning of their own actions. For instance, robots may need to plan their movements, while other systems may use internal planning to ensure that an adequate solution to a problem is obtained within an acceptable time scale.

According to our definition, planning involves choosing a set of operations and specifying either the timing of each or just their order. In many problems, such as planning a manufacturing process, the operations are known in advance. However the tasks of allocating resources to operations and specifying the timing of operations can still be complicated and difficult. This specific aspect of planning is termed *scheduling*, and is described in sections 9.7 - 9.8.

Some of the principles and problems of planning systems are discussed in section 9.2 and an early planning system (STRIPS) is described in section 9.3. This forms the basis for the remainder of this chapter, where more sophisticated features are described.

9.2 Classical planning systems

In order to make automated planning a tractable problem, certain assumptions have to be made. All of the systems discussed in this chapter (except for the reactive planners in section 9.9) assume that the world can be represented by taking a "snapshot" at one particular time. Systems that make this assumption are termed *classical planning systems*, as the assumption has formed the basis of most of the research to date. The aim of a classical planner is to move from a world described by an initial snapshot (the initial world state) to a different world state (the goal state). The term *state-based reasoning* is sometimes used to convey the same idea.

The inputs to a classical system are well defined:

- a description of the initial world state;
- a set of actions or operators which might be performed on the world state; and
- a description of the goal state.

The output from a classical planner consists of a description of the sequence of operators which, when applied to the current world state, will lead to the

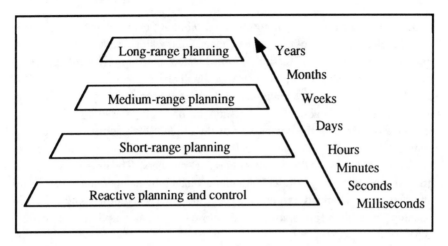

Figure 9.1 Classification by time scale of planning tasks (adapted from [2]).

desired world state as described in the goal. Each operator in the sequence creates a new projected world state, upon which the next operator in the sequence can act, until the goal has been achieved.

The assumption that a plan can be based upon a snapshot of the world is only valid if the world does not change during the planning process. Thus classical planners may be inadequate for reasoning about a continuous process, or dealing with unexpected catastrophes. If a system can react quickly enough to changes in the world to replan and to instigate the new plan, all in real time, the system is described as *reactive* (section 9.9). As reactive planners must be continuously alert to changes in the world state, they are not classical systems.

Bel et al. [2] have categorized types of planning decision on the basis of the time scale to which they apply (figure 9.1). Long-range planning decisions concern general strategy and investments; medium-term planning applies to decisions such as production planning, with a horizon of weeks or months; short-range planning or scheduling refers to the day to day management of jobs and resources. Control decisions have the shortest time horizon, and are made in real time (see chapter 10).

A significant problem in the construction of a planning system is deciding which aspects of the world state are altered by an operation (and by how much they are altered) and which are not affected at all. Furthermore, some operations may have a different effect depending on context, i.e., depending on some other aspect of the world state. Collectively, this is known as the *frame problem*. As an example, consider the operation of walking from home to the shops. Two obvious changes in the world state are firstly that I am no longer at home, and secondly that I have arrived at the shops. However, there are a number of other changes, such as the amount of rubber left on the soles of my shoes. There are also many things that will *not* have changed as a result of my walk, such as the price of oil. Some changes in the world state will depend on context. For instance, if the initial world state includes rainy weather then I will arrive at the shops wet, but otherwise I will arrive dry.

Describing every feasible variant of an action with every aspect of the world state is impractical, as the number of such interactions increases combinatorially with the complexity of the model. One approach to dealing with the frame problem is the so-called *STRIPS assumption*, which is used in STRIPS (see below) and many other classical planners. This is the assumption that all aspects of the world will remain unchanged by an operation, apart from those that are changed explicitly by the modeled operation. The STRIPS assumption is therefore similar to the closed world assumption (see section 3.5).

The planning problem becomes even more complex if we introduce so-called multiple agents. Imagine that we have programmed a robot to be capable of planning and executing a set of operations in order to achieve some goal. Suppose now that our robot is joined by several other robots that are also planning and executing various tasks. It is quite probable that the plans of the robots will interfere, e.g., they may bump into each other, or require the same tool at the same time. Stuart [3] has considered multiple robots, where each reasons independently about the beliefs and goals of others, so as to benefit from them. Other researchers such as Durfee et al. [4] have considered collaborative planning by multiple agents (or robots), where plan generation is shared so that each agent is allocated a specific task.

9.3 STRIPS

9.3.1 General description
STRIPS [5, 6] is one of the oldest AI planning systems, but it is nevertheless an informative one to consider. In its original form, STRIPS was developed in order to allow a robot to plan a route between rooms, moving boxes along the way. However, the principles are applicable to a number of planning domains, and we will consider the operational planning of a company that supplies components for aircraft engines.

Like all classical planning systems, STRIPS is based upon the creation of a world model. The world model comprises a number of objects as well as operators that can be applied to those objects so as to change the world model. So for instance, given an object *alloy block*, the operator *turn* (on a lathe) can be applied so as to create a new object called *turbine disk*. The problem to be tackled is to determine a sequence of operators that will take the world model from an initial state to a goal state.

Operators cannot be applied under all circumstances, but instead each has a set of preconditions which must hold before it can be applied. Given knowledge of the preconditions and effects of each operator, STRIPS is able to apply a technique called *means-ends analysis* to solve planning problems. This technique involves looking for differences between the current state of the world and the goal state, and finding an operator that will reduce the difference. Many classical planning systems use means-ends analysis because it reduces the number of operators that need to be considered, and hence the amount of search that is required. The selected operator has its own preconditions, whose satisfaction becomes a new goal. STRIPS repeats the process recursively until the desired state of the world has been achieved.

9.3.2 An example problem

Consider the problem of responding to a customer's order for turbine disks. If we already have some suitable disks, then we can simply deliver these to the customer. If we do not have any disks manufactured, we can choose either to manufacture disks from alloy blocks (assumed to be the only raw material) or to subcontract the work. Assuming that we decide to manufacture the disks ourselves, we must ensure that we have an adequate supply of raw materials, that staff are available to carry out the work, and that our machinery is in good working order. In the STRIPS model we can identify a number of objects and operators, together with the preconditions and effects of the operators (table 9.1).

Table 9.1 shows specific instantiations of objects associated with operators (e.g., *purchase raw materials*), but other instantiations are often possible (e.g. *purchase anything*). The table shows that each operator has preconditions that must be satisfied before the operator can be executed. Satisfying a precondition is a subproblem of the overall task, and so a developing plan usually has a hierarchical structure.

We will now consider how STRIPS might solve the problem of dealing with an order for a turbine disk. The desired (goal) state of the world is simply *customer has turbine disk*, with the other parameters about the goal state of the world left unspecified.

Let us assume for the moment that the initial world state is as follows:

- the customer has placed an order for a turbine disk;
- the customer does not have the turbine disk;
- staff are available;
- we have no raw materials;

- materials are available from a supplier;
- we can afford the raw materials; and
- the machinery is working.

Means-ends analysis can be applied. The starting state is compared with the goal state and one difference is discovered, namely *customer has turbine disk*. The STRIPS system would now treat *customer has turbine disk* as its goal and would look for an operator that has this state in its list of effects. The operator that achieves the desired result is `deliver`, which is dependent on the conditions *turbine disk ready* and *order placed*. The second condition is satisfied already. The first condition becomes a subgoal, which can be solved in either of two ways - by subcontracting the work or by manufacturing the disk. We will assume for the moment that the disk is to be manufactured in-house. Three preconditions exist for the `manufacture` operator. Two of these are already satisfied (staff are available and the machinery is working), but the

Operator and *object*	Precondition	Effect
Deliver *product*	*Product* is ready & *order* has been placed by *customer*	*Customer* has *product*
Subcontract manufacture of *product*	*Subcontractor* available & *subcontractor* cost is less than product price	*Product* is ready
Manufacture *product*	*Staff* are available, we have the *raw materials* & the *machinery* is working	*Product* is ready, our *raw materials* are reduced & the *machinery* is closer to its next maintenance period
Purchase *raw materials*	We can afford the *raw materials* & the *raw materials* are available	We have the *raw materials* & *money* is subtracted from our *account*
Borrow *money*	Good relationship with our *bank*	*Money* is added to our *account*
Sell *assets*	*Assets* exist & there is sufficient time to sell them	*Money* is added to our *account*
Repair *machinery*	*Parts* are available	*Machinery* is working & next maintenance period scheduled

Table 9.1 Operators for supplying a product to customer.
Operator names are shown emboldened and objects are italicized.

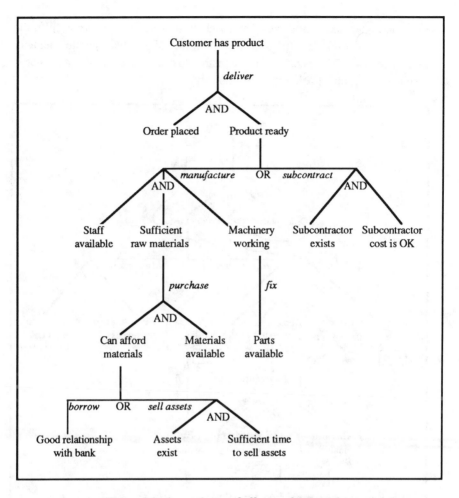

Figure 9.2 A search tree of effects and operators.

precondition that we have raw materials is not satisfied and becomes a new subproblem. This can be satisfied by the operator purchase, whose two preconditions (that we can afford the materials and that materials are available from a supplier) are already satisfied. Thus STRIPS has succeeded in finding a plan, namely:

```
purchase raw materials - manufacture product - deliver product.
```

The full search tree showing all operators and their preconditions is shown in figure 9.2, while figure 9.3 shows the subset of the tree that was used in producing the plan derived above. Note that performing an operation changes the state of the world model. For instance, the operator purchase, applied to raw materials, raises our stock of materials to a sufficient quantity to fulfil the order. In so doing, it fulfills the preconditions of another operator, namely manufacture. This operator too is then able to change the world state, since it results in the product being ready for delivery.

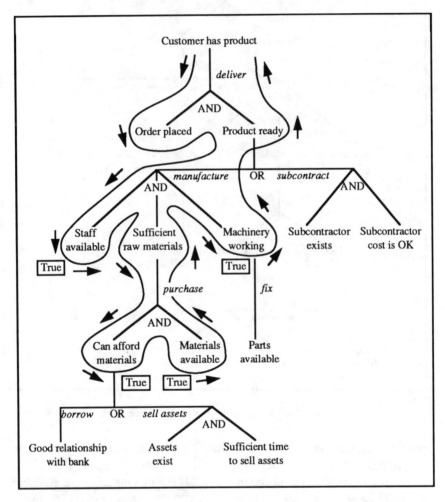

Figure 9.3   STRIPS searching for a plan to fulfil the goal *customer has product*, given the following initial world state:
- the customer has placed an order for a turbine disk;
- the customer does not have the turbine disk;
- staff are available;
- we have no raw materials;
- materials are available from a supplier;
- we can afford the raw materials; and
- the machinery is working.

9.3.3 A simple planning system in Prolog

The STRIPS system involves search, in a depth first fashion, through a tree of states linked by operators. STRIPS initially tries to establish a goal. If the goal has preconditions, these become new goals and so on until either the original goal is established, or all possibilities have been exhausted. In other words, STRIPS performs backward chaining in order to establish a goal. If it should find that a necessary condition cannot be satisfied for the branch that it is investigating, STRIPS will backtrack to the last decision point in the tree (i.e., the most recently traversed "OR" node). STRIPS is therefore heavily reliant on backward chaining and backtracking, features that are built into the Prolog language. For this reason it should be fairly straightforward to program a STRIPS-like system in Prolog*.

There are a number of different ways in which we might build a system for our example of supply of a product to a customer. For the purposes of illustration, we will adopt the following scheme:

- The sequence of operators used to achieve a goal is stored as a list, representing a plan. For instance, assuming that we have no money in our account and no raw materials, a plan for obtaining a turbine blade that is ready for delivery would be the list:

```
[borrow_money, purchase_materials, manufacture].
```

- Each effect is represented as a clause whose last argument is the plan for achieving the effect. For instance, the effect *our customer has turbine disk* is represented by the following clause:

```
has(our_customer, turbine_disk, Plan).
```

- If a particular effect does not require any actions, then the argument corresponding to its plan is an empty list. We may wish to set up certain effects as part of our initial world state, which therefore do not require a plan of action. An initial world state in which a subcontractor exists would be represented as:

```
exists(subcontractor, []).
```

---

* The actual STRIPS program described by Fikes et al. [5, 6] was implemented in Lisp. It was considerably more sophisticated than the Prolog program presented here and it used a different representation of objects and operators.

```
has (Customer, Product, Newplan) :-          % deliver product
ready(Product, Plan1),
order_placed(Product, Customer, Plan2),
merge([Plan1, Plan2, deliver], Newplan).

ready(Product, Newplan):-   % subcontract the manufacturing
exists(subcontractor, Plan1),
subcontractor_price_OK(Plan2),
merge([Plan1, Plan2, subcontract], Newplan).

subcontractor_price_OK([]):-
          % no action is required if the subcontractor's
          % price is OK, i.e. less than the disk price
price(subcontractor,Price1,_),
price(product,Price2,_),
Price1 < Price2.

ready(Product, Newplan):-
                          % manufacture the product ourselves
exists(staff,Plan1),
sufficient_materials(Plan2),
machine_working(Plan3),
merge([Plan1, Plan2, Plan3, manufacture], Newplan).

sufficient_materials([]):-
% no action required if we have sufficient stocks already
current_balance(materials,Amount,_),
Amount >= 1.

sufficient_materials(Newplan):-          % purchase materials
can_afford_materials(Plan),
merge([Plan, purchase_materials], Newplan).

can_afford_materials([]):-
% no action is required if our bank balance is adequate
current_balance(account,Amount,_),
price(materials,Price,_),
Amount >= Price.

can_afford_materials(Newplan):-                   % borrow money
bank_relationship(good, Plan),
merge([Plan, borrow_money], Newplan).
```

Box 9.1 (a)   A simple planner in Prolog (part I).

```
can_afford_materials(Newplan):-                    % sell assets
exists(assets,Plan1),
exists(time_to_sell,Plan2),
merge([Plan1, Plan2, sell_assets], Newplan).

machine_working(Newplan):-                          % fix machinery
exists(spare_parts,Plan2),
merge([Plan1, Plan2, fix_machine], Newplan).

merge([],[]):-!.

merge([ [] | Hierarchical], Flat):-
!,
merge(Hierarchical, Flat).

merge([X | Hierarchical], [X | Flat]):-
atom(X), !,
merge(Hierarchical, Flat).

merge([X | Hierarchical], [A | Flat]):-
X = [A | Rest], !,
merge([Rest | Hierarchical], Flat).

%set up the initial world state
price(product,1000,[]).
price(materials,200,[]).
price(subcontractor,500,[]).
current_balance(account,0,[]).
current_balance(materials,0,[]).
bank_relationship(good,[]).
order_placed(turbine,acme,[]).
exists(subcontractor,[]).
exists(spare_parts,[]).
exists(staff,[]).

%   The following are assumed false (closed world
%   assumption):
%       machine_working([]),
%       exists(assets,[]),
%       exists(time_to_sell,[]).
```

Box 9.1 (b) A simple planner in Prolog (part II).

- The preconditions for achieving an effect are represented as Prolog rules. For instance, one way in which a product can become ready is by subcontracting its manufacture. Assuming this decision, there are two preconditions, namely that a subcontractor exists and that the cost of subcontracting is acceptable. Thus the Prolog rule is as follows:

```
ready(Product, Newplan):-
exists(subcontractor, Plan1),
subcontractor_price_OK(Plan2),
merge([Plan1, Plan2, subcontract], Newplan).
```

The final condition of the rule shown above is the `merge` relation which is used for merging subplans into a single sequence of actions. This is not a standard Prolog facility, so we will have to create it for ourselves. The first argument to `merge` is a list which may contain sublists, while the second argument is a list containing no sublists. The purpose of `merge` is "flatten" a hierarchical list (the first argument) and to assign the result to the second argument. We can define `merge` by four separate rules, corresponding to different structures which the first argument might have. We can ensure that the four rules are considered mutually exclusive by using the cut facility (see section 2.6.3).

The complete Prolog program is shown in box 9.1. The program includes one particular initial world state, but of course this can be altered at will. The world state shown in box 9.1 is as follows:

```
price(product,1000,[]).          % Turbine disk price is $1000
price(materials,200,[]).         % Raw material price is $200 per disk
price(subcontractor,500,[]).     % Subcontractor price is $500 per disk
current_balance(account,0,[]).   % No money in our account
current_balance(materials,0,[]). % No raw materials
bank_relationship(good,[]).      % Good relationship with the bank
order_placed(turbine,acme,[]).   % Order has been placed by ACME Ltd
exists(subcontractor,[]).        % A subcontractor is available
exists(spare_parts,[]).          % Spare parts are available
exists(staff,[]).                % staff are available
```

Because it is not specified that we have assets or time to sell them, or that the machinery is working, these are all considered false under the closed world assumption.

We can now ask our Prolog system for suitable plans to provide a customer (ACME Ltd.) with a product (a turbine disk), as follows:

```
prolog> ? has(acme, turbine, Plan).
```

Prolog offers the following plans in response to our query:

```
Nº1      Plan = [subcontract, deliver]
Nº2      Plan = [borrow_money, purchase_materials, fix_machine,
                 manufacture, deliver]
No more solutions
```

We can also ask for plans to achieve any other effect that is represented in the model. For instance, we could ask for a plan to give us sufficient raw materials, as follows:

```
prolog> ? sufficient_materials(Plan).

Nº1      Plan = [borrow_money, purchase_materials]
No more solutions
```

Having discussed a simple planning system, the remainder of this chapter will concentrate on more sophisticated features that can be incorporated.

9.4 Considering the side-effects of actions

9.4.1 Maintaining a world model

Means-ends analysis (see section 9.3.1) relies upon the maintenance of a world model, since it involves choosing operators that reduce the difference between a given state and a goal state. Our simple Prolog implementation of a planning system does not explicitly update its world model, and this leads to a deficiency in comparison with the real STRIPS implementation. When STRIPS has selected an operator, it applies that operator to the current world model, so that the model changes to a projected state. This is important because an operator may have many effects, only one of which may be the goal that is being pursued. The new world model therefore reflects both the intended effects and the side-effects of applying an operator, provided that they are both explicit in the representation of the operator. All other attributes of the world state are assumed to be unchanged by the application of an operator - this is the STRIPS assumption (see section 9.2).

In the example considered in section 9.3.3, the Prolog system produced a sequence of operators for achieving a goal, namely to supply a product to a customer. What the system fails to tell us is whether there are any implications of the plan, other than achievement of the goal. For instance, we might like to be given details of our projected cash flow, of our new stocks of materials, or of the updated maintenance schedule for our machinery. Because these data are not necessary for achieving the goal (although they are affected by the planned operators), they are ignored by a purely backward chaining mechanism. (See sections 3.7 - 3.9 for a discussion of forward and backward chaining). Table 9.1 indicates that purchasing raw materials has the effect of reducing our bank balance, and manufacturing reduces the time which can elapse before the machinery is due for servicing. Neither effect was considered in our Prolog system because these effects were not necessary for achieving the goal.

9.4.2 Deductive rules

SIPE [7, 8, 9] is a planning system which is able to deduce effects that are additional to those explicitly included in the operator representation. This is a powerful capability, as the same operator may have different effects in different situations, i.e., it may be context-sensitive. Without this capability, context sensitivity can only be modeled by having different operators to represent the same action taking place in different contexts.

SIPE makes use of two types of deductive rules, namely causal rules and state rules. Causal rules detail the auxiliary changes in the world state that are associated with the application of an operator. For example, the operator purchase is intended to change the world state from *we have no raw materials* to *we have raw materials*. This change has at least one side-effect, namely that our bank account balance is diminished. This side-effect can be modeled as a causal rule.

State rules are concerned with maintaining the consistency of a world model, rather than explicitly bringing about changes in the model. Thus if the assertion *machinery is working* is true in the current world state, then a state rule could be used to ensure that the assertion *machinery is broken* is made false.

Causal rules react to changes between states, whereas state rules enforce constraints within a state. Example causal and state rules are shown in box 9.2, using syntax similar to that in SIPE. Note that the rules are passed parameters which take the place of the named arguments, making the rules more general. A rule is considered for firing if its *trigger* matches the world state *after* an operator has been applied. Thus in the case of the causal rule update_bank_balance, the trigger is the world state *we have sufficient supplies*, which is brought about by the operator purchase. Because causal rules apply to a change in world state, they also contain a *precondition*, describing the world state *before* the operator was applied (e.g., NOT(sufficient raw materials)). A causal rule will only fire if its trigger is matched after an operator has been applied and its precondition had been matched immediately before the operator was applied. State rules are not directly concerned with the application of an operator, and so do not have a

```
Causal-Rule:        update_bank_balance
Arguments:          cost,old_balance,new_balance
Trigger:            sufficient supplies of something
Precondition:       NOT(sufficient supplies of something)
Effects:            new_bank_balance = old_bank_balance - cost

State-Rule:         Deduce_fixed
Arguments:          machine1
Trigger:            machine1 is working
Other conditions:   <none>
Effects:            Not(machine1 is broken)
```

Box 9.2 Causal and state rules in SIPE.

precondition. There is, however, provision for naming further conditions (additional to the trigger) that must be satisfied.

In SIPE, when an operator is added to the current plan, causal rules are examined first in order to introduce any changes to the world model, and then state rules are applied in order to maintain consistency with constraints on the model. Other than the order of applicability, there is no enforced difference between causal and state rules. According to the syntax, both can have preconditions and a trigger, although there appears to be no justification for applying a precondition to a state rule.

9.5 Hierarchical planning

9.5.1 Description
Virtually all plans are hierarchical by nature, as exemplified by figure 9.2, although they are not represented as such by all planning systems. STRIPS (a nonhierarchical planner) may produce the following plan for satisfying a customer's order:

```
borrow money - purchase materials - fix machinery - manufacture
- deliver.
```

Some of the actions in this plan are major steps (e.g., *manufacture*), whereas others are comparatively minor details (e.g., *purchase materials*). A *hierarchical planner* would firstly plan the major steps, for example:

```
be ready to deliver - deliver.
```

The details of a step like *be ready to deliver* might then be elaborated:

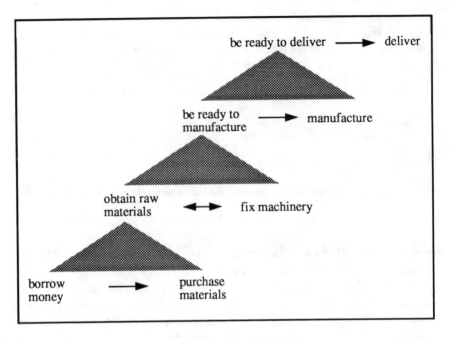

Figure 9.4 A hierarchical plan.

```
be ready to manufacture - manufacture - deliver.
```

Be ready to manufacture might be broken down into the following actions:

```
fix machinery - obtain raw materials.
```

The action *obtain raw materials* can then be elaborated further:

```
borrow money - purchase materials.
```

This hierarchical plan is depicted in figure 9.4. An action that needs no further refinement is a primitive action. In some applications *purchase materials* may be considered a primitive action, but in other applications it may be necessary to elaborate this further (e.g., pick up phone - dial number - speak to supplier - and so on...).

The distinction between a nonhierarchical planner (like STRIPS) and a hierarchical planner (like ABSTRIPS [10]), is that hierarchical planners explicitly represent the hierarchical nature of the plan. At the top of the hierarchy is a simplification or abstraction of the plan, while the lower levels contain the detailed requirements (figure 9.4). A subplan is built for achieving each action in the main plan. While the STRIPS system does recognize that the achievement of some goals is dependent on subgoals, no distinction is drawn between goals that are major steps and those that are merely details. Furthermore, as the STRIPS hierarchy is not explicitly represented, it cannot be modified either by the user or by the system itself.

The method of hierarchical planning can be summarized as follows:

i   sketch a plan that is complete but too vague to be useful; and
ii   refine the plan into more detailed subplans until a complete sequence of problem-solving operators has been specified.

Since the plan is complete (though perhaps not useful in its own right) at each level of abstraction, the term *length-first* search is sometimes used to describe this technique for selecting appropriate operators that constitute a plan.

9.5.2 Benefits of hierarchical planning
Although means-ends analysis is an effective way of restricting the number of operators that apply to a problem, there may still be several operators to choose from, with no particular reason for preferring one to another. In other words, there may be several alternative branches of the search tree. Furthermore, there is no way of knowing whether the selected branch might lead to a dead end, i.e., one of its preconditions might fail.

Consider the example of satisfying a customer's order for a product. Suppose that STRIPS has chosen to apply the manufacture operator (i.e., the left-hand branch of the tree shown in figure 9.2 has been selected). STRIPS would now verify that staff are available, plan to purchase raw materials (which in turn requires money to be borrowed), and then finally it considers the state of the manufacturing equipment. Suppose that at this point it found that the machinery was broken, and spare parts were not available. The plan would have failed, and the planner would have to backtrack to the point where it chose to manufacture rather than subcontract. All the intermediate processing would have been in vain since STRIPS cannot plan to manufacture the product if the machinery is inoperable. The search path followed is shown in figure 9.5.

Part of the expense of backtracking in this example arises from planning several operations which are minor details compared with the more important issue of whether equipment for manufacturing is available. This is a relatively important question that one would expect to have been established earlier in the plan, before considering the details of how to obtain the money to buy the raw materials. The more natural approach to planning is to plan out the important steps first, and then to fill in the details (i.e., to plan hierarchically). Hierarchical planning is therefore one way of postponing commitment to a particular action until more information about the appropriateness of the action is available. This philosophy (sometimes called the *principle of least commitment*) occurs in different guises and is discussed further in section 9.6.

Hierarchical planning requires the use of levels of abstraction in the planning process and in the description of the domain, where an abstraction level is distinguished by the granularity (or level of detail) of its description. It is unfortunate that the term "hierarchical planning" is sometimes used with different meanings. For instance, the term has been used elsewhere to describe levels of metaplanning, i.e., planning the process of creating a plan.

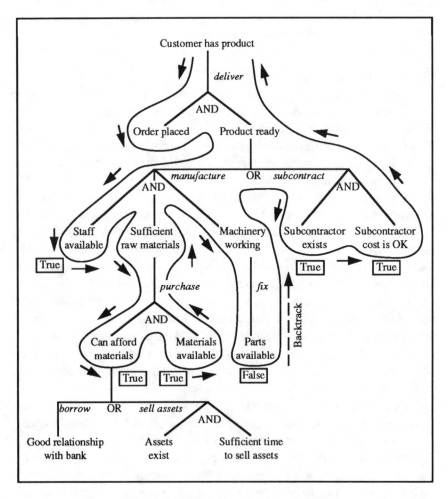

Figure 9.5 Inefficient search using STRIPS.
STRIPS backtracks on finding that there are no parts available for fixing the broken machinery.

9.5.3 Hierarchical planning with ABSTRIPS

ABSTRIPS, i.e., *abstraction-based STRIPS* [10], is an extension of STRIPS that incorporates hierarchical planning. In ABSTRIPS, preconditions and operators are unchanged from STRIPS, except that some preconditions are considered more important than others. Before attempting to generate a plan, ABSTRIPS assigns an importance rating (or criticality) to each precondition. The highest criticality is ascribed to those preconditions that cannot be altered by the planner, and lower criticalities are given to preconditions that can be satisfied by generating a subplan. Planning proceeds initially by considering only the operators which have the highest criticality, thereby generating a "skeleton" plan. To use the jargon, this is a plan in the highest abstraction space. Details of the skeleton plan are filled by progressively considering lower criticality levels. In this way, subplans are generated to satisfy the preconditions in the higher level plans, until all the preconditions in a plan have been achieved. The plan at any given level (save for the highest and lowest) is a refinement of the skeleton plan provided by the layer above, and is itself a skeleton plan for the level below.

ABSTRIPS adopts a semiautomated approach to the assigning of criticalities to preconditions. The user supplies a set of values, which are subsequently modified by ABSTRIPS using some simple heuristics. We will illustrate the process with reference to our example of supplying a product to a customer. The preconditions in our model include having something, something being affordable, or something existing. The existence or otherwise of something is beyond our powers to alter, and thus intuitively warrants the highest criticality value. On the other hand, there are a variety of different ways in which having something can be achieved, and so these preconditions might be given the lowest criticality. Thus a sensible set of user-supplied criticality values might be as follows:

Precondition	User-supplied criticality
We have an item	1
Something is affordable	2
Something exists or is available	3
Other considerations	2

ABSTRIPS then applies heuristics for modifying the criticality values, given a particular world state. The preconditions are examined in order of decreasing user-supplied criticality, and modified as follows:

(a) Any preconditions that remain true or false, irrespective of the application of an operator, are given the maximum criticality. Let's call these *fundamental preconditions.*

(b) If a precondition can be readily established, assuming that all previously considered preconditions are satisfied (apart from unsatisfied fundamental preconditions), then the criticality is left unaltered.

(c) If a precondition cannot be readily established as described in (b), it is given a criticality value between that for category (a) and the highest in category (b).

The criticality values supplied by the user are dependent only on the nature of the preconditions themselves, whereas the modified values depend upon the starting world state and therefore vary according to circumstances. Consider for instance the following world state:

customer does not have turbine disk;
customer has placed an order for a turbine disk;
staff are available;
we have no raw materials;
we have no money in the bank;
we have a good relationship with our bank;
we do not have any assets, nor time to sell assets;
the machinery is broken;
spare parts are not available;
a subcontractor exists;
the subcontractor cost is reasonable.

The following preconditions are given a maximum criticality (say 5) because they are fundamental, and cannot be altered by any operators:

order placed by customer;
subcontractor exists;
subcontractor cost is OK;
staff available;
raw materials available from supplier;
machinery parts available;
good relationship with bank;
assets exist;
sufficient time to sell assets.

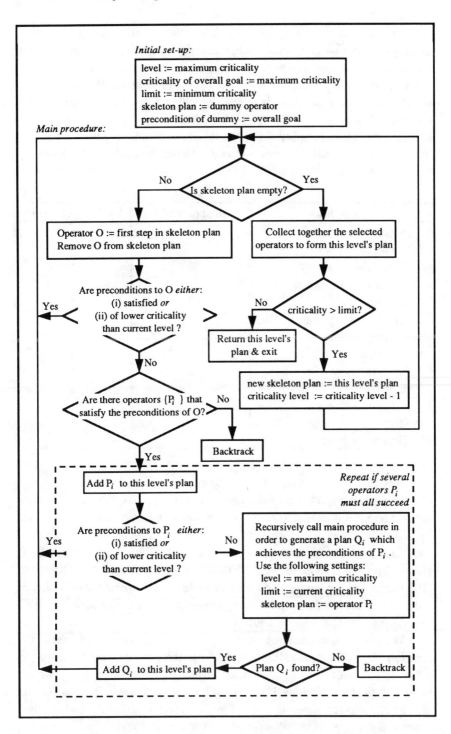

Figure 9.6 Planning with a hierarchical system based on ABSTRIPS.

The precondition *machinery working* falls into category (c) as it depends directly on *spare parts available*, a fundamental precondition which is false in the current world model. The remaining preconditions belong in category (b), and therefore their criticalities are unchanged. Although c*an afford materials* is not immediately satisfied, it is readily achieved by the operator borrow, assuming that *good relationship with bank* is true. Therefore *can afford materials* falls into category (b) rather than (c). Similar arguments apply to *product ready* and *sufficient raw materials*. Given the world model described, the following criticalities might be assigned:

Precondition	Initial criticality	Modified criticality
Staff available	3	5
Subcontractor exists	3	5
Raw materials available	3	5
Machinery parts available	3	5
Assets exist	3	5
Order placed by customer	2	5
Machinery working	2	4
Subcontractor cost OK	2	5
Good relationship with bank	2	5
Sufficient time to sell assets	2	5
Can afford materials	2	2
Product ready	1	1
Sufficient raw materials	1	1

Once the criticalities have been assigned, the process of generating a plan can proceed as depicted by the flowchart in figure 9.6. Planning at each abstraction level is treated as elaborating a skeleton plan generated at the level immediately higher. The main procedure is called recursively whenever a subplan is needed to satisfy the preconditions of an operator in the skeleton plan. Figure 9.6 is based on the ABSTRIPS procedure described by Sacerdoti [10], except that we have introduced a variable lower limit on the criticality in order to prevent a subplan from being considered at a lower criticality level than the precondition which it aims to satisfy.

When we begin planning, a dummy operator is used to represent the skeleton plan. The precondition of dummy is the goal that we are trying to achieve. Consider planning to achieve the goal *customer has product*, beginning at abstraction level 5. The precondition to dummy is *customer has product*. This precondition is satisfied by the operator deliver, which has two preconditions. One of them (*order placed*) is satisfied, and the other (*product*

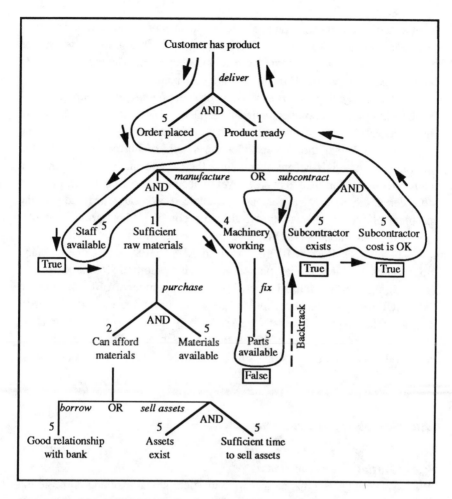

Figure 9.7 More efficient search using a hierarchical planner based on ABSTRIPS.
The figures shown alongside the preconditions are the criticality levels.

ready) has a criticality less than 5. Therefore `deliver` becomes the skeleton
plan for a lower abstraction level.

The skeleton plan cannot be elaborated in levels 4, 3, or 2, as the criticality
of *product ready* is only 1. At level 1, operators that achieve *product ready* are
sought and two are found, namely `manufacture` and `subcontract`. Both of
these operators have preconditions of the highest criticality, so there is no
reason to give one priority over the other. Supposing that `manufacture` is
selected, the main procedure is then called recursively, with the preconditions
to `manufacture` as the new goal. The precondition of the highest criticality is
staff available, and this is found to be satisfied. At the next level *machinery
working* is examined, and the main procedure is called recursively to find a

plan to satisfy this precondition. However, no such plan can be found as *parts available* is false. The plan to manufacture is abandoned at this stage and the planner backtracks to its alternative plan, subcontract. The preconditions to subcontract are satisfied and this becomes the plan.

A hierarchical planner can solve problems with less searching and backtracking than its nonhierarchical equivalent. The above example (shown in figure 9.7) is more efficient than the STRIPS version (figure 9.5), as the hierarchical planner did not consider the details of borrowing money and buying raw materials before abandoning the plan to manufacture. Since a complete plan is formulated at each level of abstraction before the next level is considered, the hierarchical planner can find dead-ends early, as it did with the problem of fixing the machinery. If more complex plans are considered, involving many more operators, the saving becomes much greater still.

The planner described here, based on ABSTRIPS, is just one of many approaches to hierarchical planning. Others adopt different means of determining the hierarchical layers, since the assignment of criticalities in ABSTRIPS is rather ad hoc. Some of the other systems are less rigid in their use of a skeleton plan. For instance, Nonlin [11] treats the abstraction levels as a guide to a skeleton solution, but is able to replan or consider alternatives at any level if a solution cannot be found or if a higher-level choice is faulty.

9.6 Postponement of commitment

9.6.1 Partial ordering of plans

We have already seen that an incentive for hierarchical planning is the notion that we are better off deferring detailed decisions until after more general decisions have been made. This is a part of the principle of postponement of commitment (or *principle of least commitment*). In the same context, if the order of steps in a plan makes no difference to the plan, the planner should leave open the option of doing them in any order. A plan is said to be *partially ordered* if it contains actions that are unordered with respect to each other, i.e., actions for which the planner has not yet determined an order and which may possibly be in parallel.

If we refer back to the Prolog planner described in section 9.3.3, we see that given a particular world state, and given the goal of supplying a product to a customer, the following plan was generated:

```
[borrow_money, purchase_materials, fix_machine, manufacture,
deliver].
```

This plan contains a definite order of events. As can be inferred from the search tree in figure 9.2, some events must occur before others. For example, the product cannot be delivered until after it has been manufactured. However, the operators `fix_machine` and `purchase_materials` have been placed in an arbitrary order. These operators are intended to satisfy two subgoals (*machinery working* and *sufficient raw materials* respectively). As both subgoals need to be achieved, they are conjunctive goals. A planning system is said to be *linear* if it assumes that it does not matter in which order conjunctive goals are satisfied. This is the so-called *linear assumption*, which is not necessarily valid, and which can be expressed as follows:

"subgoals are independent and thus can be sequentially achieved in an arbitrary order".

Nonlinear planners are those that do not rely upon this assumption. The generation of partially ordered plans is the most common form of nonlinear planning, but Hendler et al. [12] have pointed out that it is not the only form. The generation of a partially ordered plan avoids commitment to a particular order of actions until information for selecting one order in preference to another has been gathered. Thus a nonlinear planner might generate the following partially ordered plan:

$$\left[\begin{array}{c} \text{[borrow\_money, purchase\_materials]} \\ \text{fix\_machine} \end{array} , \text{ manufacture, deliver} \right]$$

If it is subsequently discovered that fixing the machine requires us to borrow money, this can be accommodated readily because we have not committed ourselves to fixing the machine before seeking a loan. Thus a single loan can be organized for the purchase of raw materials and for fixing the machine.

The option to generate a partially ordered plan occurs every time a planner encounters a conjunctive (i.e., "AND") node on the search tree. Linear planners are adequate when the branches are decoupled, so that it doesn't matter which action is performed first. Where the ordering is important, a nonlinear planner can avoid an exponential search of all possible plan orderings. To emphasize how enormous this saving can be, just ten actions have more than three million (i.e., 10!) possible orderings.

Some nonlinear planners (e.g., HACKER [13] and INTERPLAN [14]) adopt a different approach to limiting the number of orderings that need be considered. These systems start out by making the linearity assumption. When confronted with a conjunctive node in the search tree, they select an arbitrary order for the actions corresponding to the separate branches. If the selected order is subsequently found to create problems, the plan is fixed by reordering. Depending on the problem being addressed, this approach may be inefficient as it can involve a large amount of backtracking.

We have already seen that the actions of one branch of the search tree can interact with the actions of another. As a further example, a system might plan to purchase sufficient raw materials for manufacturing a single batch, but some of these materials might be used up in the alignment of machinery following its repair. Detecting and correcting these interactions is a problem which has been addressed by most of the more sophisticated planners. The problem is particularly difficult in the case of planners such as SIPE that allow actions to take place concurrently. SIPE tackles the problem by allocating a share of limited resources to each action, and placing restrictions on concurrent actions that use the same resources. Modeling the process in this way has the advantage that resource conflicts are easier to detect than interactions between the effects of two actions.

9.6.2 The use of planning variables

The use of planning variables is another technique for postponing decisions until they have to be made. Planners with this capability could, for instance, plan to purchase something, where something is a variable which does not yet have a value assigned. Thus the planner can accumulate information before making a decision about what to purchase. The instantiation of something may be determined later, thus avoiding the need to produce and check a plan for every possible instantiation.

The use of planning variables becomes more powerful still if we can progressively limit the possible instantiations by applying constraints to the values that a variable can take. Rather than assuming that something is either unknown or has a specific value (say *gearbox part number 7934*), we could start by applying the constraint that it is a gearbox component. We might then progressively tighten the constraints and thereby reduce the number of possible instantiations.

9.7 Job shop scheduling

9.7.1 The problem

As noted in section 9.1, scheduling is a planning problem where time and resources must be allocated to operators which are known in advance. The term "scheduling" is sometimes applied to the internal scheduling of operations within a knowledge-based system. However, in this section we will only be concerned with scheduling in an engineering context.

Job shop scheduling is a problem of great commercial importance. A job shop is either a factory or a manufacturing unit within a factory. Typically the job shop consists of a number of machine tools connected by an automated palletized transportation system, as shown in figure 9.8. The completion of a job may require the production of many different parts, grouped in lots. Flexible manufacturing is possible since different machines can work on different part types simultaneously, allowing the job shop to adapt rapidly to changes in production mix and volume.

The planning task is to determine a schedule for the manufacturing of the parts that make up a job. As noted in section 9.1, the operations are already known in this type of problem, but still need to be organized in the most efficient way. The output that is required from a scheduling system is (typically) a Gantt chart like that shown in figure 9.9. The decisions required are therefore:

- the allocation of machines (or other resources) to each operation; and
- the start and finish times of each operation; though it may be sufficient to specify only the order of operations, rather than their projected timings.

The output of the job-shop should display *graceful degradation*, i.e., a reduced output should be maintained in the event of accidental or pre-programmed machine stops, rather than the whole job shop grinding to a halt. The schedule must ensure that all jobs are completed before their due dates, while taking account of related considerations such as minimizing machine idle

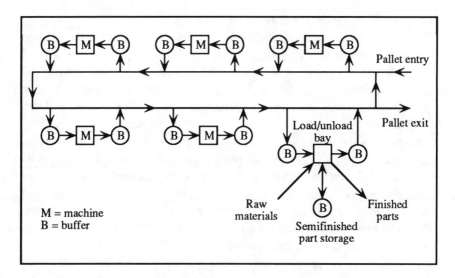

Figure 9.8 A possible job shop layout (adapted from [15]).

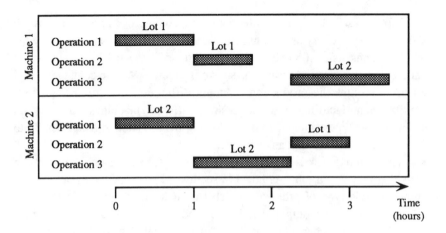

Figure 9.9 A Gantt chart.
Charts like this give a visual representation of a schedule.

times, queues at machines, work in progress and allowing a safety margin in case of unexpected machine breakdown. Some of these considerations are *constraints* which *must* be satisfied, and others are *preferences* that we would *like* to satisfy to some degree. Several researchers (e.g., Bruno et al. [15] and Dattero et al. [16]) have pointed out that a satisfactory schedule is required, and that this may not necessarily be an optimum. A similar viewpoint is frequently adopted in the area of engineering design (chapter 8).

9.7.2 Some approaches to scheduling

The approaches to automated scheduling that have been applied in the past can be categorized as either analytical, iterative or heuristic [17]. None of these approaches has been particularly successful in its own right, but some of the more successful scheduling systems borrow techniques from all three approaches. The analytical approach requires the problem to be structured into a formal mathematical model. Achieving this normally requires several assumptions to be made, which can compromise the validity of the model in real-life situations. The iterative approach requires all possible schedules to be tested, and the best one to be selected. The computational load of such an approach renders it impractical where there are large numbers of machines and lots. The heuristic approach relies on the use of rules to guide the scheduling. While this can save considerable computation, the rules are often specific to just one situation, and their expressive power may be inadequate.

Bruno et al. [15] have adopted a semiempirical approach to the scheduling problem. A discrete event simulation (similar in principle to the ultrasonic simulation described in chapter 5) serves as a test bed for the effects of action sequences. If a particular sequence causes a constraint to be violated, the simulation can backtrack by one or more events and then test a new sequence. Objects are used to represent the key players in the simulation, such as lots, events and goals. Rules are used to guide the selection of event sequences using priorities which are allocated to each lot by the simple expression:

$$\text{priority} = \frac{\text{remaining machining time}}{\text{due date} - \text{release time}}$$

Liu [17] has extended the ideas of hierarchical planning (section 9.5) to include job shop scheduling. He has pointed out that one of the greatest problems in scheduling is the interaction between events, so that fixing one problem (e.g., bringing forward a particular machining operation) can generate new problems (e.g., another lot might require the same operation, but its schedule cannot be moved forward). Liu therefore sees the problem as one of maintaining the integrity of a global plan, and dealing with the effects of local decisions on that global plan. He solves the problem by introducing planning levels. He starts by generating a rough utilization plan (typically based upon the one resource thought to be the most critical), which acts as a guideline for a more detailed schedule. The rough plan is not expanded into a more detailed plan, but rather a detailed plan is formed from scratch, with the rough plan acting as a guide.

Rather than attempt to describe all approaches to the scheduling problem, one particular approach will now be described in some detail. This approach involves constraint-based analysis (CBA) coupled with the application of preferences.

9.8 Constraint-based analysis

9.8.1 Constraints and preferences
There may be many factors to take into account when generating a schedule. As noted in section 9.7.1, some of these are *constraints* which *must* be satisfied, and others are *preferences* that we would *like* to satisfy. Whether or not a constraint is satisfied is generally clear cut, e.g., a product is either ready on time or it is not. The satisfaction of preferences is sometimes clear cut, but often it is not. For instance, we might prefer to use a particular machine. This preference is clear-cut because either it will be met or it will not. On the other hand, a preference such as "minimize machine idle times" can be met to varying degrees.

9.8.2 *Formalizing the constraints*

Four types of scheduling constraints that apply to a flexible manufacturing system can be identified:

- *Production constraints*

  The specified quantity of goods must be ready before the due date, and quality standards must be maintained throughout. Each lot has an earliest start time and a latest finish time.

- *Technological coherence constraints*

  Work on a given lot cannot commence until it has entered the transportation system. Some operations must precede others within a given job, and sometimes a predetermined sequence of operations exists. Some stages of manufacturing may require specific machines.

- *Resource constraints*

  Each operation must have access to sufficient resources. The only resource that we will consider in this study is time at a machine, where the number of available machines is limited. Each machine can only work on one lot at a given time, and programmed maintenance periods for machines must be taken into account.

- *Capacity constraints*

  In order to avoid unacceptable congestion in the transportation system, machine use and queue lengths must not exceed predefined limits.

Our discussion of constraint-based analysis will be based upon the work of Bel at al. [2]. Their knowledge-based system, OPAL, solves the static ("snapshot") job shop scheduling problem. It is therefore a classical planner (see section 9.2). OPAL contains five modules (figure 9.10):

i   an object-oriented database for representing entities in the system such as lots, operations, and resources (including machines);

ii   a constraint-based analysis (CBA) module which calculates the effects of time constraints on the sequence of operations (the module generates a set of precedence relations between operations, thereby partially or fully defining those sequences which are viable);

iii a decision support module which contains rules for choosing a schedule, based upon practical or heuristic experience, from among those that the CBA module has found to be viable;

iv   a supervisor which controls communication between the CBA and decision support modules, and builds up the schedule for presentation to the user; and

v   a user interface module.

Job shop scheduling can be viewed in terms of juggling operations and resources. Operations are the tasks which need to be performed in order to complete a job, and several jobs may need to be scheduled together. Operations are characterized by their start time and duration. Each operation normally uses resources, such as a length of time at a given machine. There are two types of decision, namely the timing or (sequencing) of operations and the allocation of resources. For the moment we will concentrate on the CBA module, which is based upon the following set of assumptions:

- there are a set of jobs (J) comprised of a set of operations (O);
- there is a limited set of resources R; and
- each operation has the following properties:
  > it cannot be interrupted,
  > it uses a subset r of the available resources,
  > it uses a quantity q_i of each resource (r_i) in the set r, and
  > it has a fixed duration d_i.

A schedule is characterized by a set of operations, their start times, and their durations. We will assume that the operations which make up a job and their durations are predefined. Therefore a schedule can be specified by just a set of start times for the operations. For a given job, there is an earliest start time (*est$_i$*) and latest finish time (*lft$_i$*) for each operation O_i. Each operation

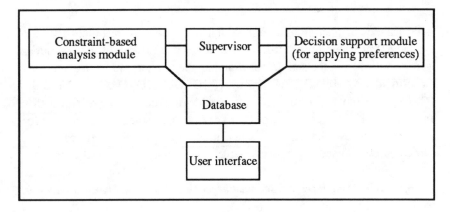

Figure 9.10 Principal modules in the OPAL scheduling system [2].

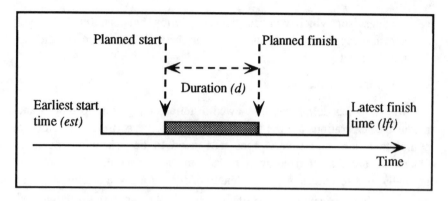

Figure 9.11   Scheduling an operation within its available time window.

therefore has a time window which it *could* occupy, and a duration within that window that it *will* occupy. The problem is then one of positioning the operation within the window as shown in figure 9.11.

9.8.3   Identifying the critical sets of operations

The first step in the application of CBA is to determine if and where conflicts for resources arise. These conflicts are identified through the use of *critical sets*, a concept which is best described by example. Suppose that a small factory employs five workers who are suitably skilled for carrying out a set of four operations (O_i). Each operation requires some number (q_i) of the workers, as follows:

	O_1	O_2	O_3	O_4
Number of workers required, q_i	2	3	5	2

A critical set of operations I_c is one that requires more resources than are available, but where this conflict would be resolved if *any* of the operations were removed from the set. In our example, the workers are the resource and the critical sets are $\{O_1,O_3\}$, $\{O_2,O_3\}$, $\{O_4,O_3\}$, $\{O_1,O_2,O_4\}$. Note that $\{O_1,O_2,O_3\}$ is not a critical set since it would still require more resources than are available if we removed O_1 or O_2. The critical sets define the conflicts for resources, because the operations that make up the critical sets cannot be carried out simultaneously. Therefore the first sequencing rule is as follows:

one operation of each critical set must precede at least one other operation in the same critical set.

Applying this rule to the above example produces the following set of conditions:

i   either   (O_1 precedes O_3) or (O_3 precedes O_1).
ii either   (O_2 precedes O_3) or (O_3 precedes O_2).
iii either   (O_4 precedes O_3) or (O_3 precedes O_4).
iv either   (O_1 precedes O_2) or (O_2 precedes O_1) or
             (O_1 precedes O_4) or (O_4 precedes O_1) or
             (O_2 precedes O_4) or (O_4 precedes O_2).

These conditions have been deduced purely on the basis of the available resources, without consideration of time constraints. If we now introduce the known time constraints (i.e., the earliest start times and latest finish times for each operation) the schedule of operations can be refined further, and in some cases defined completely. The schedule of operations is especially constrained in the case where each conflict set is a *pair* of operations. This is the *disjunctive* case, which we will consider first before moving on to consider the more general case.

9.8.4 Sequencing in the disjunctive case

As each conflict set is a pair of operations in the disjunctive case, no operations can be carried out simultaneously. Each operation has a defined duration (d_i), an earliest start time (est_i) and a latest finish time (lft_i). The scheduling task is one of determining the actual start time for each operation.

Consider the task of scheduling the three operations A, B and C shown in figure 9.12a. If we try to schedule operation A first, we find that there is insufficient time for the remaining operations to be carried out before the last *lft*, irrespective of how the other operations are ordered (figure 9.12b). However, there is a feasible schedule if operation C precedes A. This is an example of the general rule:

```
/* Rule 9.1 */
IF (latest lft - est_A) < Σ d_i
THEN at least one operation must precede A.
```

Similarly, there is no feasible schedule which has A as the last operation since there is insufficient time to perform all operations between the earliest *est* and the *lft* for A (figure 9.12c). The general rule that describes this situation is:

```
/* Rule 9.2 */
IF (lft_A - earliest est) < Σ d_i
THEN at least one operation must follow A.
```

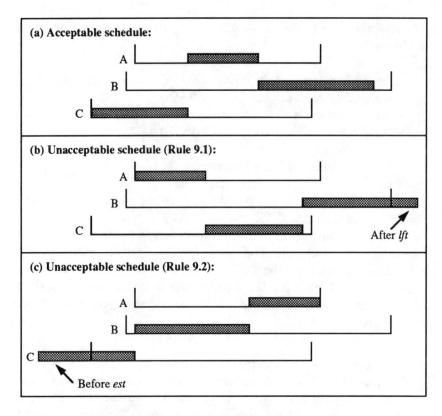

Figure 9.12   Sequencing in the disjunctive case.
        (a)   An acceptable schedule;
        (b)   "A" cannot be the first operation (rule 9.1);
        (c)   "A" cannot be the last operation (rule 9.2).

9.8.5 Sequencing in the nondisjunctive case

In the nondisjunctive case, at least one critical set contains more than two operations. The precedence rules described above can be applied to those critical sets that contain only two operations. Let us consider the precedence constraints that apply to the operations O_i of a critical set having more than two elements. From our original definition of a critical set, it is not possible for all of the operations in the set to be carried out simultaneously. At any one time, at least one operation in the set must either have finished or be waiting to start. This provides the basis for some precedence relations. Let's denote the critical set by the symbol S, where S includes the operation A. Another set of operations which contains all elements of S apart from operation A, will be denoted by the letter W. The two precedence rules that apply are as follows:

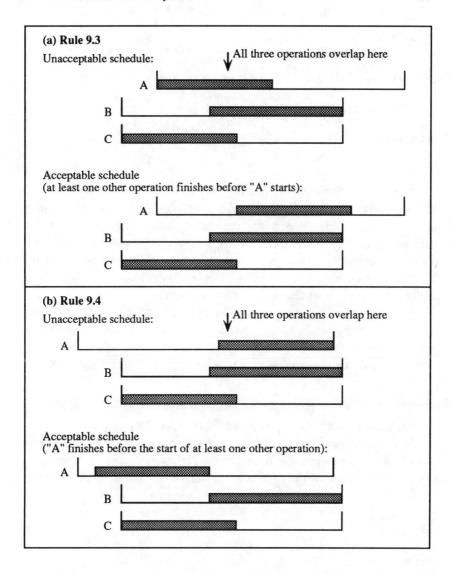

Figure 9.13 Sequencing in the nondisjunctive case.

```
/* Rule 9.3 */
IF    for every pair {O_i, O_j} of operations in set W:
      lft_i-est_j < d_i + d_j
      /* O_i cannot be performed after O_j has finished */
AND   for every operation (O_i) in set W:
      lft_i-est_A < d_A + d_i
      /* O_i cannot be performed after O_A has finished) */
THEN  at least one operation in set W must have finished before
      A starts
```

```
/* Rule 9.4 */
IF    for every pair {Oᵢ, Oⱼ} of operations in set W:
      lftᵢ-estⱼ < dᵢ + dⱼ
      /* Oᵢ cannot be performed after Oⱼ has finished */
AND   for every operation (Oᵢ) in set W:
      lftₐ-estᵢ < dₐ + dᵢ
      /* Oₐ cannot be performed after Oᵢ has finished */
THEN A must finish before at least one operation in set W
     starts.
```

The application of rule 9.3 is shown in figure 9.13a. Operations B and C have to overlap (the first condition) and it is not possible for A to finish before one of either B or C has started (the second condition). Therefore operation A *must* be preceded by at least one of the other operations. Note that if this is not possible either, then there is no feasible schedule. (Overlap of all the operations is unavoidable in such a case, but since we are dealing with a critical set there is insufficient resource to support this.)

Rule 9.4 is similar and covers the situation depicted in figure 9.13b. Here operations B and C again have to overlap, and it is not possible to delay the start of A until after one of the other operations has finished. Under these circumstances operation A *must* precede at least one of the other operations.

9.8.6 *Updating earliest start times and latest finish times*
If rule 9.1 or 9.3 has been fired, so we know that at least one operation must precede A, it may be possible to update the earliest start time of A to reflect this restriction, as shown in figures 9.14a and 9.14b. The rule that describes this is:

```
/* Rule 9.5 */
IF some operations must precede A (by rule 9.1 or 9.3)
AND [the earliest (est+d) of those operations] > estₐ
THEN the new estₐ is the earliest (est+d) of those operations.
```

Similarly, if rule 9.2 or 9.4 has been fired, so we know that at least one operation must follow operation A, it may be possible to modify the *lft* for A, as shown in figures 9.14a and 9.14c. The rule that describes this is:

```
/* Rule 9.6 */
IF some operations must follow A (by rule 9.2 or 9.4)
AND [the latest (lft-d) of those operations] < lftₐ
THEN the new lftₐ is the latest (lft-d) of those operations.
```

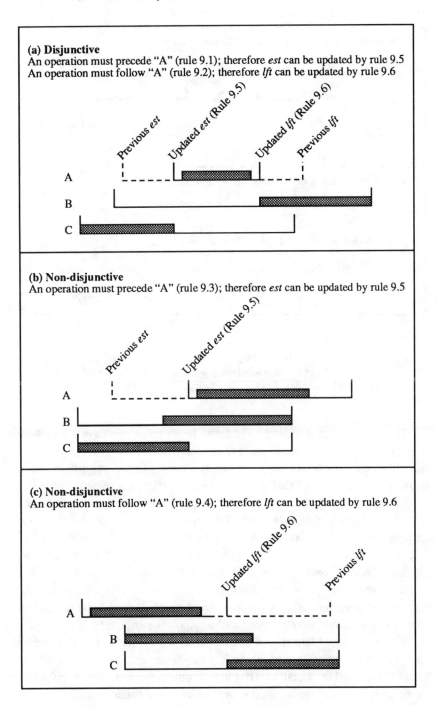

(a) Disjunctive
An operation must precede "A" (rule 9.1); therefore *est* can be updated by rule 9.5
An operation must follow "A" (rule 9.2); therefore *lft* can be updated by rule 9.6

(b) Non-disjunctive
An operation must precede "A" (rule 9.3); therefore *est* can be updated by rule 9.5

(c) Non-disjunctive
An operation must follow "A" (rule 9.4); therefore *lft* can be updated by rule 9.6

Figure 9.14 Updating earliest start times and latest finish times.

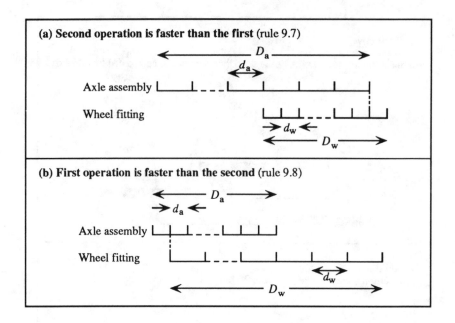

Figure 9.15 Overlapping operations in batch processing.
(a)   Rule 9.7 applies if wheel fitting is faster than axle assembly;
(b)   Rule 9.8 applies if axle assembly is faster than wheel fitting.

The new earliest start times and latest finish times can have a knock-on effect on subsequent operations. Consider the case of a factory that is assembling cars. Axle assembly must precede wheel-fitting, regardless of any resource considerations. This sort of precedence relation, which is laid down by the nature of the task itself, is referred to as a technological coherence constraint. Suppose that, as a result of the arguments described above, the *est* for axle assembly is delayed to a new time est_a. If the axle assembly takes time d_a per car, then the new *est* for wheel-fitting (est_w) will be $est_a + d_a$ (ignoring the time taken to move the vehicle between assembly stations).

However, a car plant is unlikely to be moving just one car through the assembly process, but rather a whole batch of cars will need to be scheduled. These circumstances offer greater flexibility, as the two assembly operations can overlap provided that the order of assembly is maintained for individual cars. Two rules can be derived, depending on whether axle assembly or wheel-fitting is the quicker operation. If wheel-fitting is quicker, then a sufficient condition is for wheels to be fitted to the last car in the batch immediately after its axles have been assembled. This situation is shown in figure 9.15a, and is described by the following rule:

```
/* Rule 9.7 */
IF da > dw
THEN estw = esta + Da - (n-1)dw
AND lfta = lftw - dw
```

where n is the number of cars in the batch, D_a is (nd_a), and D_w is (nd_w). If axle assembly is the quicker operation, then wheel-fitting can commence immediately after the first car has had its axle assembled (figure 9.15b). The following rule applies:

```
/* Rule 9.8 */
IF da < dw
THEN estw = esta + da
AND lfta = lftw - Dw + (n-1)da.
```

9.8.7 Applying preferences
Constraint-based analysis can produce one of three possible outcomes:

- the constraints cannot be satisfied, given the allocated resources;
- a unique schedule is produced which satisfies the constraints; or
- more than one schedule is found that satisfies the constraints.

In the case of the first outcome, the problem can only be solved if more resources are made available or the time constraints are slackened. In the second case, the scheduling problem is solved. In the third case, pairs of operations exist which can be sequenced in either order without violating the constraints. The problem then becomes one of applying *preferences* so as to find the most suitable order. Preferences are features of the solution that are considered desirable, but unlike constraints they are not compulsory. Bel et al. [2] have attempted to apply preferences by using fuzzy rules (see section 4.4 for a discussion of fuzzy logic). Their rule-based system constitutes the decision-support module in figure 9.10.

The pairs of operations that need to be ordered are potentially large in number and broad in scope. It is therefore impractical to produce a rule base that covers specific pairs of operations. Instead, rules for applying preferences usually make use of variables (see section 3.6), so that they can be applied to different pairs of operations. The rules may take the form:

```
IF
(attribute x of operation ?a) > (attribute x of operation ?b)
THEN
?a precedes ?b
```

where any pair of operations can be substituted for a and b, but the attribute x is specified in a given rule. A typical expression for x might be the duration of its available time window (i.e. *lft-est*). The rules are chosen so as to cover some general guiding principles or goals, such as:

- maximize overall slack time;

- perform operations with the least slack time first;

- give preference to schedules which minimize resource utilization; and

- avoid tool changes.

In OPAL, each rule is assigned a degree of relevance *(R)* with respect to each goal. Given a goal or set of goals, some rules will tend to favor one ordering of a pair of operations, while others will favor the reverse. A consensus is arrived at by a rather complicated scoring (or "voting") procedure. The complete set of rules is applied to each pair of operations that need to be ordered, and the scoring procedure is as follows:

- The degree to which the condition part of each rule is satisfied is represented using fuzzy sets. Three fuzzy sets are defined (*true, maybe* and *false*), and the degree of membership of each is designated μ_t, μ_m and μ_f. Each membership is a number between 0 and 1, such that for every rule:

  $$\mu_t + \mu_m + \mu_f = 1.$$

- Every rule awards a score to each of the three possible outcomes (namely "a precedes b"; "b precedes a"; or "no preference"). These scores (V_{ab}, V_{ba} and $V_{no\_preference}$) are determined as follows:

  $$V_{ab} = \min(\mu_t, R)$$
  $$V_{ba} = \min(\mu_f, R)$$
  $$V_{no\_preference} = \min(\mu_m, R)$$

- The scores for each of the three possible outcomes are totaled across the whole rule set. The totals can also be normalized by dividing the sum of the scores by the sum of the *R* values for all rules. Thus:

  Total score for ab $= \Sigma(V_{ab}) / \Sigma(R)$

  Total score for ba $= \Sigma(V_{ba}) / \Sigma(R)$

  Total score for no preference $= \Sigma(V_{no\_preference}) / \Sigma(R)$.

The scoring procedure can have one of three possible outcomes:

i   One ordering is favored over the other. This outcome is manifested by
     $\Sigma(V_{ab}) \gg \Sigma(V_{ba})$ or vice versa.

ii   Both orderings are roughly equally favored, but the scores for each are low
     compared with the score for the impartial outcome. This indicates that
     there is no strong reason for preferring one order over the other.

iii Both orderings are roughly equally favored, but the scores for each are
     high compared with the score for the impartial outcome. Under these
     circumstances there are strong reasons for preferring one order, but there
     are also strong reasons for preferring the reverse order. In other words
     there are strong conflicts between the rules.

9.8.8 Using constraints and preferences

OPAL makes use of a supervisor module (figure 9.10), which controls the
constraint-based analysis (CBA) and decision support (DS) modules. In OPAL
and other scheduling systems, constraint-based analysis is initially applied in
order to eliminate all those schedules that cannot meet the time and resource
constraints. A preferred ordering of operations is then selected from the
schedules that are left. As we have seen, the DS module achieves this by
weighting the rules of optimization, applying these rules, and selecting the
order of operations that obtains the highest overall score.

   If the preferences applied by the DS module are not sufficient to produce a
unique schedule, the supervising module calls upon the CBA and DS modules
repeatedly until a unique solution is found. The supervising module stops the
process when an acceptable schedule has been found, or if it cannot find a
workable schedule.

   There is a clear analogy between the two stages of scheduling (constraint-
based analysis and the application of preferences) and the stages of materials
selection (see section 8.8). In the case of materials selection, constraints can be
applied by ruling out all materials that fail to meet a numerical specification.
The remaining materials can then be put into an order of preference based upon
some means of comparing their performance scores against various criteria,
where the scores are weighted according to a measure of the perceived
importance of the properties.

9.9 Replanning and reactive planning

The discussion so far has deliberately concentrated on predictive planning, that
is, building a plan which is to be executed at some time in the future. Suppose

now that while a plan is being executed something unexpected happens, such as a machine breakdown. In other words, the actual world state deviates from the expected world state. A powerful capability under these circumstances is to be able to replan, i.e., to modify the current plan to reflect the current circumstances. Systems which are capable of planning or replanning in real time, in a rapidly changing environment, are described as *reactive* planners. Such systems monitor the state of the world during execution of a plan, and are capable of revising the plan in response to their observations. Since a reactive planner can alter the actions of machinery in response to real-time observations and measurements, the distinction between reactive planners and control systems (chapter 10) is vague.

To illustrate the distinction between predictive planning, replanning, and reactive planning, let us consider an intelligent robot that is carrying out some gardening. It may have planned in advance to mow the lawn and then to prune the roses (predictive planning). If it finds that someone has borrowed the mower, it might decide to mow after pruning, by which time the mower may have become available (replanning). If a missile is thrown at the robot while it is pruning, it may choose to dive for cover (reactive planning).

Collinot et al. have devised a system called SONIA [18], which is capable of both predictive and reactive planning of factory activity. This system offers more than just a scheduling capability, since it has some facilities for selecting which operations will be scheduled. However, it assumes that a core of essential operations are preselected. SONIA brings together many of the techniques that we have discussed previously. The operations are ordered by the application of constraints and preferences (section 9.8) in order to form a predictive plan. During execution of the plan, the observed world state may deviate from the planned world state. Some possible causes of the deviation might be:

- machine failure;
- personnel absence;
- arrival of urgent new orders; or
- the original plan may have been ill-conceived.

Under these circumstances, SONIA can modify its plan, or in an extreme case, generate a new plan from scratch. The particular type of modification chosen is largely dependent on the time available for SONIA to "think" about the problem. Some possible plan modifications might be:

- cancel, postpone or curtail some operations in order to bring some other operations back on to schedule;

- reschedule to use any slack time in the original plan;

- reallocate resources between operations;

- reschedule a job (comprising a series of operations) to finish later than previously planned; or

- delay the whole schedule.

A final point to note about SONIA concerns its implementation. It has been constructed as a blackboard system, as described in chapter 7 in the context of data interpretation. The versatility of the blackboard architecture is demonstrated by the variety of applications in which it is used. SONIA uses the blackboard to represent both the planned and observed world states. Separate knowledge sources perform the various stages of predictive planning, monitoring, and reactive planning. In fact, SONIA uses two blackboards - one for representing information about the shop floor, and a separate one for its own internal control information.

9.10 Summary

This chapter began by defining a classical planner as one which can derive a set of operations to take the world from an initial state to a goal state. The initial world state is a "snapshot", which is assumed not to alter except as a result of the execution of the plan. While being useful in a wide range of situations, classical planners are of limited use when dealing with continuous processes or a rapidly changing environment. In contrast, reactive planners can respond rapidly to unexpected events.

Scheduling is a special case of planning, where the operators are known in advance and the task is to allocate resources to each and to determine when they should be applied. Scheduling is particularly important in the planning of manufacturing processes.

A simple classical planner similar to STRIPS has been described. More sophisticated features that can be added to extend the capabilities of a planning system were then described, and are summarized below.

i *World modeling*
Unlike STRIPS, the Prolog program shown in section 9.3.3 does not explicitly update its world model as operators are selected. Proper maintenance of a world model ensures that any side-effects of a plan are recorded along with intended effects.

ii   *Deductive rules*

Deductive rules permit the deduction of effects that are additional to those explicitly included in the operator representation. Because they do not form part of the operator representation, they can allow different effects to be registered depending on the current context.

iii   *Hierarchical planning*

STRIPS may commit itself to a particular problem-solving path too early, with the result that it must backtrack if it cannot complete the plan that it is pursuing. Hierarchical planners can plan at different levels of abstraction. An abstract (or "skeleton") plan is formed first, such as to build a house by digging foundations, then building walls and finally putting on a roof. The detailed planning might include the precise shape, size and placement of the timber. The abstract plan restricts the range of possibilities of the detailed planning.

iv   *Nonlinearity*

Linear planners such as STRIPS make the assumption that it does not matter in which order the subgoals for a particular goal are satisfied. Partial ordering of operations is a form of nonlinear planning in which the ordering of operations is postponed until either more information becomes available or a decision is forced. In some cases is may be possible for operations to be scheduled to run in parallel.

v   *Planning variables*

The use of variables also allows postponement of decisions. Plans can be generated using variables which have not yet been assigned a value. For instance, we might plan to go somewhere without specifying where. The instantiation of *somewhere* may become determined later, and we have saved the effort of considering all of the possibilities in the meantime.

vi   *Constraints*

The use of planning variables is more powerful still if we can limit the possible instantiations by applying constraints on the values that a variable can take. Constraint-based analysis can be used to reduce the number of possible plans, or even to find a unique plan that meets the constraints.

vii   *Preferences*

If constraint-based analysis yields more than one viable plan or schedule, preferences can be applied in order to select between the alternatives.

viii *Replanning*
The ability to modify a plan in the light of unexpected occurrences was briefly discussed.

Hierarchical plans, partially ordered plans, and the use of planning variables are all means of postponing commitment to a particular plan. This is known as the principle of least commitment.

Systems that have only *some* of the above features are adequate in many situations. Some specific applications have been considered in this chapter, but much of the research effort in planning has been concerned with building general purpose planning systems that are domain-independent. The purpose of such systems is to allow knowledge relevant to any particular domain to be represented, rather like an expert system shell (see sections 1.6 and 2.2).

References

1. Charniak, E. and McDermott, D., *Introduction to artificial intelligence*, Addison-Wesley (1985).
2. Bel, G., Bensana, E., Dubois, D., Erschler, J. and Esquirol, P., "A knowledge-based approach to industrial job-shop scheduling", in *Knowledge-Based Systems in Manufacturing*, Kusiak, A. (ed.), Taylor and Francis (1989).
3. Stuart, C. J., "An implementation of a multi-agent plan synchronizer", in *9th International Joint Conference on AI (IJCAI)*, Los Angeles, p1031 (1985).
4. Durfee, E. H., Lesser, V. R. and Corkhill, D. D., "Increasing coherence in a distributed problem solving network", in *9th International Joint Conference on AI (IJCAI)*, Los Angeles, p1025 (1985).
5. Fikes, R. E. and Nilsson, N. J., "STRIPS: a new approach to the application of theorem proving to problem solving", *Artificial Intelligence*, 2, 189 (1971).
6. Fikes, R. E., Hart, P. E. and Nilsson, N. J., "Learning and executing generalized robot plans", *Artificial Intelligence*, 3, p251 (1972).
7. Wilkins, D. E., "Representation in a domain-independent planner", in *8th International Joint Conference on AI (IJCAI)*, Karlsruhe, Germany, p733 (1983).
8. Wilkins, D. E., "Domain-independent planning: representation and plan generation", *Artificial Intelligence*, 22, p269 (1984).
9. Wilkins, D. E., *Practical planning - extending the classical AI planning paradigm*, Morgan Kaufmann (1988).

10. Sacerdoti, E. D., "Planning in a hierarchy of abstraction spaces", *Artificial Intelligence*, **5**, p115 (1974).

11. Tate, A., "Generating project networks", in *5th International Joint Conference on AI (IJCAI)*, Cambridge, Massachusetts, p888 (1977).

12. Hendler, J., Tate, A. and Drummond, M., "AI planning: systems and techniques", *AI Magazine*, p61 (Summer 1990).

13. Sussman, G. J., *A computer model of skill acquisition*, Elsevier (1975).

14. Tate, A., "Interacting goals and their use", in *4th International Joint Conference on AI (IJCAI)*, Tbilisi, Georgia, p215 (1975).

15. Bruno, G., Elia, A. and Laface, P., "A rule-based system to schedule production", *IEEE Computer*, **19**, (7), p32 (July 1986).

16. Dattero, R., Kanet, J. J. and White, E. M., "Enhancing manufacturing planning and control systems with artificial intelligence techniques", in *Knowledge-Based Systems in Manufacturing*, Kusiak, A. (ed.), Taylor and Francis (1989).

17. Liu, B., "Scheduling via reinforcement", *Artificial Intelligence in Engineering*, **3**, p76 (1988).

18. Collinot, A., Le Pape, C. and Pinoteau, G., "SONIA: a knowledge-based scheduling system", *Artificial Intelligence in Engineering*, **3**, p86 (1988).

Further reading

* Proceedings of the *International Joint Conferences on AI (IJCAI)*, held in odd-numbered years since 1969.

* Allen, J., Hendler, J. and Tate, A. (ed.), *Readings in planning*, Morgan Kaufmann (1990).

* Charniak, E. and McDermott, D., *Introduction to artificial intelligence*, Addison-Wesley (1985).

* Hendler, J., Tate, A. and Drummond, M., "AI planning: systems and techniques", *AI Magazine*, p61 (Summer 1990).

* Wilkins, D. E., *Practical planning - extending the classical AI planning paradigm*, Morgan Kaufmann (1988).

chapter ten

Systems for control

10.1 Introduction

The application of knowledge-based systems to control has far-reaching implications for manufacturing, robotics and other areas of engineering. The control problem is closely allied to some of the other applications that have been discussed so far. For instance, a controller of manufacturing equipment will have as its aim the implementation of a manufacturing plan (see *systems for planning*, chapter 9). It will need to interpret sensor data, recognize faults and respond to them (see *systems for interpretation and diagnosis*, chapter 7). Similarly it will need to replan the manufacturing process in the event of breakdown or some other unexpected event (see *reactive planning*, section 9.9). Indeed, Bennett [1] treats automated control as a loop of plan generation, monitoring, diagnosis, and replanning.

The systems described in chapters 7-9 gather data describing their environment and make decisions and judgments about those data. Controllers are distinct in that they can go a step further by altering their environment. They may do this actively by sending commands to the hardware, or passively by recommending to a human operator that certain actions be taken. The passive implementation assumes that the process decisions can be implemented relatively slowly.

Control problems appear in various guises, and different techniques may be appropriate in different cases. For example, a temperature controller for a furnace may modify the current flowing in the heating coils in response to the measured temperature, where the temperature may be registered as a potential difference across a thermocouple. This is *low-level* control, in which a rapid response is required but little intelligence is involved. In contrast, *high-level* or *supervisory* control takes a wider view of the process being controlled. For instance, in the control of the manufacturing process for a steel component, a furnace temperature may be just one of many parameters that need to be adjusted. High-level control requires more intelligence, but there is often more time available in which to make the decisions.

The examples of control discussed above implicitly assumed the existence of a model of the system being controlled. Thus in building a temperature controller it is known that an increased current will raise the temperature, that this is registered by the thermocouple, and that there will be a time lag between the two. The controller is designed to exploit this model. There may be some circumstances where no such model exists, or is too complex to represent. The process under control can then be thought of as a black box, whose input is determined by the controller, and whose output we wish to regulate. As it has no other information available to it, the controller must learn how to control the black box through trial and error. In other words it must construct a model of the system through experience. We will discuss two approaches to this problem, namely the "BOXES" algorithm (section 10.7) and neural networks (section 10.8).

As well as drawing a distinction between low-level and high-level control, we can distinguish between *adaptive* and *servo* control. The aim of an adaptive controller is to maintain a steady state. In a completely stable environment, an adaptive controller would need to do nothing. In the real world, an adaptive controller must adapt to changes in the environment which may be brought about by the controlled process itself or by external disturbances. A temperature controller for a furnace is an adaptive controller whose task is to maintain a constant temperature. It must do this in spite of disturbances such as the furnace door opening, large thermal masses being inserted or removed, fluctuations in the power supply, and changes in the temperature of the surroundings. Typically it will achieve this by using negative feedback (see section 10.2 below).

A servo controller is designed to drive the output of the plant from a starting value to a desired value. Choosing a control action in order to achieve the desired output requires that a prediction be made about the future behavior of the controlled plant. This, again, requires a model of the controlled plant. Often a high-level controller is required to decide upon a series of servo control actions. This is known as *sequence* control. For instance, alloyed components are normally taken through a heat-treatment cycle. They are initially held at a temperature close to the melting temperature, then they are rapidly quenched to room temperature, and finally they are "aged" at an intermediate temperature.

10.2   Low-level control

10.2.1   Open-loop control
The open-loop control strategy is straightforward: given a control requirement, the controller simply sends a control action to the plant (figure 10.1a). The

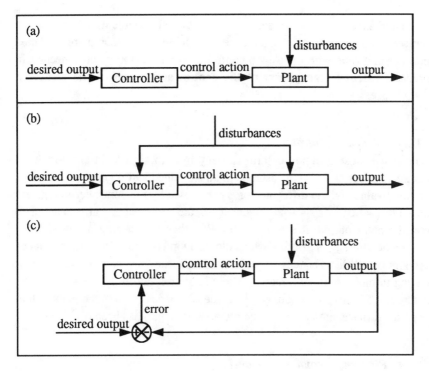

Figure 10.1 Three alternative strategies for control:
(a) open loop;
(b) feedforward;
(c) feedback (closed loop).

controller must have a model of the relationship between the control action and the behavior of the plant. The accuracy of control is solely dependent on the accuracy of the model, and no checks are made to ensure that the plant is behaving as intended. An open-loop temperature controller, for example, would send a set current to the heating coils in order to achieve an intended temperature. In order to choose an appropriate current, it would have an implicit model of the thermal capacity of the furnace and of the rate of heat loss. This strategy cannot correct for any disturbance to the plant (i.e., the furnace, in this example).

10.2.2 Feedforward control
The feedforward strategy takes account of disturbances to the plant by measuring the disturbances and altering the control action accordingly (figure 10.1b). In the example of the temperature controller, fluctuations in the mains power supply might be monitored. The nominal current sent to the coils may then be altered to compensate for fluctuations in the actual current. Note that

the disturbance is monitored, and not the controlled variable itself (i.e., not the furnace temperature). Any disturbances which are not measured are not taken into account. As with open-loop control, a model of the plant is needed in order to calculate the impact of the control action and of the measured disturbance.

10.2.3 Feedback control

This is the most common control strategy in both high-level and low-level control applications. The measured output from the plant is compared with the required value and the difference or *error* is used by the controller to regulate its control action. As shown in figure 10.1c, the control action affects the plant and the plant output affects the controller, thereby forming a closed loop. Hence the strategy is also known as closed-loop control. This strategy takes account of all disturbances, regardless of how they are caused and without having to measure them directly. There is often a lag in the response of the controller, as corrections can only be made after a deviation in the plant output (e.g., the furnace temperature in the previous example) has been detected.

10.2.4 First and second order models

It has already been emphasized that a controller can only be built if we have a model, albeit a simple one, of the plant being controlled. For low-level control, it is often assumed that the plant can be adequately modeled on first or second order linear differential equations. Let us denote the input to the plant (which may also be the output of the controller) by the letter x, and the output of the plant by the letter y. Thus in a furnace, x would represent the current flowing and y would represent the furnace temperature. The first order differential equation would be:

$$\tau \frac{dy}{dt} + y = k_1 x$$

and the second order differential equation:

$$\frac{d^2 y}{dt^2} + 2\zeta \omega_n \frac{dy}{dt} + \omega_n^2 y = k_2 x$$

where τ, k_1, k_2, ζ and ω_n are constants for a given plant, and t represents time. These equations can be used to tell us how the output (y) will respond to a change in its input (x).

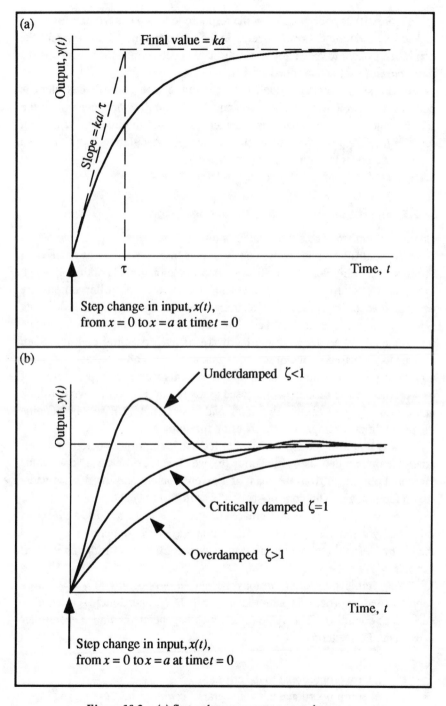

Figure 10.2   (a) first order response to a step change;
(b) second order response to a step change.

Figures 10.2a and 10.2b show the response to a step change in x for a first and second order model respectively. In the first order model, the time for the controlled system to reach a new steady state is determined by τ, which is the *time constant* for the controlled system.

In the second order model, the behavior of the controlled system is dependent on two characteristic constants. The *damping ratio* ζ determines the rate at which y will approach its intended value, and the *undamped natural angular frequency* ω_n determines the frequency of oscillation about the final value in the underdamped case (figure 10.2b).

10.2.5   Algorithmic control: the PID controller

Control systems may be either analog or digital. In analog systems, the output from the controller varies continuously in response to continuous changes in the controlled variable. This book will concentrate on digital control, in which the data are sampled and discrete changes in the controller output are calculated accordingly. There are strong arguments to support the view that low-level digital control is best handled by algorithms, which can be implemented either in electronic hardware or by procedural coding. Such arguments are based on the observation that low-level control usually requires a rapid response, but little or no intelligence. This view would therefore tend to preclude the use of knowledge-based systems. In this section we will look at a commonly used control algorithm, and in section 10.2.7 we will examine the possibilities for improvement by using fuzzy logic.

It was noted in section 10.2.3 that feedback controllers determine their control action on the basis of the error (e), which is the difference between the measured output (y) from the plant at a given moment and the desired value (the reference, r). The control "action" is often simply the assignment of a value to a variable, such as the furnace current. This is the *action variable* and it is usually given the symbol u. The action variable is sometimes known as the *control* variable, although this can lead to confusion with the *controlled* variable, y.

In a simple controller, u may be set in proportion to e. A more sophisticated approach is adopted in the PID (proportional + integral + derivative) controller. The value for u which is generated by a PID controller is the sum of three terms:

- 'P'   a term proportional to the error e;
- 'I'   a term proportional to the integral of e with respect to time; and
- 'D'   a term proportional to the derivative of e with respect to time.

Thus the value assigned to the action variable (u) by a PID controller would ideally be given by:

$$u = K_p \left(e + \frac{1}{\tau_i} \int e \, dt + \tau_d \frac{de}{dt} \right)$$

where K_p, τ_i and τ_d are adjustable parameters of the controller that can be set to suit the characteristics of the plant being controlled. K_p is the *proportional gain*, τ_i is the *integral time*, and τ_d is the *derivative time*. Since values for e are samples at time intervals (Δt), the integral and derivative terms must be approximated:

$$u = K_p \left(e(k) + \frac{\Delta t}{\tau_i} \sum_k e(k) + \tau_d \frac{e_{k+1} - e_k}{\Delta t} \right)$$

where k is the sample number, such that time $t = k\Delta t$.

The role of the 'P' term is intuitively obvious - the greater the error, the greater the control action that is needed. Through the 'I' term, the controller output depends on the accumulated historical values of the error. This is used to counteract the effects of long-term disturbances to the controlled plant. The magnitude of the 'D' term depends on the rate of change of the error. This term allows the controller to react quickly to sharp fluctuations in the error. The 'D' term is low for slowly varying errors, and zero when the error is constant. In practice, tuning the parameters of a PID controller can be difficult. One commonly used technique is the Ziegler-Nichols method (see, for example, [2]).

10.2.6 Bang-bang control

Bang-bang controllers rely on switching the action variable between its upper and lower limits, with intermediate values disallowed. As previously noted, servo control involves forcing a system from one state to a new state. The fastest way of doing this (time optimal control) is by switching the action variable from one extreme to another at precalculated times, i.e., bang-bang control. Two extreme values are used, although Sripada et al. [3] also allow a final steady-state value for the action variable (figure 10.3). Consider the control of an electric furnace. As soon as the new (increased) temperature requirement is known, the electric current is increased to the maximum value sustainable until the error in the temperature is less than a critical value e^*. The current is then dropped to its minimum value (i.e., zero) for time Δt, before being switched to its final steady-state value. There are therefore two parameters that determine the performance of the controller, namely e^* and Δt. Figure 10.3 shows the effects of errors in these two parameters.

Sripada et al. coded the three switchings of their bang-bang servo controller as a set of three rules. They acknowledged, however, that since the rules fired in sequence, there was no reason why these could not have been procedurally coded. They had a separate set of rules for adjusting the

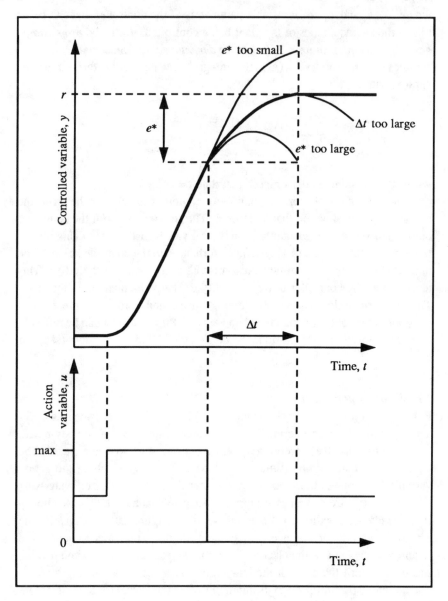

Figure 10.3 Bang-bang servo control (adapted from [3]).

parameters e^*, Δt and K_p in the light of experience. The controller was therefore *self-tuning*, and the parameter adjustment can be thought of as controlling the controller. The extent to which the parameters are adjusted is in proportion to the degree of membership of the fuzzy sets "too large" or "too small". Thus a typical fuzzy rule might be:

```
IF y overshoots r
THEN e* is too large
AND e* becomes e* - Δe.
```

The proposition "`y overshoots r`" is fuzzy, with a degree of membership between 0 and 1, reflecting the amount of overshoot. This becomes the degree of membership for the fuzzy proposition "e^* is too large", and is also used to calculate the adjustment, Δe. Techniques for scaling the adjustment (in this case Δe) to reflect the membership functions are discussed in detail in section 10.6. Sripada et al. found that their self-tuning bang-bang controller outperformed a well-tuned PI controller (i.e., a PID controller with the 'D' term set to zero).

10.3 Requirements of high-level (supervisory) control

Our discussion so far has concentrated on fairly straightforward control tasks, such as maintaining the temperature of a furnace or driving the temperature to a new set point. Both are examples of low-level control, where a rapid response is needed but scarcely any intelligence. In contrast, high-level control may be a complex problem concerning decisions about the actions to take at any given time. This may involve aspects of both adaptive and servo control. An important example of high-level control is the control of a manufacturing process. Control decisions at this level concern diverse factors such as choice of reactants and raw materials; conveyor belt speeds; rates of flow of solids, liquids and gases; temperature and pressure cycling; and batch transport.

Leitch et al. [4] have identified six key requirements for a real time supervisory controller:

- ability to make decisions and act upon them within a time constraint;
- handling asynchronous events - the system must be able to break out of its current set of operations to deal with unexpected occurrences;
- temporal reasoning, i.e., the ability to reason about time and sequences;
- reasoning with uncertainty;
- continuous operation; and
- multiple sources of knowledge.

We have come across the third requirement in the context of planning (chapter 9), and the last three requirements as part of monitoring and diagnosis (chapter 7). Only the first two requirements are new.

10.4   Blackboard maintenance

One of the requirements listed above was for multiple sources of knowledge. These are required since high-level control may have many sources of input information and many subtasks to perform. It is no surprise, therefore, that the *blackboard model* is chosen for many control applications (see chapter 7).

Leitch et al. [4] point out that since continuous operation is required, a mechanism is needed for ensuring that the blackboard does not contain obsolete information. They achieve this by tagging blackboard information with the time of its posting. As time elapses, some information may remain relevant, some may gradually lose accuracy, and some may become obsolete suddenly. There are several ways of representing the lifetime of blackboard information:

i   A default lifetime for all blackboard information may be assumed. Any information that is older than this may be removed. A drawback of this approach is that deductions made from information that is now obsolete may remain on the blackboard.

ii   At the time of posting to the blackboard, individual items of information may be tagged with an expected lifetime. Suppose that item A is posted at time t_A with expected lifetime l_A. If item B is deduced from A at time t_B, where $t_B < t_A + l_A$, then the lifetime of B, l_B, would be $t_A + l_A - t_B$.

iii   Links between blackboard items are recorded, showing the interdependencies between items. Figure 10.4 illustrates the application of this approach to control of a boiler, using rules borrowed from section 3.2. There is no need to record the expected lifetimes of any items, as all pieces of blackboard information are ultimately dependent on sensor data, which are liable to change. When changes in sensor values occur, updates are rippled through the dependent items on the blackboard. Thus in the example shown in figure 10.4, as soon as the flow rate fell, *flow rate high* would be removed from the blackboard along with the inferences *steam escaping* and *steam outlet blockage* and the resulting control action. All other information on the blackboard would remain valid.

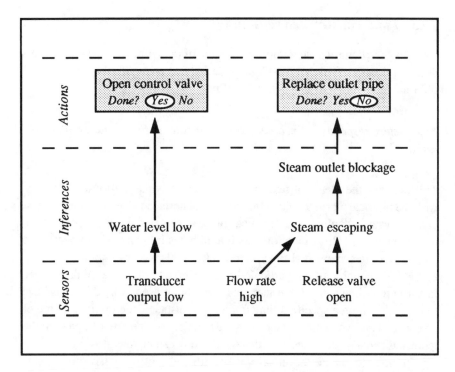

Figure 10.4 Storing dependences between items of information on the blackboard.

The third technique is a powerful way of maintaining the blackboard integrity, since it avoids unnecessary reevaluation of information. This is counterbalanced by the additional complexity of the blackboard and the computational load of maintaining the blackboard. These problems can be minimized by careful partitioning of the blackboard into levels of abstraction (from low-level statements about sensor values to high-level analysis of trends and policy) and subject groupings (low-level data about a conveyor belt is kept apart from low-level information about a boiler).

The control actions on the blackboard in figure 10.4 are shown with a flag indicating whether or not the action has been carried out. The flag is necessary because there is a time lag between an action being taken and a resultant change in the sensor data. When the action is first added to the blackboard, the flag is set to "not yet done". This is changed as soon as the action is carried out. The action is not removed at this stage, as the knowledge source that generated it would simply generate it again. Instead, the control action remains on the blackboard until the supporting evidence is removed, when the sensor reading changes.

10.5   Time-constrained reasoning

An automatic control system must be capable of operating in "real time". This does not necessarily mean "fast", but merely "fast enough". Laffey et al. [5] offer the following informal definition of real-time performance:

"the system responds to incoming data at a rate as fast or faster than it is arriving".

This conveys the idea that real-time performance is the ability to "keep up" with the physical world to which the system is interfaced. The RESCU process control system, applied to a chemical plant, receives data in blocks at five-minute intervals [4]. It therefore has five minutes in which to respond to the data in order to achieve real-time performance. This is an example of a system that is fast enough, but not particularly fast. The rate of arrival of data is one factor in real-time control, but there may be other reasons why decisions have to be made within a specified time frame. For instance, the minimum time of response to an overheated reactor is not dependent on the rate of updating the temperature data, but on the time that overheating can be tolerated.

In order to ensure that a satisfactory (though not necessarily optimum) solution is achieved within the available timescale, a knowledge-based system needs to be able to schedule its activities appropriately.   This is not straightforward, as the time taken to solve a problem cannot be judged accurately in advance.   A conservative approach would be to select only those reasoning activities which it is judged can be completed comfortably within the available time.   However, this may lead to an unsatisfactory solution while failing to use all the time available for reasoning.

Scheduling of knowledge sources is an internal control issue and would normally be kept apart from domain knowledge.   On the other hand, the time constraints are domain-specific and should not therefore be built into the inference engines or control software.   A suitable compromise is to have a special knowledge source dedicated to the real-time scheduling of domain knowledge sources.   This is the approach adopted in RESCU [4].

Some of the techniques that have been applied to ensure that a satisfactory response is achieved within the time constraints are described below.

10.5.1   Prioritization of processes and knowledge sources
In the RESCU system, processes are partitioned on two levels. Firstly the processes of the overall system are divided into "operator", "communications", "log", "monitor", and "knowledge-based system". The latter is a blackboard

system (section 7.6.2) and so it can be divided up into knowledge sources.*
This is the second level of partitioning.

The separate processes at the overall system level are considered to be independent. Thus they could run in parallel, or on a serial computer a process can be temporarily suspended while a more important process is performed. Each of the five processes is assigned a priority number between 1 and 6. The communications and monitoring processes are given the highest priorities, so these can cause the temporary suspension of the other (lower priority) activities. The application of priorities to processes is similar to the application of priorities to rules in other systems (see section 3.7.2).

The separate knowledge sources (KSs) at the knowledge-based system (KBS) level are not independent, as they all rely upon reading from, and writing to, the blackboard. Thus in RESCU, once a KS has started, it will always run to completion before another KS starts. The whole KBS process, however, can be paused. A suitable size for a KS must be small enough to ensure that the reasoning is not continuing when the data is out of date, and large enough to avoid overworking the scheduling software.

In order to provide adaptable and fairly intelligent scheduling of knowledge sources, RESCU's scheduling software is itself coded as a knowledge source. The scheduler checks the preconditions of KSs and any KSs that are applicable are assigned a priority rating. The one with the highest priority is chosen, and in the event of more than one having the highest priority then one is chosen at random. The applicable KSs that are not selected have their priority increased in the "next round" of KS selection, thereby ensuring that all applicable KSs are fired eventually.

10.5.2 Approximation

The use of priorities, described above, ensures that the *most important* tasks are completed within the time constraints, and less important tasks are only completed if time permits. An alternative approach, proposed by Lesser et al. [6] is to ensure that an *approximate* solution is obtained within the time constraints, and the solution is embellished only if time permits. Three aspects of a solution that might be sacrificed to some degree are:

- completeness;
- precision; or
- certainty.

---

* RESCU actually schedules on the basis of groups of knowledge sources, referred to as "activities".

Loss of completeness means that some aspects of the solution are not explored. Loss of precision means that some parameters are determined less precisely than they might have been. (The maximum precision is determined by the precision of the input data). Loss of certainty means that some evidence in support of the conclusion has not been evaluated, or alternatives have been ignored. Thus there is a trade-off between the quality of a solution and the time taken to derive it.

One approach to approximation would be to make a rough attempt at solving the problem initially, and to use any time remaining to incrementally refine the solution. Provided sufficient time was available to at least achieve the rough solution, a solution of some sort would always be guaranteed. In contrast, the approach adopted by Lesser et al. [6] is to plan the steps of solution generation so that there is just the right degree of approximation to meet the deadline.

Lesser et al. distinguish between *well-defined* and *ill-defined* approximations, although these names are possibly misleading. According to their definition, well-defined approximations have the following properties:

- a predictable effect on the quality of the solution and the time taken to obtain it;

- graceful degradation, i.e., the quality of the solution decreases smoothly as the amount of approximation is increased; and

- loss of precision is not accompanied by loss of accuracy. If, for instance, a reactor temperature is determined to lie within a certain temperature range, then this range should straddle the value that would be determined by more precise means.

Lesser et al recommend that ill-defined approximations only be used as a last resort, when it is known that a well-defined approximation is not capable of achieving a solution within the available time. They consider six strategies for approximation, all of which they consider to be well defined. These strategies are classified into three groups: approximate search, data approximations, and knowledge approximations. These classifications are described below.

i   *Approximate search*
Two approaches to reducing the number of alternatives which are considered (i.e., "pruning the search tree") are elimination of corroborating evidence and elimination of competing interpretations.

- *Eliminating corroborating evidence*
  Once a hypothesis has been generated, and perhaps partially verified, time

can be saved by dispensing with further corroborating evidence. This will have the effect of reducing the certainty of the solution. For corroborating data to be recognized as such, it must be analyzed to a limited extent before being discarded.

• *Eliminating competing interpretations*
Elimination of corroborating evidence is a means of limiting the input data, whereas elimination of competing interpretations limits the output data. Solutions which have substantially lower certainties than their alternatives can be eliminated. If it is recognized that some solutions will have a low certainty regardless of the amount of processing that is carried out on them, then these solutions can be eliminated before they are fully evaluated. The net result is a reduced level of certainty of the final solution.

ii   *Data approximations*
Time can be saved by cutting down the amount of data considered. Incomplete event processing and cluster processing are considered here, although elimination of corroborating evidence (see above) might also be considered in this category.

• *Incomplete event processing*
This approximation technique is really a combination of prioritization (see section 10.5.1) and elimination of corroborating evidence. Suppose that a chemical reactor is being controlled, and data are needed regarding temperature and pressure. If temperature has the higher priority, then any data which supports the estimation of the pressure can be ignored in order to save time. The result is a less complete solution.

• *Cluster processing*
Time can be saved by grouping together data items that are related, and examining the overall properties of the group rather than the individual data items. For instance, the temperature sensors mounted on the walls of a reactor chamber might be clustered. Then rather than using all of the readings, only the mean and standard deviation might be considered. This may lead to a loss of precision, but the certainty may be increased owing to the dilution of erroneous readings.

iii   *Knowledge approximations*
Changes can be made to the knowledge base in order to speed up processing. Two possible approaches are:

- *Knowledge adaptation to suit data approximations*
  This is not really a technique in its own right, but simply a recognition that data approximations (see above) require a modified knowledge base.

- *Eliminating intermediate steps*
  As noted in section 7.3, shallow knowledge represents a means of by-passing the steps of the underlying deep knowledge. Therefore it has potential for time saving. However, it may lead to a loss of certainty, as extra corroborating evidence for the intermediate steps might have been available. Shallow knowledge is also less adaptable to new situations.

10.5.3   Single and multiple instantiation

Single and multiple instantiation of variables in a rule-based system are described in section 3.7.1. Under multiple instantiation, a single rule, fired once only, finds all sets of instantiations that satisfy the condition and then performs the conclusion on each. Under single instantiation, a separate rule firing is required for each set of instantiations. Depending on the strategy for conflict resolution, this may cause the conclusions to be drawn in a different order.

In time-constrained control applications, the choice between multiple instantiation and repeated single instantiation can be critical. Consider the case of an automatic controller for a telephone network. Typically the controller will receive statistics describing the network traffic at regular intervals, Δt. Upon receiving the statistics, the controller must interpret the data, choose appropriate control actions and carry out those actions before the next set of statistics arrives. Typically there is a cycle of finding overloaded routes, planning alternative routes through the network, and executing the plan. The most efficient way of doing this is by multiple instantiation, as the total duration of the find-plan-execute cycle for all routes is smaller (figure 10.5). However, the controller must finish within time Δt. The more overloaded links that there are, the less likely it is that the controller will finish. In fact it is feasible that the controller might have found all of the overloaded links and determined an alternative routing for each, but failed to perform *any* control actions (figure 10.5b).

This problem is avoided by repeated use of single instantiation, shown in figure 10.5a, which is guaranteed to have performed *some* control actions within the available time. Thus there is a crucial difference between the two approaches in a control application. Multiple instantiation involves the drawing up of a large plan, followed by execution of the plan. Repeated single instantiation, on the other hand, involves interleaving of planning and execution.

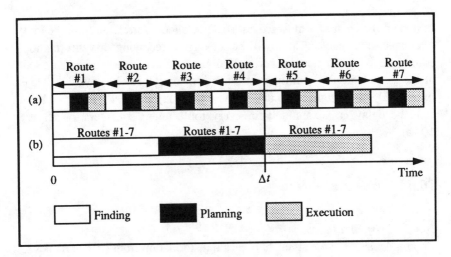

Figure 10.5 Controlling a telecommunications network within a time constraint (Δ*t*):
(a) repeated single instantiation of variables;
(b) multiple instantiation of variables.

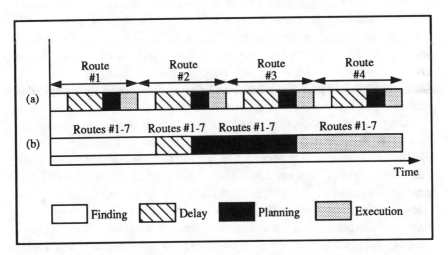

Figure 10.6 Controlling a telecommunications network where there is a delay in
receiving information:
(a) repeated single instantiation of variables;
(b) multiple instantiation of variables.

Repeated single instantiation does not always represent the better choice.
This depends on the specific application. Multiple instantiation is generally
faster as it requires the rules to be selected and interpreted once only. Multiple
instantiation can have other advantages as well. Consider the telecommunications example again, but now imagine that in order to choose a suitable

rerouting, the controller must request some detailed information from the local telephone exchanges. There will be a delay in receiving this information, thereby delaying the planning stage. If all the requests for information are sent at the same time (i.e., multiple instantiation, figure 10.6b) then the delays overlap. Under single instantiation the total delay is much greater, since a separate delay is encountered for every route under consideration (figure 10.6a).

10.6   Fuzzy controllers

10.6.1   Crisp and fuzzy control

Control decisions can be thought of as a transformation from state variables to action variables (figure 10.7). State variables describe the current state of the physical plant and the desired state. Action variables are those that can be directly altered by the controller, such as the electrical current sent to a furnace, or the flow rate through a gas valve. In some circumstances it may be possible to obtain values for the action variables by direct algebraic manipulation of the state variables. (This is the case for a PID controller - section 10.2.5.) Given suitably chosen functions, this approach causes values of action variables to change smoothly as values of state variables change. In high-level control, such functions are rarely available, and this is one reason for using rules instead to link state variables to action variables.

Crisp sets are conventional Boolean sets, where an item is either a member (degree of membership =1) or it is not (degree of membership = 0). It therefore follows that an item cannot belong to two contradictory sets, such as "large" and "small" as it can under fuzzy logic (see section 4.4). Applying crisp sets to state and action variables corresponds to dividing up the range of allowable values into subranges, each of which forms a set. Suppose that a state variable such as temperature is divided into five crisp sets. A temperature reading can belong to only one of these sets, so only one rule will apply,

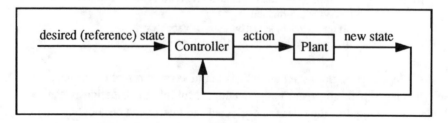

Figure 10.7   Control viewed as a transformation from state variables to action variables.

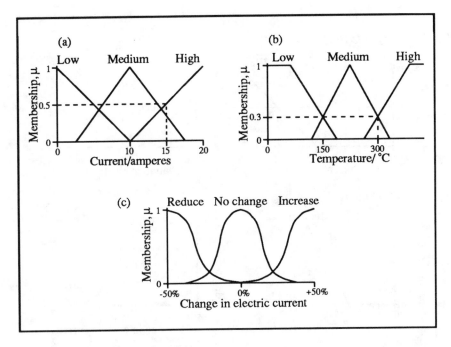

Figure 10.8 Fuzzy sets:
(a) electric current (state variable);
(b) temperature (state variable);
(c) change in electric current (action variable).

resulting in a single control action. Thus the number of different control actions is limited to the number of rules, which in turn is limited by the number of crisp sets. The action variables are therefore changed in abrupt steps as the state variables change.

Fuzzy logic provides a means of allowing a small number of rules to produce smooth changes in the action variables as state values alter. The number of rules required is dependent on the number of state variables, the number of fuzzy sets, and the ways in which the state variables are combined in rule conditions. Numerical information is explicit in crisp rules, but in fuzzy rules it becomes implicit in the chosen shape of the fuzzy membership functions.

10.6.2 Firing fuzzy control rules

Some simple examples of fuzzy control rules are as follows:

```
/* Rule 10.1f */
IF temperature is high OR current is high
THEN reduce current
```

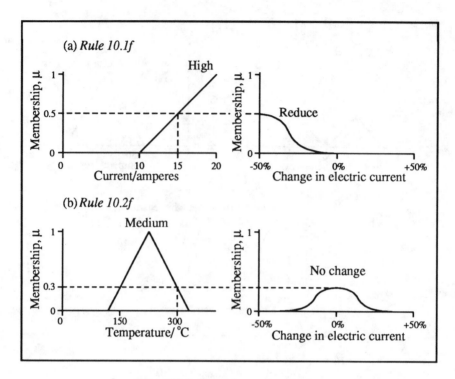

Figure 10.9 Firing fuzzy control rules.

```
/* Rule 10.2f */
IF temperature is medium
THEN no change to current

/* Rule 10.3f */
IF temperature is low and current is high
THEN no change to current

/* Rule 10.4f */
IF temperature is low and current is low
THEN increase current
```

The rules and the fuzzy sets to which they refer are, in general, dependent on each other. Some possible fuzzy membership functions (μ) for the state variables temperature and current, and for the action variable change to current, are shown in figure 10.8. Since the fuzzy sets overlap, a temperature and current may have some degree of membership of more than one fuzzy set. Suppose that the recorded temperature is 300°C and the measured current is 15 amps. Thus the temperature and current are each members of two fuzzy sets - "medium" and "high". Rules 10.1f and 10.2f will fire, with the apparently contradictory conclusion that we should both reduce the electric current and leave it alone. Of course, what is actually required is *some* reduction in current.

Rule 10.1f contains a disjunction. Using equation 4.24, the possibility value for the composite condition is:

`max{μ(temperature is high), μ(current is high)}.`

At 300°C and 15 amps, μ(temperature is high) is 0.3 and μ(current is high) is 0.5. The composite possibility value is therefore 0.5, and the corresponding membership function for "reduce current" is compressed accordingly (figure 10.9(a)). Rule 10.2f is simpler, containing only a single condition. The possibility value μ(temperature is medium) is 0.3, and so the membership function for "no change to current" is compressed as shown in figure 10.9(b).

After firing rules 10.1f and 10.2f, we have a membership function for "reduce current" and another for "no change to current". These fuzzy actions must be converted into a single precise action if they are to be of any practical use. This process is sometimes called *defuzzification*.

10.6.3 Defuzzification
The generally accepted method of defuzzification is the centroid, or center-of-gravity, method. This is easiest to visualize graphically. The membership functions are imagined to be cut out with scissors from stiff card and pasted together where (and if) they overlap. The specific action that the controller takes is indicated by the balance point of this composite shape (figure 10.10).

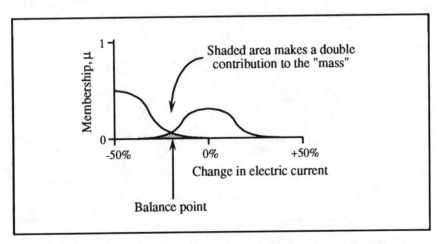

Figure 10.10 Defuzzifying a control action by the centroid method.

If the balance points for the individual membership functions are known, then determining the combined balance point (i.e., the defuzzified control action) is straightforward:

$$\text{Control action} = \frac{\sum A_i B_i}{\sum A_i},$$

where A_i and B_i are the areas and balance points respectively of the membership functions. For a given membership function, B_i is constant but A_i will change when the function is compressed, as shown in figure 10.9. The use of triangular membership functions or other simple geometries simplifies the calculations of A_i and B_i. For an isosceles triangle, the balance point is the midpoint along the base, and the area is one half of the base length multiplied by the height.

10.6.4 Tuning fuzzy controllers with genetic algorithms

Although it may be fairly easy to draw up a set of sensible fuzzy control rules, determining the most suitable shapes for the membership functions is difficult to achieve by judgment or trial and error. Karr [7, 8] has performed a number of experiments which demonstrate the viability of using genetic algorithms to determine the optimum shapes for the membership functions. (See section 6.3.4 for a discussion of genetic algorithms). Karr's membership functions were all triangular. All variables were constrained to lie within a fixed range, so the fuzzy sets "low" and "high" were both right-angle triangles (figure 10.11). The slope of these triangles was altered by moving their intercepts on

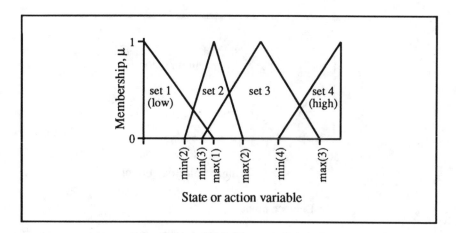

Figure 10.11 Defining triangular membership functions by their intercepts on the abscissa.

the abscissa (marked *max(1)* and *min(4)* in figure 10.11). All intermediate fuzzy sets were assumed to have membership functions that were isosceles triangles. Each is defined by two points, *max(i)* and *min(i)*, where *i* labels the fuzzy set. The "chromosome" used by Karr was a list of all the points *max(i)* and *min(i)* that determined the complete set of membership functions. These values were optimized by a combination of reproduction, mutation and crossover. In several demonstrator systems, the GA-modified fuzzy controller outperformed a fuzzy controller whose membership functions had been set manually. This is perhaps not surprising, since tuning the fuzzy sets is an optimization problem.

10.6.5 Some practical examples of fuzzy controllers
LINKman [9] is a fuzzy control system that has been applied to cement kiln control and other manufacturing processes. The amount of overlap of membership functions is deliberately restricted, thereby reducing the number of rule firings. This is claimed to simplify defuzzification and tuning of the membership functions, and to make control actions more transparent. In addition, all variables are normalized to lie within the range +1 to –1, representing the maximum and minimum extremes. A normalized value of 0 represents the normal steady-state value or set point. It is claimed that by working with normalized variables, the knowledge base can be more easily adapted to different plants.

RESCU [4] does not use fuzzy sets, but it does make use of possibility values as a means of representing levels of confidence. As with LINKman, some effort is made to limit the number of rule firings. In RESCU this is achieved by only firing a rule if its condition part has a possibility greater than some predetermined value (say 0.5).

As well as looking at servo control (section 10.2.6), Sripada et al. [3] have also addressed the application of knowledge-based techniques to low-level adaptive control. They assert that while a PID controller is adequate for reducing the drift in a typical plant output, it cannot cope with slight refinements to this basic requirement. In particular, they consider the application of constraints on the plant output, such that the output (y) must not be allowed to drift beyond $y_0 \pm y_c$, where y_0 is the set-point for y and y_c defines the constraints. Bang-bang control is required to move y rapidly towards y_0 if it is observed to be approaching $y_0 \pm y_c$.

A further requirement imposed by Sripada et al. was that control of the plant output be as smooth as possible close to the set point, therefore precluding bang-bang control under these conditions. The controller was therefore required to behave differently in different circumstances. This is possible with a system based on heuristic rules, but not for a PID controller, which has a fixed predetermined behavior.

In order to determine which type of controller action is required, and the extent of any corrective action, Sripada et al. classified the error (e) and the rate of change of the plant output (dy/dt) using the following fuzzy sets:

e = zero;
e = small positive;
e = small negative;
e = large positive;
e = large negative;
e = close to constraint;
dy/dt = small;
dy/dt = large positive;
dy/dt = large negative.

According to the degree of membership of each of the above nine fuzzy sets, a rule base was used to determine the degree of membership for each of six fuzzy sets applied to control actions:

zero change;
small positive change;
small negative change;
large positive change;
large negative change;
drastic change (bang-bang).

Incorporating the last action as a fuzzy set enabled a smooth transition to bang-bang control as the plant output approached the constraints.

10.7 The BOXES controller

10.7.1 The conventional BOXES algorithm

It has already been emphasized (section 10.1) that a controller can only function if it has a model for the system being controlled. The BOXES algorithm (described here) and neural networks (section 10.8) are techniques for generating such a model without any prior knowledge of the mechanisms occurring within the controlled system. Such an approach may be useful if:

- the system is too complicated to model accurately;
- insufficient is known about the system; or
- satisfactory control rules have not been found.

The BOXES algorithm may be applied to adaptive or servo control. Only the following information about the controlled system is required:

- its inputs (i.e., the possible control actions);
- its outputs (which define its state at any given time);
- the desired state (adaptive control) or the final state (servo control); and
- constraints on the input and output variables.

Note that no information is needed about the relationships between the inputs and outputs.

As an example, consider a bioreactor [10, 11], which is a tank of water containing cells and nutrients (figure 10.12). When the cells multiply they consume nutrients, and the rate at which they multiply is dependent only on the nutrient concentration (C_n). The aim of the controller is to maintain the concentration of cells (C_c) at some desired value by altering the rate of flow (u) of nutrient-rich water through the tank. The state of the bioreactor at any time can be defined by the two variables C_n and C_c, and thus can be represented as a point in state-space (figure 10.13). For any position in state space there will be an appropriate control action, u. By defining intervals in C_n and C_c we can create a finite number of boxes in state-space, where each box represents a collection of states that are similar to each other. A control action can then be

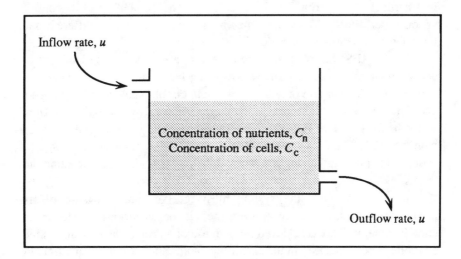

Figure 10.12 A bioreactor.

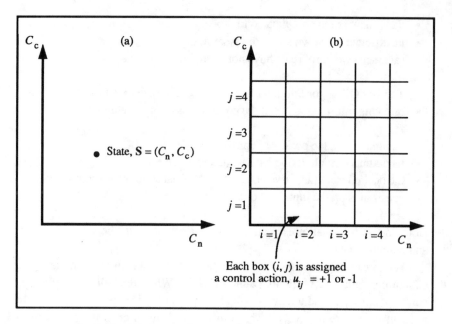

Figure 10.13   (a) state-space for a bioreactor;
(b) state-space partitioned into boxes.

associated with each box. A BOXES controller is completely defined by such
a set of boxes and control actions, which together model implicitly the
controlled system.

Control actions are performed at time $n\Delta t$, where n is an integer and Δt is
the interval between control actions. At any such time, the system state will be
in a particular box. That box is considered to be "visited", and its control
action is performed. The system may be in the same box or a different one
when the next control action is due.

The BOXES controller must be trained to associate appropriate control
actions with each box. This is easiest using bang-bang control, where the
control variables can take only their maximum or minimum value, denoted +1
and -1 respectively. In the case of the bioreactor, a valve controlling the flow
would be fully open or fully shut. For each box, there is a recorded score for
both the '+1' and the '-1' action. When a box is visited, the selected control
action is the one with the highest score. Learning is achieved by updating the
scores.

In order to learn, the system must receive some measure of its
performance, so that it can recognize beneficial or deleterious changes in its
control strategy. This is achieved through use of a *critic*, which evaluates the
controller's performance. In the case of the bioreactor, the controller's time to
failure might be monitored, where "failure" occurs if the cell concentration

(C_c) drifts beyond prescribed limits. The longer the time to failure, the better the performance of the controller. Woodcock et al. [11] consider this approach to be midway between supervised and unsupervised learning (chapter 6), as the controller receives an indication of its performance but not a direct comparison between its output and the desired output.

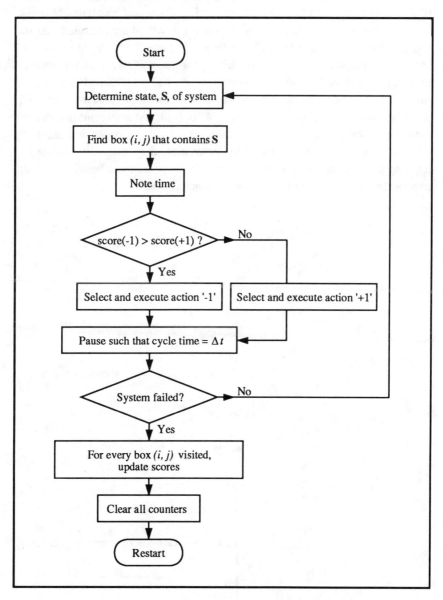

Figure 10.14 The BOXES learning algorithm.
In the example shown here, performance is gauged by time to failure.

For each box, a score is stored for both the '+1' action and the '-1' action. These scores are a measure of "degree of appropriateness" and are based on the average time between selecting the control action in that particular box and the next failure.

The learning strategy of Michie and Chambers [12] for bang-bang control is shown in figure 10.14. During a run, a single box may be visited N times. For each box, the times $(t_1...t_i...t_N)$ at which it is visited are recorded. At the end of a run (i.e., after a failure), the time (t_f) is noted and the '+1' and '-1' scores for each visited box are updated. Each score is based on the average time to failure after that particular control action had been carried out, i.e., the lifetime, l. The lifetimes are modified by a usage factor (n), a decay factor (α), a "global" lifetime (l_g), a "global" usage factor (n_g), and a constant (β), thereby yielding a score. These modifications ensure that, for each box, both alternative actions have the chance to demonstrate their suitability during the learning process and that recent experience is weighted more heavily than old experience. The full updating procedure is as follows:

$$l_g = \alpha \, l_g + t_f$$

$$n_g = \alpha \, n_g + 1$$

$$l_{(+1)} = \alpha \, l_{(+1)} + \sum_{i=1}^{N}(t_f - t_i)$$

$$n_{(+1)} = \alpha \, n_{(+1)} + N$$

$$\text{score}_{(+1)} = \frac{l_{(+1)} + \beta \dfrac{l_g}{n_g}}{u_{(+1)} + \beta}$$

$\left.\right\}$ for each box where $\text{score}_{(+1)} > \text{score}_{(-1)}$

$$l_{(-1)} = \alpha \, l_{(-1)} + \sum_{i=1}^{N}(t_f - t_i)$$

$$n_{(-1)} = \alpha \, n_{(-1)} + N$$

$$\text{score}_{(-1)} = \frac{l_{(-1)} + \beta \dfrac{l_g}{n_g}}{u_{(-1)} + \beta}$$

$\left.\right\}$ for each box where $\text{score}_{(-1)} > \text{score}_{(+1)}$

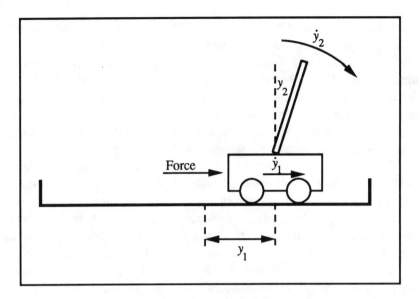

Figure 10.15 The cart-and-pole control problem.

After a controller has been run to failure and the scores associated with the boxes have been updated, the controller becomes competent at balancing in only a limited part of the state-space. In order to become expert in all regions of state-space, the controller must be run to failure several times, starting from different regions in state-space.

The BOXES algorithm has been used for control of a bioreactor as described, and also for balancing a pole on a mobile cart (figure 10.15). The latter is a similar problem to the bioreactor, but the state is described by four rather than two variables. The boxes are therefore 4-dimensional and difficult to represent graphically. In principle, the BOXES algorithm can be applied to state-space with any number of dimensions. The cart-and-pole problem, shown in figure 10.15, has been used extensively as a benchmark for intelligent controllers. A pole is attached by means of a hinge to a cart which can move along a finite length of track. The cart and the pole are restricted to movement within a plane. The controller attempts to balance the pole while keeping the cart on the length of track by applying a force to the left or right. If the force has a fixed magnitude in either direction, this is another example of bang-bang control. The four state variables are the cart's position (y_1) and velocity ($\dot{y}_1$); and the pole's angle (y_2) and angular velocity ($\dot{y}_2$). Failure occurs when y_1 or y_2 breach constraints placed upon them. The constraint on y_1 represents the limited length of the track.

Rather than use a BOXES system as an intelligent controller per se, Sammut and Michie [13] have used it as a means of eliciting rules for a rule-based controller. After running the BOXES algorithm on a cart-and-pole system, they found some clear relationships between the learned control actions and the state variables. They expressed these relationships as rules and then proceeded to use analogous rules to control a different black box simulation, namely a simulated spacecraft. The spacecraft was subjected to a number of unknown external forces, but the rule-based controller was tolerant of these. Similarly, Woodcock et al.'s BOXES controller [11] was virtually unaffected by random variations superimposed on the control variables.

One of the attractions of the BOXES controller is that it is a fairly simple technique, and so an effective controller can be built quite quickly. Woodcock et al. [11] rapidly built their controller and a variety of black box simulations using the Smalltalk object-oriented programming language. Although both the controller and simulation were developed in the same programming environment, the workings of the simulators were hidden from the controller. Sammut and Michie also report that they were able to build quickly their BOXES controller and the rule-based controller that it inspired.

10.7.2 Fuzzy BOXES

Woodcock et al. [11] have investigated the suggestion [14] that the performance of a BOXES controller might be improved by using fuzzy logic to smooth the bang-bang control. Where different control actions are associated with neighboring boxes, it was proposed that states lying between the centers of the boxes should be associated with intermediate actions. The controller was trained as described above in order to determine appropriate bang-bang actions. After training, the box boundaries were fuzzified using triangular fuzzy sets. The maximum and minimum control actions (bang-bang) were normalized to $+1$ and -1 respectively, and intermediate actions were assigned a number between these extremes.

Consider again the bioreactor, which is characterized by 2-dimensional state-space. If a particular state S falls within the box (i,j), then the corresponding control action is u_{ij}. This can be stated as an explicit rule:

```
IF S belongs in box (i,j)
THEN the control action is u_ij.
```

If we consider C_n and C_c separately, this rule can be re-written:

```
IF C_n belongs in interval i AND C_c belongs in interval j
THEN the control action is u_ij.
```

The same rule can be applied in the case of fuzzy BOXES, except that now it is interpreted as a fuzzy rule. We know from equation 4.43 that:

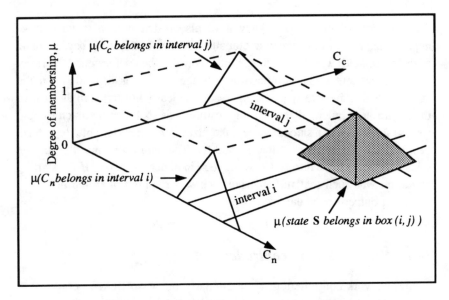

Figure 10.16 Fuzzy membership functions for boxes in the bioreactor state space.
(Adapted from [11])

$\mu(C_n$ belongs in interval i AND C_c belongs in interval j) = $\min[\mu(C_n$ belongs in interval i), $\mu(C_c$ belongs in interval j)].

Thus if the membership functions for "C_n belongs in interval i" and "C_c belongs in interval j" are both triangular, then the membership function for "S belongs in box (i,j)", denoted by $\mu_{ij}(S)$, is a surface in state-space in the shape of a pyramid (figure 10.16). As the membership functions for neighboring pyramids overlap, a point in state space may be a member of more than one box. The control action, u_{ij}, for each box to which S belongs is scaled according to the degree of membership, $\mu_{ij}(S)$. The normalized sum of these actions is then interpreted as the defuzzified action u_o:

$$u_o = \frac{\sum_i \sum_j \mu_{ij}(S)u_{ij}}{\sum_i \sum_j \mu_{ij}(S)}.$$

This is equivalent to defuzzification using the centroid method (section 10.6.3), if the membership functions for the control actions are assumed to be symmetrical about a vertical line through their balance points.

Woodcock et al. have tested their fuzzy BOXES controller against the cart-and-pole and bioreactor simulations (described above), which are both adaptive control problems. They have also tested it in a servo control application, namely reversing a tractor and trailer up to a loading bay. In none of these examples was there a clear winner between the nonfuzzy and the fuzzy boxes controllers. The comparison between them was dependent on the starting position in state-space. This was most clearly illustrated in the case of the tractor and trailer. If the starting position was such that the tractor could reverse the trailer in a smooth sweep, the fuzzy controller was able to perform best because it was able to steer smoothly. The nonfuzzy controller, on the other hand, was limited to full steering lock in either direction. If the starting condition was such that full steering lock was required, then the nonfuzzy controller outperformed the fuzzy one.

10.8 Neural network controllers

Neural network controllers tackle a similar problem to BOXES controllers, namely controlling a system using a model that is automatically generated during a learning phase. Two distinct approaches have been adopted by Valmiki et al. [15] and by Willis et al. [16]. Valmiki et al. have trained a neural network to associate directly particular sets of state variables with particular action variables, in an analogous fashion to the association of a box in state-space with a control action in a BOXES controller. Willis et al. adopt a less direct approach, using a neural network to estimate the values of those state variables that are critical to control but which cannot be measured on-line. The estimated values are then fed to a PID controller as though they were real measurements. These two approaches are discussed separately below.

10.8.1 Direct association of state variables with action variables
Valmiki et al. have applied a neural network to a control problem that had previously been tackled using rules and objects, namely the control of a glue dispenser [17]. As part of the manufacture of mixed technology circuit boards, surface mounted components are held in place by a droplet of glue. The glue is dispensed from a syringe by means of compressed air. The size of the droplet is the state variable that must be controlled, and the change in the air pressure is the action variable.

Valmiki et al. have built a 6-6-5 network (figure 10.17), where specific meanings are attached to values of 0 and 1 on the input and output nodes. Five of the six input nodes represent ranges for the error in the size of the droplet. The node corresponding to the measured error is sent a '1', while the other four nodes are sent a '0'. The sixth input node is set to '0' or '1' depending on whether the error is positive or negative. Three of the five output nodes are

used to flag particular actions, while the other two are a coded representation of the amount by which the air pressure should be changed, if a change is required. The three flags on the output are:

- increase (1) or decrease (0) pressure;
- do nothing (1) or do something (0) (overrides the increase / decrease flag);
- warning (1) or no warning (0) if the error in the droplet size is large.

The training data were generated by hand. Since the required mapping of input states to outputs was known in advance (allowing training data to be drawn up), the problem could have been tackled using rules. An advantage of a neural network approach is that an interpolated meaning can be attached to output values that lie between 0 and 1. However, the same effect could also be achieved using fuzzy rules. This would also have avoided the need to classify the state variables according to crisp sets. Nonetheless Valmiki et al.'s experiment is important in demonstrating the feasibility of using a neural network to learn to associate state variables with control actions. This is useful where rules or functions that link the two are unavailable, although this was not the case in their experiment.

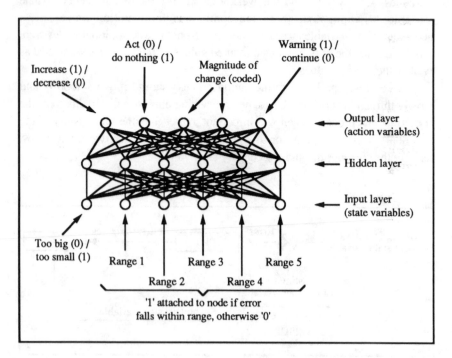

Figure 10.17 Using a neural network to map directly state variables to action variables (based on the glue-dispensing application of Valmiki et al. [15]).

10.8.2 *Estimation of critical state variables*

Willis et al. [16] have demonstrated the application of neural network controllers to industrial continuous and batch-fed fermenters, and to a commercial-scale high purity distillation column. Each application is characterized by a delay in obtaining the critical state variable (i.e., the *controlled* variable), as it requires chemical or pathological analysis. The neural network allows comparatively rapid estimation of the critical state variable from secondary state variables. The use of a model for such a purpose is discussed in section 7.5.4. The only difference here is that the controlled plant is modeled using a neural network. The estimated value for the critical state variable can be sent to a PID controller (see section 10.2.5) to determine the action variable (figure 10.18). As the critical variable can be measured off-line in each case, there is no difficulty in generating training sets of data. Each of the three applications demonstrates a different aspect to this problem. The chemotaxis learning algorithm was used in each case (see section 6.4.5).

The continuous fermentation process is dynamic, i.e., the variables are constantly changing, and a *change* in the value of a variable may be just as significant as the absolute value. The role of a static neural network, on the other hand, is to perform a mapping of static input variables onto static output variables. One way around this weakness is to use the recent history of state variables as input nodes. In the continuous fermentation process, two secondary state variables were considered. Nonetheless, six input nodes were required, since the two previous measured values of the variables were used as well as the current values (figure 10.19).

In contrast, the batch fermentation process should move smoothly and slowly through a series of phases, never reaching equilibrium. In this case, the time since the process began was important, rather than the time history of the secondary variable. Thus for this process there were only two input nodes, namely the current time and a secondary state variable.

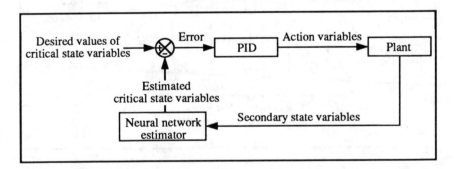

Figure 10.18 Using a neural network to estimate values for the critical state variables.

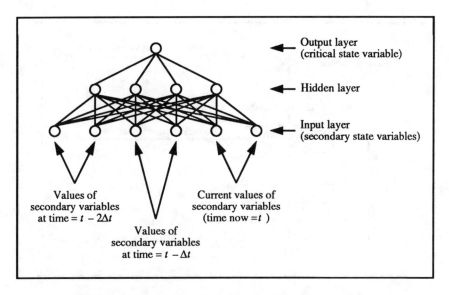

Figure 10.19 Using time histories of state variables in a neural network. (Based on the continuous fermentation application of Willis et al. [16].)

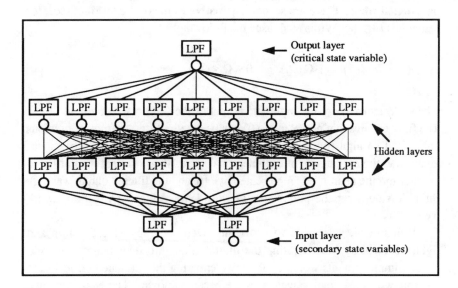

Figure 10.20 Dealing with changing variables by using low pass filters (LPF). (Based on the industrial distillation application of Willis et al. [16].)

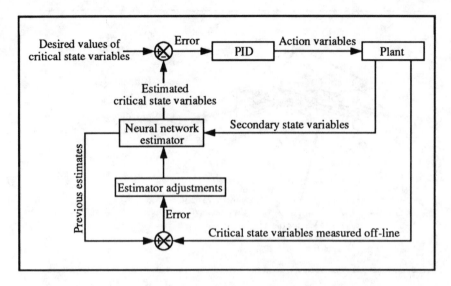

Figure 10.21 Feedback control of both the plant and the neural network estimator.

In the methanol distillation process, an alternative approach was adopted to the problem of handling dynamic behavior. As it is known that the state variables must vary continuously, sudden sharp changes in any of the propagated values can be disallowed. This is achieved through a simple low-pass digital filter. There are several alternative forms of digital filter (see, for example, [18]), but Willis et al. used the following:

$$y(t) = \Omega\, y(t\text{-}1) + (1\text{-}\Omega)x(t) \qquad 0 \le \Omega \le 1$$

where $x(t)$ and $y(t)$ are the input and output of the filter respectively at time t. The filter ensures that no value of $y(t)$ can be greatly different from its previous value, and so high-frequency fluctuations are eliminated. Such a filter was attached to the output side of each neuron (figure 10.20), so that the unfiltered output from the neuron was represented by $x(t)$, and the filtered output was $y(t)$. Suitable values for the parameters Ω were learned along with the network weightings.

Willis et al. were able to show improved accuracy of estimation and tighter control by incorporating the digital filter into their neural network. Further improvements were possible by comparing the estimated critical state variable with the actual values, as these became known. The error was then used to adjust the output of the estimator. There were then two feedback loops, one for the PID controller and one for the estimator (figure 10.21).

10.9 Statistical process control (SPC)

10.9.1 Applications

Statistical process control (SPC) is a technique for monitoring the quality of products as they are manufactured. Critical parameters are monitored and adjustments are made to the manufacturing process *before* any products are manufactured that lie outside of their specifications. The appeal of SPC is that it minimizes the number of products that are rejected at the quality control stage, thereby improving productivity and efficiency. Since the emphasis of SPC lies in *monitoring* products, this section could equally belong in chapter 7, "Interpretation and Diagnosis".

SPC involves inspecting a sample of the manufactured products, measuring the critical parameters, and inferring from these measurements any trends in the parameters for the whole population of products. The gathering and manipulation of the statistics is a procedural task, and some simple heuristics are used for spotting trends. The monitoring activities therefore lend themselves to automation through procedural and rule-based programming. Depending on the process, the control decisions might also be automated.

10.9.2 Collecting the data

Various statistics can be gathered, but we will concentrate on the mean and standard deviation[*] of the monitored parameters. Periodically a sample of consecutively manufactured products is taken, and the critical parameter (x) is measured for each item in the sample. The sample size (n) is typically between 5 and 10. In the case of the manufacture of silicon wafers, thickness may be the critical parameter. The mean, $\bar{x}$, and standard deviation, σ, for the sample are calculated. After several such samples have been taken, it is possible to arrive at a mean of means, $\bar{\bar{x}}$, and a mean of standard deviations, $\bar{\sigma}$. The values $\bar{\bar{x}}$ and $\bar{\sigma}$ represent the "normal" or set-point values for $\bar{x}$ and σ respectively. Special set-up procedures exist for the manufacturing plant to ensure that $\bar{\bar{x}}$ corresponds to the set-point for the parameter x. Bounds called *control limits* are placed above and below these values (figure 10.22). Inner and outer control limits, referred to as *warning limits* and *action limits* respectively, may be set such that:

$$\text{warning limit for } \bar{x} = \bar{\bar{x}} \pm 2\,\frac{\bar{\sigma}}{\sqrt{n}}$$

---

[*] The *range* of sample values is often used instead of the standard deviation.

action limit for $\bar{x} = \bar{\bar{x}} \pm 3\dfrac{\bar{\sigma}}{\sqrt{n}}$

Action limits are also set on the values of σ such that:

upper action limit for $\sigma = C_U\,\bar{\sigma}$

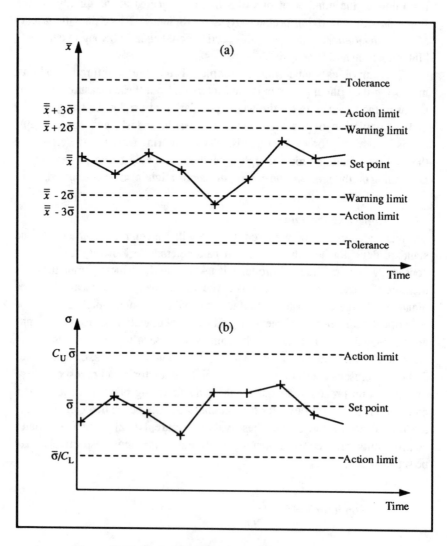

Figure 10.22 Control limits (action and warning) applied to:
(a) sample means ($\bar{x}$);
(b) sample standard deviations (σ).

lower action limit for $\sigma = \dfrac{\bar{\sigma}}{C_L}$

where suitable values for C_U and C_L can be obtained from standard tables for a given sample size, n. Note that both C_U and C_L are greater than unity. The heuristics for interpreting the sample data with respect to the control limits are described in section 10.9.3 below. Any values of $\bar{x}$ that lie beyond the action limits indicate that a control action is needed. The *tolerance* that is placed on a parameter is the limit beyond which the product must be rejected. It therefore follows that if the tolerance is tighter than the action limits, then the manufacturing plant is unsuited to the product and attempts to use it will result in a large number of rejected products irrespective of SPC.

10.9.3 Using the data

As the data are gathered, a variety of heuristics can be applied. Some typical ones are reproduced below:

```
IF a single x̄ value lies beyond an action limit
THEN a special disturbance has occurred which must be
investigated and eliminated

IF there are x̄ values beyond both action limits
THEN the process may be deteriorating

IF two consecutive values of x̄ lie beyond a worrying limit
THEN the process mean may have moved

IF eight consecutive values of x̄ lie on an upward or downward
trend THEN the process mean may be moving

IF seven consecutive values of x̄ lie all above or all below x̿
THEN the process mean may have moved

IF there are σ values beyond the upper action limit
THEN the process may be deteriorating

IF eight consecutive values of σ lie on an upward trend
THEN the process may be deteriorating

IF there are σ values beyond the lower action limit
THEN the process may have improved and attempts should be made
to incorporate the improvement permanently
```

The conclusions of these rules indicate a high probability that a control action is needed. They cannot be definite conclusions, as the evidence is statistical. Furthermore, it may be that the process itself has not changed at all, but instead some aspect of the measuring procedure has altered. Each of the above rules calls for investigation of the process, perhaps using model-based or case-based reasoning (chapter 7), in order to determine the cause of any changes.

10.10 Summary

Knowledge-based systems for control applications draw upon the techniques used for interpreting data (chapter 7) and planning (chapter 9). Frequently the stages of planning are interleaved with execution of the plans, so that the controller can react to changes in the controlled plant as they occur. This contrasts with the classical planning systems described in chapter 9, where the world is treated as a static "snapshot" Since control systems must interact with a dynamic environment, time constraints are placed upon them. There is often a trade-off between the quality of a control decision and the time taken to derive it. In most circumstances it is preferable to perform a suboptimal control action than to fail to take any action with the time limits.

The control problem can be thought of as one of mapping a set of state variables onto a set of action variables. State variables describe the state of the controlled plant, and action variables, set by the controller, are used to modify the state of the plant. Adaptive controllers attempt to maintain one or more critical state parameters at a constant value, minimizing the effects of any disturbance. In contrast, servo controllers attempt to drive the plant to a new state, which may be substantially different from its previous state. The problems of adaptive and servo control are similar, as both involve minimizing the difference (or "error") between the current values of the state variables and the desired values.

An approximate distinction can be drawn between low-level "reflex" control and high-level supervisory control. Low-level control often requires little intelligence and can be most effectively coded procedurally, for instance as the sum of proportional, integral and derivative (PID) terms. Improvements over PID control can be made by using fuzzy rules, which also allow some subtleties to be included in the control requirements, such as bounds on the values of some variables. Fuzzy rules offer a mixture of some of the benefits of procedures and crisp rules. Like crisp rules, fuzzy rules allow a *linguistic* description of the interaction between state and action variables. On the other hand, like an algebraic procedure, fuzzy rules allow smooth changes in the state variables to bring about smooth changes in the action variables. The nature of these smooth changes is determined by the membership functions that are used for the fuzzy sets.

Any controller requires a model of the controlled plant. Even a PID controller holds an implicit model in the form of its parameters, which can be tuned to specific applications. When a model of the controlled plant is not available, it is possible to build one automatically using the BOXES algorithm or a neural network. Both can be used to provide a mapping between state variables and action variables. They can also be used in a monitoring capacity, where critical state variables (which may be difficult to measure directly) are inferred from secondary measurements. The inferred values can then be used as feedback to a conventional controller. If a plant is modeled with sufficient accuracy, then predictive control becomes a possibility. A predictive controller has two goals, namely to tackle the immediate control needs and to minimize future deviations, based on the predicted behavior.

References

1. Bennett, M. E., "Real-time continuous AI", *IEE Proceedings-D*, **134**, p272 (1987).

2. Franklin, G. F., Powell, J. D. and Emami-Naeini, A., *Feedback control of dynamic systems - 2nd edition*, Addison-Wesley (1991).

3. Sripada, N. R., Fisher, D. G. and Morris, A. J., "AI application for process regulation and process control", *IEE Proceedings-D*, **134**, p251 (1987).

4. Leitch, R., Kraft, R. and Luntz, R., "RESCU: a real-time knowledge based system for process control", *IEE Proceedings-D*, **138**, p217 (1991).

5. Laffey, T. J., Cox, P. A., Schmidt, J. L., Kao, S. M. and Read, J. Y., "Real-time knowledge-based systems", *AI Magazine*, p27 (Spring 1988).

6. Lesser, V. R., Pavlin, J. and Durfee, E., "Approximate processing in real-time problem solving", *AI Magazine*, p49 (Spring 1988).

7. Karr, C. L., "Genetic algorithms for fuzzy controllers", *AI Expert*, p26 (February 1991).

8. Karr, C. L., "Applying genetics to fuzzy logic", *AI Expert*, p39 (March 1991).

9. Taunton, J. C. and Haspel, D. W., "The application of expert system techniques in on-line process control", in *Expert systems in engineering*, Pham, D. T. (ed.), IFS Publications / Springer-Verlag (1988).

10. Ungar, L. H., "A bioreactor benchmark for adaptive network-based process control", in *Neural networks for control*, Miller, W. T., Sutton, R. S. and Werbos, P. J. (ed.), MIT Press (1990).

11. Woodcock, N., Hallam, N. J. and Picton, P. D., "Fuzzy BOXES as an alternative to neural networks for difficult control problems", in *Applications of artificial intelligence in engineering VI*, Rzevski, G. and Adey, R. A. (ed.), Computational Mechanics / Elsevier, p903 (1991).

12. Michie, D. and Chambers, R. A., "BOXES: an experiment in adaptive control", in *Machine Intelligence 2*, Dale, E. and Michie, D. (ed.), Oliver and Boyd, Edinburgh (1968).

13. Sammut, C. and Michie, D., "Controlling a black-box simulation of a spacecraft", *AI Magazine*, p56 (Spring 1991).

14. Bernard, J. A., "Use of a rule-based system for process control", *IEEE Control Systems Magazine*, p3 (October 1988).

15. Valmiki, A. H., West, A. A. and Williams, D. J., "The evolution of a neural network controller for adhesive dispensing", in *IFAC workshop on computer software structures integrating AI/KBS systems in process control*, Bergen, Norway, p93 (1991).

16. Willis, M. J., Di Massimo, C., Montague, G. A., Tham, M. T. and Morris, A. J., "Artificial neural networks in process engineering", *IEE Proceedings-D*, **138**, p256 (1991).

17. Chandraker, R., West, A. A. and Williams, D. J., "Intelligent control of adhesive dispensing", *Int. J. Computer Integrated Manufacturing*, **3**, p24 (1990).

18. Lynn, P. A., *An introduction to the analysis and processing of signals*, Macmillan Press (1973).

Further reading

• Franklin, G. F., Powell, J. D. and Workman, M. L., *Digital control of dynamic systems - 2nd edition*, Addison-Wesley (1990).

• Franklin, G. F., Powell, J. D. and Emami-Naeini, A., *Feedback control of dynamic systems - 2nd edition*, Addison-Wesley (1991).

• Lee, C. C., "Fuzzy Logic in Control Systems: Fuzzy Logic Controller - Part I", *IEEE Transactions on Systems, Man and Cybernetics*, **20**, p404 (1990).

• Lee, C. C., "Fuzzy Logic in Control Systems: Fuzzy Logic Controller - Part II", *IEEE Transactions on Systems, Man and Cybernetics*, **20**, p419 (1990).

• Miller, W. T., Sutton, R. S. and Werbos, P. J. (ed.), *Neural networks for control*, MIT Press (1990).

chapter eleven

Concluding remarks

11.1 Benefits

This book has discussed a wide range of techniques and their applications. In this section we briefly look at four key benefits that are bestowed by applying these techniques.

Knowledge archiving

The knowledge base is a repository for the knowledge of one or more people. When these people move on to new jobs, some of their expert knowledge is saved in the knowledge base, which continues to evolve after their departure.

Reliability and consistency

A knowledge-based system makes decisions that are consistent with the knowledge base and the data. The knowledge-based system may therefore be more reliable than a person, particularly where repetitive mundane judgments have to be made.

Automating tedious tasks

In many applications, such as visual inspection on a production line, judgmental decision-making has to be performed repeatedly. A knowledge-based system may be able to handle the majority of cases, but it may still need to defer a decision to a person if it encounters a situation that lies beyond the scope of its knowledge. The knowledge-based system therefore allows the human to concentrate on only the most difficult cases, which are normally the most interesting.

Improved domain understanding

The process of constructing a knowledge base requires the decision-making criteria to be clearly identified and assessed. This process frequently leads to a better understanding of the problem being tackled.

These are some of the practical benefits of knowledge-based and related techniques. Although the techniques have stemmed largely from research in artificial intelligence (AI), the perceived benefits are more modest than the aims of AI, which include the construction of intelligent machines and improved understanding of the mind.

11.2 How to proceed

Advice on implementation of a knowledge-based system is unlikely to be applicable to all people in all circumstances in any application area. Nonetheless, some general observations can be made. Since knowledge-based systems are supposed to be flexible and adaptable, development is based upon continuous refinements of the initial prototype. This is the *prototype-test-refine* cycle. The key stages in the development of a system are therefore:

- decide the requirements;
- design and implement a prototype;
- continuously refine the prototype.

It is often suggested that the first prototype and its first few revisions be implemented using an expert system shell (see section 2.2) which allows rapid representation of the important knowledge. When the prototype has demonstrated its viability, the system can be migrated to a more sophisticated (and expensive) programming environment. This suggestion assumes that the shell will allow a working prototype to be built quickly, but that it will not be flexible enough to allow a complex system to be built. The approach makes some sense if a manager has to be persuaded to fund the project on the basis of the first prototype, but it also has some disadvantages. Working in a shell that lacks flexibility and representational capabilities is frustrating and can lead to convoluted programming in order to force the desired behavior. Subsequent rewriting of the same knowledge in a different style is wasteful of resources. An arguably better approach is to work from the outset with a flexible system, i.e., one that provides all the tools that are likely to be needed, or which allows extra modules to be added as required.

So far we have implicitly assumed that there is only one copy (apart from backups) of each knowledge-based system. However, many copies are frequently needed, for example if each member of a company sales team needs to use the system to configure products to meet customer requirements. In such circumstances, it is common practice for the system to be developed in a sophisticated programming environment and later distributed in compiled form for users to run on a small computer (the *delivery machine*). Consistency across the organization is ensured, since individual users cannot alter their copy of the system. If they would like changes to be implemented they must request them, so that changes are implemented in all copies of the subsequent version of the software.

Systems developed using a commercial AI toolkit (see chapter 2), may require access to some of the features of the toolkit at run-time. With this in mind, some suppliers offer both a program development toolkit and a run-time toolkit. The latter is a stripped-down (and cheaper) version of the development toolkit, and is suitable for dissemination with the delivery version of the knowledge-based system.

11.3 Trends

In many application areas, computers are being required to assist in making decisions based upon a wide view of a process or organization. This is particularly true in manufacturing, where decisions made on the production line take into account and influence design, marketing strategy, personnel data, sales orders, raw material stocks and stocks of the finished product. Use of computers to support this integrated approach to manufacturing is termed *computer integrated manufacturing*, or *CIM*. Knowledge-based systems have a key role to play in CIM, as part of large corporate software systems.

However, smaller-scale applications of knowledge-based systems are of equal or greater importance. In the form of expert systems, they serve as personal consultants to advise on design, planning, diagnosis and various other forms of decision-making. Other knowledge-based systems function silently and anonymously, performing tasks like data interpretation, monitoring or control.

In all cases, using the right software tool for each job is of prime importance. Many applications require hybrid software using a variety of techniques such as procedural algorithms, rules, objects, neural networks and genetic algorithms. One way in which such modules can be made to cooperate effectively is through the blackboard architecture, described in chapter 7.

Index